DISTRIBUTED LEARNING AND VIRTUAL LIBRARIANSHIP

DISTRIBUTED LEARNING AND VIRTUAL LIBRARIANSHIP

SHARON G. ALMQUIST, EDITOR

LIBRARIES UNLIMITED

AN IMPRINT OF ABC-CLIO, LLC
Santa Barbara, California • Denver, Colorado • Oxford, England

Library of Congress Cataloging-in-Publication Data

Distributed learning and virtual librarianship / Sharon G. Almquist, editor.
    p. cm.
   Includes index.
   ISBN 978-1-59158-906-8 (hardcopy : alk. paper) — ISBN 978-1-59158-907-5 (e-book) 1. Academic libraries—Information technology. 2. Libraries and the Internet. 3. Libraries and electronic publishing. 4. Library users—Effect of technological innovations on. 5. Public libraries—Forecasting. I. Almquist, Sharon G.
   Z678.9.D47 2011
   020.285'4678—dc23   2011018377

ISBN: 978-1-59158-906-8
EISBN: 978-1-59158-907-5

15 14 13 12 11   1 2 3 4 5

This book is also available on the World Wide Web as an eBook.
Visit www.abc-clio.com for details.

Libraries Unlimited
An Imprint of ABC-CLIO, LLC

ABC-CLIO, LLC
130 Cremona Drive, P.O. Box 1911
Santa Barbara, California 93116-1911

This book is printed on acid-free paper ∞

Manufactured in the United States of America

CONTENTS

PREFACE

When I first taught an online course called "Distributed Learning Librarianship" for the University of North Texas (UNT)[1] in 2003, I could not find a textbook for the content I wanted to present. After spending many hours doing research, chatting with my colleagues, and observing my library's efforts, I assembled a course based on written lectures supplemented by pertinent readings from various journals—all of which served as the basis for in-depth online discussions and explorations. As the course matured over the years, I realized that a one-stop textbook was something that could benefit both this course and others like it. Much of the research had already been completed and was updated as new methods and techniques were introduced. In addition, a talented group of librarians had served as guest lecturers in the course. Who better to complete a book on distributed learning and virtual librarianship than the guest lecturers as contributors and the instructor as editor?

Based on our experiences of teaching the course for several years, the guest lecturers and I assembled the book's chapters based on the course's lessons. Our intent was that professors and students could use the chapters either in a continuum or as separate entities. Each chapter addresses a unique aspect of distributed and virtual learning, yet together they form a cohesive whole.

Part of that whole was a historical background, which I considered to be of vital importance when attempting to understand the concept of distributed and virtual learning and librarianship. When initially conducting research for the course, I found the history of library support for distributed learning, open learning, correspondence courses, mailed courses, virtual solutions, and the like fascinating. This interest manifests itself in the chapter 1 annotated time line. Examining how librarians solved issues of distribution and service illustrates how librarians have always been on the cutting edge of both technology and service for all of their customers.

Speaking of cutting edge, three librarians at Eastern Kentucky University examine and discuss current issues in public and academic library support of distributed learning in chapter 2, along with an in-depth presentation of the ACRL standards for distance learning library services. They are: Brad Marcum, Distance & Online Education Program Officer; Trenia Napier, Reference Librarian and Research Coordinator for the Noel Studio for Academic Creativity; and Cindi Trainor, Coordinator of Library Technology & Data Services.

In chapter 3, Leora Kemp follows the rise of virtual universities and libraries and the role of the virtual librarian. She also describes the creation of a virtual library at the University of North Texas Dallas. As Kemp herself notes: "I'm a graduate of Duncanville (TX) High School, East Texas State University (now Texas A&M Commerce; BA in English), Southern Methodist University (master of religious education), and the University of North Texas (master of library science). After graduating from UNT, I lived and worked in Waco, TX, for ten years. Upon my return to Dallas, I was hired by Dallas Public Library, where I worked for 11 years. When I read about the opening for a librarian to head the virtual library at the Dallas Campus, I immediately applied for a position. I was very excited about being there and about the future of the Campus and the opportunity to provide some unique library services. We were truly pioneers in this venture." After an impressive career, Kemp retired in March 2011 but will remain active in library endeavors and education.

Meeting virtually, three librarians examine the impact of distributed and virtual reference services in chapter 4. All are extensively involved in reference and distance services. For example, Carla Cantagallo is the librarian to contact at the University of Kentucky. Says Cantagallo, "Whether you are a Distance Learning student or faculty, the University of Kentucky Distance Learning Library Service is available to help you with your library needs. Distance Learning Library Services can obtain research materials needed to support students with their course studies, and help faculty locate the articles they need for their courses. Primary services include: preliminary literature searches on your research topic(s), books and journal articles from the University of Kentucky (UK) Libraries and research consultation."[2] For distance learning help at the University of Mississippi, students and faculty may contact Outreach Librarian Melissa Dennis, whose job includes instruction and reference duties as well as distance learning and library outreach. Jana Reeg-Steidinger, at the University of Wisconsin Stout, serves as the Reference Work Group Leader who, along with eight other librarians, provides reference service for the Stout Community. Among her responsibilities is library instruction for graduate research students. She is also Distance Learning Librarian and is thrilled to provide library outreach.

Of special interest to distributed learning endeavors is copyright law, and in-depth details are presented in chapters 5 and 6. Jeff Clark, Emeritus Faculty and former Assistant Dean for Media Resources, James Madison University, takes us through a broad overview of copyright law and interpretation. John Schlipp, currently an Assistant Professor of Library Services and Extended Collection Services Librarian at Northern Kentucky University, and formerly the Patent and Trademark Librarian at the Public Library of Cincinnati and Hamilton County (OH), addresses the crucial issues of electronic reserves and information delivery in our networked society.

Chapters 7 and 8 investigate specific issues related to public, school, and academic libraries. Ruthie Maslin, Director of the Madison County Public Library, Kentucky, presents public, school, and state libraries' commitment to providing services for a geographically diverse clientele in chapter 7. Arne Almquist, associate provost for library services at Northern Kentucky University, looks at the frequently overlooked need for marketing and the ways in which academic libraries can fully support distributed learning.

Considering the technological, sociological, and financial impact and import of distributed learning and virtual endeavors, libraries as committed providers of free information resources and librarians as expert service providers will continue to develop in their roles—whether it is in a face-to-face or virtual capacity. Libraries long have been dubbed the "People's University," and they will continue to hold that title long into the future in whatever form best suits those who use their services.

Sharon Almquist, editor
Union, Kentucky

NOTES

1. The School of Library and Information Sciences became the Department of Library and Information Sciences within the College of Information at the University of North Texas in 2008. For more information, check out their website at http://www.ci.unt.edu/main/.

2. Carla Cantagallo, University of Kentucky, Distance Learning Library Services, http://www.uky.edu/DistanceLearning/online/libraries.php.

ACKNOWLEDGMENTS

The contributors and editor would like to thank their families, colleagues, and friends for their support during the process. Many times we thought we were done with the book, only to find that there was one more thing we wished to add and discuss. Being librarians, we strove to be as comprehensive and inclusive as possible.

We would also like to thank the students in the SLIS 5369: Distributed Learning Librarianship (University of North Texas) classes for their insightful questions and discussions. Their input helped to shape the book.

1

———◆◆◆———

DISTRIBUTED AND VIRTUAL LEARNING OVERVIEW: TERMS AND TIME LINE

Sharon G. Almquist

In this chapter we will examine distributed learning terms and present an annotated time line of significant distributed learning events in the library, education, and technology fields. While the time line is weighted toward innovations in the United States, it strives to be as comprehensive as possible in its reporting of distributed learning and associated events.

WHAT'S IN A TERM OR DEFINITION?

Trying to name a concept is just about as difficult as trying to define it. There are numerous names and definitions for distributed learning and for the degrees and means of distribution, some of which are directly linked to a specific communications medium, geographic location, or time. Others are more generic and may simply reflect an idea.

TERMS AND DEFINITIONS

Distributed Learning or Education

We use the term distributed learning in the title of the book because the term *distance* imposes a restriction or qualification as well as a geographic separation between learners, instructors, librarians, and resources.

On the other hand, distribution of information and learning materials implies that they are made available and dispersed widely without restrictions of time or place. The materials may be delivered from a central location or from several different locations by varying means of distribution, be it on the back of a donkey, on a boat, through the mail system, or by means of the World Wide Web. In this scheme, materials are pushed to the users.

In another paradigm, learners come to the materials. A central physical location such as a brick-and-mortar library or classroom distributes content and materials to the learners.

By removing restrictions of any sort, distributed learning and the dissemination of information may occur anywhere at any time. Regardless of these distinctions, distance education and distributed learning are often used interchangeably in the literature and in practice.

Given the concept of bringing information to those who need it, we could further define distributed learning as a method that allows instructors, librarians, learners, resources, and content to be located in different locations and brought together via a communications medium or physical transportation device to allow instruction, research, and learning to occur without physical or real-time constraints. Distributed learning has had a long history and will continue to hold a prominent place in future educational endeavors.

To further define and specify how online education delivers content, Allen and Seaman, in the 2009 report *Learning on Demand; Online Education in the United States*, used the definitions in Table 1.1.

Table 1   Course Classifications

PROPORTION OF CONTENT DELIVERED ONLINE	TYPE OF COURSE	TYPICAL DESCRIPTION
0%	**Traditional**	Course with no online technology used — content is delivered in writing or orally.
1 to 29%	**Web Facilitated**	Course that uses web-based technology to facilitate what is essentially a face-to-face course. May use a course management system (CMS) or web pages to post the syllabus and assignments.
30 to 79%	**Blended/Hybrid**	Course that blends online and face-to-face delivery. Substantial proportion of the content is delivered online, typically uses online duscussions, and typically has a reduced number of face-to-face meetings.
80+%	**Online**	A course where most or all of the content is delivered online. Typically have no face-to-face meetings.

Elaine Allen and Jeff Seaman. *Learning on Demand; Online Education in the United States, 2009.* (Needham, MA: Sloan-C, 2010). http://www.sloanconsortium.org/publications/survey/learning_on_demand_sr2010.

Distance Learning or Education

While distributed learning is learning without bounds, distance learning is quali-fied as a system in which instructors, learners, librarians, and content are separated by time and space. It is also a system in which materials may be distributed to the learner rather than having the learner come to the materials. Traditionally, infor-mation seekers have come to a physical location, such as a library, to find and use information. With circulating materials, learners may remove items from a physical location by checking them out and taking them home—a form of distribution. In distance learning, information is pushed to the learner by whatever means best suits the information, the learner, and the situation. Requiring physical travel to a loca-tion within a set time frame (hours of operation) is bypassed.

Distance learning is the term used by the Association of College and Research Libraries (ACRL) in its *Standards for Distance Learning Library Services*, 2008. (See chapter 2 for more information about the *Standards*.)

Earlier versions of the ACRL standards included:

- 1967: *ACRL Guidelines for Library Services to Extension Students*
- 1981: *ACRL Guidelines for Extended Campus Library Services* (Extended cam-pus library services may be considered analogous to Extended University ser-vices.)
- 1990–1998: *ACRL Guidelines for Distance Learning Library Services*
- 2000–2007: *ACRL Guidelines for Distance Learning Library Services*
- 2008: *ACRL Standards for Distance Learning Library Services*[1]

Does the term *distance learning* in this context imply a link to an institution of higher education? Yes, it does. While useful to all librarians, ACRL's standards are directed at academic libraries and are based on the access entitlement principle that demands equal services regardless of whether the provider or the learner accesses services in person or at a distance.[2]

In addition to ACRL, the Library and Information Technology Association (LITA) has supported a Distance Learning Interest Group since 1997. Its purpose is "to provide a forum for the discussion of the application of technologies to dis-tance learning activities in the library and information environment."[3]

Learning in any form may be either asynchronous or synchronous.

Asynchronous learning refers to a learning experience in which people do not have to be online or in communication at the same time.

Synchronous learning refers to a learning experience where interaction hap-pens simultaneously in real time, whether online or face-to-face.

CORRESPONDENCE COURSES

The traditional correspondence course is a form of independent study in which stu-dents receive course content by regular mail, complete assignments (usually at their own pace), and send assignments back to an instructor for grading. After grading them, the instructor returns the assignments with feedback to the student. Many correspondence courses were and remain print-based and use the postal service for delivery.

Some correspondence schools prepared and copyrighted a course package for their students' exclusive use and sent this to the students along with the lessons. Many correspondence students were willing to buy not only the required textbook but also suggested supplementary texts and other books when they could. Still, a need remained for supplemental reading materials as well as research and reference items. Librarians strove to meet these needs, as Noffsinger observed in 1926:

> Librarians frequently buy out of library funds copies of books called for by students and often use the reference lists of correspondence courses as guides to purchasing. In a number of states correspondence bureaus regularly notify public librarians when a student in their community enrolls in a course and suggest that special attention might be given his needs.[4]

ADULT EDUCATION

Adult education extends educational opportunities to adults no longer attending formalized school but who may seek further training in a specific area. Before many states enacted compulsory school attendance laws, those seeking additional training might have been as young as 13, having had all the schooling deemed necessary or financially possible. Adult education is often called continuing education and may provide vocational training, high school equivalency diplomas, literacy instruction, applied science, recreation, parenting classes, or any form of adult basic education. University extension courses fell under the adult education category.

The adult education movement in the United States evolved from the argument that adults needed to remain educated and informed in order to fully participate in a democratic society. It was also a prime motivator for the establishment of public libraries. Distributed learning was and is an expedient way to bring continuing education to many people in both urban centers and rural areas.

To enhance the adult education experience, there was a pressing need to make information accessible. This was especially true because many of the adults were enrolled in classes that had no association with institutions maintaining libraries, or they received their instruction remotely from a parent institution with remote library facilities. Should adults in correspondence courses be expected to purchase all books and materials they needed to complete their research? Should they only examine the prepackaged materials and forget about further expanding their horizons?

Support for continuing education fell heavily upon public libraries. As an American Library Association (ALA) commission report on adult education from 1926 noted: "In fact, the public library and the library agencies of the state are to the adult out-of-school student what the university or college library is to the university or college student. The necessity of providing library service for resident students and their instructors is recognized by all creditable institutions of learning."[5]

The Commission on the Library and Adult Education's recommendation from 1926 summed up public library support for adult education:

> a responsibility rests on librarians to furnish, through a readers' advisory service and through reading courses prepared to meet special and individual needs, a direct service in adult education which the library is peculiarly fitted to render. Free from all elements of grading and compulsion, it should make

an appeal to younger readers who feel a lack in their educational equipment, but who are still rejoicing, perhaps, in escape from organized supervision. . . . it should attract older readers whose rigorous daily schedule does not allow attendance at regular classes, whose interests cannot be made to fit into organized curricula, or who prefer greater independence in study than is permitted in most educational institutions.[6]

Lee echoed this idea forty years later in his 1966 history of public libraries and adult education, stating: "The public library was the first tax supported agency established in the United States for the informal education of adults. It was organized specifically to provide a means by which mature individuals could continue to learn through their own efforts."[7]

OFF-CAMPUS, EXTENDED CAMPUS, UNIVERSITY EXTENSION

These terms have been used for decades and continue to be used primarily in higher education. They illustrate how the resources of an educational institution may be extended geographically beyond the confines of the campus in an attempt to serve a widely diversified clientele within the state or region that may be considered the institution's constituent area. University extension, in particular, encompassed all of the services and activities of the university up to and including library extension. While extension programs offered college credit for individual courses, they usually did not award full degrees. One such example is the Continuing & Innovative Education (CIE) service at The University of Texas (UT) at Austin, founded in 1910 by the University's Board of Regents, which is still going strong over one hundred years later. CIE offers UT at Austin credit for its courses but does not award degrees.[8]

University or college extension programs extended the institution's offerings through distance learning and were usually part of the institution's continuing education outreach arm. Continuing education was frequently aimed at adults in an effort to encourage a routine of continuous reading and study. Both public and academic libraries were prime movers in the encouragement of adult continuing education and university extended campus programs. In 1926, the American Library Association defined university extension as "adult education of a most definite sort."[9]

LIBRARY EXTENSION

In the pre-Internet world, academic libraries charged with bringing materials to people enrolled in extension courses provided library support for college and university extension courses with the maintenance of traveling libraries, package libraries, clipping services, and direct mail. Support continues today as academic libraries make available electronic resources and services as well as sustain physical extended campus libraries in geographically dispersed locations.

In public libraries, extension services include outreach efforts that encompass a wide range of activities—from building libraries and branches to establishing traveling, prison, hospital, school, and home library programs.

Host or Originating Institution

The host or originating institution is the academic institution that offers and supports distributed learning courses. It is the credit-granting body but does not have to be the degree-granting body. The Association of College and Research Libraries (ACRL) describes the credit-granting institution as "the entity, singular or collective, and the chief administrative officers and governance organizations responsible for the offering, marketing, and/or supporting of distance learning courses and programs. Each institution in a multi-institutional cluster is responsible for meeting the library needs of its own students, faculty, and staff at the collective site."[10]

The Guidelines for Library Support of Distance and Distributed Learning in Canada (2000) provide a similar definition for an originating institution as the credit-granting entity offering courses and programs in a distributed fashion. As with other degree-granting institutions, this entity may operate from a brick-and-mortar campus or be a virtual institution.[11]

Host or Originating Library

A host or originating library is a brick-and-mortar, virtual, or hybrid academic, special, or school library supporting distributed learning courses offered from that library's institution. The ACRL *Standards* characterize the originating library as

> the library operation directly associated with the originating institution. In the case of virtual universities, the library itself may be virtual, or it may be the library of an existing traditional institution, contracted for services and materials to the students, faculty, and other personnel of the virtual institution.[12]

Open Learning

In essence, open learning is a form of correspondence course offered by technical or other institutions with few, if any, requirements for admission. A prime example of open learning is the Open University (OU) in the United Kingdom. "Born in the 1960s, the 'White Heat of Technology' era, the Open University was founded on the belief that communications technology could bring high-quality degree-level learning to people who had not had the opportunity to attend campus universities."[13]

Bringing higher education level courses and vocational training to people who could not come to a campus is not a new idea; nor is it one dependent upon electronic communications media, as we'll see throughout this and subsequent chapters.

OTHER TERMS ASSOCIATED WITH DISTRIBUTED LEARNING

The following are additional terms associated with distributed learning:

- Open and distance learning (ODL) links open and distance learning.
- Networked learning may be synchronous, asynchronous, or both, and combines information and communications technology (ICT) in order to encourage con-

nections between learners, learners and educators, and learners and resources, making it a concept uniquely applicable to an association between a librarian and a learner.

- Computer learning relies on local electronic media for content.
- Online, electronic, or virtual learning uses the web as the delivery medium.
- Independent learning or flexible learning refers mainly to self-paced distance learning, regardless of the medium of delivery.
- Tele-learning emphasizes learning via video or television.
- Radio programs feature learning by radio broadcast.
- Electronic correspondence courses. An updated and computerized version of the long-popular print-based and mailed correspondence course.
- Lifelong learning or continuing education usually involves non-credit courses geared to adult learners.
- Blended or hybrid learning is a combination of assignments and course content presented both online and in the classroom. It is a convergence of brick-and-mortar and virtual methods.
- Mobile learning (m-learning) is learning via various mobile telecommunication devices, such as cellular phones, smart phones, Blackberrys, iPhones, iPads, and the like.
- Learning management system (LMS) is used interchangeably with course management system (CMS) and virtual learning environment (VLE). These are online systems that coordinate the various facets of distributed learning online, including grade book, content, discussions, student tracking, email, and other classroom-type features. Two of the most well-known are Blackboard, Inc. and Moodle.

ADDITIONAL LIBRARY TERMS ASSOCIATED WITH DISTRIBUTED LEARNING

- Outreach

Can we consider distributed learning library support synonymous with library outreach initiatives? Both efforts are certainly related and share a common goal of reaching out to customers who may not otherwise have access to, or be able to access, library services and materials. Librarians generally view outreach as a series of services to underserved or disadvantaged populations such as those in prison or other institutions, homebound individuals, those faced with physical or mental impairments, the illiterate, or those who lack transportation. One time-honored way to reach such individuals is bookmobiles, which bring materials to people. Similar programs, such as direct delivery of books to customers and books by mail, extend a library's service beyond its physical walls. Electronic library outreach further extends a library's services, offering services and content delivered electronically to remote customers.

Historically, the term outreach, as it is defined in this context, came into use in the mid-1960s with actual outreach programs being described by that name in library literature of the early 1970s. Prior to this, outreach was synonymous with library extension in both public and academic libraries.

- Traveling, itinerating, perambulating libraries (Wanderbibliotheken or Wander-bücherein in Germany)

These terms were used in the 19th and early 20th centuries to characterize self-contained collections of books (and other materials such as lantern slides, photographs, and art works) distributed from a central point to different locations in shipping boxes that also served as book shelves. The collections usually numbered between 30 to 100 books selected for general reading or assembled to meet specific requests. The libraries were static collections that stayed in one place for a specific period of time. Most were established and supported by women's clubs in cities and sent to schools or rural areas lacking a library. As states formed library commissions, they assumed support of traveling library services and professionalized them.

Inexpensive to maintain, traveling libraries were viewed as a means to acquaint people with the services a permanent library could offer. Traveling libraries may be considered forerunners of the horse-drawn book wagon and the motorized bookmobile because they brought materials directly to people who did not otherwise have access to them.

Melvil Dewey, in his *Field and Future of Traveling Libraries* (1901), outlined many of the details of traveling libraries at that time. So inexpensive were these modern methods of communication and transportation, Dewey remarked, that the rails transported bees in their hives so that they could sample seasonal flowers in different locations. Regarding libraries, Dewey observed:

> The home library for children, the house library for rural districts, collections for shipboard, barracks, fire engine houses, police stations, lumber and mining camps, lighthouses, summer hotels, clubs and other associations are reaching every class and remote locality with library facilities on the traveling plan. . . . Any library extension that goes out on the itinerant principle is part of the traveling library idea.[14]

Writing two years later, Jessie M. Good mirrored Dewey's observations and reported:

> Traveling libraries go everywhere. To life-saving stations, to lonely lighthouses, to army barracks, to fire departments, to the home reading circles in the tenement districts of our great cities.[15]

Traveling libraries continue to be supported both by libraries and by a variety of organizations, such as individual Rotary clubs, with the goal of bringing books, magazines, and other materials, including Internet access, to underserved populations around the world.

- Deposit station libraries

Since the mid-19th century, deposit station libraries incorporated traveling libraries or collections that central libraries delivered to factories, stores, churches, post offices, nursing homes, jails, daycares, prisons, homeless shelters, schools, and just about anywhere in urban and rural areas where they could be supported. Deposit station agents were often the shopkeepers or others at the location who allocated space for the books and crates, oversaw the checking in and out of the materials, collected fines, removed books that required rebinding, reported circulation statistics, and generally served as keepers of the collections. Sometimes the central library paid station agents for their services based on the number of volumes circulated monthly.

- Package libraries

Public libraries (as part of outreach) and academic libraries (as part of the extension division) circulated carefully selected collections of newspaper and magazine clippings, pamphlets, and other ephemera on a specific subject assembled upon request. They were used most frequently by debaters, schools, and club women and were popular in the early 20th century.

- Book wagon, bookmobile, cybermobile

These transportation devices for mobile learning are basically traveling libraries housed in a truck, wagon, or van (usually motorized, but not always) that contain an organized collection of library materials for checkout. Unlike static traveling libraries shipped in crates for specific loan periods to one physical location at a time, these mobile collections follow regularly scheduled routes, make multiple stops on a single run, and present rotating collections of materials. Today many also offer access to computers or the Internet.

ANNOTATED TIME LINE OF DISTRIBUTED LEARNING

The chosen presentation is chronological and separated by century. While the time line does not list every institutional and educational endeavor or technological advancement, it should give you a general overview for understanding the history of distributed learning movements and trends as well as an idea of how that history may affect current and future trends. While we can certainly find aspects of distributed learning earlier than the 17th century, the introduction of the printing press around 1440 and medieval universities come to mind as a starting point, we'll concentrate on developments from that time forward.

17th/18th Century

1617: Napier's Rods Calculating Device (Scotland)

John Napier (1550–1617), a Scottish mathematician, created a mechanical calculating device able to perform multiplication, multiplication, division, and square roots.

1642: Blaise Pascal constructed a mechanical adding machine (France)

Pascal (1623–1662), a French mathematician and philosopher, built a mechanical adding machine called the Pascaline or Arithmetique. The device initially added and subtracted up to five-digit numbers, but with improvements, it could handle six and eight digits. Pascal developed the machine to assist his father, who was a tax collector.

1694: Gottfried Leibniz (1646–1716) constructed a mechanical calculating machine that could add, subtract, multiply, and divide (Germany)

1699–1730: English clergyman Thomas Bray (1656–1730) established traveling lending libraries in the British colonies in North America

Bray's vision was to establish a parochial library in every parish in America. In 1697, he published *An Essay Towards Promoting all Necessary and Useful Knowledge, Both Divine and Human, in all the Parts of His Majesty's Dominions, Both at Home and Abroad*, in which he presented "Proposals to the Gentry and Clergy of this Kingdom for purchasing lending Libraries in all the Deanaries of England, and Parochial Libraries for Maryland, Virginia, and other of the Foreign Plantations."[16] Steiner, in his study of Bray, called him the "first apostle of the free circulating library."[17]

Bray's lending libraries or moveable repositories (Bray used both terms) traveled in boxes with shelves, doors, and locks, making them always ready for travel. In addition to use by the clergy, ladies and gentlemen of the gentry could pay a small fee for borrowing privileges.[18] Bray himself noted: "Standing libraries will signifie little in the Country, where Persons must ride some miles to look into a Book; such Journeys being too expensive of Time and Money: But *Lending Libraries,* which come home to 'em without Charge, may tolerably well supply the Vacancies in their own studies, till such a time as these *Lending* may be improv'd into *Parochial Libraries.*"[19] Prior to 1850, books were valuable and scarce commodities especially in the American colonies.

1710: Statute of Anne (England)

The full title reads, "An Act for the Encouragement of Learning, by Vesting the Copies of Printed Books in the Authors or Purchasers of such Copies, during the Times therein mentioned." The statute was enacted in England in an attempt to restore order to a chaotic book trade. This was an important foundation to later copyright law, the ramifications of which are discussed fully in chapters 5 and 6.

The statute established defined time limits for the legal protection of the right to copy:

1. For books already in print, the stationer's (publisher's) copyright was extended to 21 years; for future works, the author (or anyone who was assigned as the author) had exclusive right to print the work for 14 years, with the right to renew for an additional 14 years.
2. For works published after the statute, the author (or anyone who was assigned as the author), if still alive, had the exclusive right to print the work for 14 years, with the right to renew for an additional 14 years.

Essentially, the statue defined who could hold the right to copy and reproduce a book and established the concept of formal copyright registration, which allowed copyright holders to be more easily located. In addition, the statue required that books formally registered be deposited in nine university libraries.[20]

1728: Advertisement for Short Hand Correspondence Course (Boston, MA, United States).

Caleb Phillips, "Teacher of the New Method of Short Hand," placed an advertisement in the March 20 edition of the *Boston Gazette* in which he offered a correspondence course with the promise: "Persons in the Country desirous to Learn this Art, may by having the several Lessons sent weekly to them, be as perfectly instructed as those that live in Boston."

1785: Agricultural Societies established (United States).

Public-minded people in several states, including Pennsylvania, Massachusetts, and South Carolina, imitated the English and Europeans by establishing agricultural societies dedicated to the education of the farmer and improvement of farming. The societies published reports and may be considered forerunners of agricultural university extension. (See also the Smith-Lever Act of 1914.)

1793: Copyright established in France.

In 1790, the Marquis de Condorcet proposed that copyright should remain in effect for the length of an author's life plus an additional ten years. Criticized by the Paris Book Guild and theater directors, who complained that their ability to publish and produce plays would be severely limited, the proposal never came to a vote. Three years later, in 1793, the proposal passed in the heat of the revolutionary spirit of respect for individual rights and property. The law was considered a compromise between the acknowledgment of literary property and the concept of public domain or non-copyrightable works.[21]

1787: Copyright established in the United States.

Copyright was established in the United States as part of the *U.S. Constitution,* which stated: "The Congress shall have Power . . . [t]o Promote the Progress of Science and the useful Arts, by securing for *limited* Times to Authors and Inventors the *exclusive* Right to their respective Writings and Discoveries."[22]

1790s: The adult education movement took form in Great Britain.[23]

1795: Massachusetts Charitable Mechanic Association organized (United States).

The Association served mechanics and manufacturers by "promoting mutual good offices and fellowship, assisting the necessitous, encouraging the ingenious, and rewarding fidelity." The Association followed the trends of the day in adult education and the diffusion of knowledge by funding a library, an evening school for apprentices, and public lectures. By 1829, the library boasted around 1,500 donated volumes. The apprentices managed the library as a committee. The library was open "to all apprentices in the city and vicinity, without charge, and without any other restriction than those usually found necessary for similar purposes among adults."[24]

1797: Anderson's Institute incorporated (Glasgow, Scotland, Great Britain).

Dr. John Anderson has been called the founder of mechanics' institutions, a form of adult education for mechanics in the physical sciences, which gradually evolved into professional schools. Anderson "was desirous that useful science should be universally studied. He saw its vast importance to every class of the community. He regarded its confinement within the walls of a college as a serious injury to society." Anderson's will initially endowed the Institute with a library.[25]

19th Century

1801:   Jacquard created a punch card system for programming looms (France).

Joseph Marie Jacquard (1752–1834) created a punch card system using metal cards with holes corresponding to the binary system of open/closed that guided weaving machines to create intricate patterns. A form of computer manufacturing, this system allowed cloth to be woven according to a set of commands. Punch card systems were used well into the 1960s.

1816:   College Instructor Offers Public Lectures (United States).

An instructor at Queens College (later Rutgers University) offered public lectures on chemical philosophy directly to students in what we might consider an early form of unofficial university extension service. It was quite common for poorly paid instructors to supplement their income by offering to lecture for a fee. Another example of instructors dealing directly with students is the Correspondence University established in Ithaca, NY, in 1883.

1817:   Samuel Brown (1779–1839) began a system of itinerating libraries with 200 volumes (Haddington, Scotland).

Itinerate: to go from place to place on a circuit like judges or preachers or, in this instance, books. Directly related to the traveling and deposit station libraries in the United States, itinerating libraries most likely influenced Josiah Holbrook of lyceum fame.

Brown worked and lived in the county of East Lothian, near Edinburgh. "His itinerating libraries idea was a consequence of his having observed the limited usefulness, in small centers of population, of small static libraries, local interest in whose contents was soon exhausted."[26]

Instead of a static assortment of works, Brown assembled collections of about fifty books and circulated them every two years in an attempt to diffuse useful knowledge to those who did not have access to it. To further increase ease of access, anyone over the age of 12 could borrow a book. In a letter dated May 5, 1835 to Rev. Dr. Lorimer, Brown wrote: "The regular removal and supply of new division has excited and kept up such a disposition to read, that in several stations during the winter months, scarcely a volume is left in the book-case."[27]

Brown also visited local jails to read to prisoners and to encourage literacy among the inmates. "The jail in Haddington later became a station for an itinerating library, its jailer acting as voluntary librarian." Brown continued to support the itinerating libraries and by the early 1830s had enough money to supply them at a minimal cost to anyone agreeing to locally manage them. "In all he supplied nearly 100 such libraries not only to Scotland and England, but to Ireland, Russia, South Africa, and the West Indies."[28]

1823:   Mechanics Institute established by the Gaslight Chartered Company of Glasgow, Scotland (Great Britain).

This institute offered adult instruction designed to promote education of mechanics.

1823 and 1834:   Charles Babbage (1792–1871) created mechanical computers powered by steam (England).

In 1823, Babbage assembled the mechanical Difference Engine, a huge calculator that was never finished. Eleven years later, in 1834, Babbage completed the Analytical Engine, which was capable of storing numbers, was accurate to six decimal places, and used Jacquard's punched metal cards for its programming. The engine weighed three tons and contained four thousand mechanical and interrelated pieces.

1834:   First computer algorithm written (England).

Lady Ada Byron Lovelace (1815–1851), daughter of the poet Lord Byron, wrote the first algorithm intended to be processed by a calculating machine. She is generally regarded as the world's first computer programmer. In 1979, the United States Department of Defense named its universal computer programming language "ADA" in her honor.

1826–1850:   American Lyceum Movement flourished from 1826 to around 1850 (United States).

1826:   Millbury Branch No. 1 of the American Lyceum organized, marking the beginning of the American Lyceum movement (United States).

As in England, the first American adult education efforts stemmed from non-university sources. The lyceum was one of the first channels for the diffusion of learning, self study and improvement, and the quest for effective universal public education. As noted in the "lyceums" entry from an early 20th century edition of *The Cambridge History of English and American Literature:* "The leaders of thoughts in every walk of life participated in this adult form of education, and much of the most important literary expression of the period was originally published through this channel."[29]

Josiah Holbrook (1788–1854) of Derby, CT, is generally credited as the founder of the American Lyceum movement. In 1826, Holbrook established the first lyceum at Millbury, MA. A graduate of the 1810 Yale class with Chauncey Goodrich and Samuel F.B. Morse, Holbrook made his living as a traveling lecturer who encouraged small groups of people to assemble outside of formal schools for sustained study in specific subjects. Holbrook himself lectured on geology, mineralogy, and other natural sciences. An advocate of hands-on learning, he designed and manufactured a collection of aids for mathematics teaching in homes and schools. His goal was to help students learn the names of simple solids, basic rules for calculating the area of various surfaces, and elementary drawing. Holbrook advertised that his equipment was "[g]ood enough for the best, and cheap enough for the poorest." Thousands of schools adopted his teaching aids.

Holbrook experimented with various schools by combining manual training, farming, and formal instruction. After the failure of his Agricultural Seminary in

1825, he began lecturing on popular scientific subjects and edited *Scientific Tracts* (1830–32) and *The Family Lyceum* (1832–33).

Undaunted by previous setbacks, he established the Lyceum Village in Berea, OH, in 1837. Although the village failed after a few years, Holbrook continued to promote the lyceum movement until his premature death from drowning in 1854.

Holbrook's vision for the lyceum movement was a broad one in which he visualized town, county, and state lyceums becoming part of a national lyceum. Semiannual meetings of representatives from various town lyceums in each county would appoint committees "to inquire how books, apparatus and instruction by lecturers or otherwise can be procured by the several towns' lyceums; and to learn the state of the schools in the several towns where they are placed, and what measures can be taken to improve them."[30] One of Holbrook's goals was to introduce "a uniform system of books and instruction into our public schools."[31]

Town lyceums provided for a number of important ideals, such as:

1. The improvement of conversation.
2. Directing amusements—The lyceum was perceived as providing decent entertainment for young people that would keep them out of saloons.
3. Saving of expense—Low cost of the lyceum in terms of money with high return in increase in knowledge.
4. Calling into use neglected libraries, and giving occasion for establishing new ones—"It has been a subject of general regret, that public libraries, after a short time, fall into neglect and disuse." Lyceums, though their reliance on lecture and debate, created interest and demand for books leading to the creation and expansion of libraries.
5. Providing a seminary for teachers—Assisting teachers to increase their knowledge and marketability.
6. Benefiting academies—Experienced guest lecturers featured at lyceums brought knowledge directly to students in local academies and seminaries at little or no cost.
7. Increasing the advantages, and raising the character of district schools—Older children could take courses in small groups directly from the traveling lecturers and increase their knowledge.
8. Compiling of town histories.
9. Town maps.
10. Agricultural and geological surveys.
11. State collections of minerals.[32]

The lyceum movement, despite detractors, was an effective means of adult educational extension, which sought to supply the diffusion of useful knowledge. Highly popular, democratic, and spontaneous, lyceums inspired the formation of public schools and libraries. Even after its decline, other initiatives, such as the Chautauqua movement, carried on the concept of public lectures and open forums of debate.

1828: Movement toward international copyright code.

Reciprocal treaties introduced in Denmark between several countries awarded foreign authors the same protection as native authors in each country.

1829: Mechanic's Institute of Lexington, Kentucky, established (United States).

As with the lyceum movement, the association of libraries with mechanics institutions and as part of the American adult education movement is a strong one. When the Lexington Mechanic's Institute was established "one of the first steps of the Board of Managers was to provide a Library, the delivery of Public Lectures, and a Apprentices' School."[33]

1833: Advertisement for correspondence study by post (Sweden) .

An advertisement in English in *Lunds Weckoblad,* no. 30, a weekly newspaper published in the university city of Lund, offered "Ladies and Gentlemen" an opportunity to study "Composition through the medium of the Post."[34]

1834: Lyceum movement expands (United States).

Three thousand town lyceums flourished in the United States from Maine to Florida by 1834.

1831–1839: National American Lyceum (United States).

The National American Lyceum flourished from 1831 to 1839. At its first convention in New York City, representatives from well over a thousand towns attended. Its primary goal supported "the advancement of education, especially in the common schools, and the general diffusion of knowledge."[35] Although short-lived, the National American Lyceum was a powerful advocate for the establishment of public schools and libraries.

1837: Copyright: An act protecting property in works of science and arts is introduced in Prussia (Europe).

This act counted a term of copyright from the life span of an author and his or her immediate heirs. *Post mortem auctoris* (after the author's death) terms were introduced.

1837: The American Seamen's Friend Society placed libraries on ships leaving the Port of New York (United States).[36]

1838: Lowell Institute of Boston (United States).

John Lowell, Jr. (1799–1836) endowed a series of public lectures by leaving half of his fortune, roughly $250,000, in a trust for "the promotion of popular education through lectures, and in other ways." The resulting Lowell Institute was highly successful and its lecturers "included many of the ablest men in this and other countries. The work of the Lowell Institute has also included free lectures for advanced students given in connection with the Massachusetts Institute of Technology, science lectures to the teachers of Boston, and a free drawing school."[37]

1839: The American Seamen's Friend Society deposited libraries on ships leaving the ports of New York, Boston, Philadelphia, and New Orleans (United States).[38]

1839: English scientist John Benjamin Dancer (1812–1887) produced micro-photographs, an early type of microform.

By 1853, Dancer sold microphotographs on slides that could be viewed with a microscope.

1840s: Morse Code invented.

Morse Code was a communications medium that used small bursts of energy to break down words into their simplest form with a slow burst for a dot and a longer burst for a dash. It was a Base-2 number system like binary code.

1840: Shorthand Correspondence Courses (England).

British schoolmaster Isaac Pitman (1813–1897) taught shorthand by correspondence through the "Penny Post." (The Penny Post refers to the single postal rate of one penny.) Pitman sent post cards with instructions to his students. The students transcribed those passages, which were mainly taken from the Bible, into shorthand and sent the transcriptions back to him for correction. In 1843, Pitman formed the Phonographic Correspondence Society to continue the shorthand courses. It later evolved into the Sir Isaac Pitman Correspondence Colleges. Many writers believed that Pitman should be heralded as the first modern distance educator.[39]

1852: Benn Pitman founded the Phonographic Institute in Cincinnati, OH (United States).

Like his brother, Isaac, Benn taught shorthand through correspondence.

1842: Talfourd's or Lord Mahon's copyright act established (United Kingdom).

Copyright protection extended to a total of 42 years including at least seven years after the copyright holder's death.

1843: Scottish inventor and clockmaker Alexander Bain (1811–1877) patented the concept of a facsimile machine.

1844: Folk High School established in Schleswig (Denmark).

Lutheran Bishop Nikolai Grundtvig (1783–1872) championed the idea of folk high schools (*folkehojskole*) as a protest against the existing Latin school system. Using the term "a school of life," these schools focused on the spoken word as the primary means of teaching and allowed the needs of the community to determine the curriculum. Although not technically distance education, the folkehojskole were a unique form of adult education, brought to rural communities to better the lives of those living there.

The school's goals were:

- to stimulate the intellectual life of young adults from 18 to 25 years of age in rural Denmark
- to foster patriotism and strengthen religious conviction
- to provide agricultural and vocational training.

Interest was high with over 5,000 enrolled in the 1890s and 7,000 participating in the 1920s.[40]

1844: A practical telegraph system based on the electromagnet was introduced by the American Samuel Morse (1791–1872).

Although providing an additional communication medium, the telegraph was not used to a great extent in libraries. One notable exception occurred in 1902 in "a special legislative library that used telegraphy to rely crucial information to legislators."[41]

1845: Adult Schools of the Society of Friends in England (1845) fostered the education of the poor.

1851: Perambulating Library began operation funded by merchant and philanthropist George Moore (Warrington, England).

Moore (1805–1876) viewed the perambulating or traveling library as "a simple, cheap, and efficient method of maintaining adult education in the country districts, and of keeping reading people in contact with the pure and healthy literature of the time." This proved successful and a paid messenger delivered books to stations every six weeks. Reports indicated that "the books were nearly always out, and the country people were thus induced to read good books."[42] Each village had its own librarian and subscribers to the service paid one penny per month.

1854: Boston Public Library opened its doors to the public (Boston, MA, United States).

1856: Languages Taught Through Correspondence (Berlin, Germany).

Charles Toussaint, a Frenchman teaching French in Berlin, and Gustav Langenscheidt, a German writer and member of the Society of Modern Languages, founded a school for teaching languages by correspondence. The self-study teaching system used practical phonetic transcription.[43] While students were offered opportunities to submit questions, they were not encouraged to do so because "it would hardly be necessary since everything is fully explained in the course."[44]

1858: The External System of the University of London established (England and Worldwide).

The University of London, founded in 1836, was a revolutionary player in the distance education field and may well be considered the first global university. When Queen Victoria signed the University's fourth Charter on April 9, 1858, the External System was effectively established. The External System allowed the University of London to offer distance-learning degrees to students unable to come to a brick-and-mortar university. A year later, in 1859, the University held examinations outside of London at Queen's College in Liverpool and Owens College in Manchester. In 1865, the System broadened its scope to include study outside of England. The first country to host examinations was the island nation of Mauritius located off the African coast. The report of the examiners noted that "eleven candidates presented themselves at the examination: of whom six have passed." In 1873, the University of London awarded its first degrees to distant students in Mauritius.[45]

The External System continued to expand from its London base with examinations for non-collegiate students held in Gibraltar (1867), Canada (1868),

Tasmania and the West Indies (1869), India (1880), Ceylon (Sri Lanka, 1882), Hong Kong (1888), with 18 centers worldwide by 1899.

Degree by examination was the key component, as noted in the July 16, 1859, issue of the periodical *All the Year Round,* edited by Charles Dickens. In the article "The English People's University," the anonymous author commented on the new charter's verbiage, remarking that "every hard worker who can prove his competence may come for a degree to the University of London," and "nobody ever ridiculed the test of intellectual competence through which only men can arrive at association with the University of London. Having passed by a light examination to the degree of Bachelor of Arts in one of our old universities, the graduate may advance without any examination at all through the series of higher terms of honour. They belong to a question of little more than time and money. In the People's University every degree has to be stoutly fought for." The examination schedule was grueling. The Bachelor of Arts degree required students to pass two four-day exams a year apart. For the honors program, each exam lasted eight days.[46]

In 2001, the University opened an online library charged with the mission "to develop and maintain online resources and services in support of the present and future teaching, learning and research needs of the University of London's Distance learning Community."[47] In 2005, the University established a Centre for Distance Education. Still going strong, the External System celebrated its 150th anniversary in 2008.

1858: American Seamen's Friend Society (ASFS) introduced revolving traveling libraries to ships' crews (United States).

The ASFS library outreach program operated from 1858 to 1967; the Society itself officially ceased operation in 1986. Called the "Little Red Box" until the 1940s, ASFS libraries held approximately 50 books. Rental costs were reasonable, with a charge of $5.00 being levied before World War I. In 1878, John S. Pierson, nicknamed the "Andrew Carnegie of the Seas," published the Society's collection development policy. There were four goals named in Pierson's order of importance and with Pierson's justification for their inclusion in the library:

1. Recreation—"Even a bit of healthy humor, once in a while, will not be begrudged him . . . the first point is, to awaken a taste for reading. When that is once formed, the somewhat sensational story or narrative, with its pictures, exciting curiosity and compelling a perusal, may be expected to give place to the more solid book of history or travel."[48]
2. Humanization or civilizing books to touch the imagination and the heart as a counter to rough and coarse habits and tastes. Pierson denounced non-educational novels: "The novel, in the popular meaning of that word, does not find place in the ship's library."[49] Sailors did, however, bring their own dime novels aboard and in 1862 the ASFS publication *The Life Boat* noted: "The first two months the crew seemed to be afraid of them [the library books], till all the novels and bad books were read, when they all found delight in reading the library books."[50] Pierson was not alone in his condemnation of novels. Librarians of this era also shunned them.
3. Books featuring stories of voyages and travels, history, biographies, geography, and atlases.

4. Religious instruction was fourth on Pierson's list but first in terms of true importance to him. According to Pierson, "The greatest attention, of course, is given to the selection of these [religious books]: for, though it is made to refresh, to form a taste for reading, to humanize, to educate, the noblest aim of the ship's library is the conversion of the soul."[51]

As might be expected, the crews responded both positively and negatively to the ASFS library program, as can be seen in this librarian's report: "Books read by all hands. I have not heard an oath from any of our men since the library came on board. The men used to swear and drink. I think it a blessed thing to have these good books to read, for it keeps the mind occupied, and keeps the men from vice."[52] On the other hand, some captains complained that there were no foreign language books for their non-English speaking crews. One sailor described the books Pierson sent as "heavy enough to sink a ship." Many went unread and some went overboard.

When Pierson retired and William Elling took over, the following appeared in the March 30, 1907, Saturday edition of the *New York Times:* "Under the old librarian [Pierson] books filled with sober, solemn, elevating thoughts formed the bulk of the volumes in the libraries sent to the ships; under the new librarian (Elling) their places will be taken by thrilling tales of trouble, adventure, and intrigue—real stories; not preachments."[53]

1858:   First transatlantic cable laid between Newfoundland and Ireland.

The insulated copper wire cable allowed telegraphic communications across the Atlantic Ocean. This first cable remained operational for only a few weeks and was replaced in 1866 with a more robust version. Cyrus Field (1819–1892) staked both ventures as well as several others that were not successful.

1859:   Public Libraries in Australia circulated traveling libraries.

Beginning in 1859, public libraries in Australia set up a system of traveling libraries to serve those unable to come to a central library. This system served as one of the models for traveling libraries in the United States. From Adelaide, the public library circulated eight boxes of 30 books each among 20 country libraries. Melbourne sent out 20 libraries of 1,000 volumes each. In some instances, traveling libraries also included boxes of minerals, intended to acquaint people with the kinds of natural resources that might be readily available in their area. "These minerals are labeled, and a descriptive hand-book accompanies each cabinet which tells under what conditions each mineral is likely to be discovered."[54]

In addition to government-sponsored book collections, private funds supported the circulation of framed art prints. While the libraries reached many people, the collections were somewhat generic and could not be customized to meet the specific needs of clubs and others. To remedy this, a librarian named Mr. Anderson was attempting through donations to add "books of a general and lighter character, books that will awaken the interest of people unused to reading anything but a weekly newspaper, while some boxes will be made up for schools and juvenile reading."[55]

1859: French photograph, inventor, and optician, René Dagron (1819–1900) was granted the first patent for microfilm (France).

To illustrate the effectiveness and portability of the micro format, Dragon attached microfilmed messages to carrier pigeons that flew across German lines to Paris while the city was besieged during the Franco-Prussian War in 1870–71.

1861: On October 24, the first transcontinental telegraph system began operation in North America and connected the eastern United States to California. (See also 1844, the practical telegraph.)

1861–1865: The Civil War, also known as The War Between the States (United States).

Providing reading materials to troops on active service and recovering in hospitals was a concern during the American Civil War. The Young Men's Christian Association (YMCA) responded to this need in the fall of 1861 when it formed the United States Christian Commission of the Army and Navy (USCC). The charge of the USCC was "to take active measures to promote the spiritual and temporal welfare of the soldiers in the army, and the sailors and marines in the navy, in cooperation with chaplains and others."[56] Part of this charge involved sending books and pamphlets to the Union troops on land and at sea. To that end, the Commission prepared and distributed libraries in the general hospitals, at permanent posts and large forts, and on navy war ships. Chaplain John M. Morris of the Eighth Connecticut Volunteers remarked: "Day before yesterday, I received a box of pamphlets from the Commission. There were half a dozen men ready to open the box, and twenty more at hand to superintend the process and share the contents. The demand for reading is four times the supply."[57] Major George Haven Putnam observed that "two English grammars were eagerly read and passed along among the men shut up in Libby prison."[58]

Some regiments, such as those from Connecticut, received libraries as part of their regimental equipment. Regimental libraries were housed in strong, portable, lockable cases accompanied by a written catalog. By July 1862, these libraries contained over 1,200 volumes and 5,000 magazines. Materials covered a wide variety of subjects and were timely. The Chaplain of the Tenth Connecticut Volunteers observed: "You will always find ten to fifty men in the tent, reading and writing. The library is just the thing needed. The books are well assorted, and entertaining."[59]

In September, 1863, General George H. Thomas appointed Chaplain Thomas as the general reading agent for the Army of the Cumberland. The Chaplain worked with some 75 publishers of major newspapers and magazines to buy copies at half price. In January 1864, Chaplain Thomas contracted for half-price books from major publishers to be sold to the Christian Commission (USCC) loan libraries. Thomas spent weeks "studying publishers' catalogues and 'dictionaries of authors' and examining the books themselves in bookstores and libraries" and selected those he deemed most suitable for the libraries. When questioned about his decisions, Thomas "replied that none but the best, most suitable, and cheapest editions were chosen. Although he admittedly borrowed the idea from the American Seamen's Friend Society the book stock of his libraries contained more secular books than did the Seaman's Friend 'Sea Missions.'" The libraries increased in number throughout the war and were generally well received. After the war, many of the libraries were lost, but those salvaged were installed at permanent posts, in forts, and on warships.[60]

1862: United States Department of Agriculture established; Morrill Act (United States).

The establishment of the U.S. Department of Agriculture reflected the adult education movement for farmers that had begun as early as 1785 with the establishment of the agricultural societies. Over time the federal Department of Agriculture evolved into a kind of national university.[61]

The Morrill Act provided a land endowment for each of the states for the creation of colleges of agriculture and mechanic arts, which were dubbed land-grant universities or colleges. Each land-grant university was directly responsible for educating the people of its state and charged with solving problems through academic, research, and extension programs and activities. To accommodate the mandate to incorporate research and practical application, many of these institutions created agricultural experiment stations for exploring and testing improved farm practices. In 1907, Dr. W. E. Stone, president of Purdue University, commented on the growth in education as a result of the Morrill Act: "The impulses set in motion by the Morrill Act have developed in a remarkable short time a new education; have achieved great popularity and influences; have appealed to the democracy; and have proved it inestimable value to the industries."[62] (See also 1914: Smith-Lever Act.)

1867: Invention of the typewriter by Christopher Sholes (United States).

A year later, 1868, Sholes, Carlos Glidden, and Samuel Soule received a patent for the type writing machine. Other dates of note:

1872: Thomas Alva Edison builds the first electric typewriter.

1873: Remington & Sons mass produce the Sholes patented typewriter.

1978: Olivetti Company and the Casio Company developed an electronic typewriter.

1868: First traveling railroad library established on the Boston and Albany line (United States).

The "Circulating and Consulting Library for the Officers and Employees of the Boston and Albany Railroad Company" was intended only for use by railroad employees. Two years (1870) after its inception, the collection contained well over 1,200 volumes. The object of the collection was to provide books on the railway system, industrial arts, general science, and literature. The oversight Library Committee of five divided the library into two departments: consulting (reference, noncirculating) and circulating.

Similar railroad libraries included the Cleveland and Pittsburgh Railroad Reading-Room Association (Wellsville, OH) and the Vermont Central Railroad Library. The Baltimore and Ohio (1885) and the Southern Pacific railroads also supported libraries. The Seaboard Air Line Railroad placed station agents in charge of the libraries and allowed open access.[63]

1873–1897:   Society to Encourage Study at Home (United States).

In 1873 at the age of 50, Anna Eliot Ticknor (1823–1896), daughter of a Harvard University professor who was also one of the founders of the Boston Public Library, established the Boston-based "Society to Encourage Study at Home." According to the biographical note in one of the Society's publications (1897), Ticknor was

> at once secretary, treasurer, and president, writer of reports, framer of courses and of book lists, purchaser for the library, and active in all sorts of details. More important still was her correspondence with the students of the Society . . . It will be seen that she was a teacher, an inspirer, a comforter and, in the best sense, a friend of many and many a lonely and baffled life.[64]

Although the program was not affiliated with any academic institution, it enrolled more than 7,000 women in university-level correspondence courses and was self-supporting. Ticknor, assisted by about 200 volunteers, "laid out and directed courses of study over the country. By a well-organized system of distribution, she [Ticknor] sent books, engravings, photographs, maps, all that makes the outfit of thorough instruction, to the doors of families living far from museums, libraries, or colleges."[65]

The courses featured readings and tests offered to all who were interested in a noncompetitive environment based on monthly correspondence. Courses taught in order of interest included:

- History
- English Literature
- German
- Art
- French
- Science

Ticknor has been hailed as the "mother of American correspondence study." A member of the Massachusetts Library Commission (the first state library commission in the United States, founded in 1890) and passionately concerned with literacy, Ticknor did not neglect books. To support the Society's studies, she "collected a large lending library; and though these books were constantly on the road and passed through many hands they were rarely lost, and, with few exceptions, they were returned uninjured."[66] The Society effectively ended with Ticknor's death in 1897. Although popular, it was criticized for a failure to adapt its methods of instruction to the abilities and requirements of its students. Competition from expanding university extension courses as well as multiple correspondence opportunities combined with the loss of Ticknor's dynamic personality to seal the Society's fate.

1873: University of the Cape of Good Hope established in South Africa (Africa).

This was the first university established in South Africa. Modeled on the University of London, it awarded degrees through examination. In 1916, it was renamed the University of South Africa (UNISA) and in 1946 the Division of External Studies was launched. In 2004, UNISA merged with Technikon Southern Africa, added the distance education component of Vista University (VUDEC), and became the new UNISA, a open distance education institution.

1874: Chicago Public Library initiated the Delivery Station system of outposts (Illinois, United States).

The Chicago Public Library delivered books by horse-drawn carriage to library deposit stations housed in candy or drug stores. Employees at the stores administered the circulations and over time the store owners were paid a small amount to house and oversee the collections. Deposit stations located in businesses, churches, and factories were also popular. Reading rooms were set up in "Chicago's many community park field houses or on the upper floors of businesses. By the early 1900s Deposit Stations accounted for two-thirds of the entire circulation of the Chicago Public Library."[67] People were able to request specific books and have them delivered to the location nearest to them.

Librarian John Cotton Dana (1856–1929) equivocally commented on the importance of delivery stations in an address titled *Making a Library Known* that was delivered before the Long Island Library Club in 1905:

> Delivery and deposit stations bring the library to the very doors of many people in the city who never can visit the main building itself. Delivery stations seem a particularly unsympathetic way of getting books into people's hands. The arm's length method of selecting through a catalogue, the many disappointments because of the constant demand for the new books, of which the supply is always inadequate, these alone discourage many from the continued use of the delivery station. The deposit station, a small collection of books placed in a store on open shelves and cared for by the storekeeper—this seems more successful.[68]

1874–current: Chautauqua Institution (Chautauqua, NY, United States).

The Chautauqua Institution, originally called the Chautauqua Lake Sunday School Assembly, is located on Lake Chautauqua in southwestern New York State. Bishop John H. Vincent and Lewis Miller originally established the assembly as a normal school for Sunday School teachers in 1874. Active during the summer months, it was an experiment in vacation education.

From its beginnings as an opportunity for summer Bible study, courses expanded to cover a wide variety of subjects geared to adults who no longer attended formal school. Going one step farther into the realm of extension, the Chautauqua College of Liberal Arts Correspondence Department offered university-level correspondence study and conferred degrees from 1885 to 1891. William Rainey Harper of Yale (later the first president of the University of Chicago) served as the inaugural principal of the Chautauqua system.

The Chautauqua Scientific and Literary Circle (CLSC), organized in 1878, provided a medium for continuing education during the months away from the Institution. The CLSC is heralded as the longest continuously running book club in America.

The adult education activities of the Chautauqua Institution gave rise to the Chautauqua movement, which epitomized the concept of distributed adult education and informative lectures. Traveling Chautauquas appeared throughout the United States in the late 19th century and remained popular until the 1930s. So influential was the movement that some visiting lecture series carry the title "Chautauqua" even today.

The Chautauqua Institution in New York, a center for the arts, education, religion, and recreation, is still going strong in the present day. In each nine-week summer session, it supports a wide variety of courses, a resident orchestra, and an opera company, which has produced operas performed in English since 1929. The Smith Memorial Library provides library services to residents year-round.

1876: Telephone invented.

Even though the telephone made its debut in the latter part of the 19th century, libraries didn't use it extensively until the early 20th century. Restrictions in coverage limited service to cities and high costs made it expensive for the average citizen.

The "Moorish" Barn, around 1900. Chautauqua Institution. Courtesy of Chautauqua Institution Archives

Given libraries' interest in and acceptance of technology, however, it was no surprise that libraries embraced this new form of outreach as soon as it was feasible. As early as 1908 the Newark, NJ, Free Public Library welcomed phone calls and publicized its service in newspaper advertisements. The library proudly displayed its phone number on all printed materials. In spite of advertising, support, and interest on the part of the library, not many patrons called with reference questions. Nonetheless, an advocate for bringing information to people, the Newark Library responded to requests for books by sending them by special courier to any address in its service area while charging only a small fee for the service. A borrower could keep a book up to 30 days, but needed to come to the library to renew it. The library didn't feel comfortable renewing books by phone at this point.[69]

In 1911 the East St. Louis Public Library printed and distributed 2,000 telephone lists, which marketed the library's services and declared: "Best information bureau in town is the East St. Louis Public Library. Call—if there is anything about any subject you want to know." Also on the list was this text: "We loan books for home reading (26,000) to residents of East St. Louis. Ask how to get them."[70]

From the 1920s onward telephone usage and coverage increased steadily and allowed libraries to more fully develop telephone reference service policies and to integrate the telephone into their reference activities. Reflecting both the use of the telephone and the increased collection of sound recordings by libraries, a Wisconsin librarian observed: "In addition to strange reference questions, librarians never know if they will hear a few notes whistled into their ear for identification, when picking up the telephone receiver."[71]

Charles Cutter in his visionary 1883 article, "The Buffalo Public library in 1983," illustrated his perception of a future use telephone library services:

if I want a Cincinnati paper I telephone to the public library there to set a searcher at work to hunt up the matter in question. When she has found it she may either copy it or read it off to me through the telephone, or, better still, read it to a fonograf and transmit the foil. She sends the charge for her time, which is moderate, to the librarian here, and I pay him. This exchange is going on all the time between the different libraries.[72]

1876: American Library Association (ALA) founded by Melvil Dewey during the Centennial Exposition in Philadelphia on October 6 (United States).

1876: Portable libraries introduced in the Light-House Establishment (Michigan, United States).

In Michigan, and elsewhere, traveling libraries were sent to lighthouses to supply reading material to those staffing lonely outposts. The collections were selected with the families in mind and included fiction, literature, and, when requested, technical books.[73]

1878: Oxford University organized an extension department (England).

Like most extension efforts, one of the goals of Oxford's university extension teaching was to promote continuing education, reading, and study. Also like others, the effort heavily relied on public libraries to supply guidance for these newly created readers. (It is interesting to note that Oxford did establish traveling libraries in 1885 to support its extension services.) Most extension courses incorporated lectures, classes, a printed syllabus, and lists of recommended books for additional study.[74]

1878: Skerry's College founded (Edinburgh, Scotland).

Skerry's College was a correspondence school dedicated to the preparation of candidates for civil service examinations.

1878: Thomas Alva Edison (1847–1931) received a patent on a sound recording and playback device he called a phonograph (United States).

Edison used cylinders for the recording medium.

1880: Inventor Herman Hollerith (1860–1929) created a system of recording and retrieving information on punched cards (United States).

The U.S. census of 1890 made use of Hollerith's invention to tabulate results. In 1896, Hollerith founded the Tabulating Machine Company, which became IBM, the International Business Machines Company.

1883: The Correspondence University (Ithaca, NY, United States).

An association of 32 professors from various colleges and universities, including Harvard, Johns Hopkins, and the University of Wisconsin, formed an organization they called a "Correspondence University." Instruction took place directly between the instructor and the learner with "no disadvantage in remoteness of locality."[75]

Learners paid instructors a monthly fee based on the nature of the study undertaken as well as an additional equal sum to the organization to support advertising. The professors hoped to attract:

- graduates doing advanced work
- those preparing for college
- persons living in rural areas
- officers and men in the United States Army and Navy
- persons taking civil service exams
- men and women in stores, shops, or on farms who wanted to learn but could not leave their work to attend school or had no intention of entering college. "To these the Correspondence University offers the opportunity of carrying on their preparatory studies without seriously interfering with their other business."[76]

The word "university" in the name referred to the range of studies, rather than to the organizational structure. The group was not chartered and was not authorized to confer degrees. "The plan might be more appropriately called a bureau of education, as it simply serves as a means of bringing pupils and professors into communication," reported a contemporary newspaper.[77]

How did the classes work? An article in the October 12, 1883, edition of *The Cornell Daily Sun* discussed a typical algebra correspondence class:

> The professor who gives instruction in I algebra sends to his pupil, at the beginning of the week, a minute syllabus of questions and examples on five lessons. The pupil works, perhaps two hours a day for five days and answers all the questions he can, making a note of every difficulty. At the end of the week he sends to the professor such difficulties as he cannot finally clear up. The last of the week, the professor sends him a syllabus for the second week, and as soon as he learns of the difficulties, he solves them and sends the solutions to the student.[78]

Despite high expectations, the experiment was not successful. Apparently it was too invisible as well as too expensive to attract the students it needed to survive and flourish.

1884: Foulks Lynch Correspondence Tuition Service (London, England).

A correspondence school for accountants.

1885: Oxford University began to provide traveling libraries (England).

Oxford added a system of traveling libraries to support its extension service, which had been established in 1878. Oxford's traveling libraries contained "books of reference bearing on the course of lectures."[79]

1885: Traveling Railroad library established by the Baltimore and Ohio Line (United States).

Intended for use by rail employees only, this library circulated around 50,000 volumes in 1884 and boasted that the "average time from the placing of an order until the book is in the borrower's hands is 24 hours."[80]

1886: Berne Convention for the Protection of Literary and Artistic Works (Switzerland).

Each member of the Berne Union agreed to afford authors from other members the same intellectual property protections as in its own country. The United States joined in 1988.[81]

1886: Chichester A. Bell and Charles Sumner Tainter received a patent on a sound recording/playback device called a graphophone.

1887: University Correspondence College, Cambridge (Cambridge, England).

Prepared students for University of London external degrees.

1887: Children's Aid Society established home libraries (Boston, MA, United States).

A home library consisted of a case of 20 books aimed at children aged 9 to 15 in poor families. Small pictures and games might also be included. The oldest child in the family was made the librarian. A worker, called a visitor, from the Society came to the home once a week and guided their reading. Other successful home library systems were set up in Providence, RI (1898), Albany, NY (1892), and Pittsburgh, PA (1898), and in 1900:

- as part of the traveling library division of the circulating department of the New York Public Library,
- Brooklyn (NY) as a cooperative effort between the Pratt Institute Free Library, the Brooklyn Public Library, and the Children's Aid Society,
- Buffalo (NY) library club,
- Syracuse (NY) organized by the central New York branch of the Association of Collegiate Alumnae in cooperation with the children's department of the Syracuse Public Library,
- Chicago (IL) circulated by the Bureau of Charities in the West Side district and a committee of the Library Club,
- Helena (MT) through the public library.[82]

1887: Emile Berliner (1851–1929) patented a disc-playing sound playback system called a gramophone.

Gramophone discs were originally pressed on vulcanized rubber and it was not until ten years later, in 1897, that shellac was introduced as a more suitable medium for commercial sound recordings.

1887: Hatch Act (United States).

The Act established agricultural experiment stations to inform farmers about new developments.

1890: American Society for the Extension of University Teaching (United States).

Established in Philadelphia in June 1890; incorporated in 1892.
The goals of this group, as articulated in 1902, were

1. to extend higher education to all classes of people
2. to extend education through the whole of adult life
3. to extend thorough methods of study to subjects of everyday interest.[83]

1890: General Federation of Women's Clubs formed by ratification of women's clubs throughout the country (New York, NY, United States).[84]

1890: First commercial sound recording cylinders went on sale for the Edison phonograph.

1890–1925: University Extension becomes an organized movement (United States).

1891: The Edison Company introduced the Kinetoscope (United States).

The Kinetoscope allowed one person at a time to view a moving picture.

1891: International Correspondence Schools (ICS) of Scranton, PA, incorporated (United States).

This private correspondence school was founded by Thomas J. Foster, proprietor and editor of the *Mining Herald,* a weekly newspaper published in the coal mining district of eastern Pennsylvania. Foster established the school to educate miners, in the hope of avoiding accidents and loss of human life in the coal fields. Foster also sought to assist miners to pass the required state examinations on mine safety. In its heyday, the school offered over 300 courses on coal mining, mine surveying, mine machinery, and other pertinent issues. The school's students were working men and women seeking education that would lead them to success and make them marketable. This strategy made the school financially successful and by 1926 it had an enrollment of approximately two million students. To cater to specific needs, ICS did not rely on standard textbooks but instead distributed its own curriculum, which it called "Instruction and Question Papers." These papers gave students the basic and most important information needed for the task at hand and limited questions to the specific area under study.

The mission of the school was to provide "practical men with a technical education, and technical men with a practical education." The language used in the curriculum was simple and included many illustrations acknowledging that many of the school's clientele were not native English speakers. Materials were delivered by independent parcel delivery companies before the U.S. postal service initiated parcel post in 1913. In 1908 the school asserted: "Our courses are all prepared from a utilitarian standpoint; that is, it is always kept in view that the reason the student is taking one of our courses is that he desires to put the knowledge obtained into immediate practical use. We are not aiming to train the mind, but to give the student such information regarding the principles, theory, and practice as he can use with the position he is aiming to fill." [85] After reaching a high in 1926, enrollments gradually decreased throughout the late 1920s when more Americans were able to attend formal, free, public high schools in or near their homes. With a changed emphasis and a smaller operation, ICS is still in operation today and is called Penn Foster Career School.[86]

1892: Correspondence Division, Department of Education, University of Chicago (United States).

Dr. William Rainey Harper (1856–1906), formerly of the Chautauqua Institution, became president of the University of Chicago and established a correspondence division of the Department of Education.

1892: Pennsylvania State College established Correspondence Teaching in Agriculture (reading course) (United States). Correspondence teaching made use of the rural free delivery system to transport educational materials to students, who worked at their own pace.

1892: Melvil Dewey (1851–1931), librarian at the State Library in New York, inaugurated a practical and economical system of library extension that became known as traveling libraries.

1892: University of Wisconsin at Madison used the term *distance education* in a catalog (United States).

1894:   Diploma Correspondence College (later Wolsey Hall) (Oxford, England).

According to the College's *Prospectus* from 1914, the goal was to encourage self-confidence in the students while teaching the student "to exert his faculties to the utmost and to rely upon himself without receiving too much help before he performs his task."[87]

1894:   First commercial sound recording discs went on sale.

1895:   Louis Lumière (1864–1948) invented the Cinématographe, a three-in-one portable motion picture camera, processor, and projector (France).

1895–1914:   Wisconsin Free Library Commission (WFLC) (United States).

The WFLC was an excellent example of distributed library services and was nurtured by three unique individuals: (1) Wisconsin state senator James Huff Stout (1848–1910), who was instrumental in ensuring that the bill creating the WFLC passed the Wisconsin legislature in 1895; (2) Frank Avery Hutchins (1851–1914), one of the founders of the Wisconsin Library Association (WLA) in 1891, secretary of the WFLC from 1897 to 1899, and chief executive officer until poor health forced him to resign in 1904; (3) Lutie Eugenia Stearns (1866–1943), librarian, suffragist, and progressive radical. These individuals viewed the WFLC as a stop-gap measure between traveling libraries and the establishment of permanent, free, public libraries. The WFLC's charge was to provide "advice and counsel to all free libraries in the state, and to all communities which may propose to establish them, as to the best means of establishing and administering such libraries, the selection of books, cataloging and other details of library management."[88]

The idea first took form when Hutchins and Stearns met Melvil Dewey, then state librarian of New York, at the 1893 World's Columbian Exposition in Chicago, and learned about Dewey's work with traveling libraries in New York. Beginning in 1896, they targeted poor, rural counties, many of which were depressed after lumber mills closed. In Dunn county (population 25,000), Stout paid all expenses for a series of traveling libraries. Because of the WFLC traveling libraries, many residents, who could not easily get to the public library in Menomonie, received library services. Stout's example was followed throughout the state and by 1902 there were 305 traveling libraries statewide. Of these 305, 134 were overseen by the WFLC and the others were organized by private groups and individuals. By 1903, when the Wisconsin legislature created a department of Traveling Libraries under Katharine I. MacDonald, fewer libraries were organized by private groups.[89]

Hutchins and Sterns traveled a great deal on WFLC business promoting the libraries, delivering books in the library wagon (in pre-1913-parcel post days), and visiting rural areas. Hutchins reported that people were enthusiastic about reading, but also admitted that persuading them to read "good" (also called "wholesome" and "useful") books was a problem. Sometimes the circulation statistics were disappointing. Hutchins wrote that after the lumber mills left "the dwellings are falling into decay. A widow with small children can rent one of these houses for twenty-five or fifty cents a month and manage with a garden and poultry to keep her family together and out of the dreaded poor house. She cannot, however, give them good reading."[90]

Stearns was also concerned about the types of books offered and mentioned this to Mary Smith, librarian at Eau Claire Public Library, in a letter from 1909. "We have been going through some of our traveling library records here of late and we find that many of the classified books that are really interesting are not issued at all, while some of the works of fiction have a circulation of twenty-seven and thirty issues."[91]

The traveling libraries held between 30 and 100 volumes in locked book cases. Most collections were for general public use, but special collections were developed for lumber camps, tuberculosis sanitariums, and orphanages. With the many immigrants to serve, collections contained books in many languages—German, Yiddish, Polish, Bohemian, and others. A library might remain as long as six months and was housed in farm houses, post offices, railway stations, and stores.

The librarian for each collection was a local volunteer. The duties were simple:

• oversee circulation

• keep simple, but accurate, records

• correspond with the WFLC.

Some advocates of the library profession noted that the project would be hampered without providing proper library training for volunteers, and as early as the summer of 1895, the WFLC began training sessions for librarians. By 1906, a full-fledged library school went into operation, which later became the library school at the University of Wisconsin, Madison.

1896: Experimental Free Rural Delivery from the Post Office is begun (West Virginia, United States).

1896: Free Library of Philadelphia, PA, sent out traveling libraries (United States).

1896: The Edison Manufacturing Company introduced the Vitascope film projector, the first commercially successful motion picture projector in the United States.

The Vitascope allowed large audiences to view a motion picture and paved the way for the development and marketing of competing projectors.

1897: Kentucky State Federation for Women's Clubs appointed a committee for a traveling libraries project (United States).

When the Kentucky State Federation of Women's Clubs appointed a committee for a Traveling Libraries Project, they targeted the many mountainous and remote areas of their state. Their goal was to bring books to the people, wherever they might reside. This movement, both in terms of goals and implementation, was a precursor of the Pack Horse Library Project of the 1930s and bookmobiles of the 1950s.

Kentucky traveling libraries were fairly standard in construction, with books housed in a wooden box. The club women selected the books, concentrating on histories, biographies, poetry, wholesome fiction, and magazines. Several railroad companies transported the book boxes without charge to the end of their lines.

From there, transportation was by horseback, in wagons, or by boat to the final destination at a cabin door in the mountains.

The club wanted to exchange the library every three months, but given the transportation difficulties and costs, the libraries stayed in place for at least six months. As a justification for this length of time, the club women noted that three months was just "too short a time for a satisfactory use of the books."[92]

1897: New York Free Circulating Library formed a Traveling-Library Department (United States).

It was later called the New York Public Library Traveling Office Library.

1897: American School of Correspondence (later renamed the American School) established (Chicago, IL, United States)

The American School was established as a "go to school at home" correspondence institution offering a high school diploma in as little as two years of study. The nonprofit school is still in operation and offers a high school completion program through correspondence, self-study courses.[93]

1898: Appropriations from state legislatures established traveling libraries in Michigan and Iowa (United States).

1898: State Federations of Women's Clubs, subsidiaries of the General Federation of Women's Clubs, arranged to circulate traveling libraries in Alabama, Arkansas, Connecticut, Illinois, Missouri, South Carolina, Texas, Utah (United States).

The efforts of club women in Alabama and South Carolina illustrate the important steps these women made toward expanding literacy and the distribution of information in the southern United States.

As Kate Hutcheson Morrissette, who served on the traveling library committee of the No Name Club, in Montgomery, AL, noted in 1898:

> As is the case the wide world over, it is the women who are the first awake, who are first endeavoring to set in order a new institution. . . . The women of Alabama through the Traveling Libraries will urge the people to bring *man* to *his* highest form of value, and will help to accomplish this by education of the young people of the State.[94]

Alabama: The Alabama Federation of Women's Clubs (organized in 1895) established a traveling library collection originally consisting of 25 bound books and 15 magazines. At first, the collection circulated to any women's club with a transportation charge of one dollar and a circulation time of three to four months. By 1901, 12 traveling libraries were circulating throughout the state. As club demand dropped, the libraries were sent to towns, churches, and schools for use by the public. By 1903, the Library Committee of the Alabama Education Association assisted the club women in identifying the schools that could make the best use of the libraries.[95]

Morrissette further noted that traveling libraries brought education and information to people who could not attend school in person because of "poverty, business, or home cares; it continues the education of the graduates; and it displaces the poisonous cheap literature sown broadcast through the land by publishing houses whose only object is pecuniary gain and whose frequent advertisement is 'forty novels for twenty-five cents.'"[96]

During its eight years of support for traveling libraries, the Alabama Club's committee on Traveling Libraries had as many as 4,000 books in circulation in rural schools and communities. Unfortunately, the Club could not adequately supervise the transportation of the materials; some were damaged and transportation costs were high because the railroad refused to transport the libraries free of charge—a service enjoyed in other states. By 1905, the Club had donated much of the collection to school libraries and the remaining 1,700 books, nine book cases, and $9.81 were deposited with the Alabama Library Association, which took over the work of traveling libraries in the state.[97]

When the state legislature passed the Library Act in 1907, it also established library extension and assumed responsibility for traveling libraries. With state support and control now available, the Club dissolved its traveling library committee. The state's traveling libraries were "intended to meet an immediate local need, in rural communities and in the rural schools." The collections numbered between 25 and 35 books. While there was no rental charge, customers were charged for transportation costs and could retain the collection for as long as four months.[98]

South Carolina: Louisa B. Poppenheim (1868–1957) served as the second president of the South Carolina Federation of Women's Clubs (SCFWC). Educated at Vassar College in Poughkeepsie, NY, she felt it was the duty of women to oversee social services and that "every Club woman [must] recognize her individual responsibility for the conditions which confront her in her own community. . . . This club ideal calls us away from the individual and the selfish, and lifts us up out of personalities into principles, and teaches us that 'we never give but giving get again.'. . . The Club movement is in iteself a crusade to carry to less fortunate individuals material help and strength." Two of Poppenheim's passions were libraries and education, especially for girls.[99]

Questions that comes to mind while examining traveling libraries in the segregated southern United States include, "What about other customers, particularly African-Americans?" and "How were they served?" Fultz sums it up succinctly in his 2006 article "Black Public Libraries in the South in the Era of De Jure Segregation:"

> In 1913 only Delaware and Kentucky were reported as having traveling libraries that served African Americans; in Delaware the service was coordinated by the state's black land-grant college, and in Kentucky the state library commission sponsored two fifty-volume traveling collections. By 1926 an American Library Association survey indicated that the states of Kentucky, North Carolina, and Texas had small traveling libraries for African Americans. Earlier, around 1910, a privately sponsored extension service was coordinated by Atlanta University.[100]

1898:   The Minneapolis Women's Council established a system of traveling libraries for Hennepin County, MN (United States).

1898:   The Woman's Club of Rochester created a traveling library association (New York State, United States).

The library started with a gift of $100.00 and enough books to fill eight separate libraries holding 44 books each. To borrow a library, an individual paid one dollar for transportation and had to have "the assurance of ten responsible people." If a person came to pick up the library "in his wagon, the fee paid is added to the general fund of the association. In 1900 the libraries visited eight places, all small town or country districts almost destitute of reading matter."[101]

1898:   Hermod's correspondence courses created (Sweden).

H. S. Hermod created courses based on self-instruction independent of correspondence education as it was evolving elsewhere. The Hermod's prospectus from 1908 reflects the familiar theme of self-improvement associated with distributed learning at that time:

> Our correspondence teaching meets an important need. It affords anyone an opportunity to educate himself/herself further; it gives to young men and women anxious to make progress an opportunity to reach an independent position and to poor people a possibility to work themselves free of their poverty. The student can learn without neglecting his daily work, make use of his leisure time and in this way acquire valuable, practical knowledge. Each student constitutes his own school class. He can choose what time suits him for his study and can at will use any hour available to learn.[102]

1898:   Branch Library Movement (United States).

We've examined the efforts of club women and librarians to bring books to those in remote and rural locations, but it is also important to point out that this move to provide all members of a community with library services was not limited to the rural populations. Public libraries in the larger American cities deposited library collections in outlying neighborhoods before branch libraries were built. These efforts benefited many people who did not own an automobile, could not travel to the downtown library because of long working hours, or lived beyond the streetcar lines.

Around the turn of the 20th century, roughly beginning in 1898, there was an active movement to set up county library systems. In the 1890s, branch libraries began to open in the larger cities. In many cases, the deposit station libraries preceded the actual branch library buildings.

While additional branch libraries were built in the 1920s, deposit station libraries still remained a popular and relatively inexpensive way to distribute books to people. As the editors of the journal *Public Libraries* observed in 1902:

> Nothing seems more certain . . . than that the future will see, in every city of any considerable size, a system of public libraries installed in numerous buildings in various parts of the town, in much the same manner as the public school system is managed today. The day of one colossal building,

serving the people inadequately, and standing more for a place of exhibition and the resort of scholars of leisure than a people's university is certainly passing.[103]

1899: Cincinnati Public Library began administrating deposit station libraries (Ohio, United States).

The large, urban, and busy Cincinnati Public Library began to serve its more remote customers in 1899 with deposit station libraries—an innovation that was less expensive and more portable than a building. Deposit stations remained popular even after branch libraries were built. The last deposit station remained in Mt. Washington, on the east side of the city, until 1954. Outreach continues today, as in many public libraries, with collections sent to classrooms, nursing homes, and jails.

Like other deposit station libraries, these early collections varied in size from 50 to 700 books that were placed in book cases and housed in stores and public buildings. Interested individuals could browse the collections as well as order a book from the downtown library. Although circulation was self-serve, the shop keeper received a penny for each book that circulated as well as the anticipation of a sale because when a customer came in for a book, he or she might decide to buy something in the store.[104]

Librarian John Cotton Dana had a somewhat negative view of this process, as may be seen in his 1914 commentary prepared for the International Meeting of Librarians at Oxford, England:

In most cities libraries use deposit stations, which are small collections of books placed on open shelves, usually in drug stores, with a small bonus to owners of the stores on each book lent. They are moderately successful. But it is somewhat doubtful if this unsupervised distribution of books, chiefly recent popular novels, is worth the cost. An extension of this same method leads to the traveling library, so-called, perhaps, because it travels from the library to its appointed place and back again in one package; whereas the deposit station books stay where put, save as they are changed in part from day to day or week to week, as borrowers may make requests.[105]

1899: Bill introduced to create a Public Library Commission (Nebraska, United States).

The bill also defined a system of traveling libraries for the state. The bill was defeated, but the Lincoln Woman's Club supported the traveling library movement and on Library Day, December 17, 1900, citizens were invited to attend programs about the need for a traveling library, and the legislation that would be necessary to maintain it. Those present signed a petition that was sent to the legislature. In 1901, the Nebraska Library Association, The Nebraska Federated Woman's Clubs, and the Nebraska Teacher's Association joined together to push for recognition of the need for a Public Library Commission. Using the newspapers to communicate the needs, they sought to promote library services to all Nebraska citizens. A new bill was introduced and signed into law in March 1901.

20th Century

Late 1800s/   Farmers' Reading Circles established as a phase of the library exten-
Early 1900s: sion movement (United States).

Farmers' institutions supplied the libraries in Illinois and Indiana from headquarters at the state capitals. Each library held between 50 and 100 books with
many devoted to farm economics. The State Library shipped libraries in Ohio
with texts chosen by the dean of the College of Agriculture and Domestic Science
of the State University. All of the titles were appropriate to farm life and ranged
from agricultural chemistry to market gardening and domestic science. Although
intended to educate farmers about innovations in their field, many recipients complained about book selections. One Indiana farmer commented that "Farmers are
no fonder than other men of reading of the beauties of ringbone and spavin to
their families gathered about the evening." He continued: "Who is better able
to appreciated Riley's 'Thoughts for a Discouraged Farmer,' and 'Neighborly
Poems,' than the farmer himself? And his wife is a cheerfuller, happier woman for
her reading of fiction, poetry, travel and art, just as are women in other walks of
life." Regarding the provision of cheerful literature, another farmer wrote that "if
farmers' wives read more cheerful literature, fewer of them would be in the insane
asylums."[106]

1900:   McGill University established a department of Traveling Libraries
          (Canada).

Traveling libraries were lent for three months to public schools, country schools,
reading or literary clubs at the request of residents in communities without public
libraries. School packages included, in addition to books, lantern slides, framed
photographs by the great masters, and illustrated lectures. A third of the general
libraries held fiction titles.[107]

1900:   Ontario Traveling Libraries and Reading Camps (Canada).

Traveling libraries sent to lumber companies were called reading camps.

1900:   Cornell University Extension Courses for Rural Women (Ithaca, NY,
          United States).

In 1900, Martha Van Rensselaer (1864–1932) came to Cornell University to
organize an extension program in home economics for New York State's rural
women. A year later, in 1901, the first bulletin of the "Cornell Reading Course
for Farmer's Wives" was distributed, and in 1903, three college-credit courses
were offered. In 1905, a noncredit course in home economics was opened to any
woman in the state, continuing until 1921. More than 20,000 women across New
York State were enrolled.
Van Rensselaer received her AB from Cornell University in 1909, and the home
economics program continued to blossom under her leadership. She and her
companion Flora Rose (1874–1959) were granted the first full professorships for
women at Cornell in 1911. In 1923, Van Rensselaer was named one of the twelve
greatest women in the country by the League of Women Voters.[108]

1901: Moody Bible Institute (MBI) instituted the Moody Correspondence School (Chicago, Illinois, United States).

The correspondence school focused on those men and women who were unable to attend the school in Chicago. In 1903, MBI inaugurated an Evening School. MBI continues to offer undergraduate, graduate, and continuing education courses through distance learning.

1901: Linguaphone Company established by Jacques Roston (London, England).

Roston used Thomas Edison's phonograph and wax cylinders to promote self-study courses that allowed students to listen to a recording of a native speaker. These recordings also permitted those who could not physically attend language courses the option of study in their own time and place. The Linguaphone Group continues its support of distributed learning today by offering full language course packages.

1901: Melvil Dewey published his tract titled *Traveling Libraries: Field and Future of Traveling Libraries.* (United States).

Dewey noted, "When I began work for public library interests in New York we had 40 free public libraries and 40,000 saloons, so that by the law of averages a boy leaving his home in the evening would pass 999 open doors with a cordial welcome to the worse influences to every *one* [open door] inviting him to the companionship and inspiration of the best books. Librarians realized that if they were to do their best work they must have [an] aggressive spirit and adopt the aggressive methods of those who make other enterprises most successful."[109]

1901: A women's club in Waco, TX, was the first in the state to establish traveling libraries (United States).

1901: A. C. Barlett from Chicago, IL, supported eight traveling libraries in Arizona (United States).

The libraries contained new books accompanied by a printed catalog. They were placed near country schoolhouses "in the care of intelligent families, who take interest in seeing that every person has a fair chance at them."[110]

1902: Rural free delivery (RFD) made permanent–Post Office (United States).

Initially RFD (the title "free" was dropped in 1906 as it was by then understood) could only carry packages up to four pounds, which somewhat limited libraries attempts at distribution. For heavier packages, libraries had to contract with private express companies, an issue Lutie Stearns of the Wisconsin Free Library found ludicrous.

1902: Houston Ladies' Reading Club supported traveling libraries (Texas, United States).

Houston already had a permanent library (one of the Carnegie libraries), so the local women's club concentrated on sending traveling libraries to schools and in support of adult education. In 1904, they "included matted art pictures to further promote culture education." By 1907 this club owned and circulated "the largest number of traveling cases of books in the state, including eight cases intended for adult use and twenty-four cases intended for Harris County [Houston is in Harris County] schoolchildren." In 1916 the Texas State Library took over the traveling libraries still active in the state.[111]

1903: Worker's Education Association (WEA) established (England).

Albert Mansbridge (1876–1952) established The Association to Promote the Higher Education of Working Men in 1903. It was renamed as the Workers Educational Association (WEA) in 1905. Mansbridge had a vested interest in education for the working class. Forced to leave school at the age of 14, he went to work as an office boy. He was able to continue his education in the evenings by attending university extension lectures and taking co-operative courses. He eventually became cashier of the Co-operative Permanent Building Society. In 1908, he worked with professors at Oxford University to devise a new method for workers' education. The resulting document was considered truly revolutionary by university standards and specified the following:

> Tutorial classes over a period of three years (seventy-two meetings), with not more than thirty students, were to be provided at a low fee; the programme was to be managed by a permanent joint committee with equal WEA and university representation; and the WEA branch was to have 'a controlling voice' in the selection of tutors for its tutorial classes. Promising worker– students would proceed from the classes to full-time study at Oxford, normally to read for one of the new diplomas to be created in economics and politics.[112]

In addition to his groundbreaking work with adult education, Mansbridge was instrumental in developing the National Central Library and served as its chairman. He was also involved in the British Institute of Adult Education as well as the Seafarers' Education Service, which supplied libraries for 600 merchant ships by 1939. Two years earlier, in 1937, the Service had instituted a correspondence school named College of the Sea.[113]

1903: Northwestern University in Chicago partnered with the Interstate School of Correspondence, also in Chicago, to offer university extension courses (United States).

1904: Free Public Lectures in New York City (United States).

Free public lectures were supported by the Department of Education of New York City.

1904: University of Chicago correspondence courses established (Chicago, Illinois, United States).

Advertisement for the Interstate School of Correspondence in its affiliation with Northwestern University, 1905

1904: West Virginia Federation of Women's Clubs (WVFWC) promoted traveling libraries (United States).

Beginning with two traveling libraries, which were sent to remote mining areas and rural locations, the WVFWC sustained 16 by 1908. Like other women's clubs, the WVFWC promoted the establishment of a State Library Commission, which was instituted in 1929. Like other clubs, the WVFWC relinquished the time-consuming logistics and maintenance of traveling library administration to those professionally trained to handle these tasks when it turned over the traveling libraries to the West Virginia University Library in 1914.[114]

1904: Books for the blind were distributed (United States).

In the early 20th century, the Postal Service was reluctant to carry too much bulky and heavy mail, which kept Braille books from being delivered directly to the home. By 1914, however, books for the blind were classified as parcels, allowing them a wider and more affordable circulation.[115]

1905: First bookmobile introduced, horse-drawn book wagon (Washington County, Maryland, United States).

"The sound of the approaching book wagon brings the family from the fields, the barns, and the house. It is an important day when the Washington County (Maryland) book wagon stops at the farm, because the family is allowed to borrow as many as thirty books at a time, from scientific treatises on farming, for father, to color picture books, for baby. The farmer and his family choose their own books with the assistance of the librarian, while deposit stations in villages and all country schools are supplied with large cases of books from the central library in the county seat."[116]

So begins the 1922 American Library Association booklet titled *Book Wagons* describing the efforts of several libraries to distribute information to those not able to come to the physical library. The publication especially highlights the efforts of the Washington County Free Library under the direction of Mary Titcomb (1857–1932), who initiated the first bookmobile in the United States. Titcomb herself noted that "No better method has ever been devised for reaching the dweller in the country. The book goes to the man, not waiting for the man to come to the book."[117]

Titcomb's first book wagon featured book shelves on the outside and in the middle, storage for crates. She recalled that it looked like a cross between "a grocer's delivery wagon and the tin peddler's cart of bygone New England days."[118] It was filled with books and drawn by two horses. The library's janitor, Mr. Joshua Thomas, drove the wagon and handed out the books. With Washington County Free Library boldly, but simply, lettered on the cart, Titcomb insisted that everything remain plain and dignified without gilt or scroll work. Unfortunately, this backfired in one instance as Titcomb reported: "As our man approached one farm house, he heard a voice charged with nervous trepidation, call out, 'Yer needn't stop here. We ain't got no use for the dead wagon here.'" Responding to this alarming depiction, Titcomb promptly had the wagon's wheels and doors painted red.[119]

In 1910, the horse-drawn book wagon was struck by a freight train at a railroad crossing and completely destroyed. Extension work came to a halt because there wasn't any money to replace the wagon. The interruption didn't last long, however, because two years later (1912) a member of the library board donated enough money to purchase a motorized truck. The truck could hold 300 books and carry four deposit station crates. The motorized book mobile was able to range farther and faster than its horse-drawn predecessor. By 1915, Titcomb was able to buy a larger truck that could carry 500 books and six deposit stations. The legacy continues today with the library's outreach efforts to the residents of Washington County with homebound services, bookmobiles, and deposit stations.[120]

1905: Package library service made available from a state library extension agency of the Oregon Library Commission (Oregon, United States).

1905: Calvert Day School offered a kindergarten curriculum by correspondence (Baltimore, Maryland, United States).

Considered by some to be the beginning of formal homeschooling in the United States, Harvard graduate Virgil Hillyer, headmaster of the Calvert Day School, offered the school's curriculum as a correspondence program to "parents who, unable to send their young sons and daughters to Calvert, could nonetheless give their children the same educational advantage by purchasing the lessons and teaching them right in the home." With over a century of service, the Calvert School continues to offer distributed education opportunities for learners in preschool through eighth grade.[121]

1906: The University of Wisconsin extension division offered extension courses in engineering and a package library service (Wisconsin, United States).

Frank Avery Hutchins of the Wisconsin Free Library Commission served as director from 1907 until his death in 1914 and was succeeded by librarian Almere L. Scott, who remained director until 1946. One of the chief users of the package loan libraries were women's clubs and secondary schools. In 1922, Scott discussed the question of package library content:

> To select the material for the package judiciously, we must know for whom, why and when the information is desired. The same material cannot be used to the best advantage by a rural school pupil in preparing an essay, and a member of a chamber of commerce who will discuss the problem before the taxpayers in the country.[122]

Another innovation by University of Wisconsin Extension included lectures recorded on phonograph records. Professors recorded their lectures and the records were mailed to remote students.

1907: University of Oregon established Correspondence Teaching (United States).

1907: The Evanston Public Library began to circulate pianola rolls (player piano) rolls for home use (Illinois, United States).

1908: Telephone use increased in public library reference service in an effort to provide timely information.

1908: Yamaguchi Public Library supported traveling libraries (Japan).

The library maintained three departments: reference, circulation, and traveling libraries. By 1912, the library had 27 agencies serving as stations for the traveling libraries. Forty-three percent of the books borrowed from traveling libraries were juvenile literature.[123]

1909: University of Kansas, University of Minnesota, University of Nebraska, and University of Texas at Austin established Correspondence Teaching (United States).

1909: Correspondence learning for secondary students via the postal service began in Victoria, Australia.

1909: Frederick Griggs established The Fireside Correspondence School (Maryland, United States).

As with most distributed learning endeavors, Fireside sought to provide educational opportunities to people who were unable to attend a traditional school.

By 1916, the school had reached students throughout North America and had expanded to 10 additional countries. In 1990, the school named its academic divisions Home Study Elementary School, Home Study High School, and Griggs University. Griggs offers accredited courses for K–12 and college degrees.

1909: U.S. Copyright Act allowed works published without a copyright notice to go into the public domain upon publication.

1910: University of Missouri and University of North Dakota established Correspondence Teaching (United States).

1911: The University of Queensland, Australia, established a Department of External Studies.

1912: University of Colorado, Indiana University, and the University of Washington established Correspondence Teaching; Pennsylvania State College established Correspondence Teacher Training, a reading course (United States).

1912: The University of Virginia (UVa) began a series of extension courses (Charlottesville, Virginia, United States).

The first extension courses were offered by faculty members who taught at sites away from the central campus. Within three years (1915), the University had appointed its first director of extension services. Four years after that, 1919, UVa offered the first extension course bearing college credit.

To support the University's extension efforts, the University Library established a Package Library Service, which flourished in the 1920s and 1930s. In addition, the library sent books that were neither on reserve or rare to distant learners.

1913: University of California, Iowa State College, and University of Oklahoma established Correspondence Teaching (United States).

1913: The Gary Public Library began the circulation of player-piano rolls (Indiana, United States).

Patrons could use the player-piano rolls in the library on the Steinway piano with Gulbransen player mechanism or take them home. By 1915, the library owned over 500 rolls of popular music, light opera, and classical music. The collection remained popular well into the 1940s.[124]

1913: United States Parcel Post went into service.

Parcel post not only freed up time and money for libraries distributing materials but paved the way for the rise of mail-order purchases with to-your-door-delivery. Former restrictions were lifted and Parcel Post accepted packages weighing more than four pounds.

1914–1918: World War I.

1914: Correspondence education via the postal service for students at the primary level began in Victoria, Australia.

Children in remote areas who had never been to school received an education through distance learning. Teachers were usually based in cities and sent the students lessons in the mail, the students completed them, mailed them back to the teachers, and the teachers returned the lessons to the students with corrections and comments.

1914: Correspondence Courses in Art (United States).

The Bureau of Engraving, Inc. founded the Art Instruction Schools (originally named the Federal Schools) to train illustrators for the Bureau and for the growing printing industry. The institution continues to offer correspondence courses in art. Perhaps their most famous graduate is Charles Schulz, creator of the famous "Peanuts" comic strip. Schulz also worked at the school as an instructor after serving in the U.S. Army.

1914: Cooperative Extension Service established through the Smith-Lever Act (United States).

The Smith-Lever Act established the Cooperative Extension Service at the federal, state, and county levels. The goal was to offer publicly supported adult education in the latest developments in agriculture, home economics, and the like. Funding came primarily from the United States Department of Agriculture with matching state funds funneled through land-grant universities. The Act pulled together a number of overlapping activities to ensure a diffusion of information—from researchers at universities to local county extension agents who synthesized the information and demonstrated techniques to farmers who practically applied the methods.

1914: University of North Carolina established Correspondence Teaching (United States).

1914: First documented sound recording (record) collection in a public library established at the St. Paul Public Library (Minnesota, United States).

1914–1956: Package Loan Library flourished at the University of Texas at Austin (Texas, United States).

The Board of Regents established the UT at Austin Extension Division in 1909. Need for materials in support of extension activities prompted the development of the Extension Loan Library, which was not a traditional library housing rows of bound volumes. Instead, it was a Package Loan Library with each individual library consisting of a package made up of newspaper clippings, periodical articles, pamphlets, bulletins, and other timely items on a specific subject. Between 1914 and 1954, the Division of Extension personnel were the largest group served by the Package Library, accounting for 45 percent of all loans. Women's clubs, a form of adult education, borrowed 38 percent of all packages. Libraries were parcel post size and cost from eight to twenty cents to mail.[125]

In 1956, demand for extension library services was still high. "Perhaps because of the slow development of libraries in Texas or because of inadequate resources in libraries which do exist, the Library is still supplying many thousands of people with materials which are difficult, if not impossible, for them to obtain elsewhere."[126]

It was felt that the resources of the Library supplemented rather than substituted for the resources and services of other libraries in the state such as school libraries and smaller public libraries. These other libraries frequently lacked the staff and facilities for handling the types of materials found in the UT Extension Library. If a local library existed, the borrower was required to make his/her request through it. This was one way of encouraging the use of local libraries. If the Extension Library could not supply information for a request, but that same information could be found in books, the request was referred to the State Library for supplementary book services.

Consider the logistics of inventorying complete package libraries. Missing individual articles were checked to make sure that they had not been misfiled. When articles were lost, as was inevitable, the librarians attempted to locate identical articles. If an entire package was lost, it was replaced completely and as closely to the original as possible. The collection generally was weeded in the summer as each item was examined for timeliness as well as its historical and research value. Those deemed no longer appropriate were discarded.

1916: University of London examinations held in Ruhleben Internment Camp, Germany, where up to 5,500 male civilians (mainly British) were interned during the World War I.

1916: YMCA (Young Men's Christian Association) developed a library program for American troops on the Mexican border (United States).

Relying on librarians at the New York Public Library for expertise, the YMCA assembled collections of materials for the troops' education and entertainment.[127]

1916: Die fahrende Kriegsbücherei (Traveling War Library) established (Germany).

Traveling libraries were assembled and delivered by wagon to German soldiers on the front lines. Friedel, in discussing the libraries' catalog, wrote: "With the advantage of a chosen group of books and the inspiration of a trained officer or instructor, the possibilities to which the traveling library may be put are enormous. Again, traveling libraries are advantageous and useful because of their aid in breaking the monotony of camp life."[128]

1917: The American Library Association (ALA) Executive Board formed the Committee on Mobilization and War Service Plans to give military personnel swift and easy access to books, newspapers, and magazines (United States).

Formed shortly after the United States declared war on Germany on April 6, 1917, and later named the War Service Committee, it was initially directed by Library of Congress librarian Herbert Putnam and later was headed by Carl H. Milam. In the three years between 1917 and 1920, ALA organized two successful financial campaigns, raising over $5 million dollars through private donations along with additional donations of over three million books selected for the Books for Soldiers campaign.[129]

This was quite an accomplishment for the ALA of 1917, which was an organization of 3,300 members with an annual budget of $24,000. The young and relatively small organization tackled the mission of supplying reading material to over a million military personnel. ALA's successful efforts brought it recognition and praise and transformed it "from a relatively unknown professional society into a public service organization with national aspirations for leadership and service."[130]

ALA was able to supply reference books for soldiers who wished to continue their studies as well as those undergoing extensive instruction while in the war training camps. As a contemporary noted: "The training camp of today is not essentially different from a big university. The fellows work and study a good deal harder in the training camps than they would in a university. This war [World War I] is a highly specialized affair. It's a modern science which the men must learn by studious application to the problems of drill and trench. They acquire the habit of study, of application, in the training camp of today."[131]

Currently the Federal and Armed Forces Libraries Round Table (FAFLRT) serves as an official ALA round table and is charged with promoting library and information services and the library and information profession in the federal and armed forces communities. FAFLRT's charge is to promote "appropriate utilization of federal and armed forces library and information resources and facilities; and to provide an environment for the stimulation of research and development relating to the planning, development, and operation of federal and armed forces libraries."[132]

1915: National University Extension Association (NUEA) established (United States).

NUEA was the oldest and largest of the national university professional organizations focusing on higher education. It is still active today under the name the

Completed tower of books collected by ALA for war library service. Folder "WWI, 1914–1918—ALA Activities (2)." Box 12, Theodore W. Koch papers. Bentley Historical Library, University of Michigan.

National University Continuing Education Association (NUCEA). Many extension services evolved into continuing education departments.

1915: University of Arizona and University of West Virginia established Correspondence Teaching (United States).

1917: University of Utah established Correspondence Teaching; Pennsylvania State College established Correspondence Teaching in Engineering, a reading course (United States).

1918: University of Iowa established Correspondence Teaching (United States).

1918: Air mail service began (United States).

1918: The American Library Association established a library in Paris, France, for American soldiers, sailors, and war workers

The library was made permanent in 1920 and named the American Library in Paris, a name it still bears today. Established with a core collection of wartime books, the library's charter emphasized American literature and culture. American author Edith Wharton served as one of the first trustees of the Library.[133]

1919: University of Arkansas, University of Florida, University of Kentucky, Columbia University, University of South Dakota, and State College of Washington established Correspondence Teaching (United States).

1919: The Madison Free Library opened factory deposit station libraries (Wisconsin, United States).

The Association of Commerce approached the Madison Free Library and requested that it establish factory deposit libraries in support of a community educational program. The Library stationed its first library in the French Battery Co. (renamed Rayovac in the 1930s) "in the care of a welfare worker, an educated woman, thoroughly interested in the books as well as in the 300 men and women employees." Volumes numbered around 200 and covered general and technical topics. The collection grew through requests.[134]

1920: University of Alabama established Correspondence Teaching (United States).

1920: KDKA, Pittsburgh, the first commercially operated radio station, began broadcasting (Pennsylvania, United States).

1920s: University of Wisconsin's School of the Air established (United States).

The educational use of AM radio broadcasts began between the 1920s and the 1940s.

1920s: With the dawn of radio broadcasting, Penn State launched a high-power radio station that offered live radio courses to students around the country (Pennsylvania, United States).

1921: Brigham Young University established a Bureau of Correspondence to provide opportunities for students to begin home study courses (Provo, Utah, United States).

1921: The Seattle Public Library opened deposit station libraries in two hospitals as an experiment in extension services (Washington State, United States).

1922: University of Georgia established Correspondence Teaching (United States).

1922: Free Public Library Service of Vermont initiated bookmobile service (United States).

Like Kentucky and Nebraska, Vermont also made use of the bookmobile to serve its rural population. In 1922, the Free Public Library Service of Vermont (later the state Department of Libraries) sent the state's first book wagon on its route. It is interesting to note that funding for this wagon came from donations from the statewide Federation of Women's Clubs. The book wagon delivered books to small libraries and loaned books directly to individuals in towns lacking a library. In the 1940s the service continued, still funded by the Federation of Women's clubs. In 1974, when the State board of Libraries voted to discontinue state library-operated bookmobiles in Vermont, the newest bookmobile was eight years old.[135]

1923: University of Tennessee established Correspondence Teaching in Engineering (United States).

1923: Chicago Public Library advertised a special advisory service for students and serious readers (Illinois, United States).

When the Chicago Public Library advertised a special advisory service for students and serious readers, the response overwhelmed the staff. Although they promptly stopped advertising, the readers kept coming.

1924: Louisiana State University and the Ohio University established Correspondence Teaching (United States).

1925: Rutgers University established Correspondence Teaching (United States).

1925: The Indiana University High School (IUHS) distance education program founded (Bloomington, Indiana, United States).

Fifty years (1975) after the establishment of the IUHS, the Indiana University School of Continuing Studies (SCS) was established to further address the needs of nontraditional students, both adult learners and high school students in Indiana and outside of the state. The SCS administered the IUHS curriculum and instituted an IUHS diploma program in 1999. Still active today, IUHS classes are not directly supported by the Indiana University Libraries, but any Indiana resident may use the university libraries.[136]

1925: The John C. Campbell Folk School was established in Brasstown, NC (United States).

In 1908–09, John Campbell and his wife visited rural mountain counties from Georgia through West Virginia to study social conditions in those areas. This was a popular undertaking because "[a]t the turn of the century, the Southern Appalachian region was viewed as a fertile field for educational and social missions." The Campbells wanted to start a school in Appalachia as "an alternative to the higher-education facilities that drew young people away from the family farm."

After John Campbell's death in 1919, his widow, Olive Dame Campbell, and her friend Marguerite Butler traveled to Denmark and Sweden to study the folk school (*folkehojskole*) concept. Returning to the United States, they established the John C. Campbell Folk School in rural western North Carolina. Instruction at the Folk School was structured to be noncompetitive, with neither credits nor grades offered. Still engaging today, "the Folk School offers a unique combination of rich history, beautiful mountain surroundings, and an atmosphere of living and learning together."[137]

1925: George McCarthy, New York City banker, awarded a patent for his invention, the Checkograph machine (United States).

McCarthy initiated the first practical use of commercial microfilm with his Checkograph machine, which was designed to make permanent film copies of cancelled checks. McCarthy used motion picture film and a conveyor belt for the process. In 1928, Eastman Kodak's Recordak Division bought the rights to McCarthy's invention and marketed it under the name Recordak. Microfilm provided a popular medium for the preservation of library materials.[138]

1925: American Library Association (ALA) Committee on Library Extension established with the goal of extending library services to unserved areas, primarily rural, in the United States.

1926: American Library Association (ALA) formed the Board of Library and Adult Education to support library services for adult learners.

The Board underwent several name changes as various ALA activities were synthesized:

- 1937—Adult Education Board
- 1946—Adult Education Section of the Division of Public Libraries
- 1959—Adult Services Division
- 1972—The Adult Services Division merged with the Reference Division and created the Reference and Adult Services Division (RASD)
- 1996—Reference and User Services Association (RUSA).

1926: American Association for Adult Education established (United States).

The AAAE, originally organized by the Carnegie Corporation, combined with the Department of Adult Education of the National Education Association in 1951 to become the Adult Education Association of the United States (AEA-USA). In 1982, the AEA-USA merged with the National Association for Public Continuing Adult Education to form the American Association for Adult and Continuing Education (AAACE). The group works to promote education as a lifelong learning process as well as to systematize the methods and philosophy of the field. It publishes the journals *Adult Learning* and *Adult Education Quarterly*.

1926: National Home Study Council formed (United States).

The Council, formed under the cooperative leadership of the Carnegie Corporation of New York and the National Better Business Bureau, set out to promote sound educational standards and ethical business practices within the distance education field. One of the original members was the Art Instruction Schools. An independent accrediting commission was established in 1955, which was approved by the U.S. Department of Education as a recognized accrediting agency.

In the 1990s, the National Home Study Council changed its name to the Distance Education and Training Council. DETC serves as a clearinghouse of information about the distance study/correspondence field and sponsors the Accrediting Commission of the Distance Education and Training Council. The Accrediting Commission is also recognized by the Council for Higher Education Accreditation. DETC member institutions offer more than 500 different academic, vocational, and vocational courses by mail or by telecommunications.[139]

1927: Texas Technical College established Correspondence Teaching in Engineering (United States).

1928: University of New Mexico established Correspondence Teaching (United States).

1928: The public library system of Munich promoted a traveling mobile streetcar library—the Städtische Wander-Bücherei München (Munich, Germany).

The streetcar library traveled on a regular daily route with set stops at fixed times. The collection consisted of "approximately five thousand books, ranging from current novels to standard reference works," with new titles frequently added. Customers paid a small fee for the service.[140]

1928: Aerial Medical Service with radio support began operation (Australia).

Originally called the Aerial Medical Service (renamed the Flying Doctor Service in 1942 and the Royal Flying Doctor Service [RFDS] in 1955), founder Reverend John Flynn (1880–1951) created a flying ambulance service that provided much-needed medical services to those living in the remote Australian frontier. Just a year after its inauguration (1929), communication issues were overcome with the addition of a radio powered by a pedal-operated generator invented by Alfred Traeger. With this radio, the RFDS established an extensive radio network across the Australian outback. The service continues to this day, with bases all across Australia. Most of the radio schools operating in Australia initially used RFDS facilities and equipment.[141]

1929: University of Nebraska at Lincoln established the Independent Study High School (Nebraska, United States).

The first courses featured print-based correspondence study. Still flourishing, ISHS offers an accredited high school curriculum in both print and online formats along with a high school diploma available to both Nebraska residents and non-residents.

1929: School of the Air (SOA) movement (Australia, United States).

Schools of the Air were operated by commercial broadcast networks, state universities and departments or colleges of education, and local school boards. Although branded by some educational scholars as failures, the SOAs in the United States "reached approximately 2.5 million students nationwide (nearly 10 percent of the nation's school children) and involved tens of thousands of teachers and children directly in radio broadcasting." They brought education to isolated people who would not otherwise have had access to schools. They were especially popular in Australia, where many children lived miles away from the nearest school. SOAs intended for in-school use:

- Presented courses of study (series) in a subject that was parallel to or integrated with either a specific or typical school curricula
- Arranged programs in a series to assist in cumulative learning
- Designed individual program series for specific grade levels
- Developed broadcast schedules that coincided with the school year
- Distributed learning support materials such as teacher and student guides
- Designed series for students between kindergarten and grade 12[142]

1930s: Library extension efforts increased (United States).

University and college extension services were in full swing in the United States by the 1930s. As in the past, librarians were concerned about supporting these distributed university courses, especially in terms of supplemental reading materials as well as research and reference items.

In response to this need, the University of Chicago, long a leader in distributed learning, instituted a system of lending books for a small rental charge and reported that it was very successful. The University also lent phonograph records to aid in teaching French as well as microscopes, balances, and sets of apparatus to students of physics, chemistry, geology, zoology, and botany.

The report, "Books for the Extension Student," appeared in the 1931 *Bulletin of the American Library Association* and indicated that textbooks should be purchased by the student. It also acknowledged the difficulty the host library might encounter when asked to supply reference books "such as cyclopedias, dictionaries, and atlases, to which students in classes or in solitary study may have occasion to go."[143] Librarians were especially concerned with removing reference works from the home campus and sending them away for even short periods of time. How, then, did libraries meet the remote need for reference materials? Just as in the past, this was achieved through cooperation with public and state libraries.

Reporting in 1938, Almere Scott noted that university library extension could easily work to support correspondence students in a cooperative environment:

> When a correspondence student registers, two copies of the reference list are sent to the librarian, suggesting that one be returned indicating the volumes available to the student. The librarian may be able to purchase some books, thus building up the resources in economics, sociology, or whatever field the student is interested in. Publicity calling attention to the availability of such volumes has not only increased the circulation but has encouraged serious systematic study by others.[144]

1930s: Paperback books introduced.

1930: University of Virginia established Correspondence Teaching (United States).

1930–1934: The Carnegie Corporation of New York funded a demonstration program in Canada to promote the idea of regional libraries in the rural areas of Fraser Valley, British Columbia, Canada.

Dr. Helen Gordon Stewart served as director for the program, using the traveling library system model and a custom-built bookmobile. With these, "she brought the idea of public libraries to rural residents at deposit stations and newly established branches. The success of the travelling 'demonstration' libraries led to the establishment of other regional library units."[145] This demonstration library led to the establishment of the Fraser Valley Regional Library System (FVRL) in 1930, which is today the largest public library system in British Columbia.

1931: The University of Michigan established Correspondence Teaching (United States).

At the University Library Extension Round Table meeting in 1937, Edith Thomas reported that the University of Michigan Library Extension Service, under the direct administration of the university library, was studying civic, economic, social, and general educational problems. Their goal was to collect and make available timely materials for Michigan citizens. Thomas noted that this type of service was "characteristic of practically all the library service offered by or through the extension division of state universities in the Middle West."[146]

1932: Highlander Folk School established by Myles Horton (1905–1990) (Tennessee, United States).

1933: First Educational Television Courses offered from the University of Iowa (Iowa City, Iowa, United States).

Early broadcasts included oral hygiene and identifying star constellations.

1935: *The New York Times* published on microfilm by the Eastman Kodak Recordak division (United States).

1935: The Pack Horse librarians of Kentucky, a WPA program, flourished from 1935 until 1943 (Kentucky, United States).

Traveling libraries delivered on horseback were not a new concept when the pack horse library program was established by the Works Progress Administration (WPA) in eastern Kentucky in 1935. Like many other traveling libraries, this project sought to provide people living in rurally isolated spots a connection with the outside world through reading. They also delivered materials to schools, some of which had no books at all.

Generally, the pack horse collection relied on donations. Each headquarters administered between 200 to 800 books and magazines. Some titles had been discarded from libraries because they were too worn or soiled for further circulation; people wishing to help donated others. The librarians themselves were almost all women who lived in the communities they served. Called the "book women" by their customers, they could read, but they were not necessarily trained in library techniques.

Librarians earned a salary of about $28.00 a month paid by the Works Progress Administration (WPA). Their duties included:

1. maintaining a headquarters library, usually at the county seat
2. carrying books and magazines on horseback, muleback, or on foot throughout the county to remote locations where there were no roads.

The rationale behind the establishment of the Pack Horse Project was the demographics and socioeconomic status of Kentucky. During the 1930s and 1940s, Kentucky was one of the poorest states in the union and was even harder hit during the Great Depression than many other areas. The countryside was quite rocky and mountainous in the eastern regions, with few roads available to serve a highly scattered rural population.

By the late 1920s, other states were already serving their rural populations with motorized bookmobiles. This remained a challenge in Kentucky: how did you drive a car up a steep incline covered with broken rocks? Or, if not a door-to-door service as the Pack Horse Librarians offered, how to get remotely located people, who were very busy just making ends meet, come to you at a location that had a road? It was not until the roads were improved in the 1950s that the Friends of Kentucky Libraries could use bookmobiles to increase service to rural areas.[147]

A Pack Horse Librarian on her rounds in Owen County, KY. (Photographer, George Goodman, 1876–1961). Reproduced with permission from the University of Kentucky Archives: KUKAV-64M1-3963.

First Lady Eleanor Roosevelt visited the Pack Horse Library in West Liberty, KY, May 24, 1937. (Photographer, George Goodman, 1876–1961) Reproduced with permission from the University of Kentucky Archives: KUKAV-64M1-4965.

Similar circumstances to those in Kentucky prevailed in Mississippi during the Great Depression. Mississippi ranked second in rural population in the United States, but almost last in assessed valuation per capita. A statewide project was implemented to bring libraries to the people. "The people are book hungry," said one of the librarians who had a reading-room in her home. "A little boy knocked at my door at six o'clock in the morning to borrow *The Dutch Twins*. I passed a house the other day where a little girl was sitting on the porch reading aloud to her family of five people, not one of whom could read. An old man who was once a school teacher and a young girl who loves reading are each walking miles carrying books to share with people who otherwise would be without them."[148]

1937: The Australian Institute of Librarians created (Australia).

In 1949, the Association changed its name to the Library Association of Australia and in 1989 to the Australian Library and Information Association.

World War II: 1939–1945

Universities and libraries supported the provision of reading materials to soldiers as they had done in the past. Most notably, the University of London–External

System assisted soldiers interned in prisoner-of-war camps to continue their education, which also helped to alleviate the boredom of captivity.

Captain Hamson, imprisoned during World War II, recalled:

> The most striking phenomenon in officer prisoners-of-war camps . . . was the demand for education. It was so widespread as to be almost universal, and it was both tenacious and urgent. Though by profession a University don, I have not in peacetime encountered its equal. However, some part at least of this demand was a psychological reaction against captivity—that is to say, it was a method of escape from the immediate circumstances of prison life.[149]

1939:   Canadian Library Book Rate introduced (Canada).

The Library Rate, usually referred to as the Library Book Rate, went into service in 1939 in Canada. It was a great help in extending library services to rural and remote areas. This discounted rate applied to libraries mailing print materials to their users or to other libraries.

1939:   France created a state correspondence school (Europe).

When Germany invaded France during World War II, many schools were closed and children were dislocated. One answer to the education issue was to make use of distributed learning through a state correspondence school. This experiment in correspondence became the Centre National d'Enseignement à Distance (CNED). It is still active today, offering distributed vocational and academic classes.[150]

1941:   The Republic of Trinidad and Tobago developed library distribution agencies (Caribbean).

When Dr. Helen Gordon Stewart, a Canadian librarian, was appointed Director of the Central Library Services, she established a successful "network of distribution agencies consisting of book van stops, branch libraries, and deposit collections."[151]

1943:   Colossus, the first large-scale special-purpose electronic digital computer, began operation (England).

Built by Thomas H. Flowers and a team of engineers in London, Colossus was kept secret during the World War II and for quite some time thereafter. While an important step forward in computing, Colossus lacked two important characteristics found in later computers: (1) it had no internally stored programs, so that it had to be physically re-wired for different programs; (2) it was designed for a specific task, cracking codes. The original Colossus effectively and reliably used 1,600 vacuum tubes, the first machine to do so. One of its successors, Colossus II, was put into service in mid-1944 and used 2,400 vacuum tubes.[152]

1944:   Librarian Fremont Rider (1885–1962) introduced the opaque microcard storage medium while serving as the director of the Olin Library at Wesleyan University, Middletown, CT (United States).

The microcard consisted of a positive microprint reproduced on a 3 x 5 card storing up to 40 images. When first introduced it was heralded as "the first significant change in books since the substitution of the codex for the roll."[153] While many publications were released on microcards, the format was obsolete by the early 1970s when microfiche became the predominant method for microformat sheet reproduction.[154]

While easy to store and transport, microcards, like other microformats, could not be read without the aid of a reader. Printing from microcards required yet another type of device, the reader/printer. Did libraries send microcards to support distributed learning endeavors of individuals? Highly unlikely, although sending a printed copy from a microcard was a useable alternative.[155]

1945: Vannevar Bush (1890–1974) published his vision of the future of information retrieval (United States).

In the article, "As We May Think," Bush illustrated a system for associative information retrieval later called hypertext as well as the memex, which Bush described as "a device in which an individual stores all his books, records, and communications, and which is mechanized so that it may be consulted with exceeding speed and flexibility. It is an enlarged intimate supplement to his memory."[156]

1946: The Canadian Library Association/Association canadienne des bibliothèques incorporated (Canada).

1946: University of South Africa initiated distance learning (South Africa).

The University of South Africa (UNISA) opened its Division of External Studies on February 15, 1946. It began with a few thousand students and a handful of staff; by 2000 it had grown to about 3,000 staff members. Among UNISA's graduates are former RSA State President Nelson Mandela, who completed his LLB while in prison, and Nobel Laureate Bishop Desmond Tutu.

1946: ENIAC, the Electronic Numerical Integrator & Computer, began operation (United States).

ENIAC may be considered the first successful general digital computer. Modular, large, heavy (weighing in at around 30 tons) and complex, ENIAC drew on more than 17,000 vacuum tubes.

1947: Transistors available.

Invented by Bell Laboratories, transistors were put into operation and replaced large, hot, short-lived vacuum tubes. Unlike vacuum tubes, transistors were small and compact, used less electricity, and were more reliable.

1948: First working electronic stored-program digital computer (Manchester, England)

In June 1948, the Computing Machine Laboratory at the University of Manchester inaugurated the Manchester Small-Scale Experimental Machine (SSEM), nicknamed the Manchester Baby; the machine ran the first stored computing program.[157]

By 1940s standards, the Baby was a relatively small computer and processed only 17 instructions. The Baby was "greeted with hilarity" by the NPL [National Physical Laboratory] team developing the much more sophisticated Pilot Model

ACE.[158] The Baby, while the first, was perhaps the least of the programmable computers and quickly was succeeded by the Manchester Mark I, a brainchild of Alan Turing (1912–1954), a mathematician and computer scientist. Turing had also designed the advanced Pilot Automatic Computing Engine (ACE) and written a number of extended programs for that machine.

1948: Brigham Young University reorganized its Bureau of Correspondence, founded in 1921, into the Bureau of Home Study (Provo, Utah, United States).

The Bureau expanded its course offerings to include high school curricula.

1950: The Ford Foundation offered grants for educational programs distributed via television.

1950s: Penn State installed a live instructional television system (Pennsylvania, United States).

The television system initially connected 24 classrooms with a studio featuring one-way video and two-way audio for distribution of courses on campus.

1950s: The Juneau Rotary Club sponsored the "book boat"—a traveling library with boxes of books that visited 20 villages in Southeast Alaska (United States).[159]

1951: The Alice Springs School of the Air established at the Flying Doctor Base, Alice Springs, Northern Territory, Australia.

The first of its kind in Australia, this correspondence school brought education to isolated children in the Australian outback. Opening as a school of the air and using the equipment at the Flying Doctor Base in Alice Springs, the school broadcast lessons via radio one-way from teachers at the school to remote learners. It wasn't long before "a question and answer time was added to the end of each broadcast. Sometimes a microphone was taken into one of the classrooms at the school and the Outback children could listen in to specially prepared lessons or dramatisations. Three half-hour sessions are broadcast each week." In 1956, the school added two radio sessions for secondary students and established the school library sending books to the students via the post. By 1974, the school had become fully independent and served as the correspondence school for Central Australia. Using its own frequencies, the school reported that "correspondence work is now sent out to students, marked and returned from Alice Springs. There are now enough students to have a teacher for each class. Patrols are now made by class teachers to each of their students once a year." The school supported a library trailer in 1980 with the goal of bringing the library to remote students but abandoned the effort soon after as not workable in so large an area. The school library returned to posting books, CD-ROMs, and DVDs by mail along with correspondence lessons. The Alice Springs School of the Air has been heralded as "the world's biggest classroom."[160]

1961 to 1968: Midwest Program on Airborne Television Instruction (MPATI) began operation (Indiana, United States).

Located at Purdue University, MPATI first began operations financed by a Ford Foundation grant. It used the "flying classroom model," in which planes broadcast instructional programs to school systems, universities, and the general public in Indiana and five surrounding states. The project generated enough interest that upon its demise in 1968, several Education Television (ETV) stations were started in its stead.[161]

1953:   National University Extension Association (NUEA) Survey (United States).

In 1953, the National University Extension Association (NUEA), established in 1915, conducted a survey of 76 institutions of higher education in order to determine how they provided extension services and support for individuals and groups not in residence at a physical university.

NUEA had three major purposes in conducting this study:

1. to obtain a complete and detailed account of university extension services in the United States
2. to determine the place of extension in the structure of contemporary colleges and universities
3. to identify and distinguish the place of university extension in the total adult education pattern of the United States.

Their findings on library support were interesting. First of all, the majority of institutions (22 of 38) did not provide separate office space for correspondence study services. Only 12 set aside examination rooms for correspondence students, while 10 provided storage space for books, records, and supplies. The space allocated to the library lending services numbered between 1,000 and 2,000 square feet with a shelf space averaging about 1,500 linear feet. Almost without exception, extension librarians reported that the space allotted to them was inadequate and that the physical facility was not conductive for library lending services.

The report also found that more than half the library lending services maintained collections of materials separate from the main university library. Only about 40 percent indicated that their materials were listed in and belonged to the main library collection. In addition to books, the reporting institutions held an average of: 200,000 loan packages or clipping files, 60,000 pamphlets, 30,000 books, 15,000 periodicals, and an assortment of pictures, and sound recordings.[162]

The report found that many university extension lending departments incorporated visual aid services into their efforts. Visual services primarily served public schools, rather than correspondence students, since audio visual items, such as slides, films or micro formats, required special viewing equipment. Films were a significant expense since they were much more expensive than books and 31 institutions reported an average annual investment in new films alone of around $6,000 per year.[163]

Visual Aid Services also reported an average of about 2,000 square feet for their use. (This varied from 600 sq. ft. at one place to 20,000 sq. ft. at another.) Facilities generally included office space, photographic studio, shipping room, film storage room and racks, projection room, dark room, and workroom. In some cases, all of the above operations were crammed into a single room. Not surprisingly, "About half the directors of visual aid services believed the present space available for these activities was inadequate."[164]

The report concluded that both library and visual services played a major role in assisting their clientele, but that both were understaffed and underfunded.

1953: Book boat service inaugurated in the Archipelago of Stockholm (Sweden).

Beginning with a military boat from the coast artillery that had been equipped with shelves, the resulting book boat conveyed books to people in isolated communities in the Stockholm archipelago, which consists of about 150 islands. Following in this path several years later the *Gurli*, a passenger steamer, was outfitted with shelving for about 3,000 children's and adult books. In addition to books, the boat made available lessons and storytelling sessions for children and films and lectures for adults. The *Gurli* made two trips a year for five days each visiting 25 jetties on a set schedule. The boat spent between 30 minutes to three hours at each dock, based on the estimated number of visitors. Librarians onboard included a children's librarian and a library assistant, who were local individuals. Kjerstin Thulin wrote in *Book Boat Service in the Archipelago of Stockholm,*: "These contact persons handle circulation of the books to borrowers; they also collect the books before the book boat returns next time." Boat libraries have flourished, and continue to flourish, in other areas in Scandinavia (Finland, Norway) and from Thailand to Canada to Venezuela.[165]

1954: The Friends of Kentucky Libraries inaugurated a bookmobile program (United States).

Following in the footsteps of such programs as the Pack Horse Librarians, Kentucky continued to support outreach and distributed services. The Friends of Kentucky Libraries, with help from a variety of different organizations, individuals, and Former Governor Lawrence Wetherby, inaugurated a bookmobile program on September 16, 1954. Through the efforts and donations of this group, counties throughout Kentucky received 100 bookmobiles.[166]

1955: Traveling High School Science Libraries (United States).

Many American high schools lacked adequate supplementary reading and reference materials to support the study of science. To rectify this deficiency, a grant from the National Science Foundation allowed traveling high school libraries to be assembled and dispersed. With few exceptions, textbooks were not included in the collection, which encompassed a broad range of subject matter "so that a student may acquaint himself with the major branches of science and discern the practical application of the sciences and mathematics in research, in the professions, and in industry."[167]

1956: Book Boat Service Established in Gothenburg and Bohuslan County (Sweden).

Similar to the Stockholm Archipelago Book Service inaugurated in 1953, this traveling boat library served the western coast of Sweden. The boat brought juvenile and adult materials in a variety of languages to a clientele consisting primarily of immigrants and refugees. The boat held roughly 7,000 books, but visited only once a year.[168]

1958: Jack Kilby introduced the integrated circuit or silicon chip (United States).

The integrated circuit contained thousands of transistors etched into a silicon chip.

1960:   Kimberley School of the Air (KSOTA) commenced operation (Australia).

1961:   Carl Carlson, an employee at the Dayton, OH, National Cash Register Company, invented microfiche (United States).

Microfiche: A micro reproduction on a flat, single sheet of film. "Users are generally attracted by the suitability of microfiche as a unit record for documents less than a few hundred pages in length and by the development of microfiche standards that have made possible the production of inexpensive, high-quality readers and reader/printers."[169]

1963:   Douglas Engelbart (1925–) designed first computer mouse introducing the concept of point and click computing (United States).

Engelbart's mouse was wooden and had one button.

1964:   AIM (Wisconsin, United States).

AIM, University of Wisconsin's Articulated Instructional Media Project, used various media for teaching off-campus students who accessed local library resources to supplement their education.

1964:   First public demonstration of online bibliographical retrieval (Library/ USA Exhibit, New York World's Fair).

Using a computer and regular telephone lines, people could interact remotely with librarians.

1965:   Telephone-Based Distance Education (United States).

The University of Wisconsin began a statewide telephone-based distance education program for physicians.

1966:   Katherine School of the Air began operation (Australia).

This school offered correspondence and radio programs as a combination to bring education to students in remote areas.

1966–1998:   Educational Radio Broadcasts (Germany).

In 1966, the Hessian Broadcasting Corp. (Hessischer Rundfunk) and the University of Frankfurt along with the German Institution for Distance Education (Deutsche Institut für Fernstudien-DIFF-at the University of Tübingen) established a system of radio broadcasts beginning with "Towards an Understanding of Modern Society" (Zum Verständnis der modernen Gesellschaft). Students were able to receive certificates through radio-distributed learning. Although successful, German broadcasting companies lost interest in carrying educational content and the program ceased in 1998.[170]

1967:   British Open University Established (United Kingdom).

The British Open University, established by Royal Charter, admitted its first students in 1971. Heralded as the United Kingdom's largest university, it served over

200,000 students in 1997/98 and offers distance education courses throughout the world.

1967: Corporation for Public Broadcasting (PBS) formed (United States).

PBS's goal was to promote noncommercial television use.

1967: OCLC established (United States and worldwide).

OCLC (first named the Ohio College Library Center) was established, and remains, a nonprofit, membership, computer library and research organization. It made possible cooperative, shared, online cataloging for libraries in Ohio beginning in 1971 and extended that service worldwide in 1977. In 1981, OCLC was renamed OCLC Online Computer Library Center, Inc. In 2007, the RLG (Research Libraries Group) Union Catalog (RLIN), and OCLC's World Cat merged.

1968: Stanford Instructional Television Network created at Stanford University (California, United States).

The Network broadcast the first credit and professional education courses to school, university, and industry sites worldwide.

1969: ARPANET (Advanced Research Projects Agency Network) created by the Defense Advanced Research Projects Agency (DARPA) of the United States Department of Defense (United States).

The ARPANET was the world's first operational packet switching network, a forerunner of the Internet. Like the Internet, ARPANET evolved into a human communication medium. According to Licklider and Vezza, two early computer pioneers, ARPANET had many advantages over print mail and telephone calls because "in an ARPANET message, one could write tersely and type imperfectly, even to an older person in a superior position and even to a person one did not know very well, and the recipient took no offense. The formality and perfection that most people expect in a typed letter did not become associated with network messages, probably because the network was so much faster, so much more like the telephone."[171]

1971: Electronic mail (Email) is invented by Ray Tomlinson for use on ARPANET.

1971: The concept of e-books and Project Gutenberg, the first distributor of free e-books, pioneered by Michael Hart (United States).

1972: Computer conferencing is introduced.

1974: The Research Libraries Group (RLG) founded by cooperation between the New York Public Library and three universities: Columbia, Harvard, Yale (United States).

A year later, in 1975, RLG incorporated as a nonprofit membership consortium of research institutions. With expanding membership, RLG supported a shared cataloging database called the RLIN Union Catalog in 1980. In 1991, RLG launched the Ariel system for interlibrary loans. In 2007, the RLIN Union Catalog merged with OCLC's World Cat.

1974:   First edition of *Bears' Guide to Earning Degrees by Distance Learning* published (United States).

When John Bear (born John Klempner in 1938) completed the first edition of his guide to distance learning titled *College Degrees by Mail: A Comprehensive Guide to Nontraditional Degree Programs,* he drew prospective students' attention to opportunities for nontraditional and distributed learning programs. As part of his studies, Bear also exposed diploma mills and illegitimate programs. Considered by many to be overly opinionated, Bear and his co-authors have published frequent editions of the *Guide* with the most recent, 16th edition, appearing in 2006.

1974:   A consortium of nine Midwestern universities called the University of Mid-America joined forces to produce and deliver courses through distributed methods focusing on television (Nebraska, United States).

Based on the concepts of Britain's Open University, but without granting degrees or maintaining a faculty, the University of Mid-America pulled together the resources of several major universities in Nebraska, Kansas, Iowa, South Dakota, and Missouri. The concept originated in 1971 when the president of the University of Nebraska appointed a committee to study how the Nebraska educational television system could "reach people interested in college education but living too far from a campus to attend classes. The committee proposed the creation of an open learning, extension network called the State University of Nebraska (SUN)." SUN's expansion from local to regional service provided the impetus for the establishment of the University of Mid-America.

The television component was a major element of the distributed classroom, even though it was not based on the lecturing professor model. R. Douglas Hurt noted in "The University of Mid-America": "Instead, a host introduces various television segments, and together with location photography, interviews, newsreels, and other techniques presents related subject matter to the student."[172] Telecourses produced by this group were later made available through the Great Plains Network (GPN).

Although the University received substantial support from the National Institute of Education, it could not sustain itself and ceased operations in 1982.

1974/1975:   The Altair 8800 minicomputer introduced (United States).

When the Altair 8800 appeared on the front cover of the January 1975 *Popular Electronics* magazine, it was heralded as a "Project Breakthrough! World's First Minicomputer Kit to Rival Commercial Models." Hitting the newsstands just in time for Christmas 1974, the magazine invited enthusiasts to purchase the Altair 8800 kit for $397. For those technically less inclined, a fully assembled version was available for $498. The minicomputer held 65,000 directly addressable words and could be used with a CRT terminal.[173]

1975:   Bill Gates and Paul Allen founded Microsoft Corporation (United States).

1975–current: The FernUniversität (Open University) established in Hagen (Germany).

Based on Britain's Open University model, the FernUniversität offered flexible degree programs to those who could not attend a physical university.

1976: Steve Wozniak and Steve Jobs released the Apple I computer and started Apple Computers (United States).

1976: U.S. Copyright Act signed into law (United States).

The law specified that works published on or after January 1, 1978, were not required to display a copyright notice in order to be legally protected by copyright. The law also contained the provision for Fair Use of a copyrighted work, established a uniform term of protection for works, and clarified the exclusive rights of the copyright holder.

1976: The University of Phoenix became the first American university to offer course work online (United States).

1977: The first complete personal computer, the Commodore PET (*Personal Electronic Transactor*) introduced.

1978: The first Multi-User Domain (or Dungeon), MUD1, went online.

1978: The Bulawayo Public Library instituted a mobile library service (Rhodesia before 1980; Zimbabwe after 1980).

When it first went into operation, the Bulawayo Public Library's mobile service made do with an ancient converted bus. The library replaced the original vehicle with a more modern bus in 1984. In 1996, the Netherlands donated a bookmobile, which allowed the library to expand its mobile services to schools, many of which lacked any sort of library. One bus served 19 schools and held shelving for at least 3,500 books. The total inventory in 1998 totaled around 5,500 books, with at least 2,000 in circulation at any one time. These mobile units were cost-effective because "to provide a library of 2,000 books at each of the 19 schools visited by this vehicle would take no less than 38,000 books, while the cost of providing rooms and furnishings for 19 different libraries would be an enormous additional expenditure." In addition, a qualified librarian staffed each bookmobile, again allowing for economies based on distribution of time, staff, and resources. Unfortunately, the bookmobile's stops were limited to one hour each week.[174]

1980s: Computer Output Microfim (COM) in use.

1981: IBM introduced the first Personal Computer (PC).

The 1981 model of the IBM Personal Computer was the size of a typewriter and sold for $1,565, offering a striking contrast to many previous computers, which cost more than $9 million, were large, and required special physical space and staff. The PC development team dubbed the PC "a mini-compact, at a mini-price, with IBM engineering under the hood."[175]

1981: MS-DOS (MicroSoft Disk Operating System) 1.0 released with the IBM PC.

1981: Citizens' High School established (Orange Park, Florida, United States).

Citizens offered an accredited independent study program leading to a high school diploma for students in their teens to senior citizens.

1983: Microsoft Corporation released the first version of its GUI (graphical user interface) operating system called Windows.

1983:   University Alaska–Fairbanks (UAF) established an Off-Campus Library Services initiative (United States).

UAF supports six extended campuses and seven other units, which together make up the College of Rural Alaska. Using the U.S. Postal Service, email, fax, or the Internet for delivery, the library service delivers to students and faculty "who do not have access to appropriate information resources in their community" according to the off-campus librarian. Just as with past endeavors, the key to success is cooperation in rural Alaska. "Faxes can still be sent to tribal offices, employers, the local schools, and the extended campuses. They all allow people to use their Internet access. It's a community effort. It's just amazing what they do with very few resources, sharing and cooperating." For individuals who have never seen or stepped into a physical library or even traveled far from their own village, this service allows them to expand their skills and education in a large, rural state with a harsh climate and a scattered population.[176]

1984:   Apple Computer launched the Macintosh, the first successful mouse-driven computer with a graphic user interface.

1984–1990:   The Amstrad CPC (*Colour Personal Computer*) released to compete with other personal computers (Europe).

1985:   Indonesia Open Learning University (Universitas Terbuka = UT) established (Jakarta, Indonesia).

"The vision of Universitas Terbuka (UT) is to be the Center of Excellence in the area of management, research, and development, and to be an information clearinghouse in the field of distance and open higher education systems. The library of UT, as the learning resource and information center, should support the realization of this vision." The library established cooperative efforts with other university libraries, the Network of The Indonesia National Library, and used electronic resources to support distributed learning.[177]

1985:   Commodore Amiga PC launched with a retail cost of $1,295.00 (United States).

1986:   Odyssey Academy created (United States).

Odyssey Learning Services, incorporated 1984, established Odyssey Academy to provide K–12 distributed learning classes with several options, including teacher support and a diploma program.

1987:   Glenn Jones established the Mind Extension University (ME/U) (United States).

Jones began his efforts in distributed learning when he used a basic cable television channel to bring courses to students in K–12 and college. The undergraduate and graduate courses were accredited and although ME/U did not award credit itself, students enrolled in partner universities received course credit from their universities. In 1993, Jones founded Jones International University (JIU) taking advantage of distributed learning through the Internet. JIU was the first wholly online university to receive regional accreditation in 1999. Jones also established the Jones e-global virtual library. Although originally created for JIU faculty and students, it is available "for license by universities, corporations and individuals around the world."[178]

1987:   The American Center for the Study of Distance Education established in Penn State's College of Education.

Long an advocate for distributed learning, Penn State's Center researched distributed learning communication systems such as computer, audio, and video conferencing. The school established a Department of Distance Education in 1994.[179]

1987:   HyperCard (hypertext program) added to the Apple-Macintosh.

The HyperCard application was basically a database system in which information was stored on cards, which could be linked to each other the way hyperlinks are used to link different pages on the web. The HyperCard boasted an easy-to-understand and user-friendly interface. Many companies, schools, and libraries used the HyperCard system for catalogs, inventories, and teaching. Apple withdrew the HyperCard system in 2004.

1989:   Internet Protocol Suite (TCP/IP) initiated as a global system of Internet communication.

1989:   Tim Berners-Lee developed the Hyper Text Markup Language (HTML) and the concept for the World Wide Web (WWW) at the European Organization for Nuclear Research, known as CERN (Geneva, Switzerland).

1989:   The Berne Convention Implementation Act, Copyright (March 1).

The Act specified that works published without a copyright notice between January 1, 1978, and March 1, 1989, could claim copyright only if a copyright registration was made within five years. For anything created after 1989, no notice was needed worldwide. Any knowledge set down in a tangible medium was copyrighted at the moment of creation, with or without a copyright notice.

1989:   University of Phoenix Online campus inaugurated online degree programs (United States).

The University of Phoenix was the first private university to distribute master's and bachelor's degree programs using an asynchronous online technology.

1992:   The World Wide Web brought online as part of the Internet.

1992:   Veronica (search tool) released by University of Nevada (United States).

1992:   European Lifelong Learning Initiative (ELLI) (Europe).

The goal of ELLI, an international professional association, was to foster lifelong learning in Europe.

1992:   The LOUISiana Digital Library established (Louisiana, United States).

1992:   Mobile Library Services initiated in Bangkok (Thailand).

1992:   New York University's School of Continuing and Professional Studies (NYU SCPS) formed The Virtual College (New York, United States).

The Virtual College offered online classes in management, foreign language translation, creative writing, and IT. Its classes reach students throughout the United States and internationally.

1993:   The University of Nebraska–Lincoln instituted an online doctoral program in Educational Leadership and Higher Education (United States).

1993: The Australasian Association of Distance Education Schools (AADES) formed (Australia and New Zealand).

Still active today, AADES is a professional organization that represents school-level distance learning.

1993: The Graduate School of America, a for-profit distance education institution, is founded (Minnesota, United States).

Renamed Capella University in 1991 and accredited by the Higher Learning Commission in 1997, the school originally offered online graduate degrees in management, education, and human services. Today Capella offers over a thousand courses along with full undergraduate and graduate (including Ph.D.) online degree programs.

1993: Marc Andreessen, NCSA (National Center for Supercomputing Applications), and University of Illinois develop introduced Mosaic, the first graphical web browser (United States).

1994–1998: Digital Library Initiative, Phase 1 (United States).

Phase 1 involved three U.S. federal agencies and focused on collecting, storing, and organizing information in digital formats and making it available for search, retrieval, and processing through communication networks.

1995: Sun launches JAVA programming.

1995: *D-Lib Magazine* launched.

An entirely online publication (http://www.dlib.org/), *D-Lib Magazine* concentrates on all aspects of digital libraries.

1995: Perseus Digital Library at Tufts University established (Massachusetts, United States).

Planning for this project began in 1985. The digital library is currently an open source web-based product highlighting the history, literature and culture of the Greco-Roman world with focus on three prominent languages: Greek, Latin, and Arabic.

1995: Virtual High School established in Kitchener, Ontario (Canada).

1996: Noosa Mobile Library offered Internet service (Queensland, Australia).

Australia has long been a leader in mobile library services and distributed learning. When the Noosa mobile library was wired for Internet, it was the first in Australia. Mobile librarian Richard Yeates noted: "With selected CD-ROMs . . . adding cream to the cake of the Internet, Noosa Library mobile operators are in a very strong position to give comprehensive answers to any question that may come their way at most of the ten mobile stops throughout the Shire."[180]

1996: Camel Library Service implemented (Kenya, Africa).

The Kenya National Library Service (KNLS) inaugurated its Camel Library Service (CLS) to serve residents in areas where rough terrain and poor roads could not support motorized vehicles. Camels were loaded with books and other library materials packed into four boxes, which totaled about 300 items. Three camels traveled in a caravan and carried books, a tent, chairs, a table, and an umbrella to predetermined stops such as village centers. Leading the caravan was a librarian with two assistants accompanied by a skilled camel herdsman. Arriving at their destination, the group unloaded books, pitched a tent, spread a floor cover inside the tent to provide seating, and placed the books on shelves. The library was open for business.[181]

1996: WebCT online learning environment presented at the 5th International World Wide Web conference (Paris, France).

In 2006, WebCT was acquired by Blackboard, Inc., another course management distributor.

1997: California Virtual University (CVU) opened a consortium of California colleges and universities offering distributed courses (United States).

CVU provided a portal for online courses offered by public institutions in California. Succeeded by the California Virtual Campus (CVC), it continues to maintain a catalog of distributed learning courses offered by higher education institutions in California.

1997: Western Governors University (WGU) (United States).

The Western Governors Association, a nonprofit, fully accredited online university, was formed by a partnership between 19 states in the United States The WGU began enrolling students in the summer of 1998 and offers bachelors and masters degrees.[182]

1997: The African Virtual University (AVU) (Africa).

AVU was inaugurated in Washington, DC (U.S.) as a World Bank Project and transferred, in 2002, to Kenya. A year later (2003) it became an intergovernmental organization when five African governments (Kenya, Senegal, Mauritania, Mali, and Cote d'Ivoire) created a Charter. The AVU provides an extensive digital library. The AVU called itself a university without walls that used "modern information and communication technologies to give the countries of sub-Saharan Africa direct access to some of the highest quality learning resources throughout the world. AVU is bridging the digital divide by training world-class business managers, engineers, technicians, scientists and other professionals who will promote economic and social development and help propel Africa into the knowledge age."[183]

1997: Farmington Community Library (FCL) introduced its CyberSeniors Program (Michigan, United States).

FCL brought Internet instruction to senior centers and assisted-living facilities.[184]

1997: The Florida Virtual School (FLVS) established (United States).

FLVS is an accredited, Internet-based public high school providing K–12 courses without charge to students in Florida and on a tuition basis for students outside of Florida.

1998:   Blackboard Inc. unveiled (United States).

Blackboard provides e-learning products particularly the Blackboard Course Management System for online learning used by many K–12 and higher education distance learning programs.

1998:   Extensible Markup Language (XML) introduced.

1998:   E-book provider NetLibrary distributed content to libraries (Colorado, United States).

In 2002, OCLC (Online Computer Library Center, Inc.) bought NetLibrary saving it and many libraries' subscriptions from bankruptcy. OCLC NetLibrary for e-books and e-Audiobooks was purchased by EBSCO Publishing in 2010 and continues to be a major provider of e-content.

1998:   Rocket E-Book Reader, the first portable, self-contained e-book reader released (United States).

Not a success itself, the first e-book reader paved the way for future endeavors.

1998:   National Library of Australia Online Digital Services Project initiated (Australia)

1998:   Kaplan University's Concord Law School is established as an online school (United States).

1998:   Sonny Bono Copyright Term Extension Act (CTEA) (United States).

CTEA extended copyright protection to life of author/creator plus seventy years, a 20-year extension over the former law of life plus 50 years in the United States.

1998:   Digital Millennium Copyright Act (DMCA) signed into law as Public Law No: 105–304, October 28 (United States).

This Act essentially made the use of works in digital form more difficult for all Internet service providers and their users, by disallowing circumvention of any electronic access controls that protect works regardless of public domain or fair use exemptions."

1998:   The Muncie Public Library (MPL) established a cybermobile service (Indiana, United States).

MPL took bookmobile service and distributed learning one-step further with the cybermobile, a bookmobile fitted out as a rolling computer resource featuring six wireless Internet workstations. The bookmobile offered computer instruction in various applications on board and brought computer classes to senior centers, apartment complexes, schools, and community centers.[185]

1998–current: Blue Trunk Library (BTL) Project established by the World Health Organization (WHO).

With unreliable or nonexistent access to electricity, many health care providers in remote and inaccessible locations in Africa and other developing countries rely primarily on print materials. The BTL project fulfills this need by providing traveling libraries of books shipped in a blue metal trunk.[186]

1998: Mohammed Rezwan founded Shidhulai Swanirvar Sangstha (SSS), a non-profit boat organization (Bangladesh).

Expanding on his original organization in 2002, Rezwan introduced a boat school that allowed children to go to school during the annual monsoon season, which typically lasts three to four months. During this time, the SSS brought school to children since the children could not come to the school. To accomplish this goal, Rezwan equipped boats and loaded them with books, computers, printers, phones, and projectors. Using solar energy for power, these mobile schools traveled to remote communities using the waterway system.[187]

1998–2003: Digital Library Initiative, Phase 2 (United States).

Expanding on phase I (1994–98) Phase 2 involved nine agencies including the National Library of Medicine and the Library of Congress.

1999: Desire2Learn eLearning Solutions established (United States).

Desire2Learn offers a commercial learning management system providing web-based e-learning solutions for K–12 and higher education.

1999: Biblioburro (the donkey library) began operation (La Gloria, Colombia).

Seeing a need and responding to it, teacher Luis Soriano created the Biblioburro, a way to share books from his own library collection with children and adults in villages around La Gloria. On weekends, Soriano and his two donkeys, Alfa and Beto, visit villages and bring "the transformative power of reading" to those who have no access to books or other information sources. Soriano noted in 2008 "I started out with 70 books, and now I have a collection of more than 4,800."[188]

1999: Department of Non-Formal Education, Information Education Promotion Center, Ministry of Education, initiated the Public Library Project (Thailand).

The public library project highlighted mobile floating libraries on boats. The first was the Nang Noppamas, which held more than 1,500 books and offered a computer with Internet access. Three librarians oversaw services and allowed visitors to read books on deck or use a table below. If someone became seasick, he or she was allowed to take the book ashore.[189]

1999: Term "Web 2.0" introduced by Darcy DiNucci in the article "Fragmented Future." *Web 2.0* describes how people may share information interactively using the established World Wide Web through various communications media, such as social net-working.

The 21st Century

2000: The ANGEL Learning Management System is released by CyberLearning Labs, Inc. (United States).

ANGEL, originally developed as OnCourse at Indiana–Purdue University Indianapolis (IUPUI) in 1996, was renamed ANGEL Learning, Inc. and released commercially. In 2009, competitor Blackboard Inc. acquired the company.

2000:   Cyber Seniors Program established at the Multnomah County Library (Oregon, United States).

With the aid of a grant from telephone provider U.S. West, the Library loaded up its cybermobile with PCs to bring computer and Internet instruction to senior citizen centers. Well-trained volunteers set up the PCs at each center and conducted the training sessions that included up to six seniors at a time.[190]

2000:   National High School began offering online courses (Georgia, United States).

The National High School, an accredited private high school based in Atlanta, offers computer-based high school instruction. Like many previous distributed educational endeavors, the NHS supports the belief that "all students have the right and the opportunity to earn a high school diploma, while recognizing that not all students are able to accomplish this in a traditional educational setting."[191]

2000:   K12 founded by Ron Packard (United States and worldwide).

K12 is listed as America's largest provider of personalized virtual web-based public and private schooling for students in grades K–12. As an educational company, K12's curriculum, management services, and support supply the backbone for many virtual public charter schools across the United States. K12 International Academy is the accredited private school component offering full-grade packages as well as individual courses.[192] K12 acquired KC Distance Learning, Inc. (KCDL) in July 2010. KCDL provides distributed learning for middle and high school students through several venues, including the Keystone School. An accredited private online school, Keystone was established in 1974 to provide a flexible learning environment offered by certified teachers for full- and part-time students.[193]

2000:   The Kentucky Virtual High School (KVHS), part of the Kentucky Virtual Schools, established by the Kentucky Department of Education (Kentucky, United States).

The Virtual Schools are served by the Kentucky Virtual Library, established in 1999.

2000:   The Michigan Virtual School (MVS) funded by the Michigan Legislature (United States).

2001:   Donkey Drawn Electro-Communication Library Carts (Zimbabwe)

The donkey libraries serviced the Nakyi District in the northwestern area of Zimbabwe. Because of such library efforts, the literacy rate in this area was about 86 percent—much higher than in areas without the service. The carts not only carried books, but provided a one-stop source for communications using radio, telephone, fax, and the Internet. Solar panels on the cart's roof provided electricity for a self-contained unit. Some carts also carried a satellite dish.[194]

2001:   The Bangkok Metropolitan Administration (BMA) introduced home libraries (Thailand).

2001:   The Kalamazoo Public Library contracted with Audible.com to loan digital audio books (Michigan, United States).

2001: Branson School Online (Colorado, United States).

Online public school established with children learning in their homes. Laptop computers are rented at low cost to families.

2002: TEACH Act signed into law (United States).

The Technology, Education and copyright Harmonization Act (TEACH), part of the larger Justice Reauthorization legislation (H.R. 2215), was signed into law. TEACH clarified and redefined the terms and conditions by which accredited, nonprofit education institutions throughout the United States could use copyrighted materials in distance education. (Chapters 5 and 6 examine TEACH and its ramifications for libraries and copyright.)

2002: Moodle open source course management system released.

A competitor to Blackboard and other commercial course management systems, Moodle is freely available open source software. Although copyrighted, Moodle may be copied, used, and modified according to its license.[195]

2002: Elephant Libraries receive UNESCO literacy prize for 2002 (Thailand).

Elephants provided the power behind bookmobiles in Northern Thailand. Carrying books, computers, satellite dishes, and generators, the elephant libraries brought information and educational materials to remote villages.[196]

2003: The Cleveland Public Library began circulation of e-books (Ohio).

2003: Schools of the Air embraced satellite technology (Australia).

2004: First Distance Education Network hosted at the Modern Institute for the Humanities (Moscow, Russia).

Gilat Skystar partnered with the open university, Modern Institute for the Humanities with a student body of over 145,000, to bring satellite-based distributed learning to 155 remote sites.[197]

2004: Telecom Company Cable & Wireless offers distance education to Seychellois through its virtual academy (Republic of Seychelles).

2004: Caribbean Association for Distance and Open Learning (CARADOL). Established with financial support from UNESCO.

2004: National Open University of Nigeria (NOUN) founded (Africa).

2004: LOCKSS (Lots of Copies Keep Stuff Safe), based at Stanford University Libraries, CA, released into production after development beginning in 1999 (United States).

2004: Sakai Project initiated in January, involving a partnership between the University of Michigan, Indiana University, MIT, and Stanford, to create a collection of open source tools for online course management (United States).

The Sakai Project, currently administered by the Sakai Foundation, is a group of over 100 members from educational institutions. Sakai is an open source learning management system similar to Moodle.

2004: Google partnered with libraries to launch a massive book digitization project (Worldwide).

Google Inc. in partnership with several major research libraries (Harvard, Stanford, University of Michigan, University of Oxford) and the New York Public Library began digitally scanning books in an effort to make them searchable worldwide via Google. Scanned items included both out-of-print, public domain, and copyrighted works. The latter effort has prompted several copyright controversies.

2005: European Digital Library launched an integration of the bibliographic catalogs and digital collections of the national libraries of Europe.

2005: Embedded Librarian model gains momentum (Worldwide).

Librarians are embedded into online courses giving students immediate access to library instruction and reference services.

2005: Nicholas Negroponte of MIT (Massachusetts Institute of Technology) introduced the One Laptop per Child concept (United States).

2005/6: PDF/A, a digital format for long-term archiving certified by the International Organization for Standardization.

PDF (portable document format) files called PDF/A and developed by Adobe Systems Incorporated was adopted as suitable for long-term archiving.

2005: ProQuest digitized 19th-Century Collection of British House of Commons Parliamentary Papers from 1801 to 1900.

2005: The rise of Library 2.0.

Library 2.0 operates on the supposition that information should be available at all times.

2005: The University of Florida introduced outdoor mobile reference stations (Florida, United States).

In addition to the mobile efforts at Florida, librarians at Brandeis and Harvard Universities take laptops to academic departments and set up office hours, increasing librarians' interaction with the teaching faculty.[198]

2005: New York University's School of Continuing and Professional Studies (NYU SCPS) launched the university's first fully online undergraduate degree program for adult students (New York, United States).

2005: Mobile Donkey Libraries Established (Ethiopia, Africa).

Very similar to attempts in other countries with remote and relatively inaccessible areas, the Ethiopian Books for Children and Educational Foundation (EBCEF) established mobile donkey libraries to bring books and reading to schools and villages without library services. The donkey cart stored books, stools for seating, and food for the donkey. A trained librarian or library assistant distributed the books to the children during scheduled stops. Children read to themselves or aloud with the librarian's guidance. When the visit was over, the librarian packed up the materials to take to the next destination. Librarian Yohannes Gebregoergis reported that the mobile libraries were a success because they "connected the children with books and have given them a sense of empowerment."[199]

2006: SONY launched an electronic book store on the Web called Connect E-Book.

2006: Michigan required high school students to complete at least one course online calling it the Online Learning Experience (United States).

2007: Amazon.com introduced the wireless e-book reader Kindle and marketed it as easy to use, needing no computer, no cables, and no syncing with external devices.

2007: The Ministry of Training, Colleges and Universities established the elearnnetwork.ca (Ontario, Canada).

The goal of the network was to provide online access to students in small and rural communities across Ontario.

2007: Bibliomulas (book mules) established in Venezuela (South America).

The University of Momboy initiated the idea of the bibliomulas or books mules. These mule bookmobiles transported books to remote mountain villages to encourage reading. Some mules also carried laptops and projectors, making them effective cyber mules and cine mules. "We want to install wireless modems under the banana plants so the villagers can use the internet," reported Robert Ramirez, of the University's Network of Enterprising Rural Schools.[200]

2009: Barnes & Noble released its e-book reader called the Nook.

2009: University of the People (UoPeople) established as the world's first tuition-free online academic institution.

UoPeople is "dedicated to the global advancement and democratization of higher education."[201]

2009: Open High School launched (Utah, United States).

The Open High School is a public charter school serving Utah high school students. The school is free and charges only a few fees to cover equipment and yearbooks. It is unique in that is uses open content coursework created by its instructors. This approach results in courses that are fairly inexpensive to produce and more easily updated than expensive textbooks. There are no physical classrooms and content is available online 24/7.

2009–2010: Library in a Box service operated in Bandung, West Java, Indonesia.

The Centerville Rotary Club of Ohio supported outreach services to children by providing traveling libraries. The library in a box was delivered by motorcycle in the city of Bandung and in the surrounding mountains that are inaccessible to cars. Each box holds between 250 and 300 children's books in Indonesian. The Centerville Rotary Club bought the books in Indonesia and supported 25 delivery sites.[202]

2010: Online courses and enrollments increase significantly.

According to the report *Learning on Demand: Online Education in the United States, 2009,* the number of students taking online courses increased significantly over the last six years. The report noted that: "Over 4.6 million students were taking at least one online course during the fall 2008 term; [this is] a 17 percent increase over the number reported the previous year." A further observation showed

2009–2010: Library in a Box service in Bandung, West Java, Indonesia

Centerville Rotary Club's book project in Indonesia. Courtesy of Mae E. Berkel-Avé.

that "more than one in four higher education students now take a least one course online."[203]

2010: Sony released several e-book readers.

E-book readers proliferate, offering a variety of services, including downloads from libraries.

2010: Apple released the iPad.

Apple's iPad features a touch screen and built-in applications, including iBooks. Apple had previously brought out its first tablet computer, the Newton Message-Pad 100, in 1993, and ceased its production in 1998. Also of interest, were the iPod, launched in 2001, and the iPhone, released in 2007.

2010: The Applied Engineering and Technology Library at the University of Texas at San Antonio opened as a bookless library (Texas, United States).

With a building designed to be bookless, the UTSA library planned to provide "pre-loaded collections of EBooks on EReader devices such as iPad or Kindle for students to check out and take home."[204]

2010: Students in rural schools viewed math and science content on computer screens during long bus rides (Pope County District, Arkansas, United States).

Mobile learning allowed students with long bus commutes to and from school an opportunity to study using ceiling-mounted computer screens.[205] Not a new idea, other initiatives to provide laptops and Internet access have made the wired, mobile bus a reality for many students.

2010: E-book sales continued to rise.

2010: Google launched Google eBooks.

Google's Ebookstore allowed a variety of readers to access over three million titles, some free, others available for purchase. Purchased titles were stored in the cloud on Google servers. Called Google eBooks.

2010: Amazon announced Kindle for the web.

Similar to Google's e-bookstore, Amazon's service allowed access to the full text of Kindle books in a web browser.

2011: BitTorrent and Khan Academy collaborated to offer free educational videos.

The free application offered access to videos in math, science, and the humanities. Khan Academy operates as a not-for-profit corporation and presents this opportunity in support of its mission to provide "a world-class education to anyone, anywhere."[206]

2011: Blackboard launched CourseSites.

Commercial course management system provider Blackboard launched a free service called CourseSites. Aimed at faculty in K–12 as well as higher education, the system is totally free.

2011: Rise of the Lendle and other loaning sites for Kindle e-book users.

Beginning in 2011, Kindle users could lend their e-books one time. According to the Kindle Community:

> Each book can be lent once for a loan period of 14-days and the lender cannot read the book during the loan period. Additionally, not all e-books will be lendable—this is solely up to the publisher or rights holder, who determines which titles are enabled for lending.[207]

Sites like Lendle and book lending.com allowed lending of Kindle e-books.[208]

NOTES

1. ACRL, *Standards for Distance Learning Library Services* (Chicago: American Library Association, 2008). http://www.ala.org/ala/mgrps/divs/acrl/standards/guidelinesdistancelearning.cfm. It is interesting to note that in the ACRL report titled *ACRL 2009 Strategic Thinking Guide for Academic Librarians in the New Economy,* http://www.ala.org/ala/mgrps/divs/acrl/issues/value/acrlguide09.pdf (p. 8), the term distributed is used instead of distance to describe the concept of multiple points of diffusion of access to and sharing of content.

2. ACRL, *Standards.*

3. LITA, Distance Learning Interest Group, http://www.ala.org/ala/mgrps/divs/lita/litamembership/litaigs/distancelearningb/distancelearning.cfm.

4. John S. Noffsinger, *Correspondence Schools, Lyceums, Chautauquas* (New York: Macmillan, 1926), 304. Internet Archive, http://www.archive.org/details/correspondencesc 028298mbp.

5. American Library Association, Commission on the Library and Adult Education, *Libraries and Adult Education: Report of a Study Made by the American Library Association* (Chicago: ALA, 1926), 42.

6. Ibid., 38.

7. Robert Ellis Lee, *Continuing Education for Adults through the American Public Library 1833–1964* (Chicago: ALA, 1966), 1. Many schools lacked libraries or even books. Edmund J. James, president of the University of Illinois from 1904 to 1920, had this to say about American education in 1892: "It is well known that in many of our rural districts . . . the educational facilities are of the most meager description. . . . the great bulk of children drop out of school before they have reached the age of thirteen or fourteen. It is estimated that only one per cent of the pupils who enter the primary grades reach the last year in the high school, and a very small proportion of the pupils, indeed, ever pass beyond the lower grammar grades." In discussing university extension, James noted: "The term University Extension has become very generally known, of late, in this country and abroad, as the name of a great educational movement. . . . it calls attention . . . to one of the most important aspects of the moment . . . the attempt to utilize for purposes of popular education, to a larger extent than at present, the facilities of existing higher institutions of learning." Edmund J. James. "University Extension in the United States." *Our Day: A Record and Review of Current Reform* 9 (1892): 79–80, http://books.google.com/books?id=l7QRAAAAYAAJ& dq=%22University%20Extension%20in%20the%20United%20States%22&pg=PA79#v=one page&q=%22University%20Extension%22&f=false.

8. University of Texas at Austin University Extension, *Online Courses: Overview*, http://www.utexas.edu/ce/uex/online/.

9. ALA, *Libraries and Adult Education*, 145. Adult education and the effectiveness of its outcomes varied greatly. William S. Learned of the Carnegie Foundation commented on both the wealth and breath of educational opportunities in *The American Public Library and the Diffusion of Knowledge,* published in 1924, when he wrote about the vast opportunities available to adults no longer attending formal education: "There are books and periodicals in profusion; the great American 'lecture' habit is still tenacious; universities offer numberless correspondence and extension opportunities, while the efforts of religious groups, "Chautauquas," women's clubs, workingmen's associations, community forums, and similar undertakings seem to indicate a feverish intellectual activity" (6). While Learned commended this activity, he lamented that much of it lacked discipline or lasting value. "A vague ambition or sheer boredom in face of mental idleness impels many to 'take up' year after year what proves to be an unrelated series of ill-chosen fragments of study offered without alternative and really well suited to but few of the participants. Made up on a democratic basis, the group usually includes such wide extremes of ability and preparation as to rob the course of genuine pertinence for any, and is often held together, if at all, by social rather than by intellectual considerations" (6). Still, the availability and popularity of adult education inspired public libraries to meet the needs of its many and diverse students. Learned singled out the Milwaukee Library, which attempted to meet the needs of adult students enrolled in: "1. Americanization classes. 2. Educational classes of the trade unions. 3. Educational departments of stores and factories. 4. Educational clubs and organizations of the churches, and 5. Advanced students in university extensions and high school evening classes" (41). The library's outreach efforts to the first two groups included bringing classes to its main branch, visiting classes to discuss library services, preparing "special collections suited to their needs" and "organizing library committees in each group or union to promote the use of library books" (41). William S. Learned, *The American Public Library and the Diffusion of Knowledge* (New York: Harcourt, Brace and Company, 1924), http://ia700202.us.archive. org/20/items/americanpublicli007473mbp/americanpublicli007473mbp.pdf.

10. ACRL, *Standards*.

11. CLA, *Guidelines for Library Support of Distance and Distributed Learning in Canada* (Canadian Library Association, 2010), http://www.cla.ca/AM/Template.cfm?Section=Position_Statements&Template=/CM/ContentDisplay.cfm&ContentID=3794.

12. ACRL, *Standards*.

13. The Open University, *History of the OU*, http://www.open.ac.uk/about/ou/p3.shtml.

14. Melvil Dewey, *Field and Future of Traveling Libraries* (Albany, NY: Univ. of the State of NY, 1901), 9, http://books.google.com/books?id=y9tRt3MaMZ8C&pg=PA1#v=onepage&q&f=false.

15. Jessie M. Good, "The Traveling Library as a Civilizing Force," *The Chautauquan* 36 (Sept. 1902–March 1903), 77.

16. Thomas Bray, *An Essay Towards Promoting all Necessary and Useful Knowledge, Both Divine and Human, in all the Parts of His Majesty's Dominions, Both at Home and Abroad* (London: Printed by E. Holt for Robert Clavel, at the Peacock in St. Paul's Church-Yard, 1697), 1, http://www.archive.org/details/essaytowardsprom00bray.

17. Bernard C. Steiner, "Rev. Thomas Bray and his American Libraries," *The American Historical Review* 2, no. 1 (1896): 63, http://www.jstor.org/stable/1833614.

18. Bray, *An Essay*, 3.

19. Steiner, 63.

20. *An Act for the Encouragement of Learning, by Vesting the Copies of Printed Books in the Authors or Purchasers of such Copies, during the Times therein mentioned* (London: Printed by the assigns of Thomas Newcomb, and Henry Hills, deceas'd; printers to the Queens most excellent Majesty, 1710). Available at Wikisource, "Copyright Act 1709," http://en.wikisource.org/wiki/Copyright_Act_1709.

21. John Ewing, "Copyright and Authors," *First Monday* 8, no. 10 (2003): http://firstmonday.org/htbin/cgiwrap/bin/ojs/index.php/fm/article/view/1081/1001.

22. *U.S. Constitution*, Article I, Section 8, Clause 8.

23. M. K. Smith wrote, "Adult schools and the making of adult education" in *The Encyclopedia of Informal Education* (2004), http://www.infed.org/lifelonglearning/adult_schools.htm. Smith offered a concise and informative discussion of adult education trends in England, Scotland, and Wales beginning with the Society for Promoting Christian Knowledge in 1699. As a part of the movement, for the first time, "the Church of England [was] making an attempt to encourage the formal teaching of adults to read."

24. "Intelligence," *American Journal of Education* 4 (1829): 66.

25. "Mechanics' Institutions," *American Journal of Education* 1 (1826): 134. A comprehensive discussion of mechanics institutes in England, with many references to libraries, may be found in Mabel Phythian Tylecote's *The Mechanics' Institutes of Lancashire & Yorkshire Before 1851* (Manchester: University of Manchester, 1957).

26. *Encyclopedia of Library and Information Science*, "Iterating Libraries," 154–56.

27. The letter appears in "Ministers of the Respective Parishes, under the Superintendence of a Committee of the Society for the Benefit of the Sons and Daughters of the Clergy," *The New Statistical Account of Scotland*, v. 2. (Edinburgh: Blackwood, 1845), 17.

28. Taylor Brown, "Samuel Brown and his Libraries," *Library Review* 8, no. 4 (1941): 125–29, http://www.emeraldinsight.com/10.1108/eb012910.

29. *The Cambridge History of English and American Literature in 18 Volumes* (1907–21), v. 17: Later National Literature, part 2, 23: Education: 46. Lyceums, http://www.bartleby.com/227/1646.html. David Mead, in a discussion about the Ohio lyceum, noted: "The lyceum came to be looked upon as a panacea for all the dissolute tendencies of the young, and as a pleasurable means of engendering literary tastes and culture. The social importance of the lyceum was widely recognized. On January 5, 1852, Governor Reuben Wood, in his annual message before the Ohio legislature on the conditions of the state, requested that the

General Assembly provide funds to promote the organization of lyceums and literary associations. Such a policy, declared the Governor, 'would certainly have a tendency to prevent dissipation by the desertion of places tending to immoralities, and cause young men to store their minds with useful knowledge and elevate themselves in their own self-dignity and self-respect.'" David Mead, *Yankee Eloquence in the Middle West: The Ohio Lyceum 1850–1870* (East Lansing: Michigan State College Press, 1951), 179.

30. Noffsinger, *Correspondence Schools,* 100.

31. Ibid., 101.

32. *American Lyceum, or Society for the Improvement of Schools and Diffusion of Useful Knowledge* (Boston: Perkins & Marvin, 1826), 5–10. Thomas Wyse, "The Lyceum System in America, with a Consideration of its Applicability to Mechanics' Institutions in England," *The Old South Leaflets no 139. 21st series, 1903* (Boston: Old South Meeting House, 1903, original article 1838), 14–20. Regarding precept number four, the American Lyceum in 1831 expounded on the issue of neglected town libraries: "A deep and general regret has been expressed that town and village libraries are but little read, that they are entirely neglected and scattered. The cause for this regret is removed by the meetings of lyceums. The moment that young people come together for mutual instruction in subjects of useful knowledge they call for books. The old library is looked up or a new one formed, and when the members are not conversing with each other, they are perhaps conversing with their books." Herbert Baxter Adams, *Educational Extension in the United States* (Washington: Government Printing Office, 1901), 287. United States Bureau of Education. Chapter from the Report of the Commissioner of Education for 1899–1900. The term "lyceum" remains a popular name today for many public lecture and concert halls.

33. "Education in Kentucky," *American Journal of Education* 4 (1829): 545.

34. Jon Jónasson, "On-line distance education a feasible choice in teacher education in Iceland?" (Master's thesis, University of Strathclyde, 2001), http://starfsfolk.khi.is/jonj/en/skrif/mphil/2dised.htm.

35. Noffsinger, *Correspondence Schools,* 102. As Glenn Frank observed in 1919: "While the actual life of this national organization was brief, it accomplished definite results in its eight years of activity. It forwarded education in Cuba, Venezuela, and Mexico; it gave our own common schools an impetus toward better things, and left behind many educational, literary, and lecture associations founded through its influence, all of which have left their mark on the educational life of the country." He also noted that "one out of every eleven persons in the United States every year attends either a lyceum or Chautauqua program." Glenn Frank, "The Parliament of the People," *The Century Magazine* 98, no. 3 (July 1919): 406. Local lyceums remained in operation after the demise of the national lyceum, but the organizational logistics and financial accounting for reserving lyceum lecturers was a thorny proposition. In 1868, James Redpath organized the Boston Lyceum Bureau, which alleviated many of these concerns and initiated a bureau system "which gradually placed the booking of lectures upon a systematic business basis" (Frank, 407).

36. David M. Hovde, "Benevolence at Sea: Shipboard Libraries for the American Navy and Merchant Marine," in *Libraries to the People, Histories of Outreach,* eds. Robert S. Freeman and David M. Hovde (Jefferson, NC: McFarland, 2003), 52.

37. George Willis Cooke, *Unitarianism in America: A History of Its Origin and Development* (Boston: American Unitarian Association, 1910, 1902), 407–8, Internet Archive: http://www.archive.org/details/unitarianisminam00cook.

38. Hovde, "Benevolence at Sea," 52–53.

39. Börje Holmberg, "The Evolution of the Character and Practice of Distance Education," *Open Learning: The Journal of Open and Distance Learning* 10, no. 2 (June 1995), http://www.c3l.uni-oldenburg.de/cde/found/holmbg95.htm.

40. Alvah T. Canfield, "Folk High Schools in Denmark and Sweden: A Comparative Analysis," *Comparative Education Review* 9, no. 1 (1965): 18, http://www.jstor.org/stable/1186166.

41. John W. Fritch, "Electronic Outreach in America: From Telegraph to Television," in *Libraries to the People, Histories of Outreach,* eds. Robert S. Freeman and David M. Hovde (Jefferson, NC: McFarland, 2003), 166.

42. Samuel Smiles, *George Moore, Merchant and Philanthropist,* 3rd ed. (London: George Routledge, 1878), 154.

43. Noffsinger, *Correspondence Schools,* 4.

44. Holmberg, "Evolution of the Character and Practice," 7. Holmberg quoted J. A. Baath who had translated the 1901 Toussaint-Langenscheidt prospectus.

45. University of London, *External System,* http://www.londonexternal.ac.uk/150/history/history_1880.shtml.

46. Charles Dickens, ed. "The English People's University," *All the Year Round: A Weekly Journal* 1 (July 16, 1859): 279–83.

47. University of London, *Books and Library Services,* http://www.external.ull.ac.uk/about/index.php.

48. John S. Pierson, "Ship's Libraries and Ocean Colportage," *The Sailors' Magazine and Seamen's Friend* 50, no. 11 (November, 1878): 325.

49. Ibid., 326.

50. Hovde, "Benevolence at Sea," 57.

51. Pierson, "Ship's Libraries," 328.

52. Ibid., 330.

53. *The New York Times,* "Livelier Books for Ship Libraries; Something Lighter Than Bunyan Will Be Offered to the Sailors. Young Librarian's Idea Thrilling Tales of Adventure and Intrigue, Not Preachments, for the Men of the Seas," March 30, 1907, http://query.nytimes.com/mem/archive-free/pdf?_r=1&res=9B05EED9163EE033A25753C3A9659C946697D6CF.

54. Good, "The Traveling Library," 67–69.

55. Ibid.

56. USCC, *History of the USCC: Heroes of Faith During the Civil War,* http://www.usccgettysburg.org/history.asp.

57. Theodore Wesley Koch, *War Libraries and Allied Studies* (New York: G. E. Stechert, 1918), 4, http://www.archive.org/details/warlibrariesalli00koch.

58. Ibid., 3–4.

59. Ibid.

60. Carrol H. Quenzel, "Books for the Boys in Blue," *Journal of the Illinois State Historical Society (1908–1984)* 44, no. 3 (Autumn, 1951): 221, http://www.jstor.org/stable/40189150. *United States Christian Commission for the Army and Navy: Work and Incidents: First Annual Report* (Philadelphia: The Commission, 1863), 93–126, http://www.archive.org/details/annualreport123commgoog. It was interesting to note that traveling libraries were not always safe and the Christian Commission had to frequently replace materials. The *First Annual Report* (p. 251) stated: "We share with the Government both the perils and the losses incident to the forty miles mountain transportation. Seventeen wagon-loads of choice hospital stores, with a fine library and good stock of reading, are captured and burned by guerillas on the mountains. O what a world of comfort and benefit to the soldier is lost in this one mountain conflagration!"

61. Theodore J. Shannon and Clarence A. Schoenfeld, *University Extension* (New York: The Center for Applied Research in Education, Inc., 1965), 45.

62. U.S. Department of Agriculture, *Proceedings of the Twenty-First Annual Convention of the Association of American Agricultural Colleges and Experiment Stations* (Office of Experiment Stations Bulletin No. 196, issued Dec. 20, 1907), 55.

63. Frederick Converse Beach, ed. *The Americana: A Universal Reference Library.* New York: Scientific American Compiling Dept., 1912. "General Intelligence," *Journal of Social Science: Containing the Transactions of the American Association,* no. 2 (New York: Leypoldt & Holt, 1870), 256–57, http://books.google.com/books?id=TcnNAAAAMAAJ&lpg=PA2

56&ots=8IkPrH9IS9&dq=%22Railroad%20libraries%22&pg=PA256#v=onepage&q=%22 Railroad%20libraries%22&f=false.

64. *Society to Encourage Studies at Home: founded in 1873 by Anna Eliot Ticknor: born June 1st, 1823, died October 5th, 1896.* [Boston]: Society to Encourage Studies at Home, 1897; Cambridge: Riverside Press. Available from the Harvard University Library Page Delivery Service, 3, http://pds.lib.harvard.edu/pds/view/3284561?n=1&imagesize=1200& jp2Res=.25.

65. Ibid., 5–6.

66. Ibid., 6.

67. Chicago Public Library, *History,* http://www.chipublib.org/aboutcpl/history/ index.php.

68. John Cotton Dana, "Making a Library Known, Address Delivered before the Long Island Library Club, 1905," in *Libraries Addresses and Essays by John Cotton Dana* (White Plains, NY: Wilson, 1916), 120.

69. *Public Libraries,* "Use of Telephones in Libraries," 1908, 361.

70. The East St. Louis Public Library also issued a bookmark containing lists of books on various topics. Bookmark no. 12 contained "a list of things 'You ought to know.' The direction 'Use these for a book-mark instead of turning down the leaves' is printed in black-face type." *Public Libraries,* "News from the Field, Central," 16, no. 7 (July 1911): 179.

71. The comment was made by Josephine Machus in "Recordings in Public Libraries, Three Success Stories," *Wisconsin Library Bulletin* 54 (July/August 1958): 260, as quoted in Sharon Almquist, *Sound Recordings and the Library.* Occasional Papers 179 (Champaign, IL: University of Illinois, 1987), 19.

72. Cutter, C. A., "The Buffalo Public Library in 1983," *Library Journal* (August 1883): 213.

73. Michigan Lighthouse Conservancy, "USLHE Traveling Library," http://www. michiganlights.com/lhlibrary.htm.

74. Thomas Greenwood, *Public Libraries: A History of the Movement and a Manual for the Organization and Management or Rate-Supported Libraries,* 4th ed. (London: Cassell & Co., 1891), 474.

75. Advertisement, *The Cornell Daily Sun,* April 25 1884, http://cdsun.library.cornell. edu/cgi-bin/newscornell?a=d&srpos=11&cl=search&d=CDS18840425.2.2.3&e=—_ cgiargdatfq_——20—1-DA—%22correspondence+university%22-all.

76. Noffsinger, *Correspondence Schools,* 5–6.

77. The Badger, "A New Educational Scheme," *The Cornell Daily Sun,* September 26, 1883, 2, http://cdsun.library.cornell.edu/cgi-bin/newscornell?a=d&srpos=1&cl=sea rch&d=CDS18830926.2.2.2&e=---_cgiargdatfq_-----20--1-DA---%22correspondence+ university%22-all.

78. "The Correspondence University," *The Cornell Daily Sun,* October 12, 1883, 1–2, http://cdsun.library.cornell.edu/cgi-bin/newscornell?a=d&d= CDS18831012.2.1.3&cl=& srpos=0&st=1&e=--------20--1-----all. In *The Cornell Daily Sun* (April 27, 1884) the following appeared: "A letter was received some time since from a girl in Indiana, who thought that the Correspondence University was a matrimonial bureau. It is almost needless to add that the secretary did not receive a second letter from this young lady." Another amusing look at issues at the Correspondence University appeared in the September 24, 1884 issue of The *Cornell Daily Sun*: "The Correspondence University has lost a patron. A lady taking work in Zoology received from that department a specimen of the Necturus [commonly known as Waterdogs and Mudpuppies] with instruction for dissecting and making drawings of the same. In a subsequent letter she touchingly detailed how after handling the specimen she was so haunted in her dreams and waking thoughts by images of the disgusting animal that she could obtain no peace of mind and enjoy her dinner only by abandoning the study."

79. M. G. Brumbaugh, "University Extension, History of the English Movement," *Education, A Monthly Magazine Devoted to the Science, Art, Philosophy and Literature of Education* 13 (September 1892–June, 1893): 422.

80. Good, "The Traveling Library," 77.

81. The full text of the Berne conference, formally known as the International Convention for the Protection of Literary and Artistic Works, is available on the WIPO (World Intellectual Property Organisation) website, http://www.wipo.int/treaties/en/ip/berne/trtdocs_wo001.html.

82. Myrtilla Avery, "Summary of New York and Other Traveling Library Systems," in *Field and Future of Traveling Libraries,* Melvil Dewey (Albany, NY: University of the State of New York, 1901), 130ff.

83. *World Almanac & Book of Facts,* 1902, in "University Extension," 322.

84. General Federation of Women's Clubs, "History and Mission," http://www.gfwc.org/gfwc/History_and_Mission.asp.

85. University of Scranton, Weinberg Memorial Library, *International Correspondence Schools of Scranton, Pennsylvania, 1897–1996. Finding Aid. 25 May 2005.* International Correspondence Schools of Scranton, Pennsylvania History, 1891 to the Present, http://www.academic.scranton.edu/department/wml/icsfinding.htm#3. Also of interest on this website: "the state of Pennsylvania passed the Mine Safety Act of 1885, requiring miners and inspectors to pass examinations on mine safety. The test was exhaustive and the language was incredibly confusing, especially for miners who spoke little or no English. One of the questions on the test read: 'A fan is designed to produce a current of 175,000 cubic feet of air per minute; what should be the diameter of its central orifice if it receives its air upon each side?'" Also see The *Coal and Metal Miners' Pocketbook of Principles, Rules, Formulas, and Tables,* 9th ed., rev. and enl., with original matter (1905) published by International Correspondence Schools, Scranton, Pa. It, and many others, are available through The Internet Archive: http://www.archive.org/details/coalmetalminersp00inteuoft. There are more publications at The Open Library, http://openlibrary.org/a/OL2119100A/International_Correspondence_Schools_Scranton_Pa. See also: James D. Watkinson, "Education for Success: The International Correspondence Schools of Scranton, Pennsylvania," *The Pennsylvania Magazine of History and Biography* 120, no. 4 (Oct., 1996), 343–69, http://www.jstor.org/stable/20093071.

86. Ibid. Penn Foster Career School, "Our History," http://www.pennfoster.edu/history.html.

87. *Wolsey Hall Prospectus,* 9, quoted in Holmberg, 1986, 17.

88. Christine Pawley, "Advocate for Access: Lutie Stearns and the Traveling Libraries of the Wisconsin Free Library Commission, 1895–1914," *Libraries and Culture* 35 (2000): 441.

89. Ibid., 442.

90. Ibid., 446. In 1910, Stearns complained about "the ridiculous sight . . . of the rural mail carrier . . . driving along the country road closely followed . . . by the traveling library delivery wagon" (Pawley, 454).

91. Ibid., 452.

92. Constance L. Foster, "Looking back: 1976," *Kentucky Libraries* 59 (1995): 6.

93. American School, http://www.americanschoolofcorr.com/. In an advertisement in the April 1903 edition of *The Cosmopolitan,* the American School of Correspondence billed itself as a technical school in partnership with the brick-and-mortar Armor School of Technology. Together they offered "ambitions young men, who are unable to attend a resident school, an opportunity for self-improvement under competent instructios, men who have the laboratories and facilities of a high-grade college of engineering at their command." Students in the correspondence school were assisted in "securing positions in Chicago, which will enable them to take advantage of the excellent opportunities for laboratory and shop practice, offered in the evening classes of the Armour Institute of Technology." This

combination of correspondence work with evening classes provided interesting opportunities for those not able to attend full blown technical institutions. "Technical Education," advertisement, *The Cosmopolitan* 34, no. 6 (April 1903): 737.

94. Kate Hutcheson Morrissette, "Traveling Libraries in Alabama," *The Sewanee Review* 6, no. 3 (July 1898): 345, 348.

95. Kenneth R. Johnson, "The Early Library Movement in Alabama," *The Journal of Library History* 6, no. 2 (April 1971): 120–12, http://www.jstor.org/stable/25540285.

96. Morrissette, "Traveling Libraries," 346.

97. Johnson, "The Early Library Movement," 120–32.

98. Thomas McAdory Owen, *History of Alabama and Dictionary of Alabama Biography* (Chicago: The S.J. Clarke Publishing Co., 1921), 58: 574. Dr. Thomas McAdory Owen (1866–1920), director of the State Department of Archives and History and founder of the state library association, was instrumental in bringing information to many counties that lacked a library. In 1911, the Alabama legislature increased the extension division's appropriation by $5,000. Owen enlarged the extension service division and initiated services to the deaf and blind.

99. Joan Marie Johnson, "Louisa B. Poppenheim and Marion B. Wilkinson: The Parallel Lives of Black and White Clubwomen" in *South Carolina Women:Their Lives and Times,* vol. 2, eds. Marjorie Julian Spruill, Jalinda W. Littlefield, and Joan Marie Johnson (Athens, GA: The University of Georgia Press, 2010), 111. The quotes are from Poppenheim's "Address to the Eighth Convention of the South Carolina Federation of Women's Clubs" held in May, 1910. In 1901, Poppenheim reported that the South Carolina club women had donated 3,000 books to support free traveling libraries and had created 48 stations. Commercial travel lines, such as the Southern Railroad, donated free transportation for the libraries in South Carolina. Louisa B. Poppenheim, "The South Carolina Federation of Women's Clubs," *The Educational* 1, no. 3 (April 1902): 70.

100. Michael Fultz, "Black Public Libraries in the South in the Era of De Jure Segregation," *Libraries & the Cultural Record* 41, no. 3 (Summer 2006): 355–56.

101. Avery, "Summary," 107.

102. Börje Holmberg, *The Evolution, Principles and Practices of Distance Education,* Studien und Berichte der Arbeitsstelle Fernstudienforschung der Carl von Ossietzky Universität Oldenburg, vol. 11 (Oldenberg: BIS-Verlag der Carl von Ossietzky Universität, reprint 2008): 19, http://www.mde.uni-oldenburg.de/download/asfvolume11_eBook.pdf.

103. Paul Dickson, *The Library in America* (New York: Facts on File Publications, 1986), 41.

104. John Fleischmann, *Free and Public: One Hundred and Fifty Years at the Public Library of Cincinnati & Hamilton County, 1853–2003* (Cincinnati, OH: Orange Frazer Press, 2003), 93. William Frederick Poole was head of the Cincinnati Public Library from 1869 to 1873. He came from Boston where he was director of the Boston Athenaeum. In Cincinnati, he bought novels "because he knew the public wanted fiction even if certain members of the Board of Education feared novels were the devil's calling cards." He also opened the library on Sundays, "making Cincinnati the first city with a legal public amusement on the Sabbath besides church, or illegal ones such as public drinking, profane swearing, shooting in town, running horses, exhibiting puppet shows, wire dancing, cock fighting, juggling, or tenpin bowling" (Fleischmann, 34). Poole was famous for inventing the Cincinnati-Chicago model of public libraries as well as compiling the first general index to U.S. periodicals, *Poole's Index to Periodical Literature,* in 1848. He edited two other editions (1853, 1882). Later editions were edited by W.J. Fletcher; the last appeared in 1907. This index was replaced by the *Readers' Guide to Periodical Literature.*

105. John Cotton Dana, "The Legitimate Field of the Municipal Public Library, prepared for the International Meeting of Librarians at Oxford, England, August 31 to September 4, 1914," in *Libraries Addresses and Essays by John Cotton Dana* (White Plains, NY: Wilson, 1916), 273.

106. Good, "The Traveling Library," 71.

107. Avery, "Summary," 137.

108. Cornell University, *Timeline of the New York State College of Home Economics, 1900–1969,* http://rmc.library.cornell.edu/homeEc/timeline.html; Cornell University, *Faculty Biographies: Martha Van Rensselaer,* http://rmc.library.cornell.edu/homeEc/bios/marthavanrensselaer.html.

109. Dewey, *Traveling Libraries, Field and Future of Traveling Libraries,* 6.

110. Good, "The Traveling Library," 74–75.

111. Jennifer Cummings, " 'How Can We Fail?' The Texas State Library's Traveling Libraries and Bookmobiles, 1916–1966," *Libraries and the Cultural Record* 44, no. 3 (2009): 303.

112. Bernard Jennings, "Mansbridge, Albert (1876–1952)," *Oxford Dictionary of National Biography,* (Oxford: Oxford University Press, 2004), http://www.oxforddnb.com/view/article/34859.

113. Ibid.

114. Barbara J. Howe, "West Virginia Women's Organizations, 1880s–1930 or "Unsexed Termagants . . . Help the World Along," *West Virginia History* 49 (1990): 81–102, http://www.wvculture.org/history/journal_wvh/wvh49-7.html.

115. Arthur E. Bostwick, *The American Public Library* (New York: D. Appleton, 1917), 31.

116. *Book Wagons: The County Library with Rural Book Delivery* (Chicago: American Library Association, 1922), 2. While there is no author attribution on the title page, the following appears at the bottom of page 2: "This little booklet is made up of material furnished by Miss Mary L. Titcomb of the Washington County Free Library, Hagerstown, Md., and Miss Mary Frank of the New York Public Library."

117. Mary Titcomb, *The Story of the Washington County Free Library* (Hagerstown, MD: Press of Hagerstown Bookbinding & Print. Co., 1931), as quoted at *The Bookmobile Collection,* Western Maryland's Historical Library, http://www.whilbr.org/bookmobile/index.aspx.

118. Ibid.

119. Ibid.

120. Ibid.

121. Calvert School, "Calvert School History and Philosophy," http://homeschool.calvertschool.org/about-calvert/historyphilosophy.

122. Quote from Almere L. Scott, Department of Debating and Public Discussion, Extension Division, University of Wisconsin, Madison, University Library Extension Service Round Table meeting at the American Library Association, 1922. See also Martin P. Andersen, "The Loan Package Library: A Tool for Implementing Adult Education in a Democracy, *The Library Quarterly* 20, no. 2 (Apr., 1950): 119–26, http://www.jstor.org/stable/4303871.

123. "News from the Field," *Public Library* 17 (1912): 426.

124. Sharon Almquist, *Sound Recordings and the Library.* Occasional Papers 179 (Champaign, IL: University of Illinois, 1987), 10.

125. Mary Akin Cochran, "The University of Texas Package Loan Library, 1914–1954" (Master's thesis, University of Texas, 1956), 2. E. S. Goree, "The Extension Loan Library and List of Free Bulletins," *University of Texas Bulletin* 1726 (May 5, 1917): 4. Let's consider a few additional comments about direct mail services of package libraries and individual books. Mailing books directly to the reader was best adapted to meet the needs of isolated adult students or readers. One of the problems was the cost of postage. The library paid to ship the book out and the borrower had to pay to return it. Another was that a library received requests in writing and it was often difficult to judge the nature of the request without further discussion—meaning that the librarian did not send back a letter asking for clarification. (Consider the time lag as the mail was delivered—snail mail—as opposed to

almost instant responses via e-mail.) As a result of not having additional interaction, misunderstandings were frequent and this lead to a perception of unsatisfactory library service.

Mailing materials was an expensive service for libraries because in addition to postage, there was the preparation time: check the book out to a remote user, wrap it, type a label, take it to the mail room or post office. "Few states have sufficient books and personnel to develop this service so that it can really meet the need. It is one thing to lend an occasional book to fill an urgent request, but quite another to serve all of the people who have no local library" (American Library Association, Commission on the Library and Adult Education, *Libraries and Adult Education*, 79).

In the 1940s, the Nebraska Library Commission mailed books to individuals through their Books by Mail program. The instructions told borrowers who did not live close to a public library to simply fill out a post card. Books circulated for one month and the borrowers were responsible for mailing back the books. Charges were usually only four to six cents; the borrower paid the postage both ways submitting stamps with the returned book. A slogan read: "It's your library—as close to you as your mailbox" (Nebraska Library Commission, Books by Mail, http://www.nlc.state.ne.us/centennial/1900s/19401949/ BooksbyMail.html).

126. Cochran, Package Loan Library, 137–38.

127. David M. Hovde, "YMCA Libraries on the Mexican Border, 1916," *Libraries and Culture* 32, no. 1 (Winter 1997): 113, http://www.jstor.org/stable/25548492.

128. J. H. Friedel, "The Traveling Library in the European War," *The Library Journal* (September 1916): 662.

129. American Library Association, "Library War Service," http://wikis.ala.org/profes sionaltips/index.php/Library_War_Service.

130. Arthur P. Young, "Aftermath of a Crusade: World War I and the Enlarged Program of the American Library Association," *The Library Quarterly* 50, no. 2 (April 1980): 192, http://www.jstor.org/stable/4307216. Additional praise for ALA's efforts "to furnish any book in any language to any American soldier, sailor or marine in any country" was voiced by the Rotarians "who of all men, value efficiency and admire a big job thoroly well done. "The American Library Association is the sole agent thru which the American army and navy can get books, and wherever books are found, in army camps and cantonments, naval stations, coast defense bases, war ships and transports, they are there by virtue of the Library War Committee." Charles E. Rush, "Any Book for Any Soldier Anywhere," *The Rotarian* 13, no. 5 (Nov. 1918): 216.

131. Theodore Wesley Koch, *War Service of the American Library Association* (Washington, DC: Library of Congress, 1918), 3–4. Koch quoted Mr. Raymond B. Fosdick.

132. American Library Association, "Federal and Armed Forces Libraries Round Table," http://www.ala.org/ala/mgrps/rts/faflrt/governance/index.cfm.

133. The American Library in Paris, *History of the Library*, http://www.americanlibrary inparis.org/about-the-library/history-of-the-library.html.

134. Bob Kann, "2. The Personalities of Places and Things," *All Their Ways are Helping Ways: Stories from the History of the Madison Public Library*, 2001, http://www.madison publiclibrary.org/kann/personalities.html.

135. Sybil Brigham McShane, "Mobile Library Literacy: Solutions for a Rural Environment," *First Monday* 6, no. 4 (April 2001): http://firstmonday.org/htbin/cgiwrap/bin/ ojs/index.php/fm/article/viewArticle/845/754.

136. Anne J. Haynes, e-mail message to author, January 13, 2011. The Wells Library circulation policy may be found online at http://www.libraries.iub.edu/index. php?pageId=941.

137. John C. Campbell Folk School, "A Unique History," https://www.folkschool. org/index.php?section=articles&article_cat_id=21&article_id=5. The Campbell school offers over 860 week-long and weekend classes in subjects ranging from Basketry to Broom

Making to Music to Quilting to Writing. The classes remain non-competitive and feature a hands-on approach.

138. Geroge M. Eberhard, ed., *The Whole Library Handbook* (Chicago: American Library Association, 2006), 421.

139. Distance Education and Training Council, "DETC History," http://www.detc. org/theassociation.html#history.

140. Redmond A. Burke, "German Librarianship from an American Angle," *The Library Quarterly* 22, no. 3 (July, 1952): 185, http://www.jstor.org/stable/4304131.

141. Royal Flying Doctor Service, "Our History," http://www.flyingdoctor.org.au/ About-Us/Our-History/.

142. William Bianchi, "Education by Radio: America's Schools of the Air," *TechTrends* 52, no. 2 (April 2008): 36.

143. "Books for the Extension Student—Report by the Joint Committee on Cooperation," *Bulletin of the American Library Association* 25 (October 1931): 676.

144. Almere L. Scott, "University Extension Division Point of View," *Bulletin of the American Library Association* 32 (1938): 979.

145. Jennifer M. Joseph and Claudia Hill, "From Then 'til Now: The Development of Rural Library Services in Trinidad and Tobago," in *Caribbean Libraries in the 21st Century: Changes, Challenges, and Choices,* eds. Cheryl Peltier-Davis and Shamin Renwick (Medford, NJ: Information Today, Inc., 2007), 15.

146. Edith Thomas, University of Michigan Library. Paper presented at the University Library Extension Round Table meeting, American Library Association. *Bulletin of the American Library Association* 31 (1937): 901–3.

147. According to James A. Nelson, Kentucky State Librarian (1980–2006), the Pack Horse Project had employed 96 women and 11 men. James A. Nelson, Libraries," *The Kentucky Encyclopedia* (Lexington, KY: The University Press of Kentucky, 1992), 553–54. An excellent discussion of the pack horse librarians may be found in a juvenile literature book: Kathi Appelt and Jeanne Canella Schmitzer, *Down Cut Shin Creek: The Pack Horse Librarians of Kentucky* (New York: Harper Collins, 2001).

148. Beatrice Sawyer Rossell, "Book Relief in Mississippi," *The Survey* 71, no. 3 (1935): 5, http://newdeal.feri.org/survey/s353.htm.

149. University of London External System, "Wartime Education," http://www.london external.ac.uk/150/history/wartime.shtml.

150. Holmberg, *Evolution, Principles and Practices of Distance Education,* 20.

151. Joseph and Hill, "From Then 'til Now," 5.

152. Jack Copeland, "Alan Turing 1912–1954," in *The Essential Turing: Seminal Writings in Computing, Logic, Philosophy, Artificial Intelligence, and Artificial Life plus The Secrets of Enigma,* ed. B. Jack Copeland (Oxford: Oxford University Press, 2004), 2.

153. Donald Coney, "The Promise of Microprint: A Symposium Based on *The Scholar and the Future of the Research Library," College and Research Libraries* 6 (March 1945): 179, quoted in Klaus Musmann, *Technological Innovations in Libraries, 1860–1960: An Anecdotal History* (Westport, CT: Greenwood Press, 1993), 118.

154. One source noted: "However, not until five years after Rider's death in 1965 was the microcard abandoned in favor of the microfiche." Alan Marshall Meckler, *Micropublishing: A History of Scholarly Micropublishing in America 1938–1980* (Westport, CT: Greenwood Press, 1982), 56.

155. There were three opaque microform formats: Microprint, Microlex, and microcards. Microprint was a proprietary product of the Readex Corporation, with images reproduced on a 6 x 9 inch card. It achieved the widest distribution, especially in academic circles. Microlex was a product of the Microlex Corp. Its card measured 6.5 x 8.5 inches and held about 200 images per side. It was used mainly for legal publications and was essentially obsolete by the late 1970s. William Saffady, *Micrographics* (Littleton, CO: Libraries Unlimited Inc., 1978), 56.

156. Vannevar Bush, "As We May Think," *Atlantic Monthly* (July 1945): 6, http://www.theatlantic.com/magazine/archive/1969/12/as-we-may-think/3881/4/.

157. Copeland, "Alan Turing 1912–1954," 2.

158. Jack Copeland, "Lecture on the Automatic Computing Engine (1947)," in *The Essential Turing: Seminal Writings in Computing, Logic, Philosophy, Artificial Intelligence, and Artificial Life plus The Secrets of Enigma,* ed. B. Jack Copeland (Oxford: Oxford University Press, 2004), 367.

159. Catharine M. Gleason, "Here Comes the Book Boat!" *The Rotarian* 80, no. 2 (February, 1952): 28.

160. *Australia* (Singapore: APA, 2007), 270. Alice Springs School of the Air, *Overview,* http://www.assoa.nt.edu.au/_HISTORY/history.html.

161. University of Maryland Libraries, "Archives of The Midwest Program on Airborne Television Instruction (MPATI)," http://www.lib.umd.edu/NPBA/papers/mpati.html.

162. National University Extension Association. *University Extension in the United States.* A study by the National University Extension Association, made with the assistance of a grant from the Fund for Adult Education, John R. Morton, Director (Birmingham, AL: University of Alabama Press, 1953), 66–67.

163. Ibid.

164. Ibid.

165. Kjerstin Thulin, "Book Boat Service in the Archipelago of Stockholm," *Resource Sharing and Information Networks* 7, no. 2 (1992): 83.

166. Kentucky Department for Libraries and Archives, "Kentucky's Bookmobile Program," http://www.kdla.ky.gov/resources/KYBookmobiles.htm.

167. Hilary J. Deason, "Traveling High-School Science Libraries," *Science,* New Series, 124, no. 3230 (November 23, 1956): 1013.

168. Thulin, "Book Boat Service," 84.

169. William Saffady. *Micrographics* (Littleton, CO: Libraries Unlimited Inc., 1978), 45.

170. Hans-Henning Kappel, Burkhard Lehmann, and Joachim Leoper, "Distance Education at Conventional Universities in Germany," *International Review of Research in Open and Distance Learning* 2, no. 2 (January 2002): 4.

171. J.C.R. Licklider and Albert Vezza, "Applications of Information Networks," *Proceedings of the IEEE* 66, no. 11 (November, 1978): 43–59.

172. R. Douglas Hurt, "The University of Mid-America: An Open University Approach to Higher Education," *Peabody Journal of Education* 54, no. 2 (January 1977): 120–22, http://www.jstor.org/stable/1491852.

173. H. Edward Roberts and William Yates, "Exclusive! Altair 8800 the Most Powerful Minicomputer Project Ever Presented—Can be Built for Under $400," *Popular Electronics,* January 1975, 33.

174. Robin W. Doust, "Provision of School Library Services by Means of Mobile Libraries—The Zimbabwe Experience," 64th IFLA General Conference August 16–August 21, 1998, http://archive.ifla.org/IV/ifla64/004-108e.htm.

175. IBM, "The Birth of the IBM PC," http://www-03.ibm.com/ibm/history/exhibits/pc25/pc25_birth.html.

176. Danianne Mizzy, "Job of a Lifetime: When Your Campus is Alaska," *C&RL News* (May 2003): 316–17. Mizzy interviewed Suzan Hahn, assistant professor of library science and off-campus librarian for the University of Alaska–Fairbanks. Hahn discussed how the Internet has allowed for increased, timely distribution of many materials: "Five years ago, very few rural students had Internet access, so everything was being photocopied and sent out via fax or in the mail, sometimes both. You might fax the paper to the local grocery store or local tribal offices. The quality of faxes was not good and, in many cases, it might cost them a dollar a page. Now, most folks have Internet access at home, school, or through work. So to send articles, we scan it and put it up on the Web in PDF or send it via e-mail."

177. Effendi Wahyono and M. Hum, "A Plan for the Development of the Library of Indonesia Open Learning University," *AAOU '98—Asian Librarians' Roundtable* (1998): 1, http://www.ouhk.edu.hk/~AAOUNet/round/effendi.pdf.

178. Jones International, "Jones Story," http://www.jones.com/pages/jones-story. The Jones e-global virtual library advertises itself as a "full-service online resource management portal" that "provides a sound, easily navigated structure within which to aggregate content specific to your institution's needs." Extensive information about the library may be found at http://www.egloballibrary.com/index.jsp.

179. Penn State, "World Campus History," http://www.worldcampus.psu.edu/About Us_History.shtml.

180. Richard Yeates, "The Wired Mobile," State Library of Queensland (April 2005), http://sss.slq.qld.gov.au/info/publib/mobile/reports/1998/wired.

181. Kenya National Library Service, "Camel Mobile Library Service in Kenya," c. 1999–2005, http://www.knlw.or.ke/camel.htm; Karin Passchier, "Camels Help Provide Library Services," IFLANET 2002, http://archive.ifla.org/V/press/pr0228–02.htm.

182. Western Governors University, http://www.wgu.edu/.

183. For more information, see the AVU website at http://www.avu.org/. Since its foundation, the AVU has trained more than 40,000 students with the ability to reach across language barriers. AVU's rector, Dr. Bakary Diallo, detailed AVU's accomplishments in a keynote address presented at the MIT LINC Conference, May 24, 2010, in Boston, MA. "What the AVU has accomplished since its inception is the development of distance and e-learning programs, management of e-learning consortiums, and development of African-based educational content. That is what I would like to talk about today: setting up distance and e-learning centers, higher education resources, quality assurance policy formulation and the digital library." AVU, "AVU Rector Makes Keynote Address at the MIT LINC Conference," http://www.avu.org/News/avu-rector-makes-keynote-address-at-the-mit-linc-conference.html. The digital library is available to all AVU faculty, researchers, and students through the AVU portal.

184. Rachel Singer Gordon, *Teaching the Internet in Libraries* (Chicago: ALA, 2001), 104.

185. Ibid., 105–6. According to Schneider's article, previous efforts at cyber connections included the use of packet radio to submit books requests and reference questions from the bookmobile to the main library at the Whitman County Library in Colfax, WA. In 1995, the Troy–Miami County Public Library in Ohio used a cellular Net connection to access circulation information. In 1997, the Topeka and Shawnee County Public Library in Kansas offered Internet access in two of its bookmobiles. One thing electronic information did was to lighten the load in bookmobiles while providing increased access through online sources. Karen G. Schneider, "The Cybermobile: A Groovy Set of Wheels," *American Libraries* 29, no. 8 (September 2008): 76–77, http://www.ala.org/ala/alonline/inetlibrarian/1998columns/september1998.cfm.

186. Pascal Mouhouelo, Auguste Okessi, and Marie-Paule Kabore, "Where There Is No Internet: Delivering Health Information via the Blue Trunk Libraries," *PLOS Medicine* (March 2006), http://www.plosmedicine.org/article/info:doi/10.1371/journal.pmed.0030077.

187. In recognition of this important work, Shidhulai received the 2005 Bill & Melinda Gates Foundation Access to Learning Award for providing free public access to computers and the Internet. Shidhulai Swanirvar Sangstha, "Our Work," 2008, http://www.shidhulai.org/ourwork.html.

188. Simon Romero, "Acclaimed Colombian Institution Has 4,800 Books and 10 Legs," *The New York Times,* October 19, 2008, http://www.nytimes.com/2008/10/20/world/americas/20burro.html?pagewanted=1&_r=3.

189. Thailand Illustrated, "Libraries on the Move," http://thailand.prd.go.th/ebook_bak/story.php?idmag=9&idstory=84.

190. Gordon, *Teaching the Internet,* 103–4.

191. National High School, "About Us," http://nationalhighschool.com/about_us.asp.

192. "Grade Expectations: Ron Packard and K12 Add Seats to the Virtual Classroom," *Smart CEO* (December 2008), http://www.k12.com/filefolder/k12.smartceo.pdf. For complete information, access the K12 website at http://www.k12.com/.

193. The Wall Street Journal Digital Network, "K12 Inc. Announces Acquisition of KC Distance Learning, Inc.," *Market Watch,* July 26, 2010, http://www.marketwatch.com/story/k12-inc-announces-acquisition-of-kc-distance-learning-inc-2010-07-26.

194. IFLANET, "Donkeys Help Provide Multi-Media Library Services," 2002, http://archive.ifla.org/V/press/pr0225-02.htm.

195. Moodle, "About," http://moodle.org/about/.

196. IFLA Mobile Section, *Newsletter* 1 (Autumn 2002), 6, http://archive.ifla.org/VII/s38/news/mobile01-02.pdf.

197. "Gilat Signs Agreement with Russia's Largest Open University, Moscow's Institute of the Humanities, for Country's First Distance Education Project," *Wireless Satellite and Broadcasting* 14, no. 4 (April 2004): 5.

198. Lee Hisle, "Reference questions in the library of the future," *Chronicle of Higher Education* 52, no. 6 (September 30, 2005): B6–B8.

199. The Global Fund for Children, Annual Report and Resource Guide, 2005–2006, *Queen Helina and the donkey Mobile Library of Awassa* (Washington, DC: The Global Fund for Children, 2006), 25, http://www.globalfundforchildren.org/pdfs/GFC_Annual Report_2005–06.pdf.

200. BBC News, "Venezuela's Four-Legged Mobile Libraries Story," August 4, 2007, http://news.bbc.co.uk/go/pr/fr/-/2/hi/programmes/from_our_own_correspondent/6929404.stm.

201. "About Us and How To Get Tuition-Free Online Education," University of the People, http://www.uopeople.org/groups/tuition-free-education.

202. Mae E. Berkel-Avé, e-mail message to author, April 26, 2010. Mae and her husband Hans, both Rotarians, purchased the first thirty books for the project and also traveled to Indonesia to assist with distribution.

203. Elaine Allen and Jeff Seaman, *Learning on Demand: Online Education in the United States, 2009.* (Needham, MA: Sloan-Consortium, 2010), 1, http://www.sloanconsortium.org/publications/survey/learning_on_demand_sr2010.

204. Christi Fish, "UTSA Opens Nation's First Bookless Library on a University Campus (September 9, 2010), http://www.utsa.edu/today/2010/09/aetlibrary.

205. "High-Tech School Bus Extends Learning," eSchool News, November 30, 2011, http://www.eschoolnews.com/2010/11/30/high-tech-school-bus-extends-learning/. The Pope County district uses the Aspirnaut™ program, which "is a partnership with rural K-12 schools to recruit and develop the science, technology, engineering and math (STEM) workforce necessary for the 21st century." Aspirnaut has offered mobile and other services since 2007. Aspirnaut, "Online Bus," http://www.aspirnaut.org/bus-online.php.

206. Joshua Bolkan, "Khan Academy Distributing Through BitTorrent," *The Journal* (February 25, 2011), http://thejournal.com/articles/2011/02/15/khan-academy-distributing-through-bittorrent.aspx.

207. Kindle Community, "Coming Soon for Kindle" October 22, 2010, http://www.amazon.com/tag/kindle/forum/ref=cm_cd_et_md_pl?_encoding=UTF8&cdForum=Fx1D7SY3BVSESG&cdMsgNo=1&cdPage=1&cdSort=oldest&cdThread=Tx2C5X2K2KCS71H&displayType=tagsDetail&cdMsgID=MxK69TLYS7TISE#MxK69TLYS7TISE.

208. See Lendle at http://lendle.me/and book lending.com at http://www.booklending.com/.

2

CURRENT ISSUES IN DISTRIBUTED LEARNING AND VIRTUAL LIBRARIANSHIP: ACRL STANDARDS

Brad Marcum, Trenia Napier, and Cindi Trainor

This chapter examines the Association of College and Research Libraries (ACRL) *Standards for Distance Learning Library Services* and introduces some of the challenges libraries face in the provision of library services to distributed students and faculty. The authors also discuss the level of support libraries provide to geographically distributed students today. Later chapters more fully discuss many of the issues introduced in this chapter.

ACRL STANDARDS FOR DISTANCE LEARNING LIBRARY SERVICES

As stated on its website, "[t]he Association of College and Research Libraries (ACRL), a division of the American Library Association, is a professional association of academic librarians and other interested individuals. It is dedicated to enhancing the ability of academic library and information professionals to serve the information needs of the higher education community and to improve learning, teaching, and research."[1]

As part of its efforts to enhance learning, teaching, and research, the ACRL publishes and regularly updates guidelines and standards intended to guide the development of excellent libraries and effective library services, including those for distance education. The document governing the provision of library services to distance students originated as the ACRL *Guidelines for Library Services to Extension Students* in 1963 and has been continually evolving and growing, keeping pace with the constantly changing technology and information needs of remote users. The guidelines have been revised and updated seven times since their creation, the latest being in 2008 when they were elevated from guidelines to standards.

The *Standards for Distance Learning Library Services* was developed to ensure equality in the provision of information and services to remote users. The underlying principle of the standards is that of access entitlement, the idea that all students should have equality of access to library resources and services. As stated in the executive summary, "[e]very student, faculty member, administrator, staff member, or any other member of an institution of higher education is entitled to the library services and resources of that institution, including direct communication with the appropriate library personnel, regardless of where enrolled or where located in affiliation with the institution. Academic libraries must, therefore, meet the information and research needs of all these constituents, wherever they may be."[2]

While the *Standards* has always sought to encourage and ensure the provision of the highest quality services, the reality is that it is sometimes impossible or impractical to provide the exact same services to all students and faculty. The standards acknowledge this, calling for resources and services that are equivalent but not necessarily the same as those provided to users on main campuses. This concept of "equivalency" as set forth by the *Standards* is one of the foundational principles of distance learning library services. To support equivalency, the *Standards* provides guiding principles and best practices for providing library services to geographically distributed faculty and students in eight areas: Fiscal Responsibilities, Personnel, Library Education, Management, Facilities and Equipment, Resources, Services, and Documentation. It is important to note that compliance with the *Standards* is voluntary, not compulsory. As such, varying degrees of compliance may exist among institutions.

Fiscal Responsibilities

The standards place responsibility for fiscal matters solely on the originating institution, which is defined as the credit-granting body responsible for offering, marketing, and/or supporting distance learning courses and programs. The originating institution must "provide continuing, optimum financial support for library services to the distance learning community;" in this instance, "optimum" indicates that the support must be sufficient to meet the specifications outlined by the *Standards* and any other applicable ACRL standards or guidelines (e.g., ACRL's *Standards for Libraries in Higher Education* and ACRL's *Information Literacy Competency Standards for Higher Education*) as well as applicable standards and guidelines established by professional, state, and regional accrediting agencies.[3] It is also imperative that the originating institution consider "the mandate for equal program and service access for users with disabilities and compliance with appropriate federal and state laws, such as the Americans with Disabilities Act (ADA) and Title 504 of the Rehabilitation Act" when establishing budgets.[4]

The standards maintain that financing for distance learning library services must correspond "to the formally defined needs and demands of the distance learning program," and must be "designated and specifically identified as such within the originating institution's budget and expenditure reporting statements."[5] Additionally, finances for distance learning library services must be allocated on a schedule consistent with the originating institution's budgeting cycle. In essence, there should be a line item in the library's budget for each cycle that is expressly designated and defined for distance learning library services.

Personnel

Effective management and coordination of distance learning library services require the expertise of library administrators and key administrative and support personnel from the originating institution; these personnel participate on the main campus and at distance learning sites and must include the staff who provide support services for people with disabilities. The originating institution is responsible for clearly defining the responsibilities of these professional and paraprofessional staff. Personnel assigned to distance learning library services must be sufficient in number and skills to meet and respond to the distance learning community's information needs and any goals and objectives set for them by the institution. The originating institution must also ensure that appropriate planning, implementation, and evaluation of resources and services are conducted. Distance learning library personnel must have classification, employment status, salary scales, workloads, and professional growth and development opportunities equivalent to that of other comparable library employees. Finally, policies must be written to establish status, rights, and responsibilities of distance learning personnel.

Library Education

The standards call for schools of library and information science to incorporate "courses and individual course units concerning the provision of distance learning library services to distance learning communities in their curriculum"[6]; however, while the charge to teach distance learning issues is admirable, the reality is less promising. The authors surveyed the course catalogs of the top ten programs in library and information studies as identified by *U.S. News & World Report*[7] in order to identify courses and/or individual course components pertaining to the provision of distance learning library services. Four schools tied for the 10th slot in the *U.S. News & World Report* rankings, so 13 schools were included. Of these 13 schools of library and information studies, only one, the Graduate School of Library and Information Science at the University of Illinois–Urbana-Champaign (number one in the rankings), offered an entire course devoted to the provision of distance learning library services. Only four offered courses with an easily identifiable distance learning library services component.

Management

Regardless of the number of personnel assigned to distance learning library services, "care must be taken [. . .] to ensure that none of the essential functions of the librarian-administrator [. . .] are omitted."[8] Essential management functions include:

- developing missions, goals, and objectives for the distance learning library program;
- linking these to the originating institution's missions, goals, and objectives;
- creating strategic planning documents;
- regularly evaluating services and resources, including needs and outcomes assessments pertaining to users and their use of services;
- promoting services and resources to the distance learning community;
- developing and revising collection development and acquisition policies;
- fostering cooperation and collaboration with administration, teaching faculty, and other internal and external constituents;
- serving as an advocate for the distance learning community.

Facilities and Equipment

Similar to the treatment of fiscal responsibilities, the standards charge the originating institution with providing "sufficient facilities, equipment, and communication tools to attain the objectives of distance learning programs."[9] The size, number, scope, and accessibility of such facilities and equipment must also "be sufficient to provide timely access to all students, including those with disabilities"[10] and must be equivalent to that provided to the non-distance learning community. Suitable arrangements may include the establishment of satellite libraries; agreements with local and virtual non-affiliated libraries, including public libraries; available and accessible electronic database searching; interlibrary loan services; and online services such as web-based virtual libraries, electronic communication tools, and involvement in course management software.

Resources

In addition to ensuring equality of access to library services, the access entitlement principle underlying the *Standards* also dictates that the originating institution ensure "that the distance learning community has access to library materials equivalent to those provided"[11] to the traditional—or on-site, non-distance—learning community. Such resources must be sufficient in "quality, depth, number, scope, and currency"[12] to meet all students' needs in fulfilling course assignments. Sufficiency may be determined by any one or more of a number of constituents, from administrators in the library or larger originating institution to an accrediting organization, and thus varying degrees of service may exist. The resources must also enrich the academic programs, meet teaching and research needs, facilitate the acquisition of life-long learning skills, accommodate varying levels of technological access, and accommodate other information needs as needed.[13]

Services

The distributed learning and virtual community is diverse, exhibiting a wide range of information and instruction needs. The exact combination of services and delivery methods for each of these needs will vary from community to community and may be governed by standards and guidelines other than those from ACRL. Services provided by the originating institution to its distance constituents must be equivalent (though not necessarily identical) to those offered to traditional on-campus students. Services must include reference assistance; online instruction and information services; reliable, rapid, and secure access to online resources; reciprocal and/or contractual borrowing or ILL services using the broadest applications of copyright; adequate hours; prompt delivery of items to users; and point-of-use assistance.[14]

Documentation

The library and the librarian-administrator must maintain and make available proper documentation that demonstrates compliance with the standards. This documentation includes user guides and other instructional material; mission and purpose statements; policies, regulations, and procedures; collection statistics; facilities and collections assessment measures; and needs and outcomes assessment measures. Data regarding staff and work assignments, institutional and organizational charts, budgets, curriculum vitae of professional personnel, position descriptions of all personnel, any formal written agreements with any and all constituents, library evaluation studies, and documents and evidence of involvement in curriculum development and planning must also be included.[15]

HOW WELL DO LIBRARIES SUPPORT DISTRIBUTED LEARNING?

In the past, the format of the information gathered and held at libraries combined with limited transportation methods did not lend itself readily to distribution to remote locations and resulted in unequal (or no) service to distributed users. Traveling libraries and deposit station libraries eased this restriction somewhat, but more specifically, libraries were not comfortable in fulfilling requests for important or irreplaceable materials because it meant trusting mail or courier services to safely deliver and return these valuable items. In addition, libraries hesitated to lend archival materials to unsupervised individuals. The photocopying of articles and selected sections of books eased these concerns somewhat, but this solution introduced added expenses in staff time and materials expended in obtaining copyright clearance, copying, and delivery.

The organizational outlook of a library's parent organization greatly affects its range of responsibilities to distance constituents. Public and state libraries, while not obligated to follow the *Standards,* may also support distributed learning through outreach efforts. There are two major approaches to providing distance learning library services. Some libraries assign responsibility for administration of all distance services to a single librarian; others have a more integrated approach, spreading the distance learning library services workload across the entire institution. Those taking the integrated approach may or may not have a single librarian whose title is Distance Librarian.

Neither approach is particularly dominant among member libraries of the Association of Research Libraries. In 2005, Yang conducted a survey of 62 ARL libraries providing services to distance students. This survey found that 35 libraries (56.5%) have a librarian who either is dedicated full- or part-time to working with distance education and that 27 libraries (43.5%) provide services to distant users but do not have a librarian specifically tasked with doing so.[16]

Administratively, distance and virtual librarians hold a variety of positions within a library's organization. In the same survey, Yang found that just under half (45.7%) of distance librarians report to the head of the local reference department, while only 8 (22.9%) report directly to the library director or dean.[17] The rest either report to the head of instruction or interlibrary services.[18] As distributed education becomes more important in higher education, distance learning librarian-administrators will likely spend more of their time facilitating and planning service and less time in the trenches answering reference questions and providing library instruction.

As the World Wide Web expanded access to digitized information, the role of the library began to shift from a repository of knowledge and physical items to that of an information hub. In the wake of this change, distance librarians have shifted from serving as guardians and gatekeepers of physical items to experts in content management. They oversee the integration of library services and resources into course management systems, the navigation of the library website and electronic resources, and the delivery of information. Carrying out this responsibility requires breaking down the *silo effect* that has often historically been the mode of operation in traditional libraries and institutions. The silo effect occurs when the information and/or services an individual needs are scattered across numerous networks. In the case of libraries and the distributed learning community, the silo effect often occurs because services and resources "are created by disparate applications or groups;" libraries purchase "networked products through multiple vendors" as well as create their own content and delivery methods (i.e., websites, the online catalog, and so on), while the broader originating institution and/or teaching faculty (through the course management software, for example) are also creating and storing vital, pertinent information in multiple and unrelated online locations.[19] As a result, the distributed learning student is forced "to cope with this fragmentation by sequentially visiting several information storehouses to piece together the needed information."[20] While the integration of library resources into course management software, metasearching, and link resolvers such as SFX[21] have been successful in alleviating some of the burden, the silo effect is still an issue for the distributed learning community.

The rapid proliferation of online programs at colleges and universities has created a service vacuum as libraries struggle to provide appropriate resources for and support to these programs. As is often the case with curriculum development, the library is often not consulted when an institution is planning an online program. Library efforts to support programs after the fact can have an informal and retrofitted feel to them. The role of library support is often overlooked in the planning of distributed programs, and this lack of consideration is reflected in the literature of distributed education; to create a truly effective online education program, research support—and the librarians who provide it—must be a fundamental component of curriculum development.

WHAT MAKES A DISTANCE STUDENT "DISTANT" AND A CANDIDATE FOR DISTRIBUTED LEARNING?

Definitions of what makes a student truly "distant" and a candidate for distributed learning can vary among accrediting organizations. For example, the Southern Association of Colleges and Schools Commission on Colleges (SACSCOC), that accrediting body for degree-conferring colleges in eleven southern states, defines distance education as that in which "the majority of the instruction (interaction between students and instructors and among students) in a course occurs when students and instructors are not in the same place. Instruction may be synchronous or asynchronous."[22] The image of students at their computers, logging in to make a post to their class discussion board comes to mind. This is the classic definition of distance learning.

In contrast, the ACRL *Standards* takes a broader view by defining a distance learning community as "[a]ll individuals, institutions, or agencies directly involved with academic programs or extension services offered away from or in the absence of a traditional academic campus, including students, faculty, researchers, administrators, sponsors, and staff, or any of these whose academic work otherwise takes them away from on-campus library services."[23]

The definition of distance education or distributed learning also varies among institutions. Some universities may have remote or regional campuses served by distributed or distance education staff that are not acknowledged as *distant* by their accrediting bodies. Other institutions do not draw distinctions between students taking classes at the main campus and those enrolled online or away from campuses. This latter approach facilitates the application of online technologies in traditional classes and is useful in serving the needs of the always-connected Millennial generation.[24] This "a student is a student" approach can create some confusion when gathering and reporting statistics for assessment by accrediting groups. It is important when planning or administering distributed education services that libraries and distance librarians be mindful of which definitions have primacy.

INFRASTRUCTURE: DELIVERING SERVICES AND CONTENT IN SUPPORT OF DISTANT STUDENTS

The Internet is the backbone of modern distributed education and the libraries that support it. Today's academic and public libraries subscribe to dozens of databases, hundreds of electronic books, and thousands of online journals that are accessible to all students and faculty regardless of their location. Because on-campus users—even users inside library buildings—use the Internet to access library resources and course management systems, the line between on-campus and distributed learners has blurred. Online resources level the playing field for geographically distributed students, providing the same access to students across campus as across the country. This has facilitated the integrated approach to distributed learning library services in libraries, as the idea of accessing library services and materials remotely is no longer the purview of a small percentage of the population, many of whom were part of an institution's extension services.

Course Management Systems (CMS)

Course management systems (CMS), whether commercial or open source, have traditionally focused on delivering content created by the instructor and collecting content created by students rather than content purchased or licensed or created by the library. The circles of communication in a course management system generally involve student–instructor or student–student interaction, and while librarians have found ways of embedding themselves in individual online courses, and technology staff can build library content into a CMS,[25] doing so seamlessly and across subjects varies widely among available products. Success or failure of these products can be caused by myriad factors that are both in and out of the library's or the instructor's control.

While definitions of *distant* and *distributed* have evolved and expanded, so too has the role of the course management system on campus. The same course management system used to deliver an entire course online is used to supplement face-to-face classes[26] or to provide a space to store course-related materials such as tests and quizzes for traditional face-to-face classes on the main campus.[27] Enrolled students may access library resources directly from links embedded in their online class delivered through the course management system.

Librarians and Library Resources in the CMS

Librarian involvement in course management systems can be achieved in two ways, defined by some as the "macro" and "micro" approaches.[28] At the macro level, librarians work with information technology staff who support the CMS to add links to library resources that appear to all users, such as a tab linking to the library webpage or a link inside every course that points to librarian-created, subject-oriented research guides. A disadvantage to this approach is that all students are given the same resources, which might not necessarily be relevant given the course material.[29] On a more micro level, librarians can work with individual instructors or teaching faculty to become "embedded" in one or more courses. Embedded librarians can participate in discussion forums and in synchronous chat sessions, and they can add links to appropriate library resources and even provide library instruction and collaborate with instructors to provide research-related assignments and quizzes through the CMS.[30] This more in-depth approach can be time-consuming and is often not scalable to all courses offered at an institution or even within a specific discipline. The macro approach provides some library resources for all courses when embedding is not possible or practical because there are not enough librarians to go around.

Librarians use online resources to effectively and easily provide support for online courses by creating course-specific webpages or lists of appropriate links that may be displayed directly in a course within the CMS. Integration of reserve readings—a long-standing tradition at many institutions—can also play a role in connecting library resources to the CMS. Library reserves staff can create links, which may be posted inside a course to directly connect students to pertinent electronic books or online journal articles, and save faculty the time required to find and create these links themselves.[31] Many library reserves staff also handle copyright clearance for reserve readings or locate and clear items not owned by the library, freeing up more time for teachers.

The Library Website

As access to electronic resources has increased, library websites have been increasingly designed with distance users in mind. However, library websites in and of themselves tend to be delivery mechanisms for metadata rather than content: library hours, news announcements, catalog searches, and links to online databases and journals. The library website remains largely a portal to online content as well as in-house information rather than the container of those resources, though locally created and hosted collections are available at many institutions in their digital libraries or institutional repositories. There are products available and in use at libraries that enable simultaneous search of content existing or indexed in disparate databases, but this federated search technology, due to its slow retrieval speed, is mediocre at best.[32] An emerging trend in aggregating library content is to create a single index of all content that the library owns or has access to. Products like Serials Solutions' Summon, OCLC WorldCat Local, and EBSCO's Discovery Service create enormous indexes that search the library catalog and other locally held resources alongside electronic journal collections and abstracting and indexing databases, with and without full text.[33] These products will only be as good as the cooperation between their creators and the publishers from which they license content, and have the potential to be hampered by publishers' unwillingness to allow their content to be indexed in a competitor's product.

The library website can link to a bewildering array of databases, journals, and other resources relevant to a wide variety of subjects. Library websites are generally designed as one-size-fits-all sites, providing links to all materials that a library owns or has access to, and while most libraries attempt to arrange resources by subject or format, finding the appropriate resource to support an assignment in an online course is a needle-in-a-haystack adventure that pushes most users to search engines like Google and easily accessed websites like *Wikipedia*.[34] Librarians can step in here and create subject-specific or even course-specific guides to library resources, easy-to-use webpages that guide students to the most appropriate books, journals, databases, and other library resources that they need to complete assignments. Of even greater utility to distributed students would be a library system that enables collocation of resources that students choose, arranged how the students preferred, according to subject or by course.[35] The personalization movement of the late 1990s and early 2000s could be revived to address this need.

"Web 2.0" and "Library 2.0"

The term "Web 2.0" was originally coined by Tim O'Reilly in 2005 to distinguish a new, emerging type of World Wide Web from the dot-com bubble-era start-ups.[36] O'Reilly saw the next generation of the web as a computing platform through which users access software applications via their web browser, rather than installing them directly onto a computer. Web 2.0 sites and applications are characterized by:

- Harnessing collective intelligence and the wisdom of crowds;
- Data, which can be remixed, shared, and mashed together to form new applications or new perspectives;
- A "permanent beta" state: applications evolve quickly and implement new features as they are written rather than bundling features into an entirely new product;
- Flexible, simple, and sometimes less formal programming technologies;
- Availability on devices other than personal computers, such as cell phones, smart phones, and other mobile devices.

Web 2.0 *harnesses collective intelligence* by enabling anyone with an Internet-connected device to create, edit, and publish content on the web. Compare, for example, the print *Encyclopædia Britannica* with the online encyclopedia *Wikipedia*. *Encyclopedia Britannica*'s 32 volumes published in 2007 comprise 65,699 articles; on August 11, 2008, the English version of *Wikipedia* reached 2.5 million articles, roughly equivalent to 1,218 printed volumes.[37] In May 2010, more than 3 million articles were on the English *Wikipedia*.[38] While even *Wikipedia*'s founder, Jimmy Wales, discourages its academic use, students still flock to it in droves.[39]

At the heart of Web 2.0 applications is *data.* Leading Web 2.0 sites control and give best access to data[40] that users remix, add to, and create new perspectives on by adding their own information to the mix. Google Maps is an excellent example: the first iteration of this application comprised simple road and aerial photography maps. Since then, Google has added traffic information, public transportation and walking directions, and "Street View," photographs that enable people to see what the streets on the map look like in real life. Paired with local information already indexed by Google, Google Maps has become a powerful way to locate businesses in an area. Users with Google accounts can create "mashups" that combine geographic and business data, creating customized maps that can display for example, hotels near a conference center, complete with user ratings and user-contributed and professionally published reviews and photos.[41]

Web 2.0 has meant an *end to the software release cycle*: PC software used to come only in shrink-wrapped boxes, and new versions were revealed and put on shelves with great fanfare. Web applications are often said to be in "permanent beta," meaning they are never complete, and that there are always newly implemented features that may not work quite right. Putting these features in front of users early and as they are released means that the bugs can be worked out quickly, and that feedback by the entire user community can be solicited and utilized.[42]

Programmers of Web 2.0 applications take advantage of *lightweight programming models* like AJAX (Javascript and XML) and REST (Representational State Transfer) rather than more formal and robust web services protocol stacks like SOAP (Simple Object Access Protocol). These services enable systems to be loosely coupled together and facilitate the syndication of data outward for reuse and re-mixing (e.g., Google Maps, RSS feeds).[43]

The final and perhaps most revolutionary aspect to Web 2.0 is the idea that Web 2.0 software *exists at a level "above a single device."* Simply put, not only are web applications accessible from any Internet-connected computer, but any Internet-connected device, such as mobile phones,[44] "Internet appliances" like the Chumby, video game consoles like Nintendo Wii, even devices like the iPod Touch or the Nabaztag "smart rabbit," an expensive German toy that will read the weather, news, or even email aloud to its owner.

The term "Library 2.0" was coined by Michael Casey in 2005 as a way to describe new library services that invited and enabled participation from patrons.[45] Because the definition of "Web 2.0" applied not only to software applications but to a new way of writing software and experiencing the web, a heated debate began among library workers on the definition of "Library 2.0."[46] In the book that Casey wrote with Laura Savastinuk, *Library 2.0: A Guide to Participatory Library Service*, Casey suggests that any definition of Library 2.0 must include the ideas that Library 2.0 "is a model for constant and purposeful change," that it "empowers library users through participatory, user-driven services," and that "through the implementation of the first two elements, Library 2.0 seeks to improve services to current library users while reaching out to potential users."[47] The debate rages on whether Library 2.0 is a philosophy or a set of commonly employed technologies—or some combination of the two—but because "Library 2.0" stems from Web 2.0 and lives on the web, its utility to distant learners is obvious. Library 2.0 is another playing field leveler—all blog commenters are created equal, as it were. User location or status doesn't matter.

2.0 Technologies and Tools Support Distance Learning Library Services

The greatest impact that Web 2.0 has had on distributed education is the availability of free tools that instructors and students can use to supplement course management systems. Where instructors don't have access to a CMS, tools can even be loosely joined to create an ad-hoc CMS. The same can be said for distributed learning library services: many free tools that can be used for instruction can be used to provide access to or enhance library services and resources.

RSS, Really Simple Syndication or Rich Site Syndication

Simply put, RSS feeds display the content from one website on another website or in a desktop application capable of reading and displaying those feeds. In terms of displaying library content to distant learners, RSS feeds can be used to integrate reserve readings lists into a course management system, to list new books and resources on a website, or to bring discipline-specific journal tables of contents or news headlines into a librarian-created, web-based research guide.

Blogs and Wikis

Two technologies that enable the easy creation of websites have seen wide adoption in libraries and in education. Libraries publish internal blogs and intranet wikis aimed at staff or external blogs and wikis aimed at patrons; instructors have the option of creating a blog with free online tools or with the blog or wiki tool built into most content management systems. Blogs and wikis offer interactive components, which—like their ease of use—distinguish them from ordinary websites. Comments from authorized or anonymous users are often a vibrant part of a blog or wiki; enabling comments on library or education blogs encourages participation from students and facilitates discussion among them. Blogs are a good way for students to report work on projects; wikis facilitate collaboration across and among groups.

The best distinguishing characteristic separating a blog from a wiki is that a blog is a website comprising individual entries, or "posts," that are arranged in reverse chronological order. A wiki, at its heart, is merely a website that anyone can edit. Blog posts and wiki pages can be revised at any time by those who are authorized to do so; in the case of wikis, a running revision history of each wiki page is kept, enabling reversion to a previous edition at any time.

Blogs and wikis typically publish RSS feeds, meaning that new posts or wiki changes can be displayed on other websites or inside the CMS. Headlines from library blogs or notification of new links on the wiki could be added to a course page.

Social Bookmarking

Social bookmarking websites provide users a way to create online lists of websites to visit later. The "social" in social bookmarking comes in seeing what other users add and in the creation of a network of users who have similar interests. The most popular social bookmarking site is delicious.com, on which users bookmark favorite web destinations and assign keyword "tags" to them. Each webpage on Delicious.com is also published via RSS, enabling bookmarks to be displayed on other websites. Libraries can use Delicious bookmarks to populate a list of recommended websites for a course. The list is automatically updated as sites are added and removed in Delicious. There are other social bookmarking sites, many of which target a specific web community. For example, citeulike.com is a social bookmarking tool aimed at the education community.

The idea of user-generated tags has been put to use in libraries as well. "Next-generation" library catalog interfaces provide users with the ability to add keyword tags to items owned by an individual library.[48] Librarians can create quick course-related reading lists by tagging items with the course or instructor name. With the course tag in hand, a view of all relevant readings is only a few clicks away.

The University of Pennsylvania created a tagging application for the University community in its PennTags project, an online application to save and tag library resources and public websites and then share them with the world. Penn users create "projects" to which they add similar items. Projects or tags can be shared with colleagues or the world. PennTags is also a great way to find others on the University campus with similar interests.[49]

Perhaps the most innovative use of tags is to create a "tag cloud," which creates a visualization of the frequency with which tags appear in an application. Tag clouds are used on websites like delicious.com, the photo-sharing site flickr.com, some next-generation library catalog interfaces, and in PennTags. Tags used more frequently appear in larger fonts.

Social networking sites like Facebook[50] have become hugely popular on college campuses as a way for students to connect with each other and share information about themselves. Instructors can use Facebook groups to share information about a class or to create a course discussion board. Libraries are also experimenting with Facebook: many libraries have "pages" that students and faculty can become "fans" of; libraries can post hours, events, photos, videos, and announcements to their Facebook pages. Minnesota's Hennepin County Public Library added tabs to its Facebook page that allow anyone to search the catalog or ask a question via instant messaging. Many applications can be added to a library's Facebook page, facilitating the use of library resources from within Facebook. As of this writing, more than 40 public and academic libraries have created applications allowing users to search their library catalogs from Facebook.

Collaborating online is a natural fit for distributed learners, and is an online extension of the growth of collaborative spaces in library buildings. The idea of "library as place" is still very strong in the modern library landscape, alongside the recent move of library resources and services to the online world. The allocation and design of library spaces have evolved over the years in response to users' demand for collaborative space. In academic libraries, this is manifested in an Information Commons or space dedicated to group study. In public libraries, group study or meeting rooms are common. Collaborating online is made easy with Web 2.0 applications. Some online collaboration tools are built into course management systems, such as discussion boards, voice or text chats, Live Classrooms, and IM; there are tools freely available via the web as well for collaborative creation of documents, spreadsheets, and presentations; for sharing files with groups; for streaming audio or video of an event; and for chatting with a group of fellow students.

The Research Reality: Search Engines vs. the Library

Students and faculty alike increasingly begin information searches on the Internet. A 2005 study by OCLC found that when initiating a search for information, 84 percent of those surveyed reported starting with a search engine, compared to only 1 percent who used their library's website.[51] College students reported starting with search engines 89 percent of the time, compared with 2 percent who used their library's website.[52] Another study revealed that though students do have some understanding of authority when it comes to evaluating information, fully 48 percent of citations examined in English Composition papers were for websites.[53]

The library can promote online tools that acknowledge the new web reality and endeavor to integrate library resources more closely into the modern web experience. LibX[54] is an open source software program that libraries can customize and publicize to patrons for installation in a web browser. It provides the ability to search resources selected by the library from a browser toolbar or by highlighting text and right-clicking with the mouse. LibX embeds a library's icon in popular services like Google, Amazon, Yahoo, Barnes & Noble and *The New York Times*. Clicking the icon sends the user to their local library catalog. LibX also makes use of the OpenURL standard. If a library owns an OpenURL Link Resolver such as SFX or Article Linker, LibX will embed the resolver button into webpages, connecting users to full text articles, the catalog entry for an item, or even the Interlibrary Loan form. LibX is a powerful and time-saving tool for integrating library resources into the web browsing experience. Additionally, by using the library's icon—or a component of the library's brand identity—LibX helps further the library's PR efforts by reminding users of who supplies access to those resources.

Zotero, another open source web browser add-on, is a free citation manager.[55] Users download Zotero for free and then collect bibliographic citations directly from their web browser without purchasing additional expensive resources, such as the commercial reference management software package EndNote,[56] or web-based commercial citation manager RefWorks.[57] With Zotero, citations can be arranged into collections and tagged for later retrieval. Several other online and desktop citation managers exist for collecting and sharing research: Papers,[58] Mendeley,[59] and WizFolio[60] are a few examples.

ASSISTANCE

A rapidly changing world and amazing technological advances have significantly changed the general profile of the academic library patron; now, the academic library patron may be "local or remote students, traditional or non-traditional students who work full-time and are pursuing their academic programs via online methods, [. . .] full-time students located on the college/university campus, [. . .] full-time [students who] commute for long distances and visit their campus a limited number of days per week, [. . .] international students pursuing courses solely via the Web," or students who "live several time zones away from the campus providing their program," to name but a few.[61] Faced with these new profiles, libraries quickly discovered that traditional in-person, face-to-face reference and classroom instruction were not always viable options for many students, especially the distributed student, facing significant geographical and time constraints.

These same library users are accustomed to living an increasing amount of their lives online, including fulfilling education and research needs. Moyo points out that "the 24/7 availability of the Web provides patrons with the opportunity to conduct library research anytime," anywhere, which has "resulted in library patrons expecting 24/7 access to not only the library electronic collections, but also online help [. . .] if and when needed."[62] Furthermore, "electronic resources have generated an even greater reference and instruction need."[63] Libraries are evolving in response, modifying resources and services to meet the growing needs of ever-changing user communities. The following two sections provide a brief overview of the current reference and instruction environments, specifically for meeting the reference and instruction needs of the distant or remote library user. Reference and instruction services for distributed learning are covered in-depth in chapter 5.

Reference

Telephone reference has long been a staple of distance education library services, and for good reason. It provides an easy and inexpensive point of contact for the student who is geographically distant from the library building. Telephone reference provides a synchronous reference interaction, allowing reference interviews to proceed much as they would at a traditional reference desk. Many libraries provide toll-free or local numbers, effectively eliminating costs for the distance student, though this service has become less important with the proliferation of unlimited long-distance telephone service plans.

Phone reference does present some barriers. Visual cues present in face-to-face reference assistance that often serve as indicators of success or closure in the reference interview are nonexistent in telephone reference. Should researchers require assistance during hours the library is closed, they are forced to wait until the library opens; in some cases, distance students may be unable to contact the library during business hours due to family, employment, or other daytime commitments. For distance students geographically located in a different time zone, telephone reference may be virtually impossible. If a request is too difficult or complicated to be fulfilled within a reasonable time frame, the librarian and researcher may fall prey to a lengthy game of telephone tag to complete the transaction, possibly extending the reference interview over multiple days.

Despite its barriers, telephone reference remains a commonly offered service; however, shifts in patron needs and demands have led libraries to offer virtual reference services, such as reference services initiated electronically. Virtual reference began with Internet technology but has expanded to include reference service delivered to mobile phones via instant messaging and text messaging.[64] In fact, "[I]nternet connectivity and electronic communication forms the foundation for the new reference environment."[65] Braxton and Brunsdale report that email reference services first arrived on the scene in the mid 1980s, grew more popular in libraries as recreational use increased during the 1990s,[66] and have become a standard reference service.[67]

Email reference counteracts some of the barriers of telephone reference, most notably because it extends the hours during which questions or research requests may be submitted to the reference desk. With the advent of email reference, time constraints faced by library patrons living in different time zones or those who must conduct the majority of their research during hours the library is closed may be effectively obviated, assuming that the library patron has adequate time to wait for a response. Email reference "can be beneficial for shy students and non-native speakers,"[68] because it "allows the librarian more time to reflect on the question and find sources without the pressure of waiting users" and "serves as a tailored pathfinder to which a learner can refer back at a later date" if links to tutorials or resources are included.[69]

Email reference is not without its own barriers. First and foremost, email reference does not allow for a traditional reference interview, and it seldom occurs in real time. The visual and verbal cues that often guide the librarian in face-to-face reference interviews do not exist in email reference. Librarians are tasked with interpreting a question that may or may not be fully fleshed-out and misinterpretations may require multiple messages to clarify, causing delay. In an attempt to alleviate misinterpretations and collect as much information about a query as possible, some libraries have added web forms to their repertoire of virtual reference services, often in combination with email reference. Such web forms can serve as a surrogate reference interview and commonly require the patron to include specific details, such as resources already consulted, type of sources requested, deadlines for the information, and patron contact information. Web forms and email links may be embedded in course management systems, throughout a library's web presence, and even some third-party resources such as full-text databases and electronic journal websites.

Braxton and Brunsdale found that, much as with email reference, the increasing popularity and recreational use of chat during the 1990s spurred libraries to incorporate reference service via text chat into their reference arsenal.[70] Libraries first ventured into chat reference by utilizing popular and free instant messaging (IM) services, such as AIM, Yahoo Messenger, and MSN Messenger.[71] Commercial virtual reference software (VRS) was developed in response to certain limitations with IM, and many libraries chose to utilize VRS packages such as OCLC's QuestionPoint,[72] which is supported by OCLC's 24/7 Reference Cooperative.[73] The 24/7 Reference Cooperative "provides an around-the-clock reference service, built by a cooperative of participating libraries" whose inclusion of academic, public, and even special libraries greatly increases reference availability.[74] VRS packages provided tools beyond those offered in instant messaging software at the time: the ability to co-browse, run statistical reports, keep transaction logs, and even add video or voice to the chat reference service. The VRS technology, however, is often unfamiliar to the distance learner, and may even require that software be installed on the user's and the librarian's computers. As Kimok and Heller-Ross found, the use of commercial VRS software packages "increase[s] service costs, staff training, and the chat transaction time and [. . .] can result in librarian and user frustration."[75]

While some libraries still use commercial VRS, many have recently returned to IM for chat reference, utilizing chat aggregators such as Trillian,[76] Pidgin,[77] and Meebo,[78] which allow individuals to connect to and manage several IM providers and/or accounts through a single interface.[79] Modern chat tools are more often used by distance learners, and chat aggregators offer some expanded capability. For example, Meebo's "Meebo Me" chat widget capability allows libraries to embed an IM chat box—a widget—in webpages, blogs, wikis, and other components of their web presences. This chat widget then allows users to chat instantly and anonymously with the library's IM presence without having to download any software and without being signed into an IM account. Due to their capability to run multiple popular IM accounts (e.g., Yahoo Messenger, AIM, MSN Messenger) from one centralized aggregator account, chat aggregators are very desirable and useful; they allow libraries to reach multiple users using the chat tools with which each user is most comfortable and familiar. Unfortunately, many of these chat aggregators do not offer easy access—or any access at all—to usage statistics that libraries need to evaluate and assess their services. The library community has responded to chat aggregators with libraryh3lp, an open source chat service that utilizes public instant messaging networks like Yahoo and AOL Instant Messenger, provides chat widget capability like Meebo, and yet gives the libraries the statistics they seek to justify and assess the service.[80]

Regardless of the specific method or tools used, "online chat has become the basis of the exploding virtual reference services."[81] Chat reference has one big advantage over email reference: whereas email is asynchronous, if used effectively and efficiently, chat technologies can create a synchronous reference interview, "enabling an interactive, real-time connection" between student and librarian.[82] Chat reference can be accessed from any location as long as an Internet connection is available, making it especially beneficial and appealing to distance students. Sophisticated users may also chat through AOL Instant Messenger, Yahoo, or MSN over their mobile phones. Some libraries have realized the 24-hours-a-day, 7-days-a-week availability of chat through consortia and other collaborations with similar or like-minded institutions, alternative service providers, and chatterbots or other virtual agents, which are becoming common customer servants in the commercial sector. Providing real-time reference assistance outside librarian business hours satisfies user demands for instant gratification in ways that elude asynchronous email reference and "open hours only" telephone reference. Chat technology provides point-of-need assistance when embedded in the form of a widget within the library's web presence or in the course management system, which is critical in an electronic environment.[83]

Like other virtual reference services, chat reference has its own set of challenges. Many librarians feel pressure to answer virtual questions immediately, and in as quick a fashion as possible. There is often a prolonged dialogue back and forth between user and librarian to clarify the question, to provide instruction and resources, and to determine whether or not the information provided satisfies the reference need. Poor typing skills or speed and a lack of verbal and visual cues may also lead to slow transactions and frustration. Reference librarians often may find that their users tend to fall easily into IM lingo, leading some details to become "lost in translation." Libraries should be aware that chat has its own set of benefits and challenges, ranging from cost issues for the library to technology and accessibility issues for the distance learner.

When considering virtual reference tools and services to embed in their websites and course management systems, librarians must examine their choices closely in order to ensure that any new technologies will be compatible with existing technologies as well as accessible to their user communities. As with any VRS, "lack of education, resources and technology problems can all contribute to negative experiences."[84] As with any new service, time must be devoted to train library staff on the tools used; library staff unfamiliar with instant messaging or chat may experience difficulty with learning these technologies, and some may exhibit resistance towards the service due to their own discomfort concerning the technology.

Libraries are constantly looking to add relevant services, particularly those that reach out to students in their own online environments, a philosophy that helps traditional students and distance learners alike. Librarians are seeking out opportunities to connect with students through Web 2.0 technologies such as social networking, blogs, and wikis by embedding links to virtual reference email addresses and web forms, chat widgets, and library FAQs in such environments. Many libraries are also experimenting with providing assistance via videoconferencing, web conferencing, voice over Internet protocol (VoIP), and SMS or text messaging. With an ever-evolving array of technology, virtual reference services will continue to grow and change in the coming years. Libraries are also harnessing some of these same technologies to extend library instruction to distance education students.

Instruction

The ACRL's *Standards for Distance Learning Library Services* core concept of equal access also applies to library instruction. The *Standards* dictates that distributed and distance students' instruction opportunities must be equivalent to that provided for on-campus students. (An interesting wrinkle is whether these courses are fully online or blended courses combining online with several face-to-face meetings.) Library instruction focuses on developing and fostering information literacy skills so that students can locate, evaluate critically, and effectively use information. Providing this same experience to distance learning students is more problematic than the provision of equivalent reference services. Viggiano declared library instruction to be "one example of a service that cannot be denied to distance learners, but which cannot be provided in the traditional manner."[85] The current environment is by necessity a diverse one, and "[m]ethods for delivering library instruction range from in-person visits at off-site locations to teleconferencing and videoconferencing, from paper workbooks to online chat," and "may be high- or low-tech, synchronous or asynchronous, one-on-one or broadcast to hundreds of students on multiple campuses."[86] Library instruction to distance constituents varies from institution to institution and is driven by the geographic distance of the library or librarian relative to satellite locations, the number of personnel and resources devoted to distance learning library services, course management software and technologies employed or not employed for online or hybrid courses, the willingness of the faculty to collaborate with the librarian, and the budget allocated for support of distributed library services.

In-person library instruction provided off-site, most likely at a satellite campus, is the instruction method that librarians prefer, perhaps because of its similarities to traditional library instruction.[87] In-person library instruction is generally customized to meet specific needs as determined by the course or assignment, though general library instruction also occurs. In-person instruction provides the opportunity for student, faculty, and librarian interaction. Librarians can respond to questions, and verbal and nonverbal cues, to deliver an instruction experience tailored to the situation at hand.

In-person library instruction at remote locations is effective but not always feasible. If only one librarian is responsible for all distributed courses, there may not be adequate time to honor every instruction request in person. The off-site location may be too geographically distant to justify the cost of travel and staff time. While current trends show libraries are moving toward an integrated approach to delivery of services to distance students, in some instances the budget or personnel are already spread too thinly, and the originating institution cannot afford to commit more money or staff time to travel. Even when budgets and staffing allow for travel, the off-site location may not have adequate space, computers, or other technologies necessary to deliver library instruction in the same manner as at the main location, making instruction equivalent to that provided on-campus impractical or impossible.

An important consideration is that in-person, off-site instruction is only possible when classes meet regularly, and only then if the faculty is willing to dedicate valuable class time for library instruction. As online-only courses become more popular, students are less likely to gather together at a specified time and place.[88] The unfortunate result is the fact that in-person off-site instruction simply may not be an option for every distributed or partially distributed course.

Before technology made virtual reference and online instruction possible and popular, librarians provided instructional material to geographically distant students on paper, in the form of printed resource guides, detailed instructions on conducting research or using databases, pathfinders for a specific subject, package libraries, and library brochures providing information about resources and services. Such instruction was typically supplemented by librarian–student interaction via telephone and email, in much the same fashion as virtual reference. As distributed classes began to move into an online environment, librarians began to move instructional material online by developing subject-specific webpages, research guides and tutorials, and Frequently Asked Questions lists designed to act as a substitute for in-person library instruction. These online instruction alternatives were at first solely available on the library website; it is now common to make web-based library materials available in course management systems. However, most of these early alternatives to in-person library instruction were static and asynchronous.

The distance education environment has changed drastically since its inception and new networked, interactive, and collaborative Internet technologies are now available to innovative instruction librarians. Paper packets and static HTML tutorials, research guides, and subject-specific guides have evolved into interactive tutorials with voice narration. Screen-recording software such as Camtasia,[89] Captivate,[90] and Jing[91] allow librarians to record database or web searches, providing verbal and visual instruction. Librarians can also incorporate interactive components for the user, creating an experience similar to the search demonstration component of in-person library instruction. Librarians make use of broadcast television, webinar technologies, videoconferencing, podcasting, and streaming video to provide asynchronous library instruction more similar to face-to-face classes. Freely available tools exist to create many of these options, which can frequently be embedded within the course management system and accessed when convenient to remote students.

Many librarians are collaborating effectively with faculty, becoming fully immersed in online and hybrid courses via course management systems (CMS). Librarians embed chat widgets, interactive tutorials, videos, and podcasts in the CMS. Many participate in and start discussion threads, host virtual library instruction through chat, and create course modules that appear in the course syllabus. Web-based library instruction can also be delivered outside the CMS or the library website, online in virtual worlds, course blogs, and social networking sites such as Facebook. In addition to requiring faculty buy-in, much of the success of this creativity hinges on the institution's ability and willingness to support such innovations in terms of budget and staff time, though there are many free or low-cost options available.

LIBRARY CONTENT—EMERGING ISSUES

Electronic Books

Electronic books have been around for many years, yet they are still relatively rare compared to their paper counterparts. Due to the terrific ease with which electronic content can be copied and remixed, vendors have undertaken draconian measures to protect intellectual property by inhibiting functions in electronic books that could otherwise increase their adoption. Limits on the number of pages that can be printed, the number of characters that can be copied and pasted, and the number of users who can view an electronic book simultaneously often mar the e-book experience. These features were found by ebrary, an e-book vendor, to be the most desired improvements to the current e-book model. The only thing desired more than these features was more plentiful titles in the right areas of study.[92] Faculty also want greater subject coverage, but the ability to download an e-book is more important to them than fewer restrictions on printing and copying.[93]

Negotiating the licensing and ensuring future access to electronic books has been challenging to libraries. Electronic book collections do not have significant overlap with libraries' print holdings,[94] and unrealistic pricing and licensing models still inhibit widespread adoption.[95] Electronic books are also limited by the lack of standards governing their format, hardware requirements, distribution, and delivery.

Electronic books may be more widely adopted among younger generations who are accustomed to reading a majority of their text online. The advent of portable devices that can display e-books may also speed their adoption. These include devices dedicated to electronic texts, such as Amazon's Kindle and Sony's Ebook Reader, and devices that can display or play myriad media, such as the iPod Touch or an Ultra-Mobile PC. The development of larger-format readers, such as the Kindle DX and Apple iPad has generated buzz in the higher education community about the potential of such devices for displaying textbooks.

Video

Video has obvious applications in a distance education setting and has been mentioned here in the context of library instruction. Professors can stream their lectures over the Internet live to students at any location for immediate or delayed viewing. Streaming video obviates the need for all students to be in the same place simultaneously. Videos can be embedded in the course management system or on any webpage.

Issues surrounding video include uneven availability of bandwidth fast enough to effectively stream video—some rural areas are limited to dial-up Internet access or have no access at all. Another difficulty frequently encountered when using videos in the virtual classroom involves copyright concerns. Instructional technology staff and librarians alike are frequently forced to refuse instructors' requests to digitize and embed clips from (or entire) documentaries and films. In response, libraries have begun to license films from companies such as the Films Media Group's (FMG) Films On Demand.[96] Films on Demand is a "state-of-the-art streaming video platform."[97] Its large catalog of documentary films and educational programs can be streamed over the Internet; additionally, Films on Demand provides libraries the option to "integrate videos directly into online card catalog systems and distributed learning courseware."[98] Professors simply link to the film from within their courses.

Delivering Library Materials: Document Delivery, Interlibrary Loan, and Distance Learners

Document delivery is the provision of information to users regardless of distance or geographic location. This can encompass a variety of methods and formats, but the core concept behind document delivery as it pertains to distance education is that distance is not a prohibitively limiting factor and that materials will be delivered if possible, regardless of location, without requiring the user to ever visit the library. While delivery of library materials to distant students and the resulting copyright issues will be covered in much greater detail in chapter 7, the following delivery methods warrant mention here as the current mainstays of document delivery service.

Print delivery methods are quickly being supplanted by electronic delivery but are still required in some instances. When a student requests a print book or article owned by the library, the item is then retrieved and checked out to or photocopied for the requester and mailed or sent via fax. This option has long been the method of choice for delivery of materials to students taking online or correspondence courses but has been supplanted by electronic delivery when feasible. Many institutions with extended campuses make use of a courier service that travels between these locations and the main campus. This is a quicker, more secure, reliable, and cost-effective option for delivery to students located at these campuses. Material requested by students away from locations affiliated with the institution must be sent via ground delivery or fax.

Electronic delivery of articles and of book chapters is the method of choice for getting library materials to distance students and faculty. Libraries lease or buy photocopying equipment capable of scanning paper materials and converting the resulting file to PDF format. Libraries place electronic versions of articles on servers to be accessed by the requesters via secure logins. Electronic delivery of documents requires a fraction of the time and expense a print document delivery request requires, though start-up costs for software and equipment can be high. Once established, an electronic document delivery service saves the library time while filling the student's information need as quickly as possible.

Interlibrary Loan

The term *document delivery* generally applies to materials owned by the originating institution. Delivery of books and articles owned by another library is called interlibrary loan (ILL). This system relies on a network of agreements among libraries to fill gaps in their respective collections as requested by local users. Libraries having ILL services also lend their materials to other libraries, but only the concept of borrowing materials from other libraries is covered here. Interlibrary loan services generally comprise delivery of physical materials and electronic delivery of journal articles. Library users file requests with their local library, which then requests to borrow the item(s) from another library that owns them. The library user checks out and returns materials at his or her local library. The local library returns the items to the owning institution. From the distributed learner perspective, items borrowed via Interlibrary Loan can take longer than local-library document delivery, and loaning libraries can have varying loan periods, so borrowing periods and due dates may vary among books requested at the same time. The library-to-library-to-user delivery method required by modern Interlibrary Services is slow compared to electronic document delivery, but it is currently the best method available to put physical materials not owned by local libraries in the hands of their users.

Carl Frappaolo asked, "If a document is created, but nobody reads it, does it exist?"—drawing attention to the important role that effective and timely delivery of information play in the information literacy life cycle.[99] The awareness of a need for information is vital, the ability to find the information is critical, but the delivery of needed information to the library user in an effective and timely manner is perhaps the most important challenge of all. What benefit are information literacy skills to a student if they cannot acquire the content they need, when they need it? Despite this, Behr and Hayward found that although "the number of distance education students has increased . . . there is no corresponding increase in use of document delivery services."[100] Rather than utilize available document delivery services, students are satisfying their information needs by searching full text databases, using search engines and choosing the first reasonable option that they encounter.[101] The ease of access to online resources, good and bad, can result in students choosing the items at hand over higher-quality items that require more time and effort to retrieve.[102] While many requests can be filled in as little as one day, scores of students are impatient with this delay or with the amount of effort involved in filling out request forms (even those online) or contacting library personnel to request delivery of library materials and choose to use information that is immediately available, with less regard for its quality than its ease of access and instant delivery.

It is important for librarians to keep in mind that while the extraordinary increase in easy access to library-selected, full-text electronic resources since the late 1990s is of obvious and unquestionable benefit to distributed learners, not all articles or books are available in full text online, necessitating the delivery of physical items. It is incumbent on librarians to emphasize to students the importance of using library databases to identify quality information and to "educate students about the advantages and limitations of the free Web . . . to ensure a well-rounded information-literate student who is aware of and utilizes the best resources available, not just those that are quick and easy."[103]

Strong consortial agreements such as OhioLINK are being formed to better deliver information to library users regardless of location. OhioLINK is "a consortium of 88 Ohio college and university libraries and the State Library of Ohio that work together to provide Ohio students, faculty and researchers with the information they need for teaching and research" and serves "more than 600,000 students, faculty, and staff at 90 institutions."[104] OhioLINK has been in existence since 1987 and is a model for the future of regional partnerships to perform collaborative collection development and document delivery. Many states have formed similar consortia; California's LINK+,[105] Texas's Harrington Library Consortium,[106] and Missouri's Missouri Library Network Corporation,[107] for example, serve similar purposes.

Electronic Reserves

Academic libraries have been providing reserve services in support of course studies for many years. Traditional course reserve collections consist of physical items stored apart from the general circulating collection, either in a special reserve room or simply behind the circulation desk. Typically, library staff place items on reserve at the request of faculty; reserve lists can comprise books, photocopies of journal articles and/or book chapters, audio/video recordings, and instructor-created materials such as study guides or notes. Course reserves are considered supplemental readings and are not intended to replace textbooks. To ensure the availability of reserve materials to as many students as possible, reserve item loan periods are short, often only two to four hours, and reserve items are sometimes restricted to use within the library.

Course reserve collections benefit faculty and students but are not without their challenges. Heavily used course reserves require a great deal of staff time for the retrieval and processing of materials, the interpretation and application of fair use guidelines or outright clearance of copyright, and in repairing or replacing damaged or lost materials. Drawbacks for students include the fact that only one student can access an item at a time, long wait times for materials in high demand, long lines at the circulation desk, and frustration during times of high stress, such as midterms or finals. Restrictions placed on course reserves that restrict their use to the physical library space mean that students geographically distant may find it impossible to access and use course reserves.

As with reference services, library instruction, and document delivery, librarians have strived to put course reserves online.[108] In reviewing literature concerning student preferences and habits in regards to physical and electronic reserves (e-reserves), Isenberg discovered that the vast majority of students not only preferred e-reserves to physical reserves but were more likely to access online resources, since access to them is not restricted by location or time as long as an Internet connection is available.[109] Unlike physical reserves, multiple students can access an electronic item simultaneously, frustration and wait time are avoided, and students are not charged late fees. The library can reclaim valuable space once dedicated to reserve collections and eliminate expenses associated with loss or damage to physical items.

Benefits of e-reserves must be weighed against their costs. Libraries must realize that while they decrease staff time spent circulating, receiving returns, and re-shelving materials, the time spent initially processing e-reserves increases when requested material must be digitized by the library staff. As with electronic document delivery, start-up costs for the equipment and software required to create and provide e-reserves can be high. Funding for equipment maintenance must also be considered for long-term support of electronic resources. As with any new service, library staff must be trained in the processes required to develop, maintain, and support e-reserves as well as in the methods necessary to troubleshoot technological issues that may arise in their creation and use.

Perhaps the most complicated reserves management issues are those surrounding the interpretation and application of copyright laws and guidelines. Copyright issues are discussed in great detail in chapter 7, but library workers must be aware of applicable laws and how they can drive policy creation in their libraries. Such laws include not only the Copyright Act but the TEACH Act and the Digital Millennium Copyright Act (DMCA). Library staff must be trained in the interpretation of guidelines and their application to library policy. If the library decides to perform copyright clearance for reserve materials, adequate funding and staff time must be allotted. The library may be responsible for communicating usage guidelines to staff, faculty, and students, and may decide to implement digital rights management (DRM) technologies designed to protect and enforce predefined policies controlling access and use of digital content.

Marketing

The appropriate marketing of distributed and virtual library services is integral to their success. Libraries may most effectively market these services in terms of identifying and addressing challenges that distance students and faculty encounter. Each service offered—document delivery, electronic reserves, interlibrary loan, references assistance, and library instruction—is a selling point and plays a part in a comprehensive campaign to educate students and faculty about the services available to them from their library. Many students and faculty are not aware that such services exist, and this percentage is even higher among new students, regional campuses, and online students, as well as adjunct faculty and distance students in general. Establishing a marketing program and library brand that is a recognized part of the campus community and is embedded in the digital spaces occupied by students and faculty is a critical part of successful distance learning library services. These and other marketing issues are covered in detail in chapter 8.

EMERGING ISSUES IN DELIVERY OF CONTENT AND SERVICES

Mobile Devices, Mobile Learning

Web 2.0 enables us to access information anytime, anywhere, on any Internet-connected device. Course materials, from audio lectures in MP3 format to simple email reminders from the instructor, can be accessed from mobile phones, e-book readers, MP3 players, and of course portable computers, which range from the traditional laptop to the tiny Ultra-Mobile PC, netbooks, iPads, and tablet PCs, which features on-screen handwriting capability. The market penetration of mobile devices among students and faculty varies from 60 to 100 percent, so the time is right for moving distance education (and library services) to these devices.[110]

When considering mobile learning, it's important to look beyond the devices, at technologies that lend themselves to mobile communication and delivery of content. It is possible to compose and read email, send short text messages, and participate on social networking sites such as Twitter[111] or Facebook using a basic cell phone. All these services could be put into use by instructors and students in support of their online classes and by the librarians who in turn support them.

One of the drawbacks of today's always-on, instant-access environment is that it challenges the traditional model under which students have access to professors only during class time and office hours. Now that's it's possible to contact a professor via email, instant message, Facebook, Twitter, or countless other methods, student expectations for access to instructors has increased.[112] As we have seen, librarians have been less reluctant than some faculty to press these technologies into service. Consider this: with competition from commercial sources, is 24/7 access in the education world a desirable, realistic, and achievable goal?

Virtual Worlds as Learning Environments

Educators have been experimenting with virtual worlds such as Second Life for the delivery of lectures and course materials. Librarians have also been experimenting with providing reference, instruction, and even electronic collections in the form of documents, web links, and visual and interactive exhibits.[113] Although very well received in a study of computer science students, and though it was found to enhance traditional lectures, distributed education and library services through Second Life remain problematical.[114]

Conclusion

This chapter has provided an overview of some current issues in distributed learning and virtual librarianship, many of which will be examined in greater detail later in this text. We have examined the Association of College and Research Libraries (ACRL) *Standards for Distance Learning Library Services* and introduced some of the challenges libraries face in the provision of library services to geographically distributed students and faculty. The underlying theme of this chapter has been the evolution of library services in support of distributed faculty and students. Librarians have sought to support distributed learning for many years, but the changes brought about by the growth of new technologies enable continuously expanding delivery of information and services.

REFERENCES

Association of College and Research Libraries. "What is the Association of College & Research Libraries?" American Library Association, August 3, 2006. http://www.ala.org/ala/mgrps/divs/acrl/about/whatisacrl/index.cfm.

Association of College and Research Libraries. "Standards for Distance Learning Library Services." American Library Association, September 1, 2006. http://www.acrl.org/ala/mgrps/divs/acrl/standards/ guidelinesdistancelearning.cfm.

Behr, Michele, and Julie Hayward. "Do Off-Campus Students Still Use Document Delivery? Current Trends." *Journal of Library Administration* 48: 3/4 (2008): 277–93. doi:10.1080/01930820802289318.

"Best Library and Information Studies Schools." *U.S. News & World Report* (April 22, 2009). http://grad-schools.usnews.rankingsandreviews.com/best-graduate-schools/top-library-information-science-programs.

Black, Elizabeth L. "Toolkit Approach to Integrating Library Resources into the Learning Management System." *The Journal of Academic Librarianship* 34: 6 (2008): 496–501. doi:10.1016/j.acalib.2008.09.018.

Breeding, Marshall. "Next-Generation Library Catalogs." *Library Technology Reports* 43: 4 (2007): n.p.

Casey, Michael E., and Laura C. Savastinuk. *Library 2.0: A Guide to Participatory Library Service*. Medford, NJ: Information Today, 2007.

Chapman, Cameron. "Google maps: 100+ best tools and mashups." *Mashable: The Social Media Guide* (January 8, 2009). http://mashable.com/2009/01/08/google-maps-mashups-tools/.

Connaway, Lynn, and Wicht, Heather. "What Happened to the E-book Revolution?: The Gradual Integration of E-books into Academic Libraries." *The Journal of Electronic Publishing* 10: 3 (2007). doi:10.3998/3336451.0010.302.

Corbeil, Joseph R., and Maria E. Valdes-Corbeil. "Are You Ready for Mobile Learning?" *EDUCAUSE Quarterly* 30: 2 (2007): 51–58. http://net.educause.edu/ir/library/pdf/EQM0726.pdf.

Crawford, Walt. "Library 2.0 and 'Library 2.0.'" *Cites and Insights: Crawford at Large* 6: 2 (2006). http://citesandinsights.info/civ6i2.pdf.

Croft, Rosie, and Naomi Eichenlaub. "E-mail Reference in a Distributed Learning Environment: Best Practices, User Satisfaction, and the Reference Services Continuum." *Journal of Library Administration* 45: 1/2 (2006): 117–148. doi:10.1300/J111v45n01_07.

Driscoll, Lori. *Electronic Reserve: A Manual and Guide for Library Staff Members*. Binghamton, NY: Haworth Information Press, 2003.

ebrary. "Global Student E-book Survey." (2007): 1–46. http://www.ebrary.com/corp/collateral/en/Survey/ebrary_faculty_survey_2007.pdf.

ebrary. "2008 Global Student E-book Survey." (2008): 1–40. http://www.ebrary.com/corp/collateral/en/Survey/ebrary_student_survey_2008.pdf.

Fichter, Darlene. "Intranet Librarian—Technology Trends for Intranet Librarians." *Online* 28: 6 (2004): 45–50.

Films Media Group. "Films on Demand—FAQs—Frequently Asked Questions." *Films on Demand: Digital Educational Video.* Accessed October 28, 2009. http://www.fmgondemand.com/PortalFAQs.aspx.Frank, Ilene. "Librarians in Virtual Worlds: Why Get a Second Life?" *First Monday* 13: 8 (August 4, 2008). http://firstmonday.org/htbin/cgiwrap/bin/ojs/index.php/fm/article/view/2222/2010.

Frappaolo, Carl. "Document Delivery—The Glamour and Power of it All." *AIIM E-Doc Magazine* 21: 5 (2008): 26–34.

Hane, Paula J. "New discovery tools for online resources from OCLC and EBSCO." *News-Breaks & The Weekly News Digest* (April 16, 2009). http://newsbreaks.infotoday.com/NewsBreaks/New-Discovery-Tools-for-Online-Resources-From-OCLC-and-EBSCO-53468.asp.

Harrington, Charles F., Scott A. Gordon, and Timothy J. Schibik. "Course Management System Utilization and Implications for Practice: A Survey of Department Chairpersons." *Online Journal of Distance Learning Administration* 9: 4 (2004). http://www.westga.edu/~distance/ojdla/winter74/harrington74.htm.

Holmberg, Kim, and Isto Huvila. "Learning Together Apart: Distance Education in a Virtual World." *First Monday* 13: 10 (October 6, 2008). http://firstmonday.org/htbin/cgiwrap/bin/ojs/index.php/fm/article/view/2178/2033.

"Inspirator: Michael Casey, Gwinnett County Public Library." *Library Journal* (March 15, 2007). http://www.libraryjournal.com/article/CA6423425.html.

Isenberg, Laurie. "Online Course Reserves and Graduate Student Satisfaction." *Journal of Academic Librarianship* 32: 2 (2006): 166–172. doi:10.1016/j.acalib.2005.12.003.

Jeong, Wooseob. "Instant Messaging in On-site and Online Classes in Higher Education." *EDUCAUSE Quarterly* 30: 1 (2007). http://net.educause.edu/ir/library/pdf/EQM0714.pdf.

Kelley, Kimberly B., and Gloria J. Orr. "Trends in Distant Student Use of Electronic Resources: A Survey." *College and Research Libraries* 64: 3 (2003): 176–191. Accessed March 3, 2009. http://ala.org/ala/mgrps/divs/acrl/publications/crljournal/2003/may/kelley.pdf.

Kimok, Debra, and Holly Heller-Ross. "Visual Tutorials for Point-of-Need Instruction in Online Courses." *Journal of Library Administration* 48: 3/4 (2008): 527–543. doi:10.1080/01930820802289656.

Krug, Steve. *Don't Make Me Think: A Common Sense Approach to Web Usability.* Berkeley, CA: New Riders, 2006.

Lee, Lisa S. "Reference Services for Students Studying by Distance: A Comparative Study of the Attitudes Distance Students Have Towards Phone, Email and Chat Reference Services." *New Zealand Library & Information Management Journal* 51: 1 (2008): 6–21. http://www.lianza.org.nz/sites/lianza.org.nz/files/NZLIMJ_Vol51_Iss1_Oct_2008.pdf.

McClure, Randall, and Kellian D. Clink. "How Do You Know That?: An Investigation of Student Research Practices in the Digital Age." *Portal: Libraries and the Academy* 9: 1 (2008): 115–132.

Moyo, Lesley M. "Electronic Libraries and the Emergence of New Service Paradigms." *Electronic Library* 22: 3 (2004): 220–230. doi:10.1108/02640470410541615.

OCLC Online Computer Library Center, Inc. "College Students' Perceptions of Libraries and Information Resources: A Report to the OCLC Membership." (2006): 1–100. http://www.oclc.org/reports/pdfs/studentperceptions.pdf.

OCLC Online Computer Library Center, Inc. "Perceptions of Libraries and Information Resources: A Report to the OCLC Membership." (2005): 1–290. http://www.oclc. org/reports/pdfs/Percept_all.pdf.

OhioLINK. "What is OHIOLink?" OHIOLink. Last modified June 15, 2009. http:// www.ohiolink.edu/about/what-is-ol.html.

O'Reilly, Tim. "What is Web 2.0? Design Patterns and Business Models for the Next Generation of Software." *O'Reilly Network* (September 30, 2005). http://www.oreillynet. com/pub/a/oreilly/tim/news/ 2005/09/30/what-is-web-20.html.

PennTags FAQ. "What is PennTags?" University of Pennsylvania. (October 11, 2005). http://tags.library.upenn.edu/help.

Price, Jason S., and John D. McDonald. "To Supersede or Supplement? Profiling E-book Aggregator Collections vs. our Print Collections." (Presentation, XXVIII Annual Charleston Conference: Issues in Book and Serials Acquisitions, November 6, 2008). PowerPoint slides. http://ccdl.libraries.claremont.edu/cdm4/item_viewer. php?CISOROOT=/lea&CISOPTR=161&CISOBOX=1.

"QuestionPoint/24 7 Coop FAQs." *QuestionPoint Wiki*. Last modified January 30, 2009. http://wiki.questionpoint.org/24+7+Coop+FAQs.

Rainie, Lee, and Bill Tancer. "Wikipedia: When in Doubt, Multitudes Seek it Out." *Pew Research Center* (April 24, 2007). http://pewresearch.org/pubs/460/wikipedia.

Ritzema, Tim, and Billy Harris. "The Use of Second Life for Distance Education." *Journal of Computing Sciences in Colleges* 23: 6 (2008): 110–116.

Sadeh, Tamar. "Transforming the Metasearch Concept into a Friendly User Experience." In *Federated Search: Solution or Setback for Online Library Services,* ed. by Christopher N. Cox, 1–25. Binghamton, NY: Haworth, 2007.

Sessoms, Pam, and Eric Sessoms. "LibraryH3lp: A New Flexible Chat Reference System." *The Code{4}Lib Journal* 4 (September 22, 2008). http://journal.code4lib.org/ar ticles/107.

Shank, John D., and Nancy H. Dewald. "Establishing Our Presence in Courseware: Adding Library Services to the Virtual Classroom." *Information Technology & Libraries* 22: 1 (2003). http://www.ala.org/ala/mgrps/divs/lita/ital/2201shank.cfm.

Shumaker, David. "Who Let the Librarians Out?: Embedded Librarianship and the Library Manager." *Reference & User Services Quarterly* 48: 3 (2009): 239–42, 257.

"Size of *Wikipedia.*" *Wikipedia.* Last modified May 20, 2010. http://en.wikipedia.org/w/ index.php?title=Size_of_wikipedia&oldid=246571727.

Sodt, Jill M., and Terri P. Summey. "Beyond the Library's Walls: Using Library 2.0 Tools to Reach Out to All Users." *Journal of Library Administration* 49: 1–2 (2009): 97–109. doi:10.1080/01930820802312854.

Southern Association of Colleges and Schools Commission on Colleges. "Distance Education and Correspondence Education, Policy Statement." (June 2010). http://sac scoc.org/pdf/Distance and correspondence policy final.pdf.

Sweeney, Richard T. "Reinventing Library Buildings and Services for the Millennial Generation." *Library Administration & Management* 19: 4 (2005): 165–175.

Trainor, Cindi. "Open Source, Crowd Source: Harnessing the Power of the People Behind Our Libraries." *Program: Electronic Library and Information Systems* 43: 3 (2009): 288–298. doi:10.1108/00330330910978581.

Tweney, Dylan. "Tim O'Reilly: Web 2.0 is About Controlling Data." *Wired Magazine online* (April 13, 2007). http://www.wired.com/techbiz/people/news/2007/04/ timoreilly_0413.

Ullman, Craig, and Mitchell Rabinowitz. "Course Management Systems and the Reinvention of Instruction." *T.H.E. Journal* (October 1, 2004). http://www.thejournal. com/articles/17014.

Viggiano, Rachel. "Online Tutorials as Instruction for Distance Students." *Internet Reference Services Quarterly* 9: 1/2: (2004): 37–54. doi:10.1300/J136v09n01_04.

Virkus, Sirje, Getaneh Agegn Alemu, Tsigereda Asfaw Demissie, Besim Jakup Kokollari, Liliana M. Melgar Estrada, and Deepak Yadav. "Integration of Digital Libraries and Virtual Learning Environments: A Literature Review." *New Library World* 110: 3/4 (2009): 136–150.

Yang, Zheng Ye. "Distance Education Librarians in the U.S. ARL Libraries and Library Services Provided to Their Distance Users." *Journal of Academic Librarianship* 31: 2 (2005): 92–97. doi:10.1016/j.acalib.2004.12.004.

Young, Jeff. "Wikipedia Founder Discourages Academic Use of His Creation." *Chronicle of Higher Education: The Wired Campus* (June 12, 2006). http://chronicle.com/wiredcampus/article/1328/wikipedia-founder-discourages-academic-use-of-his-creation.

NOTES

1. Association of College and Research Libraries (ACRL), "What is the Association of College & Research Libraries?," American Library Association, August 3, 2006, para. 1, http://www.ala.org/ala/mgrps/divs/acrl/about/whatisacrl/index.cfm.

2. Association of College and Research Libraries (ACRL), *Standards for Distance Learning Library Services*, American Library Association, September 1, 2006, "Executive Summary: The Access Entitlement Principle" section, para. 1, http://www.acrl.org/ala/mgrps/divs/acrl/standards/guidelinesdistancelearning.cfm.

3. Ibid., "Fiscal Responsibilities" section, para. 1.

4. Ibid., "Philosophy: A Bill of Rights for the Distance Learning Community" section, para. 7.

5. Ibid., "Fiscal Responsibilities" section.

6. Ibid., "Library Education" section.

7. "Best Library and Information Studies Schools," *U.S. News & World Report,* April 22, 2009, http://grad-schools.usnews.rankingsandreviews.com/best-graduate-schools/top-library-information-science-programs.

8. ACRL, *Standards,* "Management" section, para. 1.

9. Ibid., "Facilities & Equipment" section, para. 1.

10. Ibid.

11. Ibid., "Resources" section, para. 1.

12. Ibid.

13. Ibid., "Resources" section.

14. Ibid., "Services" section.

15. Ibid., "Documentation" section.

16. Zheng Ye Yang, "Distance Education Librarians in the U.S. ARL Libraries and Library Services Provided to their Distance Users," *Journal of Academic Librarianship* 31, no. 2 (2005): 94, doi:10.1016/j.acalib.2004.12.004.

17. Yang, "Distance Education Librarians," 93.

18. Ibid.

19. Darlene Fichter, "Intranet Librarian—Technology Trends for Intranet Librarians," *Online* 28, no. 6 (2004): 46.

20. Ibid.

21. ExLibris SFX, http://www.exlibris.co.il/category/SFXOverview.

22. Southern Association of Colleges and Schools Commission on Colleges, "Distance Education and Correspondence Education, Policy Statement," (June 2010): p. 1, http://www.sacscoc.org/pdf/Distance and correspondence policy final.pdf

23. ACRL, *Standards,* "Definitions" section, para. 2.

24. Richard T. Sweeney, "Reinventing Library Buildings and Services for the Millennial Generation," *Library Administration and Management* 19: 4 (2005): 165–75.

25. David Shumaker, "Who Let the Librarians Out?: Embedded Librarianship and the Library Manager," *Reference & User Services Quarterly* 48: 3 (2009): 239–42, 257.

26. Craig Ullman and Mitchell Rabinowitz, "Course Management Systems and the Reinvention of Instruction," *T.H.E. Journal* (October 1, 2004), http://www.thejournal.com/articles/17014.

27. Charles F. Harrington, Scott A. Gordon, and Timothy J. Schibik, "Course Management System Utilization and Implications for Practice: a Survey of Department Chairpersons," *Online Journal of Distance Learning Administration* 9: 4 (2004), http://www.westga.edu/~distance/ojdla/winter74/harrington74.htm.

28. John D. Shank and Nancy H. Dewald, "Establishing Our Presence in Courseware: Adding Library Services to the Virtual Classroom," *Information Technology and Libraries* 22: 1 (2003), http://www.ala.org/ala/mgrps/divs/lita/ital/2201shank.cfm.

29. Sirje Virkus and others, "Integration of Digital Libraries and Virtual Learning Environments: A Literature Review," *New Library World* 110: 3/4 (2009): 37–54.

30. Elizabeth L. Black, "Toolkit Approach to Integrating Library Resources into the Learning Management System," *The Journal of Academic Librarianship* 34: 6 (2008): 496–501, doi:10.1016/j.acalib.2008.09.018.

31. Ibid.

32. Tamar Sadeh, "Transforming the Metasearch Concept into a Friendly User Experience," in *Federated Search: Solution or Setback for Online Library Services,* ed. by Christopher N. Cox (Binghamton, NY: Haworth, 2007), 3.

33. Paula J. Hane, "New Discovery Tools for Online Resources from OCLC and EBSCO," *NewsBreaks & The Weekly News Digest,* April 16, 2009, http://newsbreaks.infotoday.com/NewsBreaks/New-Discovery-Tools-for-Online-Resources-From-OCLC-and-EBSCO-53468.asp.

34. Online Computer Library Center, Inc. (OCLC), *Perceptions of Libraries and Information Resources: A Report to the OCLC Membership* (Dublin, OH, OCLC, 2005), 1–17, http://www.oclc.org/reports/pdfs/Percept_all.pdf.

35. Sweeney, "Reinventing Library Buildings and Services."

36. Tim O'Reilly, "What is Web 2.0? Design Patterns and Business Models for the Next Generation of Software," *O'Reilly Network,* September 30, 2005, http://www.oreillynet.com/pub/a/oreilly/tim/news/ 2005/09/30/what-is-web-20.html.

37. Cindi Trainor, "Open Source, Crowd Source: Harnessing the Power of the People Behind Our Libraries," *Program: Electronic Library and Information Systems* 43: 3 (2009), doi:10.1108/00330330910978581.

38. "Wikipedia: Size of Wikipedia," *Wikipedia,* Annual Growth Rate section, last modified May 20, 2009, http://en.wikipedia.org/wiki/Size_of_wikipedia.

39. Jeff Young, "Wikipedia Founder Discourages Academic Use of His Creation," *Chronicle of Higher Education: The Wired Campus,* June 12, 2006, http://chronicle.com/wiredcampus/article/1328/wikipedia-founder-discourages-academic-use-of-his-creation; Lee Rainie and Bill Tancer, "Wikipedia Users," *Pew Internet and American Life Project,* April 24, 2007, http://www.pewinternet.org/~/media//Files/Reports/2007/PIP_Wikipedia07.pdf.pdf.

40. Dylan Tweney, "Tim O'Reilly: Web 2.0 is About Controlling Data," *Wired Magazine online,* April 13, 2007, http://www.wired.com/techbiz/people/news/2007/04/timoreilly_0413.

41. Cameron Chapman, "Google Maps: 100+ Best Tools and Mashups," *Mashable: The Social Media Guide,* (January 8, 2009), http://mashable.com/2009/01/08/google-maps-mashups-tools/.

42. O'Reilly, "What is Web 2.0?"

43. Ibid.

44. Ibid.

45. "Inspirator: Michael Casey, Gwinnett County Public Library," *Library Journal* (March 15, 2007), http://www.libraryjournal.com/article/CA6423425.html.

46. Walt Crawford,"Library 2.0 and 'Library 2.0,'" *Cites and Insights: Crawford at Large* 6: 2 (Midwinter 2006), http://citesandinsights.info/civ6i2.pdf.

47. Michael E. Casey and Laura C. Savastinuk, *Library 2.0: A Guide to Participatory Library Service* (Medford, NJ: Information Today, 2007), 5.

48. Marshall Breeding, "Next-Generation Library Catalogs," *Library Technology Reports* 43: 4.

49. University of Pennslvania, "What is PennTags?," October 11, 2005, http://tags.library.upenn.edu/help.

50. Facebook, http://www.facebook.com.

51. OCLC, *Perceptions of Libraries*, 1–17.

52. Online Computer Library Center, Inc. (OCLC), *College Students' Perceptions of Libraries and Information Resources: A Report to the OCLC Membership* (Dublin, OH: OCLC, 2006), 1–7, http://www.oclc.org/reports/pdfs/studentperceptions.pdf.

53. Randall McClure and Kellian D. Clink, "How Do You Know That?: An Investigation of Student Research Practices in the Digital Age," *Portal: Libraries and the Academy* 9: 1 (2008): 115–32.

54. LibX: A Browser Plugin for Libraries, http://www.libx.org.

55. Zotero, http://www.zotero.org.

56. Endnote, http://www.endnote.com.

57. RefWorks, http://www.refworks.com.

58. Papers, http://mekentosj.com/papers.

59. Mendeley, http://www.mendeley.com.

60. WizFolio, www.wizfolio.com.

61. Lesley M. Moyo, "Electronic Libraries and the Emergence of New Service Paradigms," *Electronic Library* 22: 3 (2004): 221, doi:10.1108/02640470410541615.

62. Ibid., 221.

63. Ibid., 224.

64. Jill M. Sodt and Terri P. Summey, "Beyond the Library's Walls: Using Library 2.0 Tools to Reach Out to All Users," *Journal of Library Administration* 49: 1–2 (2009): 104, doi:10.1080/01930820802312854.

65. Moyo, "Electronic Libraries," 224.

66. Susan M. Braxton and Maureen Brunsdale, "Email Reference as a Substitute for Library Receptionist," in *Digital versus Non-Digital Reference: Ask a Librarian Online and Offline,* ed. Jessamyn West (Binghamton, NY: Haworth Press, 2004), cited in Lisa S. Lee, "Reference Services for Students Studying by Distance: A Comparative Study of the Attitudes Distance Students Have Towards Phone, Email and Chat Reference Services," *New Zealand Library & Information Management Journal* 51: 1 (2008): 7, http://www.lianza.org.nz/sites/lianza.org.nz/files/NZLIMJ_Vol51_Iss1_Oct_2008.pdf.

67. Rosie Croft and Naomi Eichenlaub, "E-mail Reference in a Distributed Learning Environment: Best Practices, User Satisfaction, and the Reference Services Continuum," *Journal of Library Administration* 45: 1/2 (2006): 118, doi:10.1300/J111v45n01_07.

68. Lisa S. Lee, "Reference Services for Students Studying by Distance: A Comparative Study of the Attitudes Distance Students Have Towards Phone, Email and Chat Reference Services," *New Zealand Library & Information Management Journal* 51: 1 (2008): 8, http://www.lianza.org.nz/sites/lianza.org.nz/files/NZLIMJ_Vol51_Iss1_Oct_2008.pdf.

69. Croft and Eichenlaub, "E-mail Reference in a Distributed Learning Environment," 119.

70. Braxton and Brunsdale, cited in Lee, "Reference Services for Students Studying by Distance," 7.

71. Sodt and Summey, "Beyond the Library's Walls," 106.

72. QuestionPoint: 24/7 Reference Services, http://www.questionpoint.org.

73. Sodt and Summey, "Beyond the Library's Walls," 106–7.

74. "Wikipedia: Size of Wikipedia," *Wikipedia,* Annual Growth Rate section, last modified May 20, 2009, http://en.wikipedia.org/wiki/Size_of_wikipedia.

75. "QuestionPoint/24 7 Coop FAQs." *QuestionPoint Wiki,* What is the 24/7 Reference Cooperative? Section, para. 1, http://wiki.questionpoint.org/24+7+Coop+FAQs.

76. Debra Kimok and Holly Heller-Ross, "Visual Tutorials for Point-of-Need Instruction in Online Courses," *Journal of Library Administration* 48: 3/4 (2008): 535, doi:10.1080/01930820802289656.

77. Trillian, http://www.trillian.im.

78. Pidgin, http://www.pidgin.im.

79. Meebo, http://www.meebo.com.

80. Pam Sessoms and Eric Sessoms, "LibraryH3lp: a New Flexible Chat Reference System," *The Code{4}Lib Journal* 4 (September 22, 2008), 2009, http://journal.code4lib.org/articles/107.

81. Moyo, "Electronic Libraries," 224.

82. Lee, "Reference Services for Students Studying by Distance," 8.

83. Moyo, "Electronic Libraries," 229.

84. Lee, "Reference Services for Students Studying by Distance," 7.

85. Rachel Viggiano, "Online Tutorials as Instruction for Distance Students," *Internet Reference Services Quarterly* 9: 1/2 (2004): 39, doi:10.1300/J136v09n01_04.

86. Viggiano, "Online Tutorials," 39.

87. Ibid., 40.

88. Ibid.

89. TechSmith Camtasia, http://www.techsmith.com/camtasia.asp.

90. Adobe Captivate, http://www.adobe.com/products/captivate.

91. TechSmith Jing, http://www.techsmith.com/jing.

92. Ebrary, "2008 Global Student E-book Survey," (2008): 1–40, http://www.ebrary.com/corp/collateral/en/Survey/ebrary_student_survey_2008.pdf.

93. Ebrary, "Global Student E-book Survey," (2007): 1–46, http://www.ebrary.com/corp/collateral/en/Survey/ebrary_faculty_survey_2007.pdf.

94. Jason S. Price and John D. McDonald,"To Supersede or Supplement? Profiling E-book Aggregator Collections vs. Our Print Collections," (presentation, XXVIII Annual Charleston Conference: Issues in Book and Serials Acquisitions, November 6, 2008), PowerPoint slides, http://ccdl.libraries.claremont.edu/cdm4/item_viewer.php?CISOROOT=/lea&CISOPTR=161&CISOBOX=1.

95. Lynn Connaway and Heather Wicht, "What Happened to the E-book Revolution?: The Gradual Integration of E-books into Academic Libraries," *The Journal of Electronic Publishing* 10: 3 (2007), doi:10.3998/3336451.0010.302.

96. Films on Demand, http://www.fmgondemand.com.

97. Films Media Group [FMG], "Films on Demand—FAQs—Frequently Asked Questions," What is Films on Demand section? The Films on Demand FAQ may be found at http://www.fmgondemand.com/PortalFAQs.aspx.

98. FMG, "Films on Demand—FAQs," What are the benefits of using Films On Demand?" section, http://www.fmgondemand.com/PortalFAQs.aspx.

99. Carl Frappaolo, "Document Delivery—The Glamour and Power of It All." *AIIM E-Doc Magazine* 21: 5 (September/October, 2007): 26.

100. Michele Behr and Julie Hayward, "Do Off-Campus Students Still Use Document Delivery? Current Trends," *Journal of Library Administration* 48: 3–4 (2008): 288, doi:10.1080/01930820802289318.

101. Steve Krug. *Don't Make Me Think: A Common Sense Approach to Web Usability* (Berkeley, CA: New Riders, 2006), 24.

102. Kimberly B. Kelley and Gloria J. Orr, "Trends in Distant Student Use of Electronic Resources: A Survey," *College and Research Libraries* 64: 3 (2003), http://ala.org/ala/

mgrps/divs/acrl/publications/crljournal/2003/may/kelley.pdf; Yang, "Distance Education Librarians."

103. Kelley and Orr, "Trends in Distant Student Use of Electronic Resources," 188.

104. OhioLINK, "What is OhioLINK?," This is OHIOLink section, para. 1, last modified June 15, 2009, http://www.ohiolink.edu/about/what-is-ol.html.

105. California's LINK+ Union Catalog, http://csul.iii.com/screens/linkplusinfo.html.

106. Texas's Harrington Library Consortium, http://www.harringtonlc.org/whoarewe.html.

107. Missouri's Missouri Library Network Corporation, http://www.mlnc.org/about.html.

108. Lori Driscoll. *Electronic Reserve: A Manual and Guide for Library Staff Members.* (Binghamton, NY: Haworth Information Press, 2003).

109. Laurie Isenberg, "Online Course Reserves and Graduate Student Satisfaction," *Journal of Academic Librarianship* 32: 2 (2006): 166–72, doi:10.1016/j.acalib.2005.12.003.

110. Joseph R. Corbeil and Maria E. Valdes-Corbell, "Are You Ready for Mobile Learning?," *EDUCAUSE Quarterly* 30: 2 (2007): 51–58, http://net.educause.edu/ir/library/pdf/EQM0726.pdf.

111. Twitter, http://twitter.com.

112. Wooseob Jeong. "Instant Messaging in On-site and Online Classes in Higher Education," *EDUCAUSE Quarterly* 30: 1 (2007): 30–36, http://net.educause.edu/ir/library/pdf/EQM0714.pdf. See also Jeffrey R. Young, "The 24-Hour Professor," *The Chronicle of Higher Education* (May 31, 2002).

113. Ilene Frank, "Librarians in Virtual Worlds: Why get a Second Life?," *First Monday* 13: 8 (August 4, 2008), http://firstmonday.org/htbin/cgiwrap/bin/ojs/index.php/fm/article/view/2222/2010.

114. Kim Holmberg and Isto Huvila, "Learning Together Apart: Distance Education in a Virtual World," *First Monday* 13: 10 (October 6, 2008), http://firstmonday.org/htbin/cgiwrap/bin/ojs/index.php/fm/article/view/2178/2033;Tim Ritzema and Billy Harris. "The Use of Second Life for Distance Education," *Journal of Computing Sciences in Colleges* 23: 6 (June 2008): 110–16, http://portal.acm.org/citation.cfm?id=1352403.

3

VIRTUAL UNIVERSITIES, LIBRARIES, LIBRARIANS, AND INTERFACES: A CASE STUDY—UNT AT DALLAS VIRTUAL LIBRARY

Leora M. Kemp

In a *Library Journal* webcast, "The Future of the Library: How the Library Eco-system is Evolving To Support 21st Century Information Demands,"[1] co-presenter Rob Mercer made two comments that describe the growing trends in education in general and distributed learning in particular:

• The Internet has changed everything.
• Today's library is user-driven.

No one in the business of education can deny either of these statements. They permeate every aspect of the delivery of educational products and services. Changes in this new way of doing things come faster and faster and often cause discomfort, confusion, and stress to all parties involved. In the 1980s and 1990s, when libraries were eliminating their physical card catalog, customers were unhappy and stressed that they had to learn a different way of locating books on library shelves—although they still could physically browse the shelves of open stack libraries and rely on serendipity to find items of interest. In the early part of the 21st century, users are seeing printed or paper books disappear from their libraries and they hardly know how to cope with the idea. Students in library school ask about the future of libraries, of books, and of librarians. They ask if there will be library jobs for them when they get their degrees. Parents, students, teachers, and the world watched as Cushing Academy (Ashburnham, MA) prep school removed its collection of 20,000 print books from the library and replaced them with computers.[2]

The library at the University of North Texas Dallas Campus was created in 2000 as a virtual library to support a newly created, small branch campus located 50 miles from the main campus. As director of that virtual library, I have seen the virtual aspect continue to increase while the print collection remains small. This is primarily a virtual library, 10 years later.

Coming into a virtual library in a physical location can be a shock to many people who may ask, "Where's the real library?" The following poem reflects this confusion.

Virtual Library

I am happy to have lived in a century
Where books were sacred
And you were told to wash your hands to use them
They did not come five-to-a-box
Like cold cereal,
With about as much nourishment
As Cocoa Puffs or Lucky Charms.
There was meat on their bones,
And you could wrap your hands
Around them like a lover
Or an old friend.

Books forgave a lot—
Graham cracker crumbs, peanut butter spots,
And an occasional child or puppy
Chewing on their binding.
You could take one to bed with you
And it would be there in the morning,
Pages slightly wrinkled,
Marker still in place

Right where you left off the night before.
The thought of libraries existing
Without books is like phone sex—
Safe, sterile, lacking flavor
Texture, touch and taste,
No flowers, no imagination
No risks and no rewards—
No waiting in line and no frustration
Predictable, boring, just a big bill
From AT&T at the end of the month
And you never even get to see a face—
Never even get to turn a page.
I need something real to hold onto—
Not an imaginary card catalog in limbo
Where I am asked to accept on blind faith
That books still live somewhere out in the ether.

What a crock of baloney!
I need to see them lined up on shelves like tin soldiers
Gathering dust, glowing under sparkling motes
Shot with sunshine from stained glass windows
In a solid library made of polished oak and
Fine leather, with a fire in the old stone fireplace,
Not microchips and prayer.

—Nancy Fitz-Gerald Viens, January 1994
(used with permission)

Nonetheless, the world has embraced the microchip, and consequently in this chapter we will examine virtual universities, virtual/digital libraries, librarians, and interfaces. We will first establish definitions for the terms *virtual, digital, electronic,* and *hybrid,* many of which are often used interchangeably. This will be followed by a discussion of the importance of licensing sources for distributed learning. The final segment offers a history of the University of North Texas System Center at Dallas (later renamed UNT Dallas) and its library to illustrate the building of a library from scratch. The development of the library and the university is interwoven.

VIRTUAL UNIVERSITIES

Adults are busy people and virtual universities appeal to them. At the very least, their lives may include one or two jobs, family responsibilities (children or the care of older parents), and college or some other form of education. Any or all of these may be barriers to them becoming full-time students who finish their undergraduate education in the traditional four years by attending face-to-face classes. Although university extension efforts of the past provided for a variety of ways that learners could earn a degree or complete certificates to improve marketability, modern technology has greatly increased the convenience to learners to study/ learn anytime, anywhere.

Tschang and Sente[3] list three kinds of educational institutions prevalent at the beginning of the 21st century:

1. the traditional campus-based college or university
2. open learning environments that serve off-campus or part-time students
3. virtual universities (VU), which in the purest form have no physical campus, but use the Internet primarily to provide distributed learning

It is only in the 21st century that the purest form has begun to flourish. Notwithstanding technological innovations, we find that many virtual universities operate within the confines of the traditional and existing brick-and-mortar institutional boundaries.

Like libraries, universities of the early 21st century are primarily hybrids, but may become fully virtual by

- becoming campus-less
- serving learning needs from a distance
- bringing and distributing knowledge to a learner regardless of geography, time, or method of access

With the emergence of a knowledge-based economy and technological change, especially the emergence of the Internet as a major global force, there is consistent and increased demand for education. Economics are being driven by increasing globalization and competitiveness, and education is essential.

While the true virtual university may be one with no physical brick-and-mortar presence, many online programs attached to such a physical presence refer to themselves (or are referred to by others) as *virtual.* These are in fact hybrid institutions combining face-to-face and online class offerings. They may be affiliated with public or private universities or for-profit entities.

Examples of those affiliated with public universities are the University of Maryland University College[4] and Penn State World Campus.[5] Examples of for-profit *virtual* universities are the University of Phoenix[6] and the Concord Law School,[7] a division of Kaplan University. Other universities have tried this model only to give it up after a variety of problems.

- California Virtual University only operated for two years (1997–1999) and then closed for lack of funding.[8]

- University of Illinois Global Campus (2008–2009) closed because of increased competition for online students and for lack of faculty support for the for-profit model.[9]

- Fathom at Columbia University (2000–2003), a consortial educational site, tried to succeed in a weak economy and with a lack of a positive public attitude toward such ventures.[10]

- NYU Online (1998–2001), with an original $21.5 million investment, ran out of money and the Board of Trustees decided not to invest more money.[11]

- Virtual Temple (1999–2001), a for-profit venture of Temple University, closed after less than two years, declaring that there is no profit to be made. Many of the faculty had expressed skepticism at the idea.[12]

Another model with only a handful of players is the *tuition-free university*, of which the University of the People has received much attention. With less than one year in operation, the university's ability to sustain itself into the future will bear watching. According to their website, this Internet-based university provides affordable access to higher education using collaborative learning and Internet resources.

The reference to *Internet resources* seems to be the only reference to any kind of learning or library *resource*s. Apparently, information needed for assignments comes from the Internet or from print sources a student can locate on his own. It will be interesting to see how librarians and other information professionals evaluate this situation as this university grows and progresses. While currently totally virtual, there are plans to establish communication centers.[13]

A major issue for UoP is that of accreditation. According to the FAQ section of their website:

> Currently, University of the People is not an accredited university. While University of the People intends to obtain accreditation, it cannot promise nor guarantee the time-frame in which this might occur. If the University is accredited at the time a degree is awarded to a student, that student would have the benefit of having graduated from an accredited institution. Prospective and current students of UoPeople should take into consideration the possibility that they will finish their studies with University of the People with no accredited degree.[14]

THE WIKI-IZED UNIVERSITY

David J. Staley (2009) discussed another type, the Wikiversity, which he considered a challenge to the traditional university.[15] A significant move toward this new platform university has come with the development of Wikiversity (http://

en.wikiversity.org/wiki/Wikiversity:Main_Page), an initiative from the Wikimedia Foundation, the stewards of Wikipedia. Like MIT's OCW (OpenCourseWare http://ocw.mit.edu/OcwWeb/web/home/home/index.htm, a form of non-credit virtual adult education), Wikiversity is a collection of learning materials; the difference is that these learning materials are produced by Wikiversity participants, who are, like their counterparts in Wikipedia, motivated volunteers. In addition, the Wikiversity course materials, unlike those made available by MIT, are editable by users. The materials are organized into *portals* or *faculties* (at present, the terms are being used interchangeably)—what we might call *colleges* in a traditional university. Each of the various portals might include any number of *schools,* and each school might have *departments. Courses* are thus organized in this very traditional fashion, with the difference being that all of the courses and learning materials are created by Wikiversity participants. There are no admissions criteria; there are no *professors* (although there are *course leaders*). Just as with an article in Wikipedia, anyone can contribute course materials, anyone can create a faculty or a school, anyone can lead a course. Wikiversity is still quite young (it began as an independent project in August 2006) and is still evolving. Indeed, we have yet to realize the full potential of the platform in a wiki-ized university.

Staley also articulates the main features of the Wiki-ized University, noting that it

- "is a platform,
- is permeable (no formal admissions process),
- consists of voluntary and self-organizing associations of teachers and students,
- consists of a self-organizing and intellectually fluid curriculum,
- does not offer tenure to professors (professors' longevity is determined by the community),
- is governed by protocols based on community values and mores rather than on administrative rules and fiats,
- does not grant diplomas or certificates,
- encourages play (and even failure),
- is governed by 'intellectual barter' and makes all knowledge created therein free to anyone,
- is managed by administrators who 'bubble up' from among the members of the community,
- is managed by administrators who maintain the platform as 'choice architects' and lead via cultivation and care, not command and control, and
- has a fluid temporal structure: there are no 'semesters;' teaching and learning are ongoing activities."[16]

Food for Thought: What Would a Wiki-ized Library Look Like?

The increasing number of virtual universities and virtual classrooms, the favorable reactions by others to online classes, changes in the expectations by regional accrediting agencies, which now accept access to resources as opposed to requiring ownership, and the anytime-anyplace nature of the classes have served to encourage the creation of more online programs by traditional colleges and universities as well as more for-profit programs. Frequently, administrators view online education as a cash cow for strapped coffers. At the same time there is an increased need to provide a variety of resources and support for distributed learners. As distributed library services continue to evolve for learners, these services benefit the face-to-face students as well.

DIGITAL, VIRTUAL, ELECTRONIC, ONLINE, AND HYBRID LIBRARIES

Digital, Virtual, Electronic, Online, and Hybrid Libraries? What do they all mean? Are they just different flavors from the same tub? Many are used interchangeably yet may refer to different methods. How can we define the differences between the types of libraries these terms represent? Perhaps we can't, but in the digital world there seem to be two general categories: Digital and Virtual/Electronic.

Digital Libraries

Digital libraries are collections of digitized or born digital (never in print) documents, images, videos, and other materials, assembled in a searchable environment. Most digital libraries are relatively specialized and include unique or archival materials. As Bearman noted: "The predominant organization of digital libraries today is by their intellectual content or disciplinary focus. The users we know and the languages they speak are specific to disciplines."[17] Many are created by state, academic, or public libraries or other entities to highlight a specific topic.

TAKE-A-LOOK PROJECT

Examples of the variety of *digital libraries* can be seen in the following:

→ Washington State Digital Library—www.digitalwa.statelib.wa.gov

→ Illinois Digital Archives—www.idaillinois.org

→ University of North Texas Digital Library—www.digital.library.unt.edu

→ Indiana University Digital Library—www.dlib.indiana.edu

→ New York Public Library Digital Gallery—www.digitalgallery.nypl.org

→ Library of Congress—www.loc.gov/library/libarch-digital.html

→ National Science Digital Library—www.nsdl.org

→ Texas Digital Library—www.tdl.org; this library is a multi-university consortium

---

Virtual/Electronic Libraries

Virtual/electronic libraries are collections of databases containing:

1. citations and full-text articles (such as EBSCOhost)
2. e-books (NetLibrary; Project Gutenberg)

3. Internet sites and other cultural artifacts in digital form (archive.org)
4. audio and video archives (Community Audio, a part of archive.org)
5. e-journals (see e-journals.org)

Virtual libraries are frequently assembled by state organizations (with public and school library access) or academic libraries to serve specific constituencies and are password protected because of licensing agreements. An example of this is the Texas State Library's TexShare database program which "provides a wealth of electronic resources to over 700 public, academic, and libraries of clinical medicine throughout the state at a significant cost savings."[18] A virtual library is also a way of accessing information, usually, but not always, from your desktop, that resides solely in electronic format on computers without respect to physical location. According to businessdictionary.com, an "electronic library" is a "physical site and/or website that provides 24-hour online access to digitized audio, video, and written material."[19]

Hybrid Libraries

Hybrid libraries are combination libraries. They are brick-and-mortar institutions located on the continuum between the conventional and virtual library, where electronic and physical information sources are used alongside each other. Most academic (and many public) libraries of the late 20th and early 21st century are hybrid libraries.

Regardless of the type of library, libraries have evolved over the years into user- rather than library-driven institutions. With the acceptance of the Internet and electronic communication devices as valuable resources, people expect to have library access 24/7. If the Internet is available all the time, so should library resources be. In most cases, the only way that 24/7 access can happen is electronically. Libraries accomplish this through library-paid subscriptions to online databases, open access resources on the Internet, the digitization of materials in special collections, and librarians' assistance in a variety of ways via the libraries' websites.

If we consider that libraries function as hybrid libraries, then they are already providing virtual library services. Online electronic resources are, for many learners and faculty, the only ones they use (or want to use), whether from dorm or office, or whether they come into the physical library to use a computer. In addition to electronic journals and books, the emphasis on digitization provides more and more online resources, and librarians are very much involved in this. Librarians, aware of the need to serve distributed learners from their websites, are involved in providing the content and/or designing a website that will be self-explanatory and as easy to use as any other site. Librarians make available 24/7 online reference services such as chat and email. Others provide streaming video and audio resources. Contrary to some perceptions, librarians have always risen to the challenge of providing access to their collections, materials, and services.

Some libraries are providing streaming video resources for specific classes, and they are providing electronic reserves that probably will increase, not decrease because of legal challenges. Just as today's libraries are changing dramatically, so are the librarians who serve and the services they provide, although, as we have seen, librarians have always risen to challenges involving access to materials.

Digital initiatives abound around the world. They involve government agencies, museums, religious organizations, libraries of all types, and for-profit companies. As they become available via the Internet, teachers can enhance student learning, researchers can look at primary sources without having to travel great distances, special collections can be preserved, and libraries can share previously unknown collections with the world. Rickey L. Erway[20] states that "[s]ince its founding in 1974, RLG [Research Libraries Group] has been a pioneer in developing cooperative solutions to the acquisition, access, delivery, and preservation challenges" faced by organizations such as universities, independent research libraries, archives, historical societies, and museums.

According to their website, Project Gutenberg, which began in 1971, was the first to offer free electronic books. While books are their primary focus, other cultural works included in their collections are movies and music. There is no particular list of books to convert to electronic format; volunteers decide what they want to work on. Part of their decision on what to include is dictated by U.S. copyright law. Books that were published before 1923 are now in the public domain and no longer under copyright protection.[21] Currently, there are approximately 33,000 free ebooks available for downloading.[22]

The lofty goal of the Internet Archive, founded in 1996, is "to build an Internet library. Its purposes include offering permanent access for researchers, historians, scholars, people with disabilities, and the general public to historical collections that exist in digital format." In late 1999, the site expanded to include "texts, audio, moving images, and software as well as archived web pages, . . . and provides specialized services for adaptive reading and information access for the blind and other persons with disabilities."[23] There is a variety of projects being worked on to increase the scope of digital items available and services provided. Archived websites are found in the Wayback Machine (http://www.archive.org/web/web.php); a web page for every book ever published will be found in Open Library (http://openlibrary.org/); a permanent archive of multilingual digitized text and multimedia material can be found in Open Content Alliance (http://www.open contentalliance.org/).[24]

One of the most controversial, yet highly effective, digitization projects is the Google Books project, which went into operation in 2005. In their plan to digitize books in partnership with a number of large public and academic libraries, Google has found itself at the center of accusations regarding copyright, access, and profit issues. In a CBC news story, Susan Noakes included background information about this project.[25] With their aim "to increase the amount of knowledge online," Google received permission from several major universities to digitize their collections. An accusation by the Authors Guild of America of "massive copyright infringement" led to a class-action lawsuit against the project. After publishers joined the lawsuit, Google decided to now show only small portions of books not yet in the public domain. (For more information on public domain and copyright, see chapter 6.) In the British electronic newspaper *Telegraph*, Henry Samuel reported on Dec. 14, 2009, that French president Nicolas Sarkozy had stepped into the fight with Google. Sarkozy warned that he "would not allow Google to carry out a massive literary land grab on French and other European literature. 'We are not going to be stripped of our heritage for the benefit of a big company, no matter how friendly, big or American it is' he said."[26]

Jens Redmer, writing in *Google Book Search: The Story,* identified how the project benefited four groups of stakeholders, noting that

- "it is good news for *authors* because it makes it easier for more people to discover their work;
- it is good news for *publishers* because they can more easily reach a wider audience;
- it is good news for *booksellers* because readers are directed to the bookshops where they can buy books; and
- it is good news for *people who read books* because they can search through every book in our index and more easily find where to buy them, or which library to borrow them from."[27]

PRESERVATION AND LICENSING

Providing online access, the heart of the virtual school, university, or library, offers many challenges As we have seen historically, the Internet has significantly changed and influenced education and learning—perhaps in the same way the printing press did in the 15th century. As different methods for delivering information, resources, materials, and education evolve and expand, libraries embrace these methods to fulfill their missions to their communities. The Internet is here to stay and remains the primary access to research sources for distributed learners. The percentage of a library's collection development budget allocation devoted to electronic resources rises every year (generally at the discretion of the library director, but driven by factors such as user demand, availability of scholarly information, and planning for future needs), while the money spent on print materials continues to decline. The very nature of electronic resources means the library no longer owns these resources; rather, they are rented or leased. But before access is given to these materials, a license agreement must be negotiated between the library and the provider. It is incumbent upon librarians to read carefully and understand the language of each license. The diversity of libraries, their users, needs, and many other factors "contribute to the complexity of license agreements."[28]

Sharon Farb's study on licensing in U.S. academic libraries discusses the differences between stewardship and licensing. "Stewardship is preservation for future generations" while "licensing is about control," and the licenses "routinely prohibit preservation copying, archiving, or perpetual access." These licenses are not a guarantee of future access.[29] Farb notes that

> Licensing grants a limited right to access and use of resources, and supports the interests of owners or publishers. Stewardship, in contrast, is action taken in trust or on behalf of another (for example, current and future generations of users), with the aim of ensuring the integrity, authenticity, and the sustainability of resources, and thus their future value and use.[30]

Users often believe that the "full-text" journals appearing in the library's electronic database subscriptions are current and complete. In reality, "print and electronic versions of the same journals are not necessarily issued simultaneously." Indexing may not appear at the same time the article is released. In order to encourage subscribers to retain their print subscriptions, many journals frequently embargo "electronic access to their recent issues."[31]

When print or other physical items were the primary media used in libraries, preservation was mostly a matter of collecting the materials and making sure they were maintained in good condition. The preservation and long-time access to electronic/digital materials is much more complicated. Most libraries have not prepared for the preservation of these materials, relying instead on third parties, such as the vendors or publishers, for such preservation. Most vendors interviewed in Farb's study "recognize these difficulties, some saying they were involved in developing a plan . . . related to digital preservation of licensed content." At this time, only the largest publishers have such plans.[32]

Are we headed for what some have termed a Digital Ice Age? Software applications that are not backward-compatible, hardware no longer available (laser discs, anyone?), the list is endless, but not entirely new to the digital environment. The difference is basically between those items that can be read or viewed as they are, that is, without mechanical assistance such as books and printed photographs, and those that are coded to be read by machines only (phonograph records, DVDs, and the like.)[33]

There are now a number of programs and organizations devoted to the digital preservation effort. (See below under "What Do You Think?" and "Useful Websites.")

> In December 2000, [the U.S.] Congress appropriated $100 million for the National Digital Information and Infrastructure Preservation Program, to be led by the Library of Congress. The legislation called for the Library to work with other federal agencies and also with a variety of additional stakeholders to develop a national approach to digital preservation.[34]

According to the Digital Preservation website, over 130 partners work with the Library of Congress in this effort, including "libraries, archives, universities, research centers, non-profit and for-profit organizations and professional associations both across the United States and the world." The three main focus areas of this program include:

1. Capturing, preserving, and making available significant digital content,
2. Building and strengthening a network of partners, and
3. Developing a technical infrastructure of tools and services.

From this website you may view a short presentation about digital preservation. You can also learn what is at risk in your library and read tips on what you might do to lower or eliminate the risk.

As always, librarians must constantly be aware of the changes and their consequences, some unintended, happening in our information-driven world. Librarians, as they have in the past, must continue to make necessary changes in their libraries, participate in preservation for future generations, and assist their patrons in understanding what is taking place. Perhaps most important, librarians must communicate to their clientele exactly why changes are happening and necessary. To be the best stewards of the resources entrusted to us, we must also think about and prepare for the future.

One example of stewardship and long-term preservation of digital content is Planets, a consortium coordinated by the British Library whose acronym stands for "preservation and long-term access project through networked services." The acronym accurately reflects its mission, which was "to build practical services and tools to help ensure long-term access to our digital cultural and scientific assets."[35]

Although the Planets project ended on May 31, 2010, it brought together European National Libraries and Archives, leading research institutions, and technology companies to address the challenges of preserving access to digital cultural and scientific knowledge. The results of the project will be maintained and developed by the Open Planets Foundation.

TAKE-A-LOOK PROJECT

Questions to consider on this topic:

- What does one preserve? Who makes that selection?
- What happens when the media deteriorate and the content is lost forever, and is this a new concept?
- What happens when you can no longer play the media because the equipment is obsolete?
- What about obsolete formats? (8-track tape, anyone?) What about planned obsolescence?
- How is content re-mastered or migrated onto (or into) different media? (78 rpm to LP, to CD, to iTunes) Is anything lost in the transfer process?
- Who will preserve it?—Goes back to access or ownership.
- Who will provide access to it and how will this be done? Remember that licensing does not assure that the licensed materials will be preserved.
- Where will the money for preservation come from? Who should do the preservation? Librarians/Publishers?
- Is going digital cost-effective?

WHAT DO DISTRIBUTED LEARNING AND VIRTUAL LIBRARIANS DO?

When considering the duties of distributed learning and virtual librarians, it might be easier to ask, "What do these librarians NOT do?" They perform all the activities common to librarianship and more. These responsibilities vary widely and can include:

- Advocacy to library administration for equivalent, high-quality services to distance students;
- Expertise in all things distance education, including online teaching and technology;
- Web page design and responsibility for Web 2.0 initiatives and applications;
- Outreach, advertising, and marketing of library services to faculty and students;

- Representation of the main library to distance constituents and in the distance librarian community;
- Library instruction, in person and virtually, via various delivery mechanisms;
- Coordination of electronic and physical delivery of library materials owned locally and via interlibrary loan;
- Development of electronic and print collections;
- Coordination between faculty and library liaisons or subject specialists to provide library support and facilitate library instruction;
- Reference work—phone, email, and online.[36]

Two studies, spanning a decade, further explain the desirable and sometimes specialized skills that virtual librarians should possess. Ultimately, a librarian should have the ability to embrace change, a willingness to try new technologies, and a firm grounding in ethics and library science principles.

In the 2000 study, the author examined and analyzed online academic librarian job advertisements. As background to the study, the author referenced Roy Tennant's list of skills for the digital librarian or cybrarian,[37] which were identified as knowledge of "imaging technologies; optical character recognition (OCR); markup languages, including HTML, SGML, and XML; cataloging and metadata; indexing and DB technology; user interface design; programming; Web technology; and project management."[38] Because many technologies will inevitably become obsolete, Tennant also identified these desirable behavioral skills: "capacity to learn constantly and quickly; flexibility; innate skepticism; propensity to take risks; abiding public service perspective; good interpersonal skills; skill at enabling and fostering change; and capacity for and desire to work independently."[39]

The study itself categorized technical skills such as website creation and maintenance, "knowledge of computer languages, computer hardware and networking, and electronic resources" in addition to "Bibliographic Utilities and Automated Library Systems." Also found were references to Distance Education, Emerging Trends, and Electronic (or digital) Libraries.[40]

The 2010 study reported that "integration of third party Web 2.0 application programming interfaces (APIs) and social networking platforms" were areas of importance. In addition, competencies in web development, database design and management; classification formats such as XML, MARC, EAD, RDF and Dublin Core; and Educational technology (ET), project management, systems development and applications, and experience were key. Although the specifics may have changed, the desirable personal characteristics were quite similar to the earlier study and included staying current with change.[41]

CREATING A VIRTUAL LIBRARY
FOR THE 21st CENTURY

When libraries in the 21st century are created, they have the opportunity to learn from the past and to incorporate many of the new features that have been discussed in this chapter. This was the case when, in 2000, a new branch of the University of North Texas (Denton) opened in southern Dallas. What follows is a history of the first 10 years of the development of the library: a development closely tied to that of the university itself. As a part of this dual development, the head librarian was involved in all phases of planning at the university and has worked assiduously to keep the library in the forefront of development instead of being an afterthought. This reflects the philosophy that librarians belong at the very center of their community, whether that community is a city, school, or university.

HISTORY OF THE UNT AT DALLAS VIRTUAL LIBRARY-PHASE I—IN THE BEGINNING . . . 1998–DECEMBER 2006

The decision to bring state-supported education to an underserved area of southern Dallas County called for innovation in a depressed economy. In September 1998, the University of North Texas (Denton) was selected from a field of three institutions vying for the opportunity to open a branch campus. Less than a year later, in January 1999, the Texas Higher Education Coordinating Board approved the UNT proposal for the establishment of a system center (upper division branch campus) in southern Dallas County.[42] In May, the Legislature appropriated the first money and on May 13, 1999, the work group to plan for the library was established at the UNT Denton Libraries.[43]

The work group examined various models and concluded that the infrastructure to build a traditional library was a very expensive and outdated model. Here was a real opportunity to do something reflective of current trends and with an eye to the future. The idea of a *virtual library* received favorable reactions from university administrators and board members, so the process was begun. Most of the information regarding the early planning came from interviews with various members of the library planning committee, led by then-Assistant Dean of Libraries, Arne J. Almquist.

A small coordinating committee of cutting-edge people was chosen, not to create the library, but to pull together those who were knowledgeable in various areas. The expertise of those in several areas was sought: Denton campus IT department, Library LAN department, and IT manager for the new facility to coordinate all the technical aspects of the planned high-tech campus; reference librarians/liaisons to recommend titles for a core collection of print reference materials, as well as remote access to enough databases to support the first program offerings; specialists in document delivery to facilitate getting other print materials to the students; the librarian who was responsible for issues concerning circulation, furniture and construction; and the staff from Technical Services who would acquire, catalog and process the print materials. There were others involved in various capacities.

In addition to those on the Denton campus, other local Dallas libraries and librarians were involved. The members of the coordinating committee enlisted the aid of community college librarians in the service area to serve the new Dallas students in the Fall 1999 semester before the new facility was opened. The committee wanted to reassure these librarians that UNT was behind them. They were provided access to the UNT databases to:

1. develop their skills with the databases, and
2. assist the students.

The libraries were impressive and the librarians very good.

Another group of people who sought information and involvement were public librarians in the new service area. A meeting was held at one of those libraries to reassure the assembled group that they would be able to assist with requests from the college students and to lay the groundwork for contacts from the future library staff.

An early plan was for a library associate to oversee a staff of graduate library assistants and student library/computer lab monitors. Reference services would be provided by reference librarians on the Denton campus via computers equipped with a camera and netMeeting software. The decision was later made to hire a professional librarian. A librarian from the Denton campus hired and trained the first staff and oversaw the library until the newly selected librarian started in February 2000.

For the first seven months, access to electronic databases (the heart of the virtual library) was very unreliable. After a new server on the Denton campus was installed, most of the problems disappeared. Only when this access problem was solved were library instruction classes possible.

An outreach librarian was hired on the Denton campus in early 2000. One of her responsibilities was to provide instruction in Dallas. It was thought that there might be too many requests for presentations for the Dallas librarian to handle and that the teaching aspect might be difficult for her because she had come to the job from a public library. However, the teaching was not a problem—she had been a teacher in the public schools and had done many presentations to patrons in public libraries. Additionally, she was not overrun with requests for instruction—she had to seek them out!

When the Southern Association of Colleges and Schools Commission on Colleges (SACSCOC) came in September 2000 for a substantive change accreditation visit, the virtual library passed with flying colors—No Suggestions, No Recommendations. (See chapter 8 for more information on accreditation.) The plans that had been so carefully developed, the positive attitudes of UNT Library administrators, the continuous assistance and feedback from Denton colleagues, the great staff of the System Center and the support and encouragement of the UNT Assistant Dean of Libraries all helped to get this Virtual Library ready to serve the students and faculty of the new campus.

In October 2002 the name was changed to UNT Dallas Campus to make it more identifiable as an educational institution (e-mail from Deborah Leliaert, "UNT Dallas Campus Approved by THECB," October 18, 2002). From the beginning, the Campus has been on a path to become a separate university: The University of North Texas at Dallas. The first major goal was to reach 1,000 full-time-equivalent (FTE) students before that plan could go forward. The school started in a leased building and served only junior, senior, and graduate students. Three nearby community colleges in Dallas, as well as others in Tarrant and Ellis counties, serve freshmen and sophomores and serve as "feeder" schools to the new campus. The primary target audience has been the nontraditional student who has an associate degree, works full time, has a family, and lives too far from a four-year public university to find the time to finish the bachelor's degree. It is for that audience that state senator Royce West worked successfully to bring such a university to the southern part of Dallas County. As a branch, the campus could not hire its own faculty, but had to rely on Denton professors and adjuncts to teach classes in Dallas or via videoconference from Denton.

When the branch opened in January 2000, the enrollment was 204 part-time (P-T) students. By Fall 2002, the enrollment was 867 P-T students, and in the Fall of 2005 the enrollment was 1,450 P-T students and an FTE of 564. In the Spring of 2009, the 1,000 FTE mark was reached, opening up a flood of activities, reports, and plans for the next steps toward separate status.

In the Fall of 2003, the Dallas Campus was given permission to pay for six faculty members who would be assigned specifically to this Campus. Each Fall since has brought an increasing number of full-time faculty members, so that by 2009 the total number of teaching faculty was 38. In July 2005 a newly created position was filled—that of Deputy Vice Provost whose primary responsibility is to oversee the daily activities of the Dallas campus. The increasing numbers of students, faculty, and staff have impacted all departments, including the library.

From February 2000 until October 1, 2003, the library was managed with one full-time librarian and several (5–7) part-time student assistants. In October 2003, another full-time librarian was hired, one who had worked at the Dallas campus as a student assistant and graduated from UNT's ALA-accredited library science program in May 2003. She was on the staff for five years before leaving in October 2008 to take another job.

After the first year or two of operation, only UNT School of Library and Information Science (SLIS) students who have had at least the basic reference course have been hired as student assistants. As the student body grew, this policy was seen as necessary in order to adequately cover the 74 hours per week the library and computer lab operated. The student assistants were frequently alone and had to be able to assist faculty and students with all their information and computer lab needs. The previous associate librarian provided excellent training for these students as well as involvement in projects to help improve library services. When they finish their work here, they have many fine experiences to put on their resumes.

Service desk at the virtual library. Photo by Leora Kemp, 2010.

In that first temporary building, the virtual library grew from a facility with 12 computers and a general access lab with 33 workstations to an additional "team lab" with 18 computers. The librarian and the head of the IT department submitted the proposal for this additional lab, which opened on April 11, 2005. In January 2005, the library began a laptop lending program with 19 computers donated by the IT department. Both the team lab and the laptop service quickly became popular with the students.

Throughout this time, the physical collection remained quite small—about 500 print reference titles. There was a very small collection of videotapes for an anthropology class. A few professors used the reserve system to bring books and videos to this campus for their students to use. Because the campus is 50 miles from the main campus, the Dallas students are considered "distance learning" students with all the privileges—and limitations—of that group. Circulating books could be requested online and sent directly to the students' homes with prepaid return envelopes. There was a courier once a week to deliver materials between Denton and Dallas. In 2005 or 2006, electronic reserves were reinstated by the UNT Library, and faculty members were advised of the service and how to use it. When the Media Library began experimenting with streaming video, some of it became available to the Dallas campus students. This exciting program will continue to be developed.

In July 2005 a newly created position was filled—that of deputy vice provost, whose primary responsibility is to oversee the daily activities of the Dallas campus. This is the person to whom the librarians report.

The virtual library. Photo by Leora Kemp, 2010.

The Dallas Campus Library staff worked very closely with the full-time faculty members (as well as many of the part-time adjuncts) to increase awareness and use of the "virtual" library. This created the nucleus of library advocates among the teaching faculty which continues to exist.

PLANNING FOR THE FUTURE

On November 14, 2001, the Dallas City Council approved the purchase of approximately 202 acres in the I-20 corridor of southern Dallas to be given to the University of North Texas System for the development of the planned University of North Texas at Dallas campus. In addition, the developers agreed to donate 57 adjoining acres for campus development. In the Fall of 2002, five additional acres at the UNT Dallas site were purchased with donated funds from Runyon Springs, Inc., Washington Mutual, and others, bringing the total amount of land available for the campus to 264 acres.

In the summer of 2004, planning for the campus master plan (see the final master plan at http://www.unt.edu/unt-dallas/plan/Documents/Final_Master_Plan.pdf) began and the librarian was part of the planning team, along with several other Dallas Campus department heads and staff. Once the campus plan was finalized, planning began for the first building. Ground for the first building was broken in July 2005 and the official groundbreaking ceremony was held on the site on October 13, 2005.

ACTIVITIES OF THE LIBRARIANS—PHASE I

From the beginning, it has been important to emphasize that the virtual library may not be a traditional library, but it is a full-service library. The library's most important function is to see that faculty, students, and staff know how to access, evaluate, and use the electronic environment. The staff has been very proactive about getting into classrooms for even the most basic *library instruction*. For the most part, these have been one-hour presentations taught by the librarians. It was shortly before moving to the new campus that library student assistants who were comfortable (or not, but who were willing) to do presentations were given the opportunity to develop this skill. With the small staff and the absence of an "information literacy" class, these one-shot classes needed to be supplemented by online components. That led to the development of basic tutorials describing how to find a book and how to locate articles.

In order to continue to reach more students, use of the *library's website* (as well as that of the Denton libraries' website) has always been important. While it has grown and improved throughout the years, there have been drawbacks. The library is responsible for the content of its pages, but has had to submit all additions and changes to a single part-time student assistant to be added. With only one part-time person working on the entire campus website, it has sometimes led to outdated information because of the backlog. The design and format are set and beyond the scope of any individual department. In addition to the two Dallas Campus tutorials, links have been provided to other tutorials in Denton, a link to the Ask-A-Librarian site, a list of the Dallas Campus core print-reference collection, and an online library instruction request form. Online versions of the

Research Guides created for Dallas Campus students are updated every semester, and new ones are created when new programs are added.

As part of the builders of a new university, the librarians became active in *networking and outreach activities* from the beginning. On-campus activities have included extensive committee work, collaboration with other departments, attendance at all functions when possible, liaison work with faculty and administrators, work-related research service to all full-time employees, and hosting workshops for area librarians. Off-campus activities have included committee service on Chambers of Commerce and other local organizations, program outreach to area libraries (academic, public, and school), speaking opportunities to talk about the new university, participation in an annual bookfest with four small public libraries, hosting an electronic mailing list for about 200 librarians, administrators, and library school students, participation in library conferences, and other activities.

PHASE II: JANUARY 2007–APRIL 2010

The first building on the permanent campus was completed in December 2006, and the move was made during December and January. The Grand Opening for the new building was on the first day of the Spring semester, January 16, 2007. The building itself is not any larger than the original temporary facility—about 78,000 square feet. Two major advantages: (1) it is located on the permanent campus, and (2) it looks more like a college building than the previous one, which was located in a business park. The space for the library is only about one-third the size of the previous space, primarily because the computer labs are now located on two other floors. It was disappointing that the previous "library commons" area was unavailable in the new setting.

Much growth took place during these three years. In Spring 2009, the 1,000 FTE goal was reached with a headcount of 2,333. By Fall 2009, the number of full-time teaching faculty had risen to 38. Program and class offerings had increased significantly, and the capacity of the building had almost reached its limits. Until UNT Dallas has its own accreditation separate from the Denton Campus by SACSCOC (Southern Association of Colleges and Schools Commission on Colleges), it will not be able to offer completely online classes. Classes can have an online component, but must be at least 51 percent face-to-face. Until that time (projected for 2012), Dallas Campus students will remain "distance learners" of UNT Denton.

With the loss of the adjacent computer labs, the library started a "roving librarian" program, using primarily the SLIS student assistants during the busiest times of the day on Mondays through Thursdays. Although many of the questions were of a technical nature, having the library represented in the main lab presented many opportunities for reference assistance that otherwise might have been lost. Statistics and specific questions were kept from the beginning to assist in evaluation of the service. For a while, the staff considered the idea of adding a texting-type service for reference purposes. However, it was decided to delay this service until freshmen and sophomores are added to the campus. With the current average age at 30+ and a very small staff, it didn't seem like the best use of staff time.

Beginning in October 2008, the library was back to one librarian and several part-time student assistants. This remained the case for more than a year, at which time the full-time staff was increased significantly. In addition to filling the vacant librarian position, a third librarian was added along with a full-time paraprofessional. The downside of this was the loss of all but two of the student assistants. With their loss, open hours went from 74 to 65 per week and the "roving librarian" service was cut significantly.

As a result of the faculty status of UNT librarians, the Dallas Campus librarians are a part of the Dallas Campus Faculty Alliance. This has provided excellent access to teaching faculty and their activities. The bond among teaching and library faculty members is quite strong. It was the teaching faculty who requested a required core course in *information literacy* for the new university. It is expected to be introduced once accreditation has been attained.

The year 2009 was a very busy and eventful one for the new university as well as the library. With plans for adding freshmen and sophomores in Fall 2010, committees were established to create programs such as the *First Year Experience* and to deal with undergraduate courses never offered at the Dallas campus before. The time line for all the preparations for submitting reports to the Southern Association of Colleges and Schools Commission on Colleges (SACSCOC) became more intense for everyone. Search committees for another 22 faculty members were formed. Almost everyone serves on multiple committees.

A very active committee for more than a year (and includes the head of the library) has been the "Second Building Committee" which has worked to establish the needs for the second building, which is slated for opening in August 2010 with the arrival of the first freshmen and sophomores. Construction began in the summer of 2009. It will include science labs as well as other classrooms, faculty offices, a police institute, cafeteria, and the library. With the adjacency of the computer lab and help desk to the library, the *information commons* concept will become a reality. This area is scheduled to be much larger than the current library space. Again, it will be a temporary space for the library until such time that a permanent "Library and Student Success Center" can be built.

Several services will continue to be provided by UNT Denton for some time, so several Interagency Agreements were written and approved for the current fiscal year, including one between the libraries. For a negotiated fee, Denton provides access to electronic resources through negotiations with vendors, all technical services, media services, access to the automated catalog and circulation systems, document delivery to UNT Dallas students, and other services. These services are paid for with the library use fee required of every UNT student. That fee is currently $16.50 per credit hour.

ACTIVITIES OF THE LIBRARIANS—PHASE II

Library instruction during this three-year period continued to be a major service, with more sessions being taught by library student assistants. This proved to be an important part of their practicum experience and was a major factor in several of them finding jobs in academic libraries, both pre- and post-graduation. The UNT Dallas teaching faculty has been very pleased with the students' abilities.

While the library staff continued to offer instruction both one-on-one and in-class, *collaboration* with other departments in this area of teaching was also expanded. One example was moving the majority of APA instruction from the library to the writing tutor in the Student Development Office. Another was the offering of workshops on technology instruction by the new IT User Services Coordinator instead of by the library staff, who still continued to assist students one-on-one when necessary. The *roving librarian* service was established in spring 2007 to take reference services to the point-of-need, which was primarily in the computer lab. Although library student assistants, who provided this service most of the time, received many technical questions, there were sufficient reference questions to justify the additional student hours. The service ran until Fall 2009, when student wages were cut so drastically that the library could no longer afford the additional hours required to have someone on duty in two separate locations.

While library space in the second permanent building will be somewhat larger, there still will not be room for any significant collection of physical books and media materials. The current long-range plan calls for the library to remain primarily *virtual*. That will certainly be the case until a separate library is built. Visitors who comment that the library isn't very big are assured that, while the space may be small when compared with traditional libraries, it is indeed a BIG library with access to thousands of electronic resources in addition to the expanding resources on the World Wide Web.

In January 2010 a new full-time *campus webmaster and designer* was added to the campus staff. The library staff will work closely with her to make significant changes and additions to the website to create a user-friendly resource for anyone needing to improve their information literacy skills. The two new librarians have experience creating workshops and online training sessions, so their skills will be useful as more online training is provided for both current on-campus students as well as future online students.

Librarians continued to be active in networking and outreach opportunities. One librarian left us in October 1, 2008 and wasn't replaced until October 28, 2009. A new entry-level librarian position was created, and it was filled on December 7, 2009. Service on campus committees and to the Faculty Alliance (equivalent to a Faculty Senate) has barely begun for them. In time, they will be added to committees, both on and off campus. One plan being tested in the Spring 2010 semester is to offer *embedded librarian* services to any faculty member with an online class component.

THE FUTURE

The future for UNT Dallas is bright and very exciting. The second building is going up rapidly, faculty and staff numbers are increasing along with student enrollment, opportunities for new ideas abound, and eventually the campus will begin offering classes that are exclusively online. The library is part of all of this, and one day, in the not-too-distant future, there will be a separate library building, for which the library staff is already planning. In April 2010, the third building was designated as the "Library and Student Success Center." With the rapid changes in technology, it is difficult to say what new services and resources will be available, but the library will play a leading role. The revolutions that are occurring in educational delivery are happening at all levels, and library services to distributed learners should be central to the plans. Librarians must reevaluate their roles and assert themselves as part of the planning and decision-making process through networking and marketing themselves outside the library.

CONCLUSION

The birth of a new university and its impact within the community comes from the attention it garners in many different ways—its ability to attract students and faculty, the interest of area citizens who show their pride in their new neighbor, and the willingness of individuals and organizations to invest their money in the venture. Likewise, the importance of a new library, configured to include many student-related services, has been recognized by enough people that it has been selected to become one of the early spaces built on campus. Although the plan is for it to remain primarily electronic in nature, there will be elements of the traditional library. The size of the print collection has increased to about 875 titles, some of which will become circulating when the library moves into the second building. At that time, RFID (radio-frequency identification, used to track materials) will be added.

The presence of UNT Dallas and its *virtual* library continues to become known throughout the region. Both the university and the library are intent on serving the community at large as well as the campus community. Librarians continue to reach out beyond the campus borders and serve the information needs of those who are not students on the campus. The library sponsors one or two events each year for area librarians. Plans are proceeding to increase the number of library-sponsored events and broaden the audiences. The electronic mailing list for area librarians has continued to grow in membership (now almost 400) and has broadened its reach beyond the local service area. Other plans include the formation of a Library Friends group, the gathering of special collections, and collaborative digitization and preservation projects.

The World Wide Web is here to stay. Libraries will continue to become more electronic and *virtual* and will need to work closely with publishers and vendors to obtain the resources necessary for their patrons. Virtual libraries *are* real libraries. If libraries are going to be able to preserve their digital resources, they will have to be involved in helping vendors and publishers understand this need as well as be a part of the solution. The future is bright for our information-infused world and *virtual* libraries will be an integral part of it.

EXERCISES: WHAT DO YOU THINK?

Check out some of these digital initiatives and report on their scope, content, strengths, and weaknesses:

- The National Digital Library Program at the Library of Congress (United States)

  http://memory.loc.gov/ammem/dli2/html/lcndlp.html
- Electronic Libraries Programme (United Kingdom)

  http://www.ukoln.ac.uk/services/elib/
- European Digital Library

  http://www.theeuropeanlibrary.org/portal/organisation/cooperation/archive/edlproject/

- Europeana
  http://www.europeana.eu/portal/
- Portal to Texas History
  http://texashistory.unt.edu/
- Project Gutenberg
  http://www.gutenberg.org/wiki/Main_Page

USEFUL WEBSITES

Council on Library and Information Resources (CLIR): http://www.clir.org/
  CLIR is an independent nonprofit organization. Through publications, projects, and programs, CLIR works to maintain and improve access to information for generations to come. In partnership with other institutions, CLIR helps create services that expand the concept of a library and supports the providers and preservers of information.
Digital Library Federation (DLF): http://www.diglib.org/
  A consortium of libraries and related agencies that are pioneers in the use of electronic information technologies to extend their collections and services.
Digital Preservation Website, U.S. Library of Congress. http://www.digitalpreservation.gov/
  The mission of the National Digital Information Infrastructure and Preservation Program is to develop a national strategy to collect, preserve, and make available significant digital content, especially information that is created in digital form only, for current and future generations.
Electronic Libraries [eLib] Programme: http://www.ukoln.ac.uk/services/elib/; http://www.ukoln.ac.uk/services/elib/background/history.html
  The main aim of the eLib programme, through its projects, is to engage the higher education community in developing and shaping the implementation of the electronic library.
International Federation of Library Associations and Institutions (IFLA), Core Activities on Preservation and Conservation (PAC): http://www.ifla.org/en/pac
  PAC was created to focus efforts on issues of preservation and initiate worldwide cooperation for the preservation of library materials.

REFERENCES

Abel, David. "Welcome to the Library. Say Goodbye to Books." *Boston Globe,* Sept. 4, 2009. http://www.boston.com/news/local/massachusetts/articles/2009/09/04/a_library_without_the_books/.
Bearman, David. "Digital Libraries." *Annual Review of Information Science and Technology,* Vol. 41, edited by Blaise Cronin, 227. Medford, NJ: Information Today, 2007.
Bleak, Jared. "Reading Between the Lines of the Obituary for NYUonline." *Academicleadership.org: the Online Journal,* Vol. 2, no. 2 (February 13, 2007). http://www.academicleadership.org/emprical_research/Reading_Between_the_Lines_of_the_Obituary_for_NYUonline.shtml.
Blumenstyk, Goldie. "Temple U. Shuts Down For-Profit Distance-Education Company." *Chronicle of Higher Education,* July 20, 2001. http://chronicle.com/article/Temple-U-Shuts-Down/23877.

Bothel, Richard. "Bringing It All Together." *Online Journal of Distance Learning Administration,* Volume IV, no. I, Spring 2001. http://www.westga.edu/~distance/ojdla/spring41/bothel41.html.

Concord Law School, a division of Kaplan University. http://www.concordlawschool.edu/.

"Digital Preservation" website, U.S. Library of Congress, http://www.digitalpreservation.gov/.

Downes, Stephen. "What Happened at California Virtual University." *Stephen's Web,* April 13, 1999. http://www.downes.ca/post/270.

"Electronic Library" definition. http://www.businessdictionary.com/definition/electronic-library.html.

Erway, Rickey L. "Digital initiatives of the Research Libraries Group." *D-Lib Magazine,* December 1996. http://www.dlib.org/dlib/december96/rlg/12erway.html.

Farb, Sharon. "Libraries, Licensing and the Challenge of Stewardship." *First Monday,* 11, no. 7 (July 3, 2006). http://firstmonday.org/htbin/cgiwrap/bin/ojs/index.php/fm/article/view/1364/1283

Google Book Search: The Story. Google, 2007. http://static.googleusercontent.com/external_content/untrusted_dlcp/www.google.co.uk/en/uk/press/files/book-search-en.pdf.

Hane, Paula J. "Columbia University to Close Fathom.com." *Information Today,* January 13, 2003. http://newsbreaks.infotoday.com/nbreader.asp?ArticleID=16813.

Internet Archive. *About IA,* http://www.archive.org/about/about.php. *Projects,* http://www.archive.org/projects/.

Joswick, Kathleen. "Electronic Full-Text Journal Articles: Convenience or Compromise." *THE Journal,* 6/1/05. http://thejournal.com/Articles/2005/06/01/Electronic-FullText-Journal-Articles-Convenience-or-Compromise.aspx?p=1.

Kolowich, Steve. "What Doomed Global Campus?" *Inside Higher Ed,* September 3, 2009. http://www.insidehighered.com/news/2009/09/03/globalcampus.

Mercer, Rob, co-presenter. "The Future of the Library: How the Library Ecosystem is Evolving Support 21st Century Information Demands." Online seminar sponsored by *Library Journal* and Serials Solutions. (Viewed November 18, 2009).

Miller, Kathryn Metzinger. "Behind Every Great Virtual Library Stand Many Great Licenses. *netConnect,* January 15, 2003. http://www.libraryjournal.com/article/CA266431.html.

Nance, Molly. "Online Degrees Increasingly Gaining Acceptance Among Employers." *Diverse Issues in Higher Education,* 24, no. 4 (2007): 50.

Noakes, Susan. "Google's Digitization of Books." *CBC News,* Nov. 9, 2009. http://www.cbc.ca/arts/books/story/2009/11/09/f-google-digitization-books.html.

Penn State World Campus. http://www.worldcampus.psu.edu/index.shtml?cid=0706_GOOLR7409_0607.

"Planets Project" website. http://www.planets-project.eu/.

Project Gutenberg—General FAQ, http://www.gutenberg.org/wiki/Gutenberg: General_FAQ. http://www.gutenberg.org/wiki/Main_Page.

Reagan, Brad. "The Digital Ice Age." *Popular Mechanics,* Oct. 1, 2009. http://www.popularmechanics.com/technology/gadgets/news/4201645.

Samuel, Henry. "Nicolas Sarkozy Fights Google Over Classic Books." *Telegraph,* Dec. 14, 2009. http://www.telegraph.co.uk/technology/google/6811462/Sarkozy-fights-Google-over-classic-books.html.

Staley, David J. "Managing the Platform: Higher Education and the Logic of Wikinomics." *EDUCAUSE Review,* vol. 44, no. 1, January/February 2009: 36–47. http://www.educause.edu/EDUCAUSE+Review/EDUCAUSEReviewMagazineVolume44/ManagingthePlatformHigherEduca/163579.

Texas State Library—TexShare—TexShare Database Program website: http://www.tsl.state.tx.us/texshare/databasespage.html.

Tschang, F. Ted, and Senta, T. Della, eds. *Access to Knowledge: New Information Technologies and the Emergence of the Virtual University.* Oxford: Elsevier Science, 2001.

Truong, Kelly. "Online University Aims to Build Sites in 6 Developing Countries." *Chronicle of Higher Education,* July 22, 2010. http://chronicle.com/blogPost/Online-University-Aims-to/25728.

University of Maryland University College, http://www.umuc.edu/index.shtml.

University of North Texas Libraries. "Administrative Council Meeting Notes," May 13, 1999.

University of North Texas System Center at Dallas *2000 Annual Report.* Published 03/08/01.

University of Phoenix, http://www.phoenix.edu/.

University of the People, http://www.uopeople.org/.

University of the People—About Us—Media Coverage. http://www.uopeople.org/ABOUTUS/NewsCenter/MediaCoverage/tabid/256/Default.aspx.

Viens, Nancy Fitz-Gerald. "Virtual Library," Unpublished poem. January 2004.

NOTES

1. Rob Mercer, co-presenter, "The Future of the Library: How the Library Ecosystem is Evolving to Support 21st Century Information Demands," Online seminar sponsored by *Library Journal* and Serials Solutions. Viewed November 18, 2009.

2. David Abel, "Welcome to the Library. Say Goodbye to Books," *Boston Globe,* Sept. 4, 2009, http://www.boston.com/news/local/massachusetts/articles/2009/09/04/a_library_without_the_books/.

3. F. Ted Tschang and T. Della Senta, *Access to Knowledge: New Information Technologies and the Emergence of the Virtual University.* (Oxford: Elsevier Science, 2001), 3.

4. University of Maryland, University College, http://www.umuc.edu/index.shtml.

5. Penn State, World Campus, http://www.worldcampus.psu.edu/index.shtml?cid=0706_GOOLR7409_0607.

6. University of Phoenix, http://www.phoenix.edu/.

7. Concord Law School, a division of Kaplan University, http://www.concordlawschool.edu/.

8. Stephen Downes, "What Happened at California Virtual University." *Stephen's Web,* April 13, 1999, http://www.downes.ca/post/270.

9. Steve Kolowich, "What Doomed Global Campus?," *Inside Higher Ed* (September 3, 2009), http://www.insidehighered.com/news/2009/09/03/globalcampus.

10. Paula J. Hane, "Columbia University to Close Fathom.com," *Information Today* (January 13, 2003), http://newsbreaks.infotoday.com/nbreader.asp?ArticleID=16813).

11. Jared Bleak, "Reading Between the Lines of the Obituary for NYUonline," *Academicleadership.org: the Online Journal* 2, no. 2 (February 13, 2007), http://www.academicleadership.org/emprical_research/Reading_Between_the_Lines_of_the_Obitary_for_NYUonline.shtml.

12. Goldie Blumenstyk, "Temple U. Shuts Down For-Profit Distance-Education Company," *The Chronicle of Higher Education* 47, no. 45 (July 20, 2001): A29.

13. Kelly Truong, "Online University Aims to Build Sites in 6 Developing Countries," Wired Campus, *The Chronicle of Higher Education* (July 22, 2010), http://chronicle.com/blogs/wiredcampus/online-university-aims-to-build-sites-in-6-developing-countries/25728.

14. University of the People, FAQ, http://www.uopeople.org/groups/faqs. Accreditation is discussed in chapter 8.

15. David J. Staley, "Managing the Platform: Higher Education and the Logic of Wiki-nomics," *EDUCAUSE Review* 44, no. 1 (January/February 2009): 36–47, http://www.educause.edu/EDUCAUSE+Review/EDUCAUSEReviewMagazineVolume44/ManagingthePlatformHigherEduca/163579.

16. Ibid., 42.

17. David Bearman, "Digital Libraries," in *Annual Review of Information Science and Technology*, v. 41, ed. Blaise Cronin (Medford, NJ: Information Today, 2007), 227.

18. Texas State Library, *TexShare*, http://www.tsl.state.tx.us/texshare/databasespage.html.

19. BusinessDictionary.com, s.v., "Electronic Library," http://www.businessdictionary.com/definition/electronic-library.html.

20. Rickey L. Erway, "Digital Initiatives of the Research Libraries Group," *D-Lib Magazine* (December 1996), http://www.dlib.org/dlib/december96/rlg/12erway.html.

21. Project Gutenberg, *General FAQ*, http://www.gutenberg.org/wiki/Gutenberg:General_FAQ.

22. Ibid., *Main page*, http://www.gutenberg.org/wiki/Main_Page.

23. Internet Archive, *About IA*, http://www.archive.org/about/about.php.

24. Ibid., Projects, http://www.archive.org/projects/.

25. Susan Noakes, "Google's Digitization of Books," *CBC News*, November 9, 2009, http://www.cbc.ca/arts/books/story/2009/11/09/f-google-digitization-books.html.

26. Henry Samuel, "Nicolas Sarkozy Fights Google Over Classic Books," *Telegraph*, December 14, 2009, http://www.telegraph.co.uk/technology/google/6811462/Sarkozy-fights-Google-over-classic-books.html.

27. Jens Redmer, *Google Book Search: The Story ([S.l.]: Google, 2006)*, 10, http://www.danskeforlag.dk/download/pdf/145aihe.pdf.

28. Kathryn Metzinger Miller, "Behind Every Great Virtual Library Stand Many Great Licenses," *Library Journal netconnect* (Winter 2003), http://vnweb.hwwilsonweb.com/hww/jumpstart.jhtml?recid=0bc05f7a67b1790e6fad286838e8a07783d27a064074cc0dc1ecd36dda2c166b34adab923fef30d7&fmt=P

29. Sharon Farb, "Libraries, Licensing and the Challenge of Stewardship," *First Monday* 11, no. 7 (July 3, 2006): 1–5, http://firstmonday.org/htbin/cgiwrap/bin/ojs/index.php/fm/article/view/1364/1283.

30. Ibid.

31. Kathleen Joswick, "Electronic Full-Text Journal Articles: Convenience or Compromise," *THE Journal* (June 1, 2005), http://thejournal.com/Articles/2005/06/01/Electronic-FullText-Journal-Articles-Convenience-or-Compromise.aspx?p=1.

32. Farb, "Libraries, Licensing and the Challenge of Stewardship," 6.

33. Brad Reagan, "The Digital Ice Age," *Popular Mechanics*, October 1, 2009, http://www.popularmechanics.com/technology/gadgets/news/4201645.

34. U.S. Library of Congress, "Digital Preservation" website, http://www.digitalpreservation.gov/.

35. "Planets Project" website, http://www.planets-project.eu/.

36. Brad Marcum, Trenia Napier, and Cindi Trainor, "What Do Distributed Learning and Virtual Librarians Do?" (2009).

37. What is a Cybrarian? The term was used by Michel Bauwens, Information Officer at BP Nutrition in Antwerp, Belgium, to describe virtual library staff in a 1993 article. Merriam-Webster indicates first use in 1991. The term combined cyber with librarian. The Special Libraries Association defines a cybrarian as "an information professional/librarian who utilizes digital and networked communications technologies to the fullest to retrieve, evaluate and disseminate information." Special Libraries Association, *Cybrarian*, http://www.sla.org/content/Help/industopics/cybrarian.cfm. A standard dictionary definition reads: "a person whose job is to find, collect, and manage information that is available on the World Wide Web." Merriam-Webster, *cybrarian*, http://www.merriam-webster.com/

dictionary/cybrarian. In 2010, Marilyn Johnson used the term in her book titled *This Book Is Overdue! How Librarians and Cybrarians Can Save Us All* (New York: Harper, 2010).

38. Linda Marion, "Digital Librarian, Cybrarian, or Librarian with Specialized Skills: Who Will Staff Digital Libraries?," in *Crossing the Divide: Proceedings of the Tenth National Conference of the Association of College and Research Libraries* (Chicago: American Library Association, 2001), 144, http://www.ala.org/ala/mgrps/divs/acrl/events/pdf/marion. pdf. See also: Roy Tennant, "The Most Important Management Decision: Hiring Staff for the New Millennium," *Library Journal Digital* (February 15, 1998), http://www.ljdigital. com/articles/infotech/digitallibraries/19980215_2276.a.

39. Ibid.

40. Ibid., 147.

41. Debra A. Riley-Huff and Julia M. Rholes, "Librarians and Technology Skill Acquisition: Issues and Perspectives," *Information Technology and Libraries* Preprint (2010), 6, http://www.ala.org/ala/mgrps/divs/lita/ital/prepub/rileyhuff.pdf.

42. University of North Texas, System Center at Dallas, *2000 Annual Report*, March 8, 2001.

43. University of North Texas Libraries, "Administrative Council Meeting Notes," May 13, 1999.

4

EXAMINING REFERENCE ASSISTANCE IN SUPPORT OF DISTRIBUTED LEARNING

Carla Cantagallo, Melissa Dennis, and Jana Reeg-Steidinger

Whether directional, research, technical, short answer, or complex in nature, librarians offer professional assistance to answer questions and offer multiple communication outlets to connect patrons with the information they seek. In his 1876 paper, "Personal Relations Between Librarians and Reader," Samuel Green wrote, "Give them as much assistance as they need, but try at the same time to teach them to rely upon themselves and become independent." Green's advice has great value: more than 100 years later, there is still a "need for an intermediary between library users and library collections,"[1] often even between users and search engines. The information universe is continually expanding and along with constantly changing technology, librarians face many challenges and opportunities.

The history of librarians as purveyors of reference services follows the evolution of public service librarianship and the profession's willing adoption and use of new resources and new methods of distribution. The resources range from resources neatly organized on library shelves in a physical location to electronic resources available throughout the entire electronic information universe. The methods vary immensely from library users requesting information from a librarian working at a traditional reference desk in a brick and mortar building to users anytime, anywhere, requesting instant access to needed information from a remote librarian. Librarians have long been concerned with effective distribution of pertinent information; Zadel's message reflects this: "We are in control of inventing the future."[2]

Virtual reference services in academic libraries have become a viable means of communication over the past five years, especially as technology continues to transform education, and this trend will surely continue. The usefulness of a variety of reference service options offered by a library is measured in how efficiently and effectively they serve our diverse user population's needs wherever they may be.

Reference service is integral to the distributed learning student community; fortunately, there are many ways for libraries and reference librarians to function as that much-needed intermediary. When examining virtual reference assistance in support of distributed learning, the following statistics not only illustrate the popularity of distributed learning but give credibility to Green's insights as well:

> In the 2006–07 academic year, 2-year and 4-year institutions reported an estimated 12.2 million enrollments (or registrations) in college-level credit-granting distance education courses. Of these distance education enrollments, 77 percent were reported in online courses, 12 percent were reported in hybrid/blended online courses and 10 percent were reported in other types of distance education courses.[3]

There is certainly a meaningful role for reference librarians to play in the world of distributed learning just as they have in the past with extension services and outreach efforts. Just as before, it remains imperative that the reference services offered by libraries be flexible, nimble, and able to meet students' (and faculty members') needs in a timely and effective manner. It further behooves librarians to use technology to make delivery as quick and seamless as possible—especially in the era of instantaneous delivery of information via search engines.

"In physical libraries, professional librarians play an important mediating role between users and collections. Users pose vague questions typical of the early stages of problem formulation. Librarians interview users to clarify and expand upon questions, using this information to rephrase or restructure user queries in ways more readily searchable. In doing so, librarians draw upon expertise in information-seeking behavior and in interpersonal communication as well as expertise in knowledge organization and in the subject disciplines of the collection. They also draw upon expertise of other librarians. Librarians share their experiences about how they solved difficult problems. They also share tips on searching specific information systems. Some of this knowledge is gathered into 'ready reference' files of frequently asked questions and tips about solving certain types of queries. In these and other ways, librarians add value to library collections and services."[4]

Search engines such as Google, Yahoo, and Bing helped to move people from accessing traditional library resources and bring them directly to the Internet for their information needs. Along with the migration of much reference information from print to digital formats was a reduction in demand for librarian-driven reference services. Campbell described this impact in which "the library is relinquishing its place as the top source of inquiry . . . As digital technology has pervaded every aspect of our civilization, it has set forth a revolution not only in how we store and transmit recorded knowledge, historical records, and a host of other kinds of communication but also in how we seek and gain access to these materials."[5]

People make use of the Internet for information about major life goals, including educational coursework, career networking, purchasing goods and services, medical information for themselves or others, and financial investments. No longer the only source in town for information, libraries and librarians have serious competition from convenient, easy to use, and accessible search engines. According to the 2005 *Perceptions of Libraries and Information Resources: A Report to the OCLC Membership,* 89 percent of college students (84% of all respondents) began their information searches using a search engine, and just 2 percent and 1 percent respectively with the library website or online database. On the other hand, 60 percent of all respondents (not just college students) labeled libraries as providers of trustworthy/credible information and 56 percent described libraries with the label: *accurate (quality information).*[6]

A search engine might bring up thousands of pages of information—some accurate, some bogus. With major life-impacting information needs, the user can become overwhelmed or lost in the information without even knowing it. Easy to access virtual reference services should be their first online destination for trustworthy assistance. As we discuss online services in this chapter, we'll look at how librarians can position their services for maximum benefit to those seeking information. After all, the reference librarian's professional training and expertise provides information seekers with a value-added service:

> For decades, professional searchers, information brokers and reference librarians have had access to powerful and precise search engines and other tools. Information professionals learned well how to wield these tools, but average web users have not had the benefit of similar training. In short, the web has brought to the general public many tools, but not much of the expertise required to use them.[7]

DEFINING ONLINE REFERENCE

Is online reference virtual, digital, electronic, distributed, distant, synchronous, or asynchronous? Although it carries many labels, reference is the key component. The *Online Dictionary of Library and Information Science* uses the term *digital reference,* which it defines as:

> services requested and provided over the Internet, usually via email, instant messaging ("chat"), or web-based submission forms, usually answered by librarians in the reference department of a library, sometimes by the participants in a collaborative reference system serving more than one institution.[8]

The American Library Association prefers the label *virtual reference.* Their definition addresses an electronically delivered service but specifies that it is often synchronous, distant, and facilitated through the use of computers. "Communication channels used frequently in virtual reference include chat, videoconferencing, Voice over IP, co-browsing, email, and instant messaging." Such interactions may be followed up with "telephone, fax, in-person and regular mail interactions, even though these modes of communication are not considered virtual."[9]

Email reference has become a commonplace way to deliver virtual assistance. As with any method involving a gap in response time, this asynchronous conversation may be less popular than a more spontaneous method. The immediacy of a face-to-face interaction between librarian and user provides for a more satisfying discussion. Approximating the face-to-face interaction are a vast array of Web 2.0 social media technologies such as Twitter, Facebook, MySpace, wikis, blogs, and text and voice messaging. Using these tools, virtual library reference services are merely clicks away from potential users.

Distributed learning is often mobile learning. Making collections and services accessible on the mobile web allows cell phones, iPads, and other portable mobile devices to become standard communication tools for library reference. Libraries like Ball State University and the University of Virginia have established a mobile web presence. The University of Richmond Libraries' mobile site enables visitors to search through their Voyager catalog, access live laptop and PC availability information, and submit email, text, or instant message reference questions.[10]

Other libraries have included reference help in online educational tutorials, YouTube videos, podcasts, and course management systems. Better names for these types of reference services would be *networked, digital reference,* or *web-based reference,* which would distinguish them from face-to-face, phone, and snail mail references without making any grandiose claims to being virtual.[11] If we contend that face-to-face reference provides the best service, then phone or instant messaging would be second-best because of their real-time response capabilities. However, tutorials, blogs, and even email offer a lot to the patron, depending on the type of question asked or the need, and these methods cannot be abandoned by libraries that are seeking multiple ways to reach users on a local or global scale.

Issues in Virtual Reference in Support of Distributed Learning

When considering the use of virtual reference in the provision of reference services to distributed learners, there are many issues that need to be addressed. Foremost among them is the precept from ACRL's *Standards for Distance Learning Library Services,* which notes that "Library services offered to the distance learning community must be designed to meet a wide range of informational, *instructional,* and user needs, and should provide some form of direct user access to library personnel."[12]

BEST PRACTICES AND STANDARDS

Every institution that wishes to offer virtual reference services must first consider its own clientele and their needs as well as examine the library's resources, including collection, staffing, and budget issues. Considering service standards should help when creating and maintaining these services. Two important standards are offered by the American Library Association through the divisions of ACRL (Association of College and Research Libraries) and RUSA (Reference and User Services Association).

- The ACRL *Standards for Distance Learning Library Services* were discussed in-depth in chapter 2 and may be found at http://www.ala.org/ala/mgrps/divs/acrl/standards/guidelinesdistancelearning.cfm.
- The RUSA *Guidelines for Implementing and Maintaining Virtual Reference Services* can be found at http://www.ala.org/ala/mgrps/divs/rusa/resources/guidelines/virtrefguidelines.cfm.

CLIENT ATTRIBUTES AND NEEDS

Who can use the virtual reference service? This seemingly simple question begets a host of other questions that, when answered, should aim to define a user profile that will allow a library to identify those who can use virtual reference services. Advertising who can and cannot use the service should be an integral part of the library marketing campaign, for all services, but especially for distributed learning support.

Questions Pertaining to the Academic Setting

In the academic setting, deciding who can use your virtual reference service is a major consideration. Do you offer it only to your institution's faculty, students, and staff or will it be available to community members? In the arena of distributed learning, enrolled students may live in different states; how does a library define the users who fit in this category? Is a distributed learning student defined as a remote student who lives a predetermined distance from campus, such as 20 miles? Or is a distributed student someone accessing the service from a dorm across the street from the library? Are there geographical limitations for using the service? Must the student be enrolled in a course with a specific suffix that identifies it as a Distance Learning course (e.g., English 601–201, the "201" identifies the course as Distance Learning according to the university)? What happens in situations where multiple universities create cooperative degree programs? Which institution is required to provide library services to the students taking these courses? Often, the answer to this question comes down to economics: the institution receiving the student's payment for taking classes is responsible for providing reference services. In the anonymous world of virtual reference, how do reference librarians staffing the service identify a user as a client entitled to receive library services? Do we ask for names, institutional IDs? How does this affect the role libraries have had in protecting user privacy? Privacy is a major issue in the provision of reference services and virtual reference should not be exempt. What to do with the identifying patron information found in service transaction logs created when using commercial or locally created virtual reference software packages?

According to RUSA's (Reference and User Services Association) *Guidelines for Implementing and Maintaining Virtual Reference Services,* (2004), respect for the privacy of library users is paramount in the virtual reference communications between librarians and patrons. Data gathered and maintained for the purpose of evaluation should protect the person's confidentiality. If reference transactions are utilized to create a knowledge database or FAQs, caution should be taken to maintain the confidentiality of any user's inquiries by stripping identifying information from the chat transcript.

A further complication in defining one's clientele is the consideration of varying user learning styles and the effect that will have on the service. For example, the "Millennials," (the generation of students born between 1977 and 1998), when attending institutions of higher learning, expect quick, convenient, personal service, and are accustomed to choices. As experiential learners, they are motivated by peers and visual stimulation. They thrive on technology, multitasking, and self-selected social interaction. They have a preference for mobile communication devices that are essential for text messaging, social networking, and gaming. Millennials grew up with computers as an integral part of school and probably also at home, with the Internet as their primary information tool.[13]

Access to full-text collections, global resources, and a desire for 24-hour service (i.e., instant gratification), is an expectation of many virtual reference users. Libraries can meet these needs as they have in the past with a thorough understanding of their users' information seeking preferences to determine the best mix of virtual resources and services.[14] One choice is joining a virtual reference consortium to provide 24/7 reference services to users.

According to the *Standards for Distance Learning Library Services* by the Association of College and Research Libraries (2008), all students enrolled in online courses and distance education classes are entitled to library service and resources equivalent to those provided to campus users.[15] The standards further call for same service to be offered to non-English speaking students and to students with disabilities. International site-based education programs, plus online programs tapped by students worldwide, raise concerns about the provision of parallel library resources and services in a variety of languages for non-native English speaking users.[16]

Another group of users librarians must consider are those with learning or physical disabilities (who frequently do not self-identify and are not readily recognized in the virtual reference environment).[17] Again, the librarian must serve as intermediary between the user and adaptive technology with the aim to provide comparatively similar access to library resources and services. Providing reference services to diverse users involves overcoming numerous barriers. However, librarians must provide unbiased and equitable service to their users, especially those requiring additional assistance in order to successfully utilize virtual reference services and library resources.

With social media trends becoming the norm, users are adapting well to shifts in reference service that embrace virtual interaction. A Pew Research Center study showed that 42 percent of adult Internet users use instant messaging (IM) and that 24 percent of that group use IM more than email. A subsequent study by Pew confirmed the growing trend of IM use among teens, noting that 75 percent of online teens use IM and 48 percent of them use it every day. Moreover, college students appear to prefer instant messaging over email because it is better for "conveying emotions, [and] building relationships," and "it is easy to use."[18]

With a target audience of adults and teenagers, libraries are using virtual reference to provide research assistance to everyone: "Virtual reference services, particularly chat service, are clearly an integral part of reference . . . it seems imperative that libraries not only understand the trends regarding usage and perception, but that they embrace them."[19] The virtual reference set-up lends itself to the multitasking nature of users; multiple online tasks can be conducted and one can still carry on an effective synchronous chat with a librarian. Virtual reference is an important mainstay within library services.[20]

Technology

The next issue to grapple with when providing virtual reference is the use of technology. In this instance, consideration must be given to the myriad computer configurations users may have. Specifically, we are frequently faced with users accessing their coursework at home over a slow and unreliable connection. These cases can pose significant support problems since distributed learning generally makes use of *bleeding edge* technologies. Still, it is distributed learning that makes education attractive and possible for students in remote rural areas. Such students may be taking K–12 classes and those at the college level may be non-traditional students returning to school after many years as members of the work force. Many are home raising a family or caring for disabled or elderly adults. Innovative technologies relying on advanced computing power and high-speed connections may be unknown and unavailable to these learners and may also increase their level of anxiety when it comes to using virtual reference services. Ease of use, as well as users' different levels of computer knowledge, should be considered when deciding to implement a virtual reference service.

The only form of virtual reference that closely mimics face-to-face reference is that of instant messaging or chat reference. Chat reference may be conducted through a variety of options: widgets (e.g., Qwidgit), chat software (e.g., Pidgin), voice over Internet (e.g., Skype, Windows Live Messenger), and virtual worlds (e.g., Second Life, Active Worlds). The end result aims to be a true virtual reference experience for users and librarians. The popular Library Success Wiki (www. libsuccess.org) lists hundreds of libraries across the United States that are using various IM clients for reference services.

Many libraries use Meebo for virtual reference, because it supports multiple IM services, including Yahoo! Messenger, .NET Messenger Service, AIM, ICQ, MySpaceIM, and Facebook Chat. Some libraries, like the Georgia State University Library, have cleverly added the Meebo interface to the catalog so patrons running a failed search are automatically prompted to chat with a librarian. This is a great step toward targeting users at their point of need rather than making them jump through multiple hoops to ask for help.[21] Other libraries, such as the Pollak Library at California State University, Fullerton, are trading Meebo for LibraryH3lp, another embeddable web chat widget designed with more library-friendly features, such as a queue for multiple chat windows and a routing system for multiple logins into the same service.

Chatting in Second Life is an example of a virtual reference service that attempts to replicate and approximate what is arguably the most intense, most useful, but also most expensive reference mode ever developed and deployed—face-to-face reference service.[22] Users connect with volunteer librarians and library students via their avatars using the open source software designed much like a video game. The social interactions of virtual world chat assuage some of the nuisances associated with text-only chat. While librarians have mostly experimented pedagogically in Second Life through virtual classrooms and virtual libraries, a few have tested virtual reference opportunities to meet patrons' information needs. On Info Island, managed by the Alliance Library System, Second Life residents have access to a variety of open source resources and buildings like the Second Life Library, where a virtual librarian waits at the reference desk. If residents prefer, they can IM the librarian from anywhere in Second Life instead of chatting near the avatar. IM in Second Life is a private message between two users; whereas chat can be "overheard" by anyone in the room.

CASE STUDY QUESTION

If you have an open IM program, such as Meebo, that allows anyone to ask a question without identifying him- or herself, does it matter if the person is unaffiliated with the University? How do you determine if the individual is one of the approved users? Ultimately, if the librarian can answer the patron's

> question, does it really matter? It may make statistics cloudy, but which is more important: asking a user for their affiliation each and every time, or just answering his or her question?

Service Parameters

What are service parameters? These are considerations made in deciding what type of questions will be answered and in what time frame the answer will be provided. When considering what type of questions will be answered, it is recommended that the librarians providing the service agree on a shared reference philosophy. William Katz, noted librarian and authority on reference work of any kind, has categorized reference questions, and these categories may help shape discussion of service parameters.

KATZ'S REFERENCE QUESTION CATEGORIES

Katz divided reference queries into two general types:

1. *The user asks for a known item.* The request is usually for a specific document, book, article, film, or other item, which can be identified by quoting certain features, such as author, title, or source. The librarian has only to locate the needed item via the card catalog, an index, or similar source.
2. *The user asks for information without any specific knowledge of the necessary source.* Such a query triggers the usual reference interview . . . Most reference questions usually fall into the second type, particularly in school and public libraries where the typical user has little or no knowledge of the reference services available.

He then categorized reference questions into four types:

Direction: Or "information booth variety." Katz called the time to answer these questions "negligible" but noted that they could "account for 30 percent or more of the queries put to a librarian in any day."

Ready Reference: Or data-type query requiring a single, usually uncomplicated answer. The answer is generally found in standard reference works.

"The time to answer this type of question is usually no more than a minute or two. The catch is that while 90 percent of such queries are simple to answer, another 5 to 10 percent may take hours of research because no standard reference source in the library will yield the necessary data."

Specific Search, requiring more research than ready reference and a more detailed response.

- "This type of query is often called a 'bibliographic inquiry' because the questioner is referred to a bibliographic aid such as the card catalog, an

---

index, or a bibliography. The user then scans what is available and determines how much and what types of material are needed. At a less sophisticated level, the librarian may merely direct the user to an encyclopedia
article, a given section of the book collection, or a newspaper index."

- The time taken to answer such questions depends on what is available in
the library or on the Internet, but also the attitude of the librarian. "If the
librarian offers a considerable amount of help, the searching may take from
10 minutes to an hour or more. Conversely, the librarian may turn the
question into a directional one by simply pointing the user in the direction
of the card catalog," [or in the direction of the Internet access computers],
[or just emailing back a URL].

- Examples of specific search questions: "Where can I find information
on building houses?" "Do you have anything on the history of atomic
energy?"

Research: Questions that are specific search may turn into research. Research and specific search differ only in the scope and amount of time involved.

"There is no way of measuring the difficulty or the average amount of
time spent on such questions. If one considers intellectual challenge, research
queries are usually more interesting for the reference librarian and certainly
suggest that the librarian is more than a directional signal. Fortunately, reference work of the future seems to be turning toward research-oriented situations."[23]

While reference librarians are generally willing to answer any question to the
best of their ability, providing virtual reference service often creates anxiety on the
librarian's part because of a strong perception that the right answer must be found
and communicated immediately. Therefore, having policies in place detailing a
response time is necessary and should be included in the marketing and advertising
of the service. Email virtual reference services may quell some of this anxiety; however, the library should still have guidelines in place and clearly explain the turnaround time. It is best practice to reply as soon as possible, letting the user know
their question has been received. Some further pressure on both library users and
librarians can be alleviated by the realization that even questions that arrive via chat
may be partly answered right away yet may require further work by the reference
librarian. Librarian and user can agree upon how and when they will get in touch
to share further information.

There exists no single model of perfect digital reference service; some libraries
choose to use only email when providing virtual reference, while others offer a
wide gamut of communication methods. Regardless of the ones used, the most
important goal is to determine and market the services and resources that best meet
user needs.

An ACRL blogger proclaimed, "Be it resolved we should do what works, keep
trying things out until we find the right combination, and keep reevaluating that

combination as times and technologies and—more importantly—cultures change."[24] The provision of excellent service to remote users is essential to the future of virtual services or any services. The delivery of quality service is good customer service regardless of medium. The satisfaction of users' information needs is the base for continued, focused and expanded virtual reference service. Connaway, Radford, and Williams, conclude that:

> When information resources were scarce, users were obliged to turn to the library . . . Now digitized information is abundant, and easily searched by a variety of web-based, intuitive search engines and social networks, so interest in library resources has decreased. . . . To remain viable, today's librarians re-engineer to accommodate users' workflows and habits. Forward-looking library professionals have found it difficult to be flexible or change quickly, because established practices have been deeply ingrained for centuries. An increasingly diverse, sophisticated and mobile society has spawned a demanding user base with an array of information-seeking habits and needs.[25]

Communication

When a remote user interacts with a computer, without the presence of a personal intermediary in the research process, *disintermediation* occurs.[26] Virtual reference can remedy disintermediation in the digital reference transaction with professional, insightful service from the responsible librarian. Although formats, locations, and delivery methods have radically evolved, the basic precepts of reference service continue: customer service, librarian expertise, and people needing guidance. In addition to the librarian's basic reference skills of resource knowledge and interview skills, communication and interpersonal skills continue to be critical in the virtual environment. Other competences for virtual reference librarians include technology and management skills, problem solving, and analytical and creative thinking. Instruction skills, previously limited to bibliographic instruction, are included in the virtual reference skill cadre because librarians must be prepared for just-in-time instruction on a wide array of topics in addition to teaching information literacy.

Communication skills are essential in order to provide an effective reference interview when users communicate their information need to the librarian and the librarian reciprocates by responding to the information need. The behavior of the librarian, as seen by the user, becomes the outstanding factor in the user's perceived success of the reference exchange. Librarian courtesy, interest, and help are crucial in providing successful reference service.[27] In addition to keeping communication channels open during the reference transaction, the reference interview is enhanced by the librarian's ethical conduct.[28]

According to Buckley, the basis is the Golden Rule: "Do unto others as you would have done unto you."[29] The empathetic reference librarian should be alert to clues indicating how a patron would like to be treated. Although criticized in the literature for oversimplification of behavior analysis, the notion of Golden Rule reference service is one of many strategies in providing positive customer-oriented service. Another strategy for positive interaction with users is the politeness theory, which both explains and predicts increased patron satisfaction. The theory accounts for remedying the affronts to face (the public self-image that a person intends to project) posed by face-threatening acts to those addressed.[30] Librarians should be vigilant not to intimidate, threaten, or demean a user. Polite interactions result in increased sensitive reference interviews and subsequent user satisfaction.

The librarian's professional demeanor is especially crucial to users in a virtual reference exchange because some users value the interpersonal aspects with the librarian in the reference exchange as much as the information they receive. They place a high level of significance on the attitude and personal qualities of the librarian giving reference service. Librarians, on the other hand, are more likely to evaluate the reference encounter on how well they answered the question. Librarians perceive relationship qualities to be important, although to a lesser degree than users. Virtual reference librarians obviously need to focus on methods to enhance user perceptions of delivery of appropriate resources.[31] Transcript analysis of chat reference interactions can offer insight into interpersonal dynamics: as is the case with face-to-face reference, librarians tend to view successful transactions as ones in which helpful resources were located. Users, on the other hand, view success through interpersonal factors such as librarian friendliness and effort.

Virtual reference users negatively respond to automated responses, FAQs, websites pushed electronically and without explanation, and redundancy of a librarian's referral to the same resources they had already searched.[32]

Redundancy is especially important in the self-service world of search engines. If librarians are to provide a value-added service, it must not be at the same level as a standard Google or Bing search. Librarians must pay specific attention to potential virtual reference challenges. Especially important to quality reference is the reference interview, but Nilson laments that the reference interview in virtual reference service has "almost disappeared."[33] Lacking a reference interview, librarians may electronically (via email or chat), send website URLs that do not contain requested information and/or have already been viewed by the users. In real-time environments, the librarian's goal of thoroughly responding to an information need conflicts with necessary limits on the time spent with any single user in order to be available to others. The desire to provide a correct answer obviously should not be the virtual reference librarian's sole objective. The professional behavior of librarians is paramount to the continued improvement of virtual reference services and the enhanced awareness of the library as the ultimate source for information access and service.

To ensure and augment librarian professionalism, *Guidelines for Behavioral Performance of Reference and Information Service Providers* (2004) was developed by the American Library Association's Reference and User Services Association (RUSA).[34] The *Guidelines* provide a framework for best practices and are an effective tool for both service assessment and professional development training. The *Guidelines* address five major focus areas:

1. Approachability: Patrons need to realize that a reference librarian is available and feel comfortable in requesting help;
2. Interest: A librarian must show a high degree of interest in the reference transaction; a librarian with a higher level of interest will create a higher level of user satisfaction;
3. Listening/Inquiring: The reference interview is the center of the reference transaction and is essential to the process. The librarian effectively determines the user's information needs in a manner that keeps the user at ease. The librarian should communicate in a cordial, encouraging tone; allow the

user to completely state the need before responding; rephrase and clarify questions and ask for confirmation; avoid jargon, encourage patrons to expand on the request; and maintain objectivity;

4. Searching: The actual search is the intersection of behavior and accuracy. As an appropriate searcher, the librarian will have asked the user what resources were already consulted. Then the librarian will construct and explain a search strategy, abide by the user's time limit, work with the user to narrow or broaden the topics, explain how to use sources, and inquire if additional information is needed;

5. Follow-up: The librarian does not prematurely finish the reference transaction but instead asks the patron if the questions have been satisfactorily answered and makes arrangements to further research the questions if necessary. The librarian also encourages the user's return with further questions and promotes other virtual reference services.[35]

Another RUSA guideline, *Professional Competencies for Reference and User Services Librarians,* focuses on librarian proficiencies essential for successful reference staff. These competencies concentrate on the abilities, skills, and knowledge that make reference librarians unique from other professionals. They remind librarians that regardless of technology or distance, "[t]he most critical element in any information service is the staff itself."[36]

INSTRUCTION

Fundamental to library services for distributed learning students is the premise of *equal access* for students who come to the library locally and those who access it remotely. Within the *Standards for Distance Learning Library Services* document, ACRL (Association of College and Research Libraries) calls this concept *The Access Entitlement Principle* and defines it as:

> Every student, faculty member, administrator, staff member, or any other member of an institution of higher education, is entitled to the library services and resources of that institution, including direct communication with the appropriate library personnel, regardless of where enrolled or where located in affiliation with the institution. Academic libraries must, therefore, meet the information and research needs of all these constituents, wherever they may be. This principle of access entitlement, as applied to individuals at a distance, is the undergirding and uncompromising conviction of the *Standards for Distance Learning Library Services.*[37]

Best practices guidelines and standards are helpful to libraries in many ways: they give librarians a framework on which to plan for and base new services, and accrediting agencies may use them when reviewing the library services of an educational institution.

Most reference librarians are comfortable with the practice of library instruction in the face-to-face environment. Generally, the reference librarian receives a request from a faculty member to conduct a library instruction session focusing on a current topic in the class, (or to complete an assignment), and, using class time, teaches the students how to use the various library resources available to them. The methods for doing this are varied. They should take into account the professor's desired learning outcomes for the session and may incorporate the librarian's particular teaching style. In these face-to-face instruction sessions, for example, reference librarians show students the steps involved in using an electronic database (via Smart Classroom technology), or the librarian may create a web page that serves as a tutorial or *pathfinder* to aid the students in their research.

Information Literacy

The value of information literacy in the academic world is fundamental for life-long learning. Library instruction continues to play an important role in academia, whether in the traditional classroom or as a part of distributed learning. In the *Presidential Committee on Information Literacy: Final Report,* a concise description of information literacy is set forth: "To be information literate, a person must be able to recognize when information is needed and have the ability to locate, evaluate, and use effectively the needed information."[38]

ACRL further expands on this concept in its *Standards for Distance Learning Library Services,* it which it notes that

> The library must provide information literacy instruction programs to the distance learning community in accordance with the ACRL *Information Literacy Competency Standards for Higher Education* . . . The attainment of life-long learning skills through general bibliographic and information literacy instruction in academic libraries is a primary outcome of higher education, and as such, must be provided to all distance learning students.[39]

To that end, how does one offer library instruction to students who may never come on campus, whose only contact with the university and library may be via the institution's web pages or course management systems, such as Blackboard?

The great news is that there really is an abundance of opportunities available to reference librarians to make their presence felt in the world of distributed education. Librarians may take advantage of asynchronous methods of interaction by creating or using:

- Tutorials
- Frequently Asked Questions / Wikis
- Research guides
- Email
- Discussion lists
- Course Management Systems, such as Blackboard or Moodle

Tutorials can be created using presentation software and screen capture utilities (all of which are fairly low-cost and convenient to use). These products allow the user to record on-screen activities (such as database searches) and to create video tutorials. When exploring these options, librarians should keep in mind the complex issues involved in using such technology, such as ease of use, staffing, and, of course, budget.

Collaborative Virtual Reference

Collaborative reference services combine digital library services among a group of libraries to combine expertise and availability. This helps libraries provide services at all hours of the day without the added pressure on human and technical resources. Examples of vendor-based consortium products are QuestionPoint, LSSI, and Docutek. Vendors of these and similar services typically offer the same thing: quality reference assistance at any hour online with the benefit of some type of management software for administrators to organize the virtual data for assessment and other purposes. These virtual collaborations help intercept reference questions at any time by multiple librarians.

If the library's front door is also its web page, then the traditional reference desk likewise becomes the virtual chat desk. For some librarians, virtual reference shifts are no less demanding than face-to-face shifts. These new job responsibilities also must be squeezed into the already full work week. What is a normal work day for academic librarians? 8:00 A.M. to 5:00 P.M.? 9:00 A.M. to 6:00 P.M.? Weekends? Late nights? Because one standard for one library may not suit another, these questions must be answered uniquely. One underlying factor usually remains the same: the clientele set the pace for reference services—whether they are online or in person. But when does the Internet close? It doesn't. Does the library homepage shut down between the hours of 2:00 A.M. and 6:00 A.M.? Should the reference desk?

In the early 2000s, online services such as Ask Jeeves (now known as simply Ask.com because most people missed the P. G. Wodehouse reference to Jeeves the butler), were claiming millions of answered questions daily, free of charge. While there is a plethora of databases available for a reference librarian to use, the licenses usually stipulate that they only be used by current faculty, students, and staff of that institution. This can prove to be frustrating if you offer your virtual reference service to the community at large—sending full-text items from these licensed, subscription-based services is not allowed.

Libraries, feeling compelled to compete with Internet services such as Ask.com, wanted users to remember that their library also had answers for free. In addition, they wanted reference services that accommodated users as much as the commercial sites did. Thus, the market for collaborative chat began. Interactive virtual reference services, where a librarian and patron interact in real time, actually migrated into the library field in 1999 to 2000 through the use of commercial business customer service software called eGain that the consortium 24/7 (now part of OCLC) and LSSI (now tutor.com) modified for library purposes.[40] The QuestionPoint virtual reference system is a collaborative reference service formed by the Library of Congress (LOC) and OCLC (Online Computer Library Center). According to the LOC's Global Reference Network website, QuestionPoint "provides libraries with access to a growing collaborative network of reference librarians in the United States and around the world" (www.loc.gov/rr/digiref).[41] This service is purchased by libraries and added to their websites so that patrons can interact with a qualified library staff member at any hour—regardless of whether the staff member is from the patron's library or not. The service was created to "enable reference librarians to share their resources and expertise with each other and with their patrons free of charge in unprecedented ways" (www.loc.gov/rr/digiref).[42] OCLC also developed QuestionPoint Enhanced, a higher-end product with voice and video, but as seen with similar products providing VoIP software, unreliability and instability create disadvantages for users and librarians alike.

Staffing the Service (Training, Scheduling, at Desk, Away from Desk)

Paramount to any successful customer service endeavor is the training and effective use of staff. While many institutions can make use of automated systems to support customer service, most people would agree that face-to-face interaction is the preferred method, as it also allows for non-verbal communication (which gives reference librarians valuable cues as to the success of a reference interview as it is being conducted. However, in our wired world users are more often than not doing their research from home, work, and often on another floor in the library and they don't want to interrupt other tasks they are doing to ask a question. This makes virtual reference ideal. Staffing the virtual reference service with librarians who are excellent at providing reference service as well as being comfortable with technology is vital.

The Reference and User Services Association[43] (RUSA is a division of the American Library Association) offers some helpful guidelines for staffing of virtual reference services:

- Virtual reference service responsibilities should be shared among staff to ensure continuity of service.
- When possible, staff should be trained for all reference services (face-to-face and virtual) to provide greater depth of knowledge and flexibility for staffing.
- Library staff conducting virtual reference should be selected on the basis of ability, interest, and availability.
- Staff should be provided time and resources for training and continuing education to ensure effective service.

How would you staff a Virtual Reference Service? Would the provision of such a service be staffed separately from the main reference desk?

At some institutions, the library assigns a specific librarian to serve the distributed or distance learning population. This allows the DL students to receive the library services to which they are entitled by directing their questions to a specific librarian. Is this always feasible or desirable? What are the pros and cons to offering a separate DL Service? How does this fit in with the precepts in the ACRL *Standards*?

Marketing

Implementing a successful virtual reference service begins with marketing it to potential users. As with marketing other library services, a good PR campaign can remind patrons that the library provides valuable resources and services that relate to the user and the university's mission. Marketing virtual reference services varies with library budgets and service types. The University at Buffalo was one of the first universities to establish a virtual reference service. Known as Instant Librarian, the chat room thrives as a major public service without placing a drain on staff or budget through extensive advertising, assessment surveys, and use of icons.[44]

Some libraries have contests for participants in their services. In 2007, ASERL (Association of Southeastern Research Libraries) held a drawing for a free nano iPod for participants in a user satisfaction survey. Each school in the consortia was given an iPod for the contest. Members found several ways to market the contest, including advertising on Facebook and their individual library pages. Facebook has become another popular social media space for libraries to reach students for virtual reference opportunities (Facebook chat or discussion boards), marketing (ads), and sharing news and events (uploading photos, videos, and flyers).

Many academic libraries have great Facebook pages, including Yale University, Stanford University, and the University of Mississippi. Benefits to libraries joining Facebook are similar to those of other social media endeavors. A broad spectrum of patrons will be able to read news updates—especially emergency updates—or flip through pictures of the library, since many libraries shift collections or service areas and need to update photos of physical spaces periodically. Libraries can also add a variety of other social media links directly to the Facebook profile: YouTube videos and Twitter automatic updates are common additions. Finally, there are a number of applications in Facebook that can be very useful for libraries and easily added to the library's Facebook page. The WorldCat "CiteMe" application can be added to help library users cite any book in a number of styles, and WorldCat can help students and faculty find a copy of the book in local libraries.

Additional types of promotional media used to encourage virtual reference services have been fairly consistent among academic libraries. University libraries have used a variety of promotional materials to market virtual reference services, including flyers (California State University at Fresno), posters (Texas A&M University), bookmarks (Cal Poly Pomona), table tents (Syracuse University), sticky notes (University of Arizona), postcards/mailings (Kansas state collaborative), brochures (Illinois state collaborative), and giveaways (ASERL). The State of Washington collaborative reference services also provided magnets, pencils and pens, bags, buttons, and static-cling stickers.[45]

One effective way of reaching virtual individuals is word-of-mouth advertising. It is inexpensive, whereas traditional advertising and publicity can overwhelm a library's budget. While traditional advertising and publicity offer rewards, costs can be more than the library can afford. Creating "walking billboards" within the college community is an excellent form of marketing that can save libraries time and money. To help get the word out, academic libraries have used the following methods to publicize virtual reference services: Information literacy classes (Case Western Reserve University), press release/news stories (Louisiana State University), newspaper ads (South Carolina), radio ads/PSAs (Washington state collaborative), electric message boards (Cal Poly Pomona), endorsements (Kansas state collaborative), sandwich boards (Washington state collaborative), and chalk messages on campus sidewalks (Saddleback College).

In 2008, Pollak Library at California State University in Fullerton planned an extensive marketing campaign for the launch of its Meebo chat service by using bookmarks, table tent advertisements, a banner on the library homepage, as well as a slide show projected on a screen behind the reference desk. Librarians were asked to mention the service during their library instruction sessions. In addition, advertisements were placed in the Campus Bulletin and the Campus Portal homepage where faculty, staff, and students log in to access their campus email and Blackboard accounts. Finally, a press release was sent to the school newspaper, which led to an article being written, and the service was presented to a variety of faculty on the University Library Committee.[46]

In his book *Going Live: Starting and Running a Virtual Reference Desk,* Steve Coffman stresses the importance of targeting markets: "[T]he first step in developing any marketing program—whether for virtual reference services or orange juice—is to sit down and segment your users, to (1) figure out what groups of users you want to serve and what their various needs and wants are, (2) determine how your services can help meet those needs, and (3) identify marketing approaches that may be best suited to reaching each of your many audiences."[47] For example, when the University of Arizona Library wanted to market its virtual reference service to distance students, it placed bookmarks in books sent to them and created flyers for satellite campus classrooms.

When seeking branding options, libraries tend to use standard names such as *Ask a Librarian, AskNow,* or *AskRef.* It is best to choose a brand that will reach the widest audience while remaining true to the service, so library jargon should be purposely avoided in order to make the brand as transparent as possible. Connecting the virtual service to the library's other reference service identities has its advantages. "In this approach, digital reference is tied graphically and intellectually to a library's in-person and telephone reference offerings. By doing so, the library hopes to capitalize on the reference reputation it has previously built."[48] College and university libraries have noted that when polled, users seem pleased with virtual reference services, but statistics are typically not as high as expected. A boost in marketing towards target markets could include educating the public about the service and how it can meet its needs.

ASSESSMENT

User satisfaction, including all patron populations, is one of the most frequently used measures of reference service effectiveness. It can be studied from several perspectives: satisfaction with the answer, perceived staff knowledge, positive service experience, and willingness to return to the service. To provide user satisfaction, the following should be the foundation of virtual reference services:

1. Deliver resources efficiently and quickly at the point of need;
2. Make our catalogs and homepages easier to use;
3. Accommodate different discovery and access preferences;
4. Offer multiple modes of service; and
5. Provide opportunities for online collaboration.[49]

Librarians are reminded by Connaway and Radford that

Library users'. . . . major concern is getting the information they need and a second major concern is to have a pleasant interaction with a librarian who is friendly, has a positive attitude, and is helpful. These particular facets of reference librarianship transcend age and technology and endure as attributes of interactions important to all types of users across all types of reference format[s].[50]

An accountability climate exists in higher education. Assessment is necessary for budget justification and accreditation purposes. Library assessment of resources and services, including virtual reference services, provides an opportunity to utilize evidence-based quality data. Evidence based librarianship is founded on the assumption that library services must be supported by the highest quality data that is reliable, valid, and useful. Assessment including evidence-based data provides an opportunity to showcase library value. Virtual reference evaluation is critical due to the complexity of delivering high-quality remote or virtual reference service.[51]

Prior to conducting an evaluation, the following factors need to be addressed: (1) evaluation targets, for example, response time or electronic resources used; (2) "stakeholders" involved, (e.g., virtual reference users, reference librarians, collection development librarians, library administrators, and key campus administrators); (3) criteria for success (e.g., user satisfaction, volume of questions, outreach); and (4) recipients of the evaluation report.[52] Also, anticipating potential assessment shortcomings produces higher-quality data. Focus points include: (1) Impress upon user study respondents the importance of their input; (2) Enhance ease of user feedback; (3) Test the survey instruments developed to identify deficiencies and accordingly adjust instruments; (4) Train evaluators in development of assessment tools and data analysis; and (5) Ensure evaluator's human relations skills and objectivity throughout the process. Jeffrey Pomerantz and colleagues wisely admonished that "being aware of assessment issues and developing strategies to improve the quality of virtual reference service is an important step to improving the usefulness and impact of the evaluations and ultimately improving the quality and usefulness of these services to the users."[53]

Virtual reference (VR) assessment instruments include user interviews and transcript analysis. Some VR software allows for a brief exit interview that reveals the user's immediate satisfaction with the reference transaction, including technological ease, prompt response, and the librarian's willingness and ability to highlight needed resources. The follow-up interview, generally two or three weeks later, determines actual use of recommended resources, information fulfillment of user's need, and the user's likelihood to again utilize the service. The transcript analysis from chat or email reference transactions provides a wealth of data on accuracy and completeness of information provided, reference interview thoroughness, and the librarian's communication style.

The final assessment report should specifically and succinctly address evaluation criteria most relevant to the identified stakeholders. Evaluators should objectively present data and recommendations to aid decision makers. A meaningful exchange of ideas among service participants can be substantiated with assessment reports of service strengths and needed enhancements. "It is critical that evaluations of online reference services be conducted well, so that they are useful to stakeholders in making decisions that can affect the very future of the service and the library itself," observes Pomerantz.[54]

Guidelines from the library profession provide a framework for assessment. As stated in the *Professional Competencies for Reference and User Services Librarians* (RUSA 2003), "Consistent assessment of resources in the context of users' need plus evaluation of the delivery of information services is necessary."[55] The *Guidelines for Implementing and Maintaining Virtual Reference Services* (RUSA 2004) state, "Evaluation of the virtual reference service should be equivalent to and part of a library's regular evaluation of reference services."[56]

The *Standards for Distance Learning Library Services* by the Association of College and Research Libraries (2008) describe the assessment responsibilities of the virtual reference librarian: (1) Prepare a written profile of users' needed information and skills; (2) Utilize an evaluation checklist for librarian and tutorial instruction to acquire feedback from users, librarians, and instructors; (3) Organize focus groups of students, instructors, and alumni, for commentary on their distance learning experiences; (4) Assess user need for electronic library resources; (5) Assess user need for library-related services, including instruction and information literacy; (6) Compare the library's distance learning program to peer libraries; and (7) Participate in campus assessment of programs.[57]

ASSESSMENT SUMMARY

Having an ongoing assessment procedure in place ensures that assessment occurs, prioritizes the procedure with other work goals, directs efforts and data toward an understandable outcome, and utilizes assessment recommendations for continual quality improvement. Pomerantz charges librarians: "Evaluation in general is not for the faint of heart. . . . Nevertheless, ongoing evaluation of virtual reference services is essential to improving those services."[58]

SUMMARY

Each library will face unique challenges in establishing and maintaining a virtual reference service at their institution. One consistent challenge of virtual reference is the general lack of a reference interview, or the distinct need to revise the traditional reference interview to fit the scale of the virtual service. Reference librarians have preached the gospel of the reference interview for decades. Library schools teach it, librarians practice it on a daily basis at the reference desk, and dozens of books and articles talk about it.

Nilsen and Ross, at the University of Western Ontario, discuss virtual reference services as a component of their long-term research project, The Library Visit Study (2006). They compare users' satisfaction with virtual reference service to similar face-to-face reference service. Their study indicates that the reference interview has almost disappeared. Among the reasons identified for staff failure to conduct reference interviews in the virtual environment are: the nature of written vs. spoken interaction, the librarian's perceived need to respond quickly in this environment, and the rudimentary nature of the forms used in email reference. "[U]sers expect things to be quick in the electronic environment—that they should be able to type in a few keywords and get an answer at the click of a button."[59] However, this idea is flawed. If that approach was going to work, the user would have simply Googled the answer and probably not sought an *Ask a Librarian* service at all. "[T]ypically users of virtual reference service have already tried and failed to answer the question on their own."[60]

For persons with disabilities, particularly visual, virtual reference creates a longer list of obstacles. As with other forms of service, libraries included, accessibility difficulties exist almost naturally. Planning and design that addresses accessibility issues from the start is not common. However, software has been especially designed for print-impaired individuals. InfoEyes Information Service is the first virtual reference program in the United States designed for blind or visually impaired (as well as print-impaired) people. "[It] would offer all the usual components of any mainstream virtual reference service that had developed by 2004. Thus, it would offer the possibility for its patrons to communicate with a librarian through email, live chat, or a live session using Voice over Internet Protocol (IP) with co-browsing and page pushing capabilities."[61] Originally planned as a component of OCLC's QuestionPoint software, creators switched to Talking Communities (iVocalize) for live sessions, co-browsing, and chat, while keeping the email and management system on QuestionPoint. As true of other virtual reference services, some degree of fallibility is inevitable. Some problems with InfoEyes have been identified: a need for more hours, promotion of services, the need to explore connections with mainstream virtual reference, and the need for additional funding.[62]

In virtual communities such as Second Life, a drawback has been the lack of support from electronic resource publishers. "When it comes to virtual reference, such as chat, libraries have a policy of 'sending no full text' articles because licensing agreements do not cover virtual users, even if the user is affiliated with the library. Therefore, the librarian needs to be familiar with open sourced materials."[63] Like real-world reference and other forms of digital reference, virtual world reference also shares the cumbersome challenges of accessibility, approachability, visibility, and usability.

Inevitably, some libraries will choose to close a virtual service based on cost, staff time, or technical difficulties. In her 2007 study, Stephanie Walker investigated the reasons behind the cessation of nine virtual reference services. Major reasons for discontinuation fell into six categories: funding problems, staffing problems, technical problems, institutional culture conflicts, low usage overall, and low usage by target populations. "In future launches of virtual reference services, both extensive pre-planning and detailed measures for evaluation could be helpful in avoiding [discontinuations]."[64]

Pohlman, Skrien, Sollien, and Waitz succinctly describe the present state of academic library services: "No academic library exists as an insular entity . . . The challenge we face is transforming the view of the library from a place that circulates books to an entity that plays a role in the academic achievement of our learners."[65] The value of electronic resources, available anytime anywhere, surpasses that of physical resources from a library user's perspective. Not limited to time and space, users voice satisfaction with the virtual libraries' "anytime" orientation. As in the past, students are not always selective regarding their sources or their authenticity. They often ignore prime print resources, choosing instead to wade through millions of search engine hits. Time is a precious commodity to them, although they often consume large amounts of it inefficiently, due to their use of search engines such as Google. The virtual reference librarian's role is to maintain and expand the interaction between the virtual user and the library professional. Staying current and familiar with search engine protocols, web resources, and present communication technologies continues to put librarians at the critical juncture of effectively uniting users with needed information. Virtual reference librarians cannot accomplish their purpose in isolation. In order for information literacy, the precursor to lifelong learning, to imprint upon our users, it needs to be an integral part of academic curriculum.

Finally, Connaway and Radford remind the virtual library profession of a continual challenge: "We are no longer the only game in town and currently are not the first to be chosen. With work, we can make our resources and services inviting to the next generation of students, scholars, teachers, and researchers."[66]

Many distance learning students who are back in school have full-time jobs and have families. Virtual reference services are an appealing and necessary part of their academic experience; librarians, using a variety of technological offerings, may not be seen, but our presence can still be felt.

MINI-CASE: FIVE LAWS OF VIRTUAL REFERENCE

Shiyali Ramamrita Ranganathan's (1892–1972) *Five Laws of Library Science* (1931) serve as the basic philosophy of the library profession: (1) Books are for use; (2) Every reader his or her book; (3) Every book its reader; (4) Save the time of the reader; (5) A library is a growing organism. The "growing organism" analogy is certainly applicable to the rapid growth of the virtual information world.

Alireza Noruzi of the Department of Information Science, University of Paul Cezanne, Marseille, France, discussed how to best apply Ranganathan's *Five Laws* to the web (2004) and suggested these "Five Laws of the Web"*: 1) Web resources are for use; (2) Every user his or her web resource; (3) Every web resource its user; (4) Save the time of the user; (5) The Web is a growing organism.

If you were to author *The Five Laws of Virtual Reference,* what would you write?

1.
2.
3.
4.
5.

---

*Alireza Noruzi, "Application of Ranganathan's Laws to the Web," *Webology* 1, no. 2 (Dec. 2004), http://www.webology.org/2004/v1n2/a8.html.

MINI-CASE: VIRTUAL REFERENCE SERVICE (VRS) DEFINITION

Dr. Joseph Janes of the Information School at the University of Washington and founding director of the Internet Public Library, articulated a philosophical question:

"Does 'reference' really mean anything to anybody these days?"

Do our users know the meaning of Virtual Reference Service?

What do you think would be a more descriptive title? Please explain your response.

MINI-CASE: ONLINE TUTORIALS

In his landmark article "Is Google Making Us Stupid," (The Atlantic, July/ August 2008, http://www.theatlantic.com/magazine/archive/2008/07/ is-google-making-us-stupid/6868/) Nicholas Carr makes the following observations:

> Over the past few years I've had an uncomfortable sense that someone, or something, has been tinkering with my brain, remapping the neural circuitry, reprogramming the memory. . . . I think I know what's going on. For more than a decade now, I've been spending a lot of time online, searching and surfing and sometimes adding to the great databases of the Internet. . . . And what the Net seems to be doing is chipping away my capacity for concentration and contemplation. My mind now expects to take in information the way the Net distributes it: in a swiftly moving stream of particles. Once I was a scuba diver in the sea of words. Now I zip along the surface like a guy on a Jet Ski. . . . . . We risk turning into pancake people—spread wide and thin as we connect with that vast network of information accessed by the mere touch of a button.

What would be your methodology to guard against becoming a pancake person?

REFERENCES

Aldrich, Alan, and Carol Leibiger. "Face It! Reference Work and Politeness Theory Go Hand in Hand." Paper presented at the Proceedings of the 14th National Conference of the Association of College and Research Libraries, Seattle, WA, 2009.

Association of College and Research Libraries. "Information Literacy Competency Standards for Higher Education." American Library Association, 2000. http://www.ala.org/ala/mgrps/divs/acrl/standards/ informationliteracycompetency.cfm.

Association of College and Research Libraries. "Standards for Distance Learning Library Services." American Library Association, July 1, 2008. http://www.ala.org/ala/mgrps/divs/acrl/standards/guidelinesdistancelearning.cfm.

Association of College and Research Libraries. "Debating the Future of the Reference Desk." http://acrlog.org/.

Atlas, Michael. "Library Anxiety in the Reference Era." *Reference & User Services Quarterly* 44, no. 4 (2005 Summer): 314–19.

Auster, Ethel, and Donna Chan. "Reference Librarians and Keeping Up-To-Date: A Question of Priorities." *Reference & User Services Quarterly* 44, no. 1 (2004 Fall): 59–68.

Bell, Steven. "Who Needs a Reference Desk?" *Library Issues,* no. 6 (2007). http://www.libraryissues.com/.

Black, Nancy. "Blessing or Curse? Distance Delivery to Students with Invisible Disabilities." *Journal of Library Administration* 41, no. 1/2 (2004): 47–64.

Bopp, Richard, and Linda Smith. *Reference and Information Services.* Third ed. Englewood, CO: Libraries Unlimited, 2001.

Borgman, Christine. "Digital Libraries and Virtual Universities." In *Access to Knowledge: New Information Technologies and the Emergence of the Virtual University,* edited by F. Tschang and T. Senta. Oxford: Elsevier Science, 2001.

Breitbach, William, Matthew Mallard, and Robert Sage. "Using Meebo's Embedded IM for Academic Reference Services: A Case Study." *Reference Services Review* 37, no. 1 (2008): 83–98.

Briscoe, E., H. Mercado, and M. Albertson. "Information Professionals in the Driver's Seat—Part 2." *Library Hi Tech News* 157 (1998 November): 5–16.

Buckley, Chad. "Golden Rule Reference: Face-to-Face and Virtual." *The Reference Librarian* 45, no. 93 (2006): 129–36.

Campbell, Jerry. "Changing a Cultural Icon: The Academic Library as a Virtual Destination." *EDUCAUSE Review* 41, no. 1 (2006): 16–31.

Casey, Anne Marie, ed. *Off-Campus Library Services.* New York: Haworth Information Press, 2001.

Chakraborty, Mou, and Johanna Tunon. "Taking the Distance Out of Library Services Offered to International Graduate Students: Considerations, Challenges, and Concerns." *Journal of Library Administration* 37, no. 1 (2002): 163–76.

Coffman, Steve. *Going Live: Starting and Running a Virtual Reference Desk.* Chicago: American Library Association, 2003.

Coffman, Steve, and Linda Arret. "To Chat or Not to Chat—Taking Another Look at Virtual Reference, Part I." *Searcher* 12, no. 7 (2004): 38.

Connaway, Lynn Silipigni. "Make Room for the Millennials." In *NextSpace: The OCLC Newsletter:* OCLC, 2008.

Connaway, Lynn Silipigni, Marie Radford, and Jocelyn Williams. "Engaging Net Gen Students in Virtual Reference: Reinventing Services to Meet Their Information Behaviors and Communication Preferences." Paper presented at the 14th National Conference of the Association of College and Research Libraries, Seattle, WA, 2009.

Dempsey, Lorcan. "Always On: Libraries in a World of Permanent Connectivity." *First Monday,* no. 1–5 (January 2009). http://firstmonday.org/htbin/cgiwrap/bin/ojs/index.php/fm/article/viewArticle/2291.

Erdman, Jacquelyn . "Reference in a 3-D Virtual World: Preliminary Observations on Library Outreach in "Second Life." *The Reference Librarian* 47, no. 2 (2007): 29–39.

Estabrook, Leigh, and Lee Rainie. "In Search of Solutions: How People Use the Internet, Libraries, and Government Agencies to Find Help." In *Pew Internet & American Life Project.* Champaign: University of Illinois, December 2007. http://www.pewinternet.org/~/media//Files/Reports/2007/Pew_UI_LibrariesReport.pdf.pdf.

Gandhi, Smiti. "Academic Librarians and Distance Education: Challenges and Opportunities." *Reference & User Services Quarterly* 43, no. 2 (2003): 138–54.

Green, Samuel S. "Personal Relations between Librarians and Readers." *Library Journal* 1 (1876): 74–81.

Janes, Joseph. "What Is Reference For?" *Reference Services Review* 31, no. 1 (2003): 22–25.

Janes, Joseph, and Joanne Silverstein. "Question Negotiation and the Technological Environment." *D-Lib Magazine* 9, no. 2 (February 2003). http://www.dlib.org/dlib/february03/janes/02janes.html.

Katz, William A. *Introduction to Reference Work: Volume I, Basic Information Sources.* II vols. New York: McGraw-Hill, Inc, 1992.

Kwon, Nahyan, and Vicki Gregory. "The Effects of Librarians' Behavioral Performance on User Satisfaction in Chat Reference Services." *Reference & User Services Quarterly* 47, no. 2 (Winter 2007): 137–48.

Lankes, R. David. *The Virtual Reference Desk.* New York: Neal-Schuman, 2004.

"Library Mobile Initiatives." *Library Technology Reports* 44, no. 5 (July 2008): 33–38.

Library of Congress. Global Reference Network. http://www.loc.gov/rr/digiref (accessed January 28, 2011).

Lukasiewicz, Adrianna. "Exploring the Role of Digital Academic Libraries." *Library Review* 56, no. 9 (2007): 821–27.

Martell, Charles. "The Elusive User: Changing Use Patterns in Academic Libraries 1995–2004." *College & Research Libraries* 68, no. 5 (September 2007): 435–45.

Mathews, Brian. "Looking for What's Next: Is It Time to Start Talking About Library 2.1?" *Journal of Web Librarianship* 3, no. 2 (April 2009): 143–47.

Mattuozzi, Robert. "Library Public Relations: Recent Articles on Marketing and Branding in University Libraries." *Public Services Quarterly* 5, no. 2 (April 2009): 135–38.

McClure, Charles. *Statistics, Measures, and Quality Standards for Assessing Digital Reference Library Services.* Syracuse: Information Institute of Syracuse, School of Information Studies, Syracuse University, 2002.

McGraw, Kathleen A., Jennifer Heiland, and Julianna Harris. "Promotion and Evaluation of a Virtual Live Reference Service." *Medical Reference Services Quarterly* 22, no. 2 (July 2003): 41–56.

Nilsen, Kirsti, and Catherine S. Ross. Evaluating Virtual Reference from the User's Perspective. *Reference Librarian* 46, no. 95/96 (September 2006): 53–79.

Online Computer Library Center. "College Students' Perceptions of Libraries and Information Resources." Online Computer Library Center, http://www.oclc.org/reports/perceptionscollege.htm.

Online Computer Library Center. "Perceptions of Libraries and Information Resources: A Report to the OCLC Membership." Dublin, OH: Online Computer Library Center, 2005.

Parsad, Basmat, Laurie Lewis, and Peter Tice. *Distance Education at Degree-Granting Postsecondary Institutions: 2006–07.* Washington, DC: National Center for Education Statistics, 2008.

Peters, Tom, and Lori Bell. "Virtual Reference Services for the Print Impaired: Separate, but Not Equal." *Computers in Libraries* 26, no. 10 (November 2006): 24–27.

Pohlman, Julie, Susan Skrien, Julia Sollien, and Emily Waitz. "Challenges for Distance Students and Distant Librarians: Taking Advantage of the Online Environment." Paper presented at the Proceedings of the 14th National Conference of the Association of College and Research Libraries, Seattle, WA, 2009.

Pomerantz, Jeffrey. "Evaluation of Online Reference Services." *ASIS&T Bulletin* (December/January 2008). http://www.asis.org/Bulletin/Dec-07/pomerantz.html.

Pomerantz, Jeffrey, Lorrie Mon, and Charles McClure. "Evaluating Remote Reference Service: A Practical Guide to Problems and Solutions." *Portal: Libraries and the Academy* 8, no. 1 (2008): 15–30.

Radford, Marie. *The Reference Encounter: Interpersonal Communication in the Academic Library.* Chicago: Association of College and Research Libraries, 1999.

Radford, Marie, and Lorrie Mon. "Reference Service in Face-to-Face and Virtual Environments." In *Academic Library Research: Perspective and Current Trends,* 1–47. Chicago: Association of College and Research Libraries, 2008.

Reference and User Services Association. "Guidelines for Behavioral Performance of Reference and Information Service Providers." American Library Association. http://www.ala.org/ala/mgrps/divs/rusa/resources/guidelines/ guidelinesbehavioral.cfm (accessed January 28, 2011).

Reference and User Services Association. "Guidelines for Implementing and Maintaining Virtual Reference Services." Chicago, 2004. http://www.ala.org/ala/mgrps/divs/rusa/resources/guidelines/virtrefguidelines.cfm.

Reference and User Services Association. "Professional Competencies for Reference and User Services Librarians." Chicago, 2003. http://www.ala.org/ala/mgrps/divs/rusa/resources/guidelines/professional.cfm.

Rossman, Linda, and Catherine A. Durivage. "Infoeyes Information Service: A Virtual Reference Service for Print-Impaired Individuals." *The Reference Librarian* 50 (2009): 73–84.

Ryan, Jenna, Alice Daugherty, and Emily Mauldin. "Exploring the LSU Libraries' Virtual Reference Transcripts: An Analysis." *Electronic Journal of Academic and Special Librarianship* 7, no. 3 (2006).

Taddeo, Laura. "R U There? How to Reach a Virtual Audience through Affordable Marketing Strategies." *Internet Reference Services Quarterly* 13, no. 2/3 (April 2008): 227–44.

Ulvik, Synnove, and Gunhild Salvesen. "Ethical Reference Practice." *New Library World* 108, no. 7/8 (2007): 342–53.

Vilelle, Luke. "Marketing Virtual Reference." *College and Undergraduate Libraries* 12, no. 1 (January 2006): 65–79.

Walker, Stephanie. "Low Volume, Funding, Staffing and Technical Problems Are Key Reasons for Discontinuation of Chat Reference Services." *Evidence Based Library & Information Practice* 2, no. 3 (October 2007): 97–100.

Wan, Gang, Dennis Clark, and John Fullerton. "Key Issues Surrounding Virtual Chat Reference Model: A Case Study." *Reference Services Review* 37, no. 1 (2009): 73–82.

Zadel, Diane. "A Reference Renaissance." *Reference & User Services Quarterly* 47, no. 2 (2007): 108–10.

Zanin-Yost, Alessia. "Digital Reference: What the Past Has Taught Us and What the Future Will Hold." *Library Philosophy and Practice* 7, no. 1 (Fall 2004): 1–16

NOTES

1. Richard E. Bopp and Linda C. Smith, *Reference and Information Services: An Introduction*, 3rd ed. (Englewood, CO: Libraries Unlimited, 2001), 4.

2. Diane Zadel, "A Reference Renaissance," *Reference & User Services Quarterly* 47, no. 2 (2007): 109.

3. Basmat Parsad, Laurie Lewis, and Peter Tice, *Distance Education at Degree-Granting Postsecondary Institutions: 2006–07* (Washington, DC: National Center for Education Statistics, 2008), 3.

4. Christine Borgman, "Digital Libraries and Virtual Universities," in *Access to Knowledge: New Information Technologies and the Emergence of the Virtual University,* ed. F. Tschang and T. Senta (Oxford: Elsevier Science. 2001), 233.

5. Jerry Campbell, "Changing a Cultural Icon: The Academic Library as a Virtual Destination," *EDUCAUSE Review* 41, no. 1 (2006): 16.

6. Online Computer Library Center, Inc. (OCLC), *Perceptions of Libraries and Information Resources: A Report to the OCLC Membership* (Dublin, OH: OCLC, 2005), 2–18 [page 70] and A-14 [page 160], http://www.oclc.org/reports/pdfs/Percept_all.pdf.

7. Joanne Silverstein, "Digital Reference: An Overview," *D-Lib Magazine* 9, no. 2 (February 2003), http://www.dlib.org/dlib/february03/02guest-editorial.html.

8. Online Dictionary for Library and Information Science, s.v. "Digital Reference," http://lu.com/odlis/odlis_D.cfm#digitalref.

9. American Library Association, Reference and User Service Association (RUSA), "Guidelines for Implementing and Maintaining Virtual Reference Services," http://www.ala.org/ala/mgrps/divs/rusa/resources/guidelines/virtrefguidelines.cfm.

10. "Library Mobile Initiatives," *Library Technology Reports* 44, no. 5 (July 2008): 33–38.

11. Tom Peters and Lori Bell, "Virtual Reference Services for the Print Impaired: Separate, but Not Equal," *Computers in Libraries* 26, no. 10 (November 2006): 24–27.

12. Association of College and Research Libraries (ACRL), *Standards for Distance Learning Library Services,* American Library Association, September 1, 2006, "Executive Summary: The Access Entitlement Principle section," para. 1, http://www.acrl.org/ala/mgrps/divs/acrl/standards/guidelinesdistancelearning.cfm.

13. CLC, *College Students' Perceptions of Libraries and Information Resources* (Dublin, OH: OCLC, 2006), http://www.oclc.org/reports/pdfs/studentperceptions.pdf.

14. Marie Radford and Lorrie Mon, "Reference Service in Face-to-Face and Virtual Environments," in *Academic Library Research: Perspective and Current Trends*, ed. Marie Radford and Pamela Snelson (Chicago: Association of College and Research Libraries, 2008), 1–47.

15. ACRL, *Standards*.

16. Mou Chakraborty and Johanna Tunon, "Taking the Distance out of Library Services Offered to International Graduate Students: Considerations, Challenges, and Concerns," *Journal of Library Administration* 37, no. 1 (2002): 163–76.

17. Nancy Black, "Blessing or Curse? Distance Delivery to Students with Invisible Disabilities," *Journal of Library Administration* 41, no. 1/2 (2004): 47–64.

18. William Breitbach, Matthew Mallard, and Robert Sage, "Using Meebo's Embedded IM for Academic Reference Services: A Case Study." *Reference Services Review* 37, no. 1 (2008): 83–98.

19. Gang Wan, Dennis Clark, and John Fullerton, "Key Issues Surrounding Virtual Chat Reference Model: A Case Study," *Reference Services Review* 37, no. 1 (2009): 81.

20. Jenna Ryan, Alice Daugherty, and Emily Mauldin, "Exploring the LSU Libraries' Virtual Reference Transcripts: An Analysis," *Electronic Journal of Academic and Special Librarianship* 7, no. 3 (2006), http://southernlibrarianship.icaap.org/content/v07n03/ryan_j01.htm.

21. Brian Mathews, "Looking for What's Next: Is It Time to Start Talking About Library 2.1?," *Journal of Web Librarianship* 3, no. 2 (April 2009): 143–47.

22. Peters and Bell, "Virtual Reference Services," 24–27.

23. William A. Katz, *Introduction to Reference Work: Volume I, Basic Information Sources*. II vols. (New York: McGraw-Hill, Inc., 1992), 11–14.

24. "Debating the Future of the Reference Desk," *ACRLog*, Association for College and Research Libraries, http://acrlblog.org/2007/03/26/debating-the-future-of-the-reference-desk/.

25. Lynn Silipigni Connaway, Marie Radford, and Jocelyn Williams, "Engaging Net Gen Students in Virtual Reference: Reinventing Services to Meet Their Information Behaviors and Communication Preferences, Paper presented at the 14th National Conference of the Association of College and Research Libraries, Seattle, WA, 2009, 10.

26. Adrianna Lukasiewicz, "Exploring the Role of Digital Academic Libraries," *Library Review* 56, no. 9 (2007): 821–27.

27. Marie Radford, *The Reference Encounter: Interpersonal Communication in the Academic Library* (Chicago: Association of College and Research Libraries, 1999), 119.

28. Synnove Ulvik and Gunhild Salvesen, "Ethical Reference Practice." *New Library World* 108, no. 7/8 (2007): 342–53.

29. Chad Buckley, "Golden Rule Reference: Face-to-Face and Virtual," *The Reference Librarian* 45, no. 93 (2006): 130.

30. Alan Aldrich and Carol Leibiger, "Face It! Reference Work and Politeness Theory Go Hand in Hand," Paper presented at the *Proceedings of the 14th National Conference of the Association of College and Research Libraries* (Seattle: ACRL, 2009), 238, http://www.ala.org/ala/mgrps/divs/acrl/events/national/seattle/papers/235.pdf.

31. Radford and Mon, "Reference Service," 1–47.

32. Smiti Gandhi, "Academic Librarians and Distance Education: Challenges and Opportunities," *Reference & User Services Quarterly* 43, no. 2 (2003): 138–54.

33. Kirsti Nilsen and Catherine S. Ross, "Evaluating Virtual Reference from the Users' Perspective," *Reference Librarian* 46, no. 95/96 (September 2006): 53.

34. RUSA, "Guidelines for Behavioral Performance of Reference and Information Service Providers," 2004, http://www.ala.org/ala/mgrps/divs/rusa/resources/guidelines/guidelinesbehavioral.cfm.

35. Ibid.

36. RUSA, "Professional Competencies for Reference and User Services Librarians," 2003, http://www.ala.org/ala/mgrps/divs/rusa/resources/guidelines/professional.cfm.

37. ACRL, "Standards." See chapter 2 for an in-depth discussion of the *access entitlement principle*.

38. Association of College & Research Libraries (ACRL). "Presidential Committee on Information Literacy: Final Report," 1989, http://www.ala.org/ala/mgrps/divs/acrl/publications/whitepapers/presidential.cfm.

39. ACRL, "Standards."

40. Peters and Bell, "Virtual Reference Services," 24–27.

41. Library of Congress, Global Reference Network, www.loc.gov/rr/digiref.

42. Ibid.

43. RUSA, "Guidelines for Implementing and Maintaining Virtual Reference Services."

44. Laura Taddeo, "R U There? How to Reach a Virtual Audience through Affordable Marketing Strategies," *Internet Reference Services Quarterly* 13, no. 2/3 (April 2008): 227–44.

45. Vilelle, "Marketing Virtual Reference," 65–79.

46. William Breitbach, Matthew Mallard, and Robert Sage, "Using Meebo's Embedded IM for Academic Reference Services: A Case Study," *Reference Services Review* 37, no. 1 (2008): 83–98.

47. Steve Coffman, *Going Live: Starting and Running a Virtual Reference Desk* (Chicago: American Library Association, 2003), 77.

48. Vilelle, "Marketing Virtual Reference," 65–79.

49. Connaway, Radford, and Williams, "Engaging Net Gen Students," 17.

50. Ibid.

51. Jeffrey Pomerantz, Lorri Mon, and Charles R. McClure, "Evaluating Remote Reference Service: A Practical Guide to Problems and Solutions," *Portal: Libraries and the Academy* 8, no. 1: (2008)15–30.

52. Ibid.

53. Ibid., 28.

54. Jeffrey Pomerantz, "Evaluation of Online Reference Services," *ASIS&T Bulletin* (December/January 2008), http://www.asis.org/Bulletin/Dec-07/pomerantz.html.

55. RUSA, "Professional Competencies."

56. RUSA, "Guidelines for Implementing and Maintaining Virtual Reference Services."

57. ACRL, *Standards*.

58. Pomerantz, "Evaluation of Online Reference Services."

59. Nilsen and Ross, "Evaluating Virtual Reference," 74.

60. Ibid.

61. Linda Rossman and Catherine Durivage, "Infoeyes Information Service: A Virtual Reference Service for Print-Impaired Individuals," *The Reference Librarian* 50 (2009): 73–84.

62. Ibid.

63. Jacquelyn Erdman, "Reference in a 3-D Virtual World: Preliminary Observations on Library Outreach in 'Second Life,'" *The Reference Librarian* 47, no. 2 (2007): 36.

64. Stephanie Walker, "Low Volume, Funding, Staffing and Technical Problems Are Key Reasons for Discontinuation of Chat Reference Services," *Evidence Based Library & Information Practice* 2, no. 3 (October 2007): 97–100.

65. Julie Pohlman and others, "Challenges for Distance Students and Distant Librarians: Taking Advantage of the Online Environment," Paper presented at the Proceedings of the 14th National Conference of the Association of College and Research Libraries, Seattle, WA, 2009: 147.

66. Connaway, Radford, and Williams, "Engaging Net Gen Students," 10.

5

·—·✦·—·

DISTRIBUTED LEARNING
COPYRIGHT ISSUES

Jeff Clark

For many librarians and their staff, the most daunting responsibility to address in meeting teaching and learning needs are copyright issues. Most of the library resources that we deal with have owners under copyright law—and as professionals who provide services related to these resources we are obliged to apply copyright (and other intellectual property) law in an ethical and consistent way. But the nature of copyright law, which strives to meet the evolution of copyrightable information formats and of owner interests and user markets, doesn't make this task easy. It isn't helped, either, by a relative absence of copyright education in library and information studies.[1]

Distributed learning over networks—whether involving true distance learners, or a blended/hybrid course strategy that mingles online learning with interaction in a physical classroom—complicates the handling of copyright-related services even further. In a networked environment, every right of control belonging to the copyright owner of a work can be impacted to a greater degree than with physical collections and campuses alone.

The distributed learning environment presents these broad challenges:

- Lack of definitive guidance from copyright law that addresses use within the typical course or learning management system environment: Apart from licensing terms (which supplant copyright law), most of the thinking and decisions we make about using copyrighted works is drawn from precedent, court decisions, and traditional practice in a physical or analog-copy environment. How we have handled copies for classroom teaching and reserves in the physical library tends to condition their use in an online environment. The law always lags behind the educational possibilities opened up by technological change.

- Need for thorough development and coordination of copyright-related service policies, sometimes across service administrative areas as well as with faculty and students: distributed learning librarians may manage instructional development and learning management systems or may only complement, advise, or use them. Regardless of librarian input, all of the services offered beyond the library's own domain should at the very least coordinate in providing copyrighted resources. If a cohesive plan institution-wide is possible, so much the better.

- Licensed resources: Licensed or subscribed library resources increasingly accommodate course management system environments, through terms of use and the provision of stable URLs or web addresses for linking. But distributed learning librarians who negotiate licenses should remain aware of changing instructional strategies that may tax the limits of a typical license that used to be sufficient for most needs.

- The relationship of course management support services with library e-reserves: This is a particularly difficult and sensitive problem—especially when each service area is administered separately and can only coordinate their policies. Can there be a difference in the purpose and practical use of e-reserves and a learning management system? Are they subject to different policy considerations under copyright law? (These and other issues are fully addressed in chapter 6, which examines e-reserves and related specific library services such as Interlibrary Loan.)

- Finally, the trend toward Web or Library 2.0 applications and activities: chapter 2 mentions RSS feeds, blogs, wikis, and delivery of content to mobile devices.[2] All of these were a step beyond the routine features of management systems until recently, and uses of copyrighted work in this extended environment often challenge licensing terms, or (where these don't apply) the application of library rights and Fair Use justification to their limits.

METHODOLOGY

First, a note on recurring acronyms. Distributed learning, and where appropriate the distributed librarianship that supports it, are referred to as DL. Course or learning management systems of all types are referred to as CMS. (Restricted access wikis, social network applications, and services may be considered equivalent in a given situation.) Orphan works, covered by copyright but without apparent owners, are referred to as OW. The copyright-free range of works that are in the public domain are referred to as PD. Traditional classroom teaching within the physical campus, involving face-to-face instruction, is referred to as F2F. And the encoded U.S. legal doctrine of fair use—so important to all users of copyrighted works, institutional and individual—has no common acronym but is always capitalized as Fair Use.

This chapter offers a basic understanding of current United States copyright law, focused on the rights of owners and exceptions to those rights that are relevant to educational institutions (as well as other users), in the context of distributed learning wherever possible.

Topics are organized into grouped sections: "What Copyright Covers" through "Complications to Infringement and Use: Licensing" sketch the development of the copyright concept in law, define the copyright owner's rights under it, and present the licensing strategy that qualifies and may extend those rights; "The Rights of Users in the Distributed Learning (DL) Environment" through "Summary Considerations in DL Support" discuss the subject of the user's complementary "rights"—in the form of limitations on the owner's exclusive rights—under U.S. copyright law. This part of the chapter offers a discussion of how copyrighted works may be used in a distributed learning environment and introduces a set of practical scenarios that involve elements of copyright law in their analysis. The chapter's second half strives to simplify and clarify strategies for addressing real service needs, always assuming that that library and DL support staff will be applying them on behalf of their faculty and students. The specifics of copyright law outlined in the first half should inform the strategies for applying it when using a given work in the distributed learning environment. Entire books have been written that address every provision of U.S. copyright law comprehensively, in a way that this chapter cannot. Instead, to support key issues in distributed learning librarianship the author has identified several important works in the References section that may extend the reader's understanding of copyright. In addition, charts, checklists, and model forms for reference when implementing services and policies are provided in them.

The author offers the usual disclaimer of one profession to another, which occurs even where opinions are based in formal legal training: my interpretation and application of the law is intended to be educational but not considered definitive legal advice. Only a lawyer dealing with the specifics of a situation, where a service activity has the potential to infringe an owner's rights, can exhaustively analyze the user's and owner's rights in regard to copyright and any other law that may apply.

What Copyright Covers

Throughout the western world, the concept of copyright has tended to focus on works of the intellect. Human expressions conveying ideas, information, emotions, enlightenment, and entertainment—sometimes all at once—are the product of human thought, experience, and an aptitude or talent for transforming them creatively into something of value to other people in society. Many of these expressions are transitory in nature, products of speech and action in our daily lives; copyright tends not to deal with them directly (see below for one qualification). However, where an expression is creative, socially useful, and is subject to widespread dissemination in order to maximize its utility, the value of the expression has come to make it resemble property—a form of *intellectual* rather than *real* property.

United States law offers protection for works of the intellect in the form of copyright for original works of authorship, patents for utilitarian inventions, and trademarks for identifying symbols or devices. We will cover only copyright in this chapter, since its impact on DL services is the most relevant.

U.S. copyright law is outlined in Title 17 of the United States Code (USC). Under 17 USC §102, the characteristics of copyrightable works are defined as these:

- containing originality in their authorship
- as being fixed in "any tangible medium of expression, now known or later developed, from which they can be perceived, reproduced or otherwise communicated either directly or with the aid of a machine or device" (17 USC §106).

- taking a traditionally recognized expressive form defined in the statute (17 USC §102):

  - literary
  - musical (including words)
  - dramatic (including music)
  - pantomimes and choreography
  - pictorial, graphic, sculptural
  - motion pictures, audiovisual
  - sound recordings
  - architectural drawings and blueprints
  - photographs
  - cartoons
  - computer software

What *cannot* be copyrighted in general are an idea, process system, method of operation, concept, principle, or discovery (historical and scientific facts), however unique. Some of these may be eligible for other forms of intellectual property protection, but not copyright. Copyright protects only the tangible expression of ideas, creative imagination, even facts when these take a particular form and organization that is both original and fixed. "Fixed" includes not only traditional publishing means in print or other hard media (such as DVDs) but also websites, emails, and other tangible expressions within a networked environment (blogs, wikis).[3]

What follows from the characteristics cited above is the commonly referenced principle of the idea/expression dichotomy. If a work contains a mix of facts and ideas along with creative elements and organization, it is protectable as a whole because of the originality involved (not the facts and ideas). In a famous Supreme Court decision, *Feist Publications v. Rural Telephone Service,* 499 US 340 (1991), the common telephone directory was found to be unoriginal enough to warrant no protection under copyright law.[4] A directory contains public or discoverable facts (names, addresses, and of course phone numbers), arranged in a logical, common-sense way—alphabetically by surname.

Above we spoke of transitory expression, which is not eligible for copyright. However, a common situation that changes this status frequently occurs in educational settings. A professor lectures her students in a physical classroom. This act has no copyright protection, unless and until: (a) the lecture is delivered from a prepared script, outline, or notes, or (b) the delivered lecture is recorded by some means. The lecture outline or notes (which presumably contain creative insight and conclusions), and the recording of the lecture's delivery (whether from an outline or improvised on the spot), each constitute a work now fixed and separate from its live (and unprotected) performance-in-the-moment by the professor. When using course management, web conferencing, or other synchronous group communications systems, this situation is often likely to apply—since participants prepare in advance and events are often archived. Therefore, lectures prepared and/or recorded qualify as fixed expressions that are copyrightable. Looking further into DL technology, synchronous chats that are archived for later review and use are also copyrightable.

One final important point about the concept of copyright treats the distinction between the expressive work of the intellect and its fixed tangible form. The encoded form makes the work eligible for copyright, but only the work itself is protected—not the *copy* in which it is fixed. We'll return to this distinction when discussing an owner's rights and the limitations on them that benefit a user.

Copyright's Origins and Purpose

The formal history of copyright began in 1710 with England's *Statute of Anne*. Its full title suggests the purpose of restoring order to the book trade: *An Act for the Encouragement of Learning, by Vesting the Copies of Printed Books in the Authors or Purchasers of such Copies during the Times therein mentioned.* Unauthorized reprinting of works was outlawed through this law.

Nearly 80 years later, in 1787, the United States articulated the power to establish its own copyright and other intellectual property law as part of its Constitution:

> The Congress shall have Power . . . to Promote the Progress of Science and the useful Arts, by securing for limited Times to Authors and Inventors the exclusive right to their respective Writings and Discoveries. (U.S. Const. art. I, §8, cl. 8)

President George Washington signed the first Copyright Act into law in 1790. Successive revisions of the Act occurred in 1831, 1909, and most substantially in 1976. The Copyright Act of 1976 set the template for subsequent modifications. Among other things, it codified the types of works covered by copyright,[5] the exclusive rights of the copyright owner, the principle of Fair Use, and it established a uniform term of protection for works, without formalities of registration, renewal, and posting of copyright notice.

Evolving national laws began to synchronize with the Berne Convention for the Protection of Literary and Artistic Works in 1886. Berne signatories agreed to coordinate national copyright law by extending to foreign copyright holders the same levels of protection they afford their own citizens. Formal adoption of Berne has spanned decades, with the United States signing over 100 years after its inception (1989).[6] The World Intellectual Property Organization (WIPO) has addressed other areas of international agreement as well, all of them in various states of coordination.[7] From this inevitable movement toward convergence, "[t]he shape of Western copyright was settled [. . .] and integrated into the global free trade area with the WTO [World Trade Organization] TRIPS [Trade Related Aspects of Intellectual Property] Agreement of 1994. The regime combines a nod to the creator—exemplified by a term of protection derived from the author's life—with the economic structure of transferable property rights, creating a market for cultural productions."[8]

Since the last full-scale revision of U.S. law in the Copyright Act of 1976, several acts have addressed specific applications of the copyright law.[9] We will mention two of the most important developments here:

• The Sonny Bono Copyright Term Extension Act (CTEA, 1998) extended additional copyright protection of 20 years to works already existing and to those created henceforth, and in so doing brought them into closer alignment with other international copyright protection.[10] Under 17 USC §108, libraries and archives open to the general public are enabled to exercise their rights (discussed in more detail below) if a work is not currently under commercial exploitation.

• The Digital Millennium Copyright Act strove to bring copyright protection into the digital age.[11] The DMCA in effect tightened restrictions on using copyrighted works in a digital environment. Its most famous provisions (in 17 USC §1201) prohibit the act of circumventing technological access controls (with a few narrow exceptions), and prohibit the traffic in devices for circumventing *access* and *use controls* (such as for copying) designed into a work.[12] In addition, the DMCA established a "take down and notice" procedure for infringement challenges that adds to the administrative burden for users defending themselves. However, conditional protection for registered Service Providers was granted. By definition educational institutions of all kinds, as well as public libraries can register as Service Providers.[13]

These two 1998 legal developments were promoted as well as criticized as measures intended to synchronize U.S. law with international obligations under WIPO and the WTO treaties and agreements.

We observed that works protected by copyright are regarded as socially useful, or (in the Constitution's language) "Promot[ing] the Progress of Science and the useful Arts." The protection of copyright law seeks to implement this benefit.

However, the notion of copyright has prompted two divergent poles of thought historically. One argues that works of the intellect are an original expression of their creators and therefore should be owned by them as a "natural right." The other views ownership of work of the mind as a privilege granted the creator by society, with society as the benefactor.

Two French thinkers of the 18th century embody these poles of thought:

• On the one hand, Denis Diderot wrote, "What form of wealth could belong to a man, if not a work of the mind . . . if not his own thoughts, . . . the most precious part of himself, that will never perish, that will immortalize him?"

• On the other, the Marquis de Condorcet opined, "There can be no relationship between property in ideas and that in a field, which can serve only one man. [Literary property] is not a property derived from the natural order . . . It is not a true right, it is a privilege."[14]

The tenor of American thought and law has tended to favor privilege via statutory law. The granting of legal powers in the U.S. Constitution to protect "Writings and Discoveries" "to Promote the Progress of Science and the useful Arts" identifies the purpose of intellectual property law not as benefit for the author, inventor, or other creator or owner of a work, but for the society of which they are part. The securing of "exclusive right" to authors and other creators in their works is in effect a utilitarian means to an end: enhancing the prospect that the fruits of intellectual activity will be shared throughout society, via a tangible benefit to the creator. As numerous scholars have observed,[15] the incentives for creative authors to share their work are varied: profits from publishing royalties and licensing fees for further uses by others (after all, a creative person is engaged in the equivalent of gainful employment if her output is of social value); further, "the sheer joy of having one's work read and enjoyed by others and [. . .] non-economic incentives in the form of increased acclaim or reputation for the author."[16] (For academics in higher education, of course, publishing is usually a necessary condition for achieving tenure and continued employment.) Human motivations for creativity are varied and even changeable over the course of a productive life.

A final notion related to American copyright is that of "balance." Our copyright law's provisions are meant to balance the needs and rights of both owners and users. This perspective almost logically follows from the original clause in our Constitution, which secures exclusive rights for authors as a means to the end of promoting "progress," or benefit to society in general. Limited rights serve the ultimate goal, as it has been aptly put: "[W]orks are relegated to the public domain to become the heritage of all humanity and copyright is simply a temporary way station to reward authors on the road to that greater good."[17] Once the limited right to protection is over, the owner's work belongs to a general public who can use it freely at will. (We will discuss the concept of public domain, or PD, in more detail in the following section "Beyond Copyright Protection: The Public Domain.")

Copyright Ownership

The initial ownership of original works of authorship under copyright falls into one of two broad categories:

1. The individual (or individuals, if joint authorship) who perform the actual creative work. Within a collective work, each contributory work is owned by its author—except as applies below. (17 USC §201(c))
2. An employer, if the creative effort is deemed to be a *work made for hire* (prepared in the course and scope of employment). An independent contractor who is *specially ordered or commissioned* to create for one of nine statutory categories, documented with a signed agreement, is also in a *for hire* relationship with regard to that work. Included are contributions to collective works, to motion pictures or other audiovisual works, as a translation, as a supplement to another work, as a compilation, an instructional text, test or answer materials, and as an atlas. (17 USC §101)

Beyond this initial assignment, the copyright owner can then:

- Transfer specific rights under copyright[18]
- License specific rights, for use over a period of time

Ownership in Higher Education—a Relevant Variation

Within higher education, when a work is produced by faculty and staff in situations not clearly *for hire* as part of employment, copyright ownership and transfer activities take two common forms:

- Initial assignment of ownership: Institutions normally make no claim on the routine scholarly output of faculty practicing their disciplines, such as research literature and textbooks, artistic works (e.g., novels, paintings, photography), even classroom lectures and handouts. For scientific research, ownership of output is normally dictated by terms of granting agencies. But DL often presents a new wrinkle to the notion of ownership of teaching activities: teaching in this way may produce many reusable instructional components and draws upon material resources provided by the institution in an unusual degree (including faculty stipends for developing online courses). Therefore, it is common for the institution to have an intellectual property policy that stipulates an ownership arrangement for course teaching elements in DL that is different than for face-to-face (F2F) teaching. Institutional policies may claim full ownership of distributed learning course materials, or more often claim a co-ownership, in the equivalent of a "non-exclusive license" that permits use of such instructional materials even if the faculty member leaves the institution and/or markets the work commercially on her own. As regards marketing a work, an institution may specify a shared profit scheme (whether or not it involves itself in the marketing directly or leaves this to the faculty to pursue).[19]

- Transfer of ownership: Even when the faculty member has full claim to ownership of the product of her scholarly activities, the traditional publishing process usually requires the transfer of rights to the publisher. This common practice in serials publishing of scholarly literature has been hotly countered by an "open access" movement in recent years. Developments include The Public Library of Science, Creative Commons Licenses (referenced in the following section "Beyond Copyright Protection: The Public Domain"), retention of faculty authors' self-archiving rights, and the encouragement by many institutions of their faculty to modify publishing contracts in ways that benefit continued independent use by the faculty (such as sharing with students and colleagues) and by their universities (such as creating institutional repositories with general public access). Nevertheless, there is also debate on open access' practical consequences for traditional publishing, and for the library and its institution's role in and ability to support alternative publishing models. At the time of this writing, the NIH (National Institutes of Health) mandate regarding PubMed Central availability of published research that is funded by its grants is being contested in the U.S. Congress.[20] The NIH mandate has been a very public, leading-edge example of the mixed reception of open access philosophy, and so the evolution of this movement may take unexpected turns in the years ahead.[21]

In sum, there are two practical lessons to draw from the nuances of copyright ownership discussed here:

- If permission to use a work is sought, the user may need to apply careful effort to determine the true owner who can grant it.
- Where work is produced in the course of academic instruction and research, faculty and their institutions should attempt to establish ownership conditions that permit it to be usable in the DL environment from the outset whenever possible.

Exclusive Rights of the Copyright Owner (17 USC §106)

Exclusive rights of the copyright holder are defined as:

Right to reproduce the work: This includes any form of copying: transcription, duplication, and digitization—whether in the same form as the original or in an alternative form that embodies the work. Take the simple example of a printed book. A copy can be transcribed by hand, by word-processor, by photocopier, by camera that photographs the pages, or by scanner that digitizes them. It is the copyright holder, usually the author or other creator, *not* the owner of the physical book, who holds the rights to make any such copies.

Right to distribute the work to the public: The reproduction right is not a public activity, but the distribution right is. Whether a work is disseminated to others in copies that are its official publication form or not, the owner's right of control applies. This distribution right may involve selling, leasing, renting or lending. Formal limitations on this right enable qualifying libraries and archives to engage in lending activities, including interlibrary loan, and certain preservation activities. Their impact on distributed learning is discussed in the section "Rights for Eligible Libraries and Archives (17 USC §108)."

Right to prepare derivative works based upon the copyrighted work: This enables the copyright holder to modify the work, to create other works based upon it or to license others to do so. The simplest example is the case of a movie based upon a novel or play. The movie is derivative of the literary work, and represents a new copyrightable work in itself. A literary work that is translated into another language is also a derivative work. Even the amateur activity of creating an unauthorized screenplay from a movie or TV show—a product that can be found readily on the Internet, provided by fans—is a derivative work, as is so-called "fan fiction" that narrates the further adventures of literary characters. A photograph of an artistic work—painting or statue, for example—may be considered a derivative work if it has sufficient original elements as part of its execution. (A web search will find many different photographs of a multi-faceted sculpture like Henry Moore's "Nuclear Energy," each of them copyrightable because of the perspective and facets of the three-dimensional work being captured in the image.) Finally, modification to an original photograph itself—very common on the Internet—may also be argued as a derivative work. A prominent recent example was the dispute over Shepard Fairey's "Hope" poster art, which modified a news photo of Barack Obama.[22] A complete legal definition of derivative works can be found in 17 USC §101.

Right to perform or display the work publicly: A creative work that unfolds sequentially in order to be experienced—a musical composition, motion picture, software application—is being performed. Performed works may also be displayed—a frame from a movie, a screen-shot of a software operation. Other works are primarily meant for display, such as fine art and photographs. Even reading a book is a performance, and visually projecting a selection of its pages is a display. When either performance or display occurs in a public setting—to an unspecific audience in general, "outside of a normal circle of a family and its social acquaintances" (17 USC §101, definition of "publicly")—this is considered a public activity controllable by the copyright holder. Entire service industries have supported this right, such as those that rent copies and license video versions of movies for public screenings. Exceptions to this right are made in the case of the teaching environment (under 17 USC §110), and we'll deal with those below.

More specific rights under 106 and 106A: These include the copyright owner's control over digital transmission of sound recordings to the public (which enables, for example, the sales activities of a service like iTunes), and the creator's control over the attribution and integrity of unique or limited-edition fine art works (often called "moral rights").

Since 1978 (the effective date of the 1976 Copyright Act) all works are protected, and the owner's exclusive rights apply, without any formal copyright notice or registration with the Copyright Office. However, registration *is* a prerequisite to litigation for statutory damages due to unauthorized infringement. The Copyright owner's posting of any form of the copyright notice on the work itself weakens a defendant's claim to innocent infringement that is not "willful." (See "Copyright Infringement: The Potential Consequences.")

Duration of Copyright Protection

Under U.S. law differences in protection remain, depending on when a work was created or published. Table 1 shows the basic framework of U.S. copyright coverage.

Table 1   When Works Pass into the Public Domain

DATE OF WORK	PROTECTED FROM	TERM
Created Jan. 1, 1978 or after	When work is fixed in tangible medium of expression	Life + 70 years[1] or if work of corporate authorship, the shorter of 95 years from publication, or 120 years from creation[2]
Published before 1923	In public domain	None
Published from 1923–1963	When published with notice[3]	28 years + could be renewed for 47 years, now extended by 20 years for a total renewal of 67 years. If not so renewed, now in public domain
Published from 1964–1977	When published with notice	28 years for first term; now automatic extension of 67 years for second term
Created before Jan. 1, 1978 but not published	Jan. 1, 1978, the effective date of the 1976 Act which eliminated common law copyright	Life + 70 years or Dec. 31, 2002, whichever is greater
Created before Jan. 1, 1978 but published between then and Dec. 31, 2002	Jan. 1, 1978, the effective date of the 1976 Act which eliminated common law copyright	Life + 70 years or Dec, 31, 2047 whichever is greater

1 Term of joint works is measured by life of the longest-lived author.
2 Works for hire, anonymous and pseudonymous works also have this term. 17 U.S.C. §302(c).
3 Under the 1909 Act, works published without notice went into the public domain upon publication. Works published without notice between 1-1-78 and 3-1-89, effective date of the Berne Convention Implementation Act, retained copyright only if efforts to correct the accidental omission of notice was made within five years, such as by placing notice on unsold copies. 17 U.S.C. §405.

(Notes courtesy of Professor Tom Field, Franklin Pierce Law Center and Lolly Gasaway.)
Chart and notes are available at: http://www.unc.edu/~unclng/public-d.htm. Laura N. Gasaway, *When Works Pass into the Public Domain* (last updated November 4, 2003), http://www.unc.edu/~un clng/public-d.htm. Permission to reproduce granted in e-mail message to author, June 9, 2009.

Further Qualifications for Copyright Duration and Coverage

UNPUBLISHED WORKS:

Works that were created but never published—a broad range that can include letters and other historical documents, raw research data, and even computer programming—had a perpetual "common law" protection before the 1976 Copyright Act. Since that time, unpublished works (originating both before and after 1976) generally receive the same protection period as published works (excepting 120 years in the case of corporate authorship). Still, caution is advised when using unpublished works without first seeking permission. In particular, most recent court rulings "have established a relatively narrow application of Fair Use to unpublished works."[23]

WORKS PROTECTED BY FOREIGN NATIONAL COPYRIGHT:

Default protection is the principle of "national treatment"—meaning that works of foreign authorship receive protection equivalent to that afforded U.S. copyright owners. When using such works in an open access environment like the Internet, however, the situation is more complex and the case law unsettled. The copyright laws of the country offering the non-U.S. work on its servers may apply for users who access it from that location, but these laws may not apply for international users who access it from other countries. For the latter, their own country's copyright laws may apply instead. Consult the details of Peter B. Hirtle's chart *Copyright term and the public domain in the United States. 1 January 2010* (http://www.copyright.cornell.edu/pub lic_domain/copyrightterm.pdf), which provides more comprehensive international copyright coverage.[24]

MULTIPLE COPYRIGHTS WITHIN THE SAME WORK:

Joint authorship is a comparatively clear instance of multiple copyright. Others are truly more complex and multilayered works. Musical compositions may involve separate authorships for music and words; recordings of the composition can involve separate artist, performer and publisher rights.[25]

Motion pictures (or other audiovisual works) are another major example frequently cited for multi-layered copyright. Copyrights normally reside in at least the following elements: the production company for the film as a whole; the musical score and soundtrack, the screenplay, and a novel or other literary work on which the screenplay may be based. Any of these separately copyrightable elements may be complicated further by exclusive contract or licensing arrangements related to them. A good illustration of variables in movie protection is the case of the classic film *It's a Wonderful Life,* which is often cited as a benefactor of multilayered copyrights. Copyright on this 1946 film lapsed during a period when renewal was a requirement (1936–1963). Thus the Frank Capra/James Stewart movie became a staple on TV during the winter holidays of the 1980s (although TV stations still paid royalties to show it), and low-cost home video versions were distributed widely. Republic Pictures inherited the film's rights and successfully reasserted control via the movie's underlying story—a 1943 literary work by Philip Van Doren

Stern, properly renewed and still protected by copyright law. Holiday TV showings diminished, as did home video versions, which were replaced by higher quality, if more expensive, authorized releases.[26]

A more recent example of multiple complications, closer to an educator's heart perhaps, is the classic documentary on U.S. civil rights, *Eyes on the Prize* (1986). Being an almost exhaustive documentary filled with historical source material of every kind, its production involved a veritable jungle of licensed elements. Because the *Prize* production company had modest means, the licensing arranged for many of these source elements was limited in term. When licensing expired, the documentary could no longer be legally distributed. Grant funding from the MacArthur Foundation restored licensing where needed and ultimately helped put *Prize* back into circulation, enabling home video distribution in the age of the DVD.[27]

COPYRIGHTABLE IMAGES OF OTHER WORKS:

Photographs can present another opportunity for multiple or at least separate copyrights. Artistic elements of the photographic process can make the photograph an expressive work separately protectable, for example, from a fine art work that is its subject. As in the example of a novel and a movie based on it, a photograph's copyright protection may exist even where its subject's copyright has long expired. Such a photograph would have to reflect "at least the modest amount of originality required for copyright protection. [. . .] But 'slavish copying', although doubtless requiring technical skill and effort, does not qualify."[28]

Orphan Works Still Under Copyright

Orphan Works (OW) are those still protected by copyright, but whose commercial exploitation has ceased, and whose owners may no longer be identifiable or reachable in order to seek permission for uses that may infringe exclusive rights. The present owner may be unaware of their possession, or may be uninterested in exploiting it, or in offering permission to another party for its use. This could make any attempt to accurately search out the present owner and to receive any response (let alone a timely one) difficult. The consequences of using the work without permission—especially when a form of republication is involved—could be a copyright infringement legal action, if a legitimate rights holder suddenly appears to challenge that use. Legislation has been under consideration in recent years (the Orphan Works Act, referenced in chapter 6) that would provide responsible users of orphan works (if they follow due diligence guidelines in seeking the owner) much more certainty that any liability damages would be minimal or limited.[29]

Libraries and archives may be able to use certain OWs with their existing rights under 17 USC §108. These are discussed in the section "Rights for Eligible Libraries and Archives."

Beyond Copyright Protection: The Public Domain

Works in the public domain (PD) are not protected by copyright. Effectively owned by society at large, PD works can be put to any creative or socially beneficial use:

made available in a freely accessible archive (as in Project Gutenberg, the Internet Archive, and much of the content in Google Books); used flexibly in teaching, learning, scholarship, or in any fannish social activity within or outside of Web 2.0. PD status does not automatically ensure a work's wide availability, but enhances opportunity for it to occur. On a seldom-remarked downside, PD status does not require attribution to creators or even the integrity of their works' form and content when reproduced.[30] Fortunately this does not appear to be common occurrence. Where such lack of attribution and/or integrity of source material occurs, it may often involve plagiarism, rather than deliberate mischief or disrespect. Ethical conduct and reputation may also be concerned when misuse occurs in a professional context.[31]

Public domain works and public domain-like conditions for works comprise these types:

- Copyright expired

Works whose copyright protection period has expired: works created or published prior to 1923, as well as exceptions since then as discussed in the section "Duration of Copyright Protection."

- U.S. federal government works

Works directly created by the U.S. federal government and its employees. These have become fewer in recent decades, as the federal government increasingly commissions and disseminates information through contract with private enterprise in the form of outside persons or companies. The contracted product does not qualify for PD status or even free access, despite the public funding that may have created it. Some state government documents may have a status comparable to federally produced documents for their public uses, but this varies with individual states. State and local laws, like federal laws, are always in the public domain.

- PD-assigned works

Works intentionally assigned by their creators to the public. PD assignment, by declaration accompanying the work, is ensured only in the pre-1978 period. Starting that year copyright protection became automatic and an author's statement of public assignment may not override this fact. An obvious practical way around this problem is for the copyright owner of record to grant all requests to use a work and to ignore other unauthorized uses: this amounts to selective public domain. A more certain way in which to minimize unwanted effects of PD status (non-attribution and corruption of the work) is to apply a formal license that permits sharing, such as a Creative Commons (CC) license.

- PD-like licenses:

Works whose creators have applied a formal legal instrument in order to effect a PD-like status granting certain common rights of use, while not forfeiting all of them. Generally, the Creative Commons provides a formal legal structure with several licensing attributes that can be mixed and matched to suit the creator's intentions (for sharing with downstream users). Creative Commons license options currently include a true PD variant ("no rights reserved"), called CCO (http:// creativecommons.org/about/cc0). As of this writing, the CC strategy for sharing specific rights has become so common that major search engines (e.g., Google, Yahoo) offer customized searching for CC licensed materials. CC itself offers search guidance at http://search.creativecommons.org/. Note that these search tools always advise the user to check the rights statement or license at its source in order to verify accuracy. Other examples of PD-like licensing include the longstanding GNU General Public License for "free software" (http://www.gnu.org/licenses/ gpl-3.0.txt) and the Free Art License (http://artlibre.org/licence/lal/en).

Caveats in Using PD Works

AN ENHANCED EDITION OR VERSION:

If a PD work is modified by re-issue with additional features—new preface, commentary, new musical score, or with a novel design of text and graphics—any of these factors may qualify that version of the PD work for its own copyright protection. In such a case, that version can't be used freely. You'll notice that archives such as Project Gutenberg (http://www.gutenberg.org/wiki/ Main_Page) avoid this pitfall, often by providing only the plain text of a work or a published edition now clearly out of copyright. For example, the Internet Archive provides a public domain version of silent comedian Buster Keaton's 1922 short film, *The Boat* (available at: http://www.archive.org/ details/TheBoat). The condition, and possibly the source, of this film transfer mirrors a commercial version distributed by Kino on Video. The difference in this instance is not in the film itself but in the musical score by Gaylord Carter in Kino's version. The inclusion of this original score enables this version of a PD film on video to be copyrighted by Kino International Corp. 1999.[32]

A VERSION ENCODED WITH INCIDENTAL TECHNICAL PROTECTION:

What happens when a PD work is republished, as part of a collection of works both PD and copyrighted, in a digital form that limits access via technical controls, such as passwords or encryption that support digital rights management? Then the free use of that PD work in this particular form is blocked by law, even when the work itself contains no enhancement that could be copyrightable. The Digital Millennium Copyright Act (the DMCA is incorporated primarily into 17 USC §1201) prohibits circumvention of technical access controls built into a digital format publication, unless the act matches very narrow purposes designated as exemptions to the law. Every three years the U.S. Copyright Office conducts hearings to review and recommend new exemptions. Unless an exception for circumventing access controls where they are applied to public domain works is recommended to and approved by the U.S. Congress, other sources for the use of these works have to be sought.[33] For example, Housman's *A Shropshire Lad* in its PD edition is also available in an Amazon.com Kindle Edition as well as in Project Gutenberg. The Kindle format edition published by Amazon.com is not be as freely usable as a Gutenberg e-text is on various other platforms.

Verifying Copyright Status

When the copyright status and owner of a work are uncertain, a search to verify them can begin with several existing tools and services. This list is presented in no all-purpose order of preference, since each search will depend on the nature of the work. Furthermore, this resource list is both selective and unable to provide definitive answers for a work's current copyright status and owner; it can only help support an informed judgment.[34]

1. Project Gutenberg (http://www.gutenberg.org/), the Internet Archive (http://www.archive.org/), or Bartleby.com (http://www.bartleby.com) can often help identify and confirm works that are not protected by copyright in the United States or which have another use-sharing status (e.g., a Creative Commons license).
2. The U.S. Copyright Office Public Catalog contains works registered since 1978 (http://cocatalog.loc.gov/cgi-bin/Pwebrecon.cgi?DB=local&PAGE=First).
3. The U.S. Copyright Office provides a search service for a fee (as do commercial services, such as Thomson CompuMark), and also guidance on conducting a search via *Circular 22* ("How to Investigate the Copyright Status of a Work"). For both, consult http://www.copyright.gov.
4. WorldCat Copyright Evidence Registry (http://www.worldcat.org/copyrightevidence/) is based on OCLC Online Computer Library Center's WorldCat, with more than 100 million bibliographic records describing items held in thousands of libraries worldwide, plus data contributed by libraries and other organizations.
5. Stanford University's Copyright Renewal Database (http://collections.stanford.edu/copyrightrenewals/bin/page?forward=home) provides copyright renewal records received by the U.S. Copyright Office between 1950 and 1992 for books published in the United States between 1923 and 1963.
6. The Copyright Clearance Center (http://www.copyright.com/) can help identify literary works still being protected and licensed for use.
7. For certain categories of work, specialized resources may be found, such as Lists of Public Domain Music—http://www.pdinfo.com/list.php; Desert Island Films, Inc. (movie lists and copies for sale)—http://www.desertislandfilms.com/[35]

COPYRIGHT INFRINGEMENT: THE POTENTIAL CONSEQUENCES

To infringe a copyright is to violate one or more of the holder's exclusive rights outlined above—in reproduction, derivative creation, distribution, and display or performance. Infringement takes one of three forms:

1. direct infringement of the exclusive rights by the user acting alone
   Example: A faculty member or student might use a self-service photocopier, computer workstation and scanner, or make an inappropriate public

performance outside of the classroom (see "Educational Allowances That Supplement Fair Use") and thereby infringe a work independently.

2. vicarious infringement, by another who profits from and has the ability to control the infringer's actions
   Example: The activity under (1) is supported by a copy center's services, which knowingly benefit from this kind of business—and thereby a direct relationship with the primary infringer is established.

3. contributory infringement, by another who is aware of the infringing activity and/or enables the conduct (induces, causes, or contributes to it)
   Example: Either the library or instructional support office might not officially approve of an infringing activity. They let it continue without taking reasonable countermeasures to control it, such as oversight of their self-service activities wherever practical, effective policy that enables support staff to make service judgments where they are directly involved in the activity, and even turning the monitored infringing activity into a educational moment for the user. This type of infringement is contributory since it involves a service relationship with the infringing conduct.

In an educational setting—especially the cluster of interrelated services that support distributed learning (the library, instructional development and CMS support offices, network services)—a "chain of liability" for direct, vicarious and/or contributory infringement can occur. Consider this situation:

1. A faculty member has assigned several management case studies and a video, which are required reading and viewing for her students. The course is online only, with students both on campus and at distant locations. They sometimes meet synchronously online, but most of the course activities are asynchronous in the CMS.

2. The case studies aren't available in the library's database resources to be linked; they *are* available to her from the publisher as faculty-use copies only, while being marketed also for student purchase. The instructor has a print copy of each study, and the video is in the library's media center collection. None of these copies will benefit her course students under available library services: The e-reserves copyright management policy declines the case studies due to the printed terms of use for these copies, and the library's media center does not even offer an equivalent e-reserves for video, as a reflection of their cautiousness over copyright compliance. The faculty member doesn't want to make her students buy the case studies, and even if digital rights are available for the videos (are these even needed? she thinks) the funding probably isn't.

3. So, with her case studies in hand, she checks out the video, telling the staff, "I just need it for the usual loan period; the CMS office has a fast turnaround so it should be back soon for the next user." She goes to the service center that provides CMS and instructional development resources. They offer two options: (1) for the technology-savvy, workstations which enable the user to create and upload documents, audio, and video in order to meet their online course needs; and (2) for those without do-it-yourself savvy, a project service under which she can submit the work and have it completed by the office, given a short turnaround time. The service request

form only requires that she confirm copyright compliance when submitting her materials. Staff take the request and her materials from there, converting and uploading to the CMS if she prefers this. She chooses (2), and asks for document and video conversion files she can use in her CMS course site—"no problem with copyright," she signs off on the form. The staff process her request without further question.

When the instructor's text and video course materials are uploaded to her account in the CMS—an activity that could be challenged as infringement—there are other points of possible culpability in the service chain. The instructor initiated the action and could be considered by law the direct infringer. On the other hand, she did have assistance from at least one office in a position to know that what she was requesting them to do was suspect—the CMS support office that took her project. The CMS office should have a copyright compliance policy in place, given the kind of service they offer, not a routine request form that asks nothing but an assenting signature that it is a valid request. If the copyright policy were aligned with the library's and media center's own policies, so much the better. Regardless, the CMS staff must have been aware of the obvious labeling on the video from the media center's collection; a quick call to consult on the copyright propriety of its use would have been in order if CMS staff themselves were unsure. The case studies could also have been questioned for their terms of use, just as the library e-reserves staff did. As for the media center staff, they may have been put in an awkward position because of her remark alluding to the CMS office. Technically, they did not know—and had no right to ask—what her use of the video program was. But she suggested it indirectly. To the extent that the media center staff are oriented to copyright compliance policy, and are familiar with the CMS office's activities, this encounter might have led to some advice on appropriate use, say, "in the future" (assuming staff confidence in offering it). Given the scant service details of this scenario, an obligation to advise the faculty member proactively on appropriate use is not warranted on the face of it. However, the more developed the copyright compliance policy of the library and its media center, the more responsible their staff are for exercising it—and the more coordinated their policy and services are with those of the CMC support office—the higher the level of awareness of possible infringing activity becomes, and the more certain the legal obligation to discourage and where possible prevent it via effectively designed services.

An inadequate, arbitrary, or uncoordinated service policy should never be the default—since for a major incident of infringing activity, every office in the chain of liability beyond the instructor could be implicated as contributors, including the institution itself. When litigation over widespread and egregious infringement occurs, the so-called deep pockets from which monetary damages can be drawn are always sought.[36]

Assuming that this instructor's behavior is *not* widespread or knowing, the law does offer relief from a possible judgment of up to $150,000 per infringement in the form of a "good faith" assessment of the situation under 17 USC §504(c)(2):

In a case where the copyright owner sustains the burden of proving, and the court finds, that infringement was committed willfully, the court in its discretion may increase the award of statutory damages to a sum of not more than $150,000. In a case where the infringer sustains the burden of proving, and the court finds, that such infringer was not aware and had no reason to believe that his or her acts constituted an infringement of copyright, the court in its discretion may reduce the award of statutory damages to a sum of not less than $200. The court shall remit statutory damages in any case where an infringer believed and had reasonable grounds for believing that his or her use of the copyrighted work was a fair use under section 107, if the infringer was: (i) an employee or agent of a nonprofit educational institution, library, or archives acting within the scope of his or her employment who, or such institution, library, or archives itself, which infringed by reproducing the work in copies or phonorecords; [. . .]

Perhaps the most notable case law decision involving widespread infringement in an educational environment, which was not deemed in good faith, was the systematic off-air taping and use of broadcast copyrighted programs by the Board of Cooperative Educational Services (BOCES) in New York.[37] Plaintiffs were granted statutory damages of $250 for each copying and performance infringement.

Good faith protection for a contributory infringer is dependent on one key factor: a reasonable belief that your action was legally acceptable, and that this belief was derived from some knowledge of copyright law and Fair Use, rather than popular assumptions about them. "Fair Use? Teaching is noble, we're nonprofit, and I'm not charging a fee, so everything should be 'fair'"—this line of reasoning does not foster a good faith defense.

Under 17 USC 506, willful infringement—that which is knowing and intentional—is a federal crime punishable by fines and/or imprisonment in varying amounts, depending on the value of the work infringed. For example, an infringing distribution by copy, electronic, or other means, of a work that has retail value of $1,000–$2,500, can result in up to a year's imprisonment or fines.

Nevertheless, Steven A. Armatas identifies factors beyond a good faith defense that make case law addressing educational infringement relatively rare. Infringements are difficult to detect, and when minor in nature may not be worth the adverse publicity of litigation. Even when the economic harm of a possible infringement is substantial, the copyright owner usually notifies the institution first to cease the offending activity. Compliance with such a request is a wise course unless the institution has good reason to believe the challenge was made in error or that their activities did adhere to a sound and defensible copyright compliance policy. Finally, where infringement litigation may be warranted, financial incentive may be low not only because of possible good faith defense under law but, in the case of state schools, the protection of sovereign immunity could be invoked.[38] (Sovereign immunity, a part of the Eleventh Amendment to the U.S. Constitution, provides that states cannot be sued by private parties unless their consent is given.)

COMPLICATIONS TO INFRINGEMENT AND USE: LICENSING

When we discussed the infringement of copyrighted works, as well as their legal uses without permission later on, we are dealing with works that have been acquired outright in commercially available or other *lawfully made* copies (as the copyright statute defines them in 17 USC §101). These copies are generally subject to the *first sale doctrine* in 17 USC §109(a), and in the case of computer programs 17 USC §117. *First sale* affirms that the owner of a legal copy in which a copyrighted work is embodied, may dispose of it in a number of ways, including re-sale and loan, without permission of the work's owner. 17 USC §109(b) permits the copy to be publicly displayed at the place where it is located. The crucial point is this: a copyrighted work that is acquired in a first sale copy—when this occurs without contract or other conditions of the exchange—is subject to copyright law under Title 17 and not to any additional terms of the work's owner. This is the situation that we focus on when discussing so-called user rights below.

Licensed works are a different matter. Contractual terms can alter user rights and set new limitations for the work being licensed. Broadly speaking, there are at least four license or license-like applications, overt or implied, that merit mention here.

1. A negotiated license in the form of a contract sets terms of product use, overrides user options under copyright law if it does not allow them, and may even set penalties for infringement apart from or in addition to those under copyright law. A common example of a practical hindrance is the electronic product (database, journal, etc.) that lacks contractual terms of use that permit direct linking of its content to facilitate CMS use. As a substitute, the CMS instructor or support staff might have to settle for providing concise instructions to students on how to locate specific articles or other resources they are entitled to access as authorized users of their institution. Therefore, if this capability is prized, negotiating a license or subscription's terms of use to maximize utility for systematic DL activities is crucial. Among commercial content vendors for specialized media, value-added capabilities that compensate for direct linking, such as creation of clips or modules from content stored in individual user accounts or profiles, are often more important. For current examples, see Films Media Group (http://www.films.com/) or Alexander Street Press (http://www.alexanderstreet.com/), both of whom have subject-specific online video collections.

2. Beyond the actively negotiated contract is the less settled legal area of the shrinkwrap or clickwrap license, often referred to as the EULA—end user license agreement. Because the conditions under which these terms are made known to purchasers may vary, the case law on the EULA's status isn't definitive and may vary by jurisdiction. Therefore, room for the application of user rights under copyright law may still exist.

3. Also consider publicly available resources with stated terms of use—a situation that involves an ethical as well as legal component. Access to the work may be unrestricted by technical means, though its owner/provider may be capable of monitoring use and asserting its terms. Let's consider two variations:

   • Nonprofit Annenberg Media provides classic educational video programming, now free for individual viewing as Video on Demand, but designed for systematic DL use. Annenberg's "FAQ on Distance Learning" makes clear when their video programs should be licensed: "If your institution plans to use any of the titles listed above as college courses offered for credit or NON CREDIT whether in an online, hybrid, broadcast, or video based format, then payment of Course License Fees or Student Only Fees will apply" (http://www.learner. org/telecourses/index.html). These terms suggest that occasional use by individual learners who have not been guided to them by specific course requirements—and possibly selected but not systematic use as part of the course's subject content—are permissible. But DL courses intentionally basing their structure and content upon Annenberg program series would be required to the license the content (while also gaining access to curricular materials that enhance the video content).

- For-profit and sometimes nonprofit distributors now offer full-length online previews of their video programming in streaming form, a benefit to educators and media collection librarians. In past years, costly programs such as training materials on human resources—usually tailored for the private-sector market but often used by educators—have involved a lengthy process of requesting a physical copy to review from the vendor, then an evaluation, and finally a purchase decision. Now complete programs can be viewed on impulse at a mouse-click within vendor websites such as those for ATS Media (http://www. atsmedia.com/) and Enterprise Media (http://www.enterpriseme dia.com/). Even nonprofit producer/distributors like Media Education Foundation (http://www.mediaed.org/) may do this. Only free registration may be required. However, at multiple points in gaining access to such programs—on a terms-of-use page, an ordering page, during the registration process, even imprinted on the program's video stream itself—the vendor signals that viewing is for the purpose of evaluation for purchase or rental only, not for classroom use. Therefore it is prudent—and educationally ethical—to take such terms at face value, and not to directly link these preview materials in a CMS, or to guide students to access them individually as a requirement of the course. Copyright commentators may differ on the legal status, and infringement risk, if terms-of-use warnings are ignored in this situation. But it is always important to consider the question: "Should I being doing this, and does it represent my institution in a responsible light if I do?" It may be more prudent to license an online version for DL training or educational use (since such vendors usually offer that alternative), or to purchase a physical copy for use if the course is a blended one rather than having true distance learners. Note that physical copies for such expensive products seldom are purchased without their own licensing terms—i.e., they are not subject to first sale status and therefore not to the application of copyright law alone in using them (which is the subject of the sections following this one). If neither measure is cost- and teaching-effective, then selecting alternative programming might be necessary.

4. Finally, copyright permission services may act as a clearinghouse for authorized online uses of works, and sometimes provide (like database aggregators) online access to the works themselves. The most ubiquitous permission

service is probably the Copyright Clearance Center (http://www.copy right.com), coordinating permissions for the widest variety of works, with institutional licensing of content for every kind of academic use and tailored interfaces for the CMS. In the specialized area of feature films, Swank Motion Pictures, Inc. (http://www.swank.com) offers Digital Campus for streaming to classes. In general, permission services contract with copyright owners to market rights to the display or performance of their works, and sometimes to incidental copying where online access is involved. These services are a convenient way in which to obtain permission for use of works without the need for making individual decisions on whether it is required for a specific academic use that may be exempted by copyright law. This, of course, leads us now to so-called user rights.

THE RIGHTS OF USERS IN THE DISTRIBUTED LEARNING (DL) ENVIRONMENT

Within the context of copyright, its purpose, duration, owner's rights, and their infringement/enforcement outlined above, we arrive at the options that a user can exercise when not limited by license or other contractual agreement. The copyright law's allowances for unauthorized uses are conveniently referred to as *rights* but are actually expressed as *limitations* on the exclusive rights of an owner. Recognizing this fact, we will consider the most salient user rights below.

Rights for Eligible Libraries and Archives (17 USC §108)[39]

Libraries and archives that qualify can engage in three activities under §108 important to their purpose with most copyrighted works:

- Preservation
- Making copies for private study
- Making copies for interlibrary loan

Qualifications are these:

- Eligibility: the library or archive must be open to the public or to non-affiliated researchers.
- Copies to honor requests in general cannot be systematic and cannot be for profit, direct or indirect.
- Copies to honor requests for private use become the requester's property, and the library displays a copyright warning notice on order forms and at the service location.[40]
- Copies made to honor ILL requests are expected to meet and apply the same standards above.
- Works *excluded* from copying for private study or ILL: musical works, pictorial, graphic, sculptural works, and motion pictures or audiovisual works.
- For preservation, *all types* of *published works* may be copied, when an "unused replacement cannot be obtained at a fair price," if either (1) its format is obsolete,

or (2) the collection's original is damaged, deteriorating, lost, or stolen. Note that in the case of a lost or stolen work, this right would permit replacement reproduction via a lawfully made copy in the collection of another library or archive. When the reason for replacement is an "obsolete" format problem, (17 USC §108(c)(2) offers only this definition of the term: "the machine or device necessary to render perceptible a work stored in that format is no longer manufactured or is no longer reasonably available in the commercial marketplace." The most generous gauge for meeting this requirement might be: (a) no current model of the device is sold in the commercial marketplace, and (b) no unused stock of a recent model is sold by any vendor. Whether librarians and educators would be obliged to seek replacement devices further into the used equipment market seems improbable.

- For preservation, unpublished works can be copied either for preservation and security (e.g., making a copy for use) at the ownership library, or for deposit in another eligible library. By intention such copies do not become the property of library users at either location.

- For preservation, scholarship or research use of a published work in its last 20 years of copyright protection, the library may reproduce, distribute, display, or perform it if the work is not available in copy at a reasonable price, not being commercially exploited, and the Register of Copyrights has not been notified by the work's owner of intention to do so.

- Finally, a digital copy limitation: All digital format copies of works, published or unpublished, must not be made available in that form outside of the library's or archive's premises. Thus preservation copies of sound recordings and audiovisual works, made on CD or DVD (as well as in networked form), would seem to be legally prohibited from routine loans for class or other individual use when occurring outside of the physical library facilities.

In the library's support of distributed learning, §108 provisions offer as much challenge as benefit.

- Using ILL service copies, the library might offer materials to individual students enrolled in the course, working with their local libraries to which the requested material is sent. But the prohibition on *systematic* reproduction comes into play: if specific materials are required for every member of the class, then this is not an option. If the materials are supplementary—requested by a course student pursuing a specific individual study need—then the option's use is more likely to be both practical and legally justified.

- Published works with 20 years or fewer of copyright protection remaining, and not commercially exploited, are in effect verified-status Orphan Works, and in fact do not have to be part of the library's own collection already in order to use them. A work of this status can arguably be offered to DL students in networked digital form, since their study activities can be viewed as a form of scholarship or research.

- The on-premises limitation for digital copies applies to use of the work in that format, under this section's preservation rights. But 17 USC §108(f)(4) does recognize applicability of Fair Use, discussed below. Fair Use would relate to case-specific individual acts of use made by staff or the library's users, as distinguished from the routine, repeated activity of loans (which constitute a service). As noted earlier, unpublished works have narrower latitude for uses without specific permission (unless terms of donation to the library or archive accommodate).

Fair Use (17 USC §107)—The Utility Doctrine for All

In U.S. copyright law, the Fair Use doctrine is both a powerful and an uncertain tool for educators to apply. It is important for being vitally connected with the free speech right of the Second Amendment to the U.S. Constitution—since its operation is independent of permission being granted, or possibly refused, by a copyright owner.[41] Fair Use is a limitation on exclusive rights in the form of an affirmative defense for a particular use of a work which the copyright owner otherwise would be entitled to control. Libraries, other DL support offices, and their faculty and student users, always need to treat Fair Use by this operating principle: decision making is not an automatic process but instead a case-by-case evaluation involving risk management because of possible infringement.

The Fair Use doctrine describes the scope of activities that may be defensible, along with four criteria for deciding whether an activity actually can be defended as fair in a given situation. Fair Use is more descriptive than prescriptive—and therefore does not tell educators exactly what they can do in any given circumstance. Its meaningful contours, one might say, are developed over time through legal decisions that treat for and against Fair Use when infringement litigation occurs. Court decisions offer interpretations that may confirm, deny, or qualify interpretations made by users when they apply Fair Use.

Looking at the scope of activities that might be regarded as fair ones, we find in 17 USC §107:

> [T]he Fair Use of a copyrighted work, including such use by reproduction in copies or phonorecords or by any other means specified by that section, for purposes such as criticism, comment, news reporting, teaching (including multiple copies for classroom use), scholarship, or research, is not an infringement of copyright. This description is not an inclusive definition, yet it offers the educator a broad field of operation to start with. Potentially, a defendable Fair Use may impact all of the exclusive rights of a copyright holder in varying degrees. It may also supplement or ignore (depending on your viewpoint) provisions that limit those rights—such as for qualifying libraries (section 108) and for educational performances (section 110, discussed below).

However, four basic criteria—or factors of Fair Use—must be examined and applied to the proposed use at hand, balancing them in an assessment of how each one impacts exclusive rights.

The Fair Use Factors

1. *The purpose and character of the use, including whether such use is of a commercial nature or is for nonprofit educational purposes*

The phrasing suggests a range of purpose and character, with nonprofit education being at the favored end. But commercial use is not ruled out automatically; such uses have been upheld in courts as fair, especially in conjunction with the character of the use.[42] Namely, where a use is "transformative" in character, it is favored: that is, the use of the work that results in something new or different from the work's own original form or purpose. A transformative use might involve re-purposing part or even all of the work's content in a multimedia lecture, or even a collaborative wiki constructed by faculty or students. Transformation in such an activity may involve not just a selective alteration of the work's substance, but also the process and outcome of its re-use. If the work is used in an instructional strategy that involves a student learning goal that is larger than the work itself, this may qualify as transformative in a Fair Use defense. Student and faculty discussion, reporting activities, and other collaborative projects stemming from the work in question would be evidence of that larger goal—as distinguished from an expected purpose for which it was created.[43]

2. The nature of the copyrighted work

Works that are predominantly factual in nature (e.g., nonfiction works of history, the sciences) tend to be protected by what is called *thin copyright* and consequently are more subject to Fair Use. Works that are creative and artistic (e.g., poetry, fiction, movies) are more resistant and would require a stronger Fair Use evaluation overall. Consumable works such as tests, worksheets, and forms meant to be used for their obvious purpose, are a specific kind of work that is not favored for Fair Use. Note also that some legal scholars have suggested that a more nuanced consideration of the nature of a work should be gauged—not simply its inherent characteristics but also the original author's incentives in creating it.[44] An examination of this aspect of a work's nature may contribute to a favorable or unfavorable evaluation in a Fair Use defense, when the original intent and audience of the work are different than or similar to its those in teaching and learning.

3. The amount and substantiality of the portion used in relation to the copyrighted work as a whole

The greater the amount of the work used, the less likely it may be Fair Use unless other factors are strongly favored in the balance to compensate. Substantiality is a characteristic as important to consider as the quantity. This quality of the portion used—referred to as the heart of the work—may be deemed so crucial to the value of the work that a Fair Use defense is weakened.[45] In terms of quantify, however, use of the entire work—even in a commercial context—is not excluded automatically from a successful Fair Use defense.[46] At the other extreme, the *de minimis* rule is sometimes legally invoked to defend copying in an amount considered so small as to be insignificant.

4. The effect of the use upon the potential market for or value of the copyrighted work

Courts have often weighed this factor more heavily than the others. Market and value can be of central importance to copyrighted works in an age of mass culture and opportunities for distribution. A 1994 decision reminds us, though, that all four factors should "be explored, and the results weighed together, in light of the purposes of copyright" (*Campbell v. Acuff-Rose Music,* 510 U.S. 569 (1994]). Setting to one side the issue of this factor's importance, a potential Fair Use can begin with this question: Can my particular (fair) use be met by a practical market that serves it—reasonable in cost and timely in convenience—and does my action deprive the copyright holder of revenue from copies or permission fees that certainly would have been paid for the use I intend? Reflecting on this question relates back to factor one (nature of the work) in the sense of its intended purpose and market, to the extent these can be determined.

An educator should assess this question by becoming familiar with the changing markets for works and their suitability for the teaching need at hand. This is where knowledgeable guidance from library professionals is crucial. Even with familiarity of markets, though, easy answers are not routine. Decisions are complicated by the prevailing assumption that the market factor in the Fair Use equation governs our thinking about the other factors—even though legislative treatment in case history has not been clear in defining potential market for or value of works on principle. The reader will also notice that in discussing factors one, two, and four above, certain concepts tend to recur across them all, explicitly or implicitly—nature, character, purpose, intent, audience, or market, and value. This pattern of thinking suggests the interdependence of these factors when examining each one's role in a very individual use of a particular work.

Some legal scholars examining the market factor, in ways sympathetic to educational Fair Use, remind us that it should not and cannot be considered the bottom line, make-or-break benchmark of Fair Use defense, if the doctrine is to have any validity and function apart from regarding a work as an economic commodity. Otherwise, educational use decisions would be routine, administrative, and financial only.[47]

In exercising Fair Use, then, every factor must be considered, weighted, and balanced with a context that includes relevant court decisions that address comparable situations and uses (though as noted earlier, case law seldom has dealt with higher education per se), common professional practice that is perceived to be acceptable or not by the communities of copyright owners and users over historical time, and the facts of the specific use at hand, scrutinized closely. The educational profession therefore looks to the law, to its resource providers (copyright holders), to its user needs, and to its own evolving role and practice in gauging the independent actions it can and should take in using copyrighted works. Even the congressional legislative reports that accompanied the proposed 1976 revision of the Copyright Act observed:

> The statement of the fair use doctrine in section 107 offers some guidance to users in determining when the principles of the doctrine apply. However, the endless variety of situations and combinations of circumstances that can rise in particular cases precludes the formulation of exact rules in the statute. The bill endorses the purpose and general scope of the judicial doctrine of fair use, as outlined earlier in this report, but there is no disposition to freeze the doctrine in the statute, especially during a period of rapid technological change. Beyond a very broad statutory explanation of what fair use is and some of the criteria applicable to it, the courts must be free to adapt the

doctrine to particular situations on a case-by-case basis. (*Historical and Revision Notes, House Report No. 94–1476, at* 62)

As the *Code of Best Practices in Fair Use for Online Video* observes: "While case law is of essential importance in establishing legal norms, it is the *trend* in case law that determines such norms. The trend in case law about Fair Use has strongly been in the direction of supporting transformativeness as a core measure of Fair Use."[48]

The Fair Use evaluation process benefits from analytical thinking about various elements involved in the four factors. A well considered Fair Use checklist that inventories all of the elements to consider, such as the one developed by Kenneth Crews and frequently adapted in higher education,[49] helps guide the thought process as well as document the decision and action taken. The overriding principle in this author's mind is that a checklist tool enables analysis of the Fair Use factors, but should not be treated as a routine scorecard. Balancing the factors may not be a simple arithmetic calculation—that is, which column, with factors favoring or opposing Fair Use, has more checks in it? Balance can be a dynamic process, in which a positive or negative judgment on a specific factor may have more or less weight in the overall evaluation than it did in the previous case, or will in the next one.

Educational Allowances that Supplement Fair Use (17 USC §110)

U.S. copyright law has two major provisions that deal with teaching activities and the display or performance of copyrighted materials.

§110(1)—FACE-TO-FACE TEACHING DISPLAY AND PERFORMANCE:

Education uses all kinds of cultural materials that may be copyrighted. If their display or performance for a classroom audience were considered public, common viewing and discussion activities would be impossible as part of in-class teaching events. §110 limits exclusive rights by allowing "performance or display [. . .] in the course of face-to-face teaching activities of a nonprofit educational institution, in a classroom or similar place devoted to instruction." This right applies to any work acquired under the first sale doctrine. Those that are licensed, rather than purchased, may have qualifying terms either comparable or more restrictive for teaching activities.

§110(2)—DISPLAY AND PERFORMANCE IN DISTRIBUTED LEARNING—THE TEACH ACT (2002)

In 1999 after the DMCA, the U.S. Copyright Office held discussions with higher education professionals and copyright holders in order to arrive at consensus that would address the needs of distributed learning and thereby provide less uncertainty than Fair Use alone.[50] As a consequence, the Copyright Office devised recommendations to Congress, and the Technology, Education and Copyright Harmonization (TEACH) Act was later passed. It then was incorporated into copyright law under this section and 112(f), dealing with ephemeral recordings that must be made as part of distance education's technology infrastructure.

The resulting law has appeared to many observers as a compromise, tending to treat the potential of distance learning as if it were an online version of the physical classroom that imitates the sequenced activities occurring throughout the semester.[51]

On its own, TEACH offers these advantages in performing copyrighted works in a DL setting:

- Permits the conversion of works from an analog format to the necessary digital format, provided the work is not also marketed primarily in a digital networked version suitable for DL
- Permits the performance of non-dramatic literary and musical works in their entirety (roughly speaking, nonfiction and non-theatrical audiovisual works, although the forms are not defined in the copyright statute)
- Permits the performance of "reasonable and limited portions" of other audio-visual works
- Permits the display of other works in amounts comparable to those used in a F2F classroom session (which could be the entire work)

But TEACH also entails obligations for its use, these being the major ones:

- To be used by a nonprofit accredited educational institution or governmental agency
- To apply only at the direction of an instructor, only for the relevant course section during which the copyrighted material is needed, and only when directly related to the content being taught
- To use only lawfully made copies as source material
- To provide technological protection measures for the works used, that "reasonably limit" further retention by users (e.g., view-only or streaming access rather than download)
- To provide accurate information and policy on copyright to the university community

Together 110(1) and 110(2) define a basic safe harbor for display and performance in the F2F class and in the online class. Neither the F2F teaching allowance nor the TEACH allowance for DL is the same as Fair Use itself for educators. As discussed earlier, Fair Use hinges on a specific case-by-case defense that may impact the exclusive rights of a copyright holder in potentially less restrictive ways for the user—including the fact that it both avoids specificity of teaching environment (i.e., physical class or virtual) and specificity of technology employed.

Comparing TEACH with Fair Use, here are some salient distinctions:

- Fair Use impacts exclusive rights as does TEACH, but can be practiced by any individual or group, private or public, nonprofit or commercial. TEACH covers only accredited nonprofit education and occurs at the instigation of the individual educator. Support services for DL cannot proactively apply TEACH. They do so only upon faculty request.

- Fair Use does not inherently limit the amount of a work used, nor the duration of its use, although educators by consensus tradition have treated it as time-limited (e.g., for only one semester), an approach certainly in agreement with content owners' interpretation of Fair Use. TEACH does suggest portions for many works that are performed (reasonable and limited, without further definition), and does require a strict time limit: works may be used only in amounts appropriate to instructional purpose and for the period that meets the instructional goal. When these are met, access to the material must be discontinued.

- Fair Use may be applied to any sort of instructional purpose—TEACH, only to materials directly related to the content being taught. Supplementary materials not required of all students to use—such as those traditional library reserves can offer—are not supported under TEACH. But this contrast with reserves raises an interesting question in Fair Use evaluation, whether in the physical or online environment, that highlights the dynamic nature of gauging the four factors. Is a Fair Use of a work more likely justified if the work is central to the teaching of a course and required of all students to use? Or would a work that is supplementary in use—suggested but not required, or required by only some of the enrolled students in working on special projects related to the course's conduct—likely have as strong or even stronger justification for a Fair Use defense? The centrally relevant work might figure into a stronger transformative use, because it relates to the entire class. But the supplementary work may still be transformative in the learning process—for example, used in learning by individual student or group collaborators and then shared in exchange with the entire class to meet a larger learning goal—and also might be viewed as lessening impact on the market/value factor four because of its more limited use within the course. The truth is that other facts of each Fair Use application, related to the work's nature and the amount being used, will influence how these questions are answered.

- Fair Use does not in fact address a lawfully made copy—it deals with the work fixed in copy—but TEACH does require a lawful copy as source for its use in a networked environment. Fair Use cannot be claimed as a rationale to gain unlawful access to a copy of a work (remember especially the DMCA anticircumvention provisions in 17 USC §1201, referenced in the previous section "Copyrights's Origins and Purpose"). But at least in argument, Fair Use might be practiced with a potentially unlawful copy that is available, as in the case of an Orphan Work (discussed in the previous section "Orphan Works Still Under Copyright").

- Fair Use requires the consideration of four criteria and favors transformative uses that repurpose the works or the parts of them being used. TEACH only requires "reasonable and limited portions" (except for nondramatic literary and musical works)—without guidance as to how to gauge these portions—and does not require transformative uses of permitted content.

- TEACH requires technological security measures and copyright education—whereas Fair Use requires neither.

Inevitably, we need to ask: what is the relationship between Fair Use in 107 and the educational performance allowance in 110? Legal opinion appears to be an unsettled matter at this time, although there are two logical approaches. The more cautious argues that TEACH probably limits the way in which courts are likely to view most DL applications of the Fair Use doctrine: that is, Fair Use cannot be practiced so generously as to mimic what an instructor can do in the traditional, physical classroom (e.g., she can screen an entire film). On the other hand, a more generous view recently promoted by pro-education legal scholars, is that both parts of 17 USC §110 may be seen by courts as conditioning Fair Use activities in a positive way.[52] If one of the enduring goals of copyright law is to create a special place for educational activities, the argument goes, then it would seem persuasive that the relative freedom of traditionally practiced classroom activities should be justifiable in the online educational environment, despite apparent qualifications in TEACH. The U.S. Copyright Office itself, in reporting to the Congress on the recommendations that resulted in the TEACH Act, commented on the relationship: "Fair use is the broadest and most general limitation on the exclusive rights of copyright owners, and can exempt distance education uses not covered by the specific instructional exemptions. It is flexible and technology-neutral, and continues to be a critical exemption for educational users in the digital world. It requires courts to examine all the facts and circumstances, weighing four nonexclusive statutory factors."[53] These remarks tend to favor the view that TEACH should not alone reflexively restrict consideration of Fair Use in the DL environment.

Within the CMS, however, DL services would be wise to consider strategies that combine both TEACH and Fair Use: that is, focus only on content central to the teaching purpose, protect copyrighted content from distribution beyond the targeted course enrollees as much as possible, and educate faculty and students on copyright—while utilizing the freer scope of Fair Use when evaluation of the teaching need and of the work involved justify that scope. The most critical element in practicing this approach, however, is to be consistent on a case by case basis, both in policy and in practice. The approach may also be applicable to other tools of the online course, such as wikis or social networking collaborative environments, when these can be similarly restricted in access and secured in the use of their content.

Guidelines that Interpret the Law

There are four sources of guidance for using copyrighted works in educational activities. First is the law itself, where it defines permissible activities that limit exclusive rights—including those for qualified libraries and archives, for educational performances, and for the First Sale doctrine. Second is the Fair Use doctrine, wider and less prescriptive in scope than the other source above, but less certain of applicability. Third are legal decisions regarding contested user activities under the law's provisions—decisions that interpret and clarify the evolving application of the law, and may relate to educational situations even when the activity in legal dispute does not. Fourth are the various guidelines that have been developed by government and professional groups to assist interpretation of Fair Use.

None of the guidelines are part of the copyright law itself. A few have more visible status by virtue of being included in U.S. congressional reports: *Agreement on Guidelines for Classroom Photocopying* (1976), *Guidelines for Off-Air Recording of Broadcast Programming for Educational Purposes* (1979), and *Fair Use Guidelines for Educational Multimedia* (1996) in particular. (The *Fair Use Guidelines* deals with multimedia use in education, and parallels *Classroom Photocopying* in its provisions, but it does not treat or apply to the online environment generally.) Important guidelines are the American Library Association's *Model Policy Concerning College and University Photocopying for Classroom, Research and Library Reserve Use* (1982) and the *CONTU Guidelines on Photocopying Under Interlibrary Loan Arrangements* (1979). Chapter 6 discusses some of these guidelines, and Steven A. Armatas describes and reproduces most of them, as well as others.[54]

These guidelines seek to establish responsible practices that meet educational needs in the F2F classroom and in library support services for reserves and interlibrary loans in particular. The guidelines do not adequately address the online classroom environment, though. They also are quantitative in focus, even when suggesting that quantities specified are minimums only under their interpretations of Fair Use. In contrast, many guidelines now being developed by education and public-interest organizations—in distinction to those by copyright industry organizations, such as the Copyright Clearance Center (http://www.copyright.com/)—favor a more flexible qualitative approach to Fair Use. See especially the guidance and "codes of best practice" documents offered by American University's Center for Social Media (http://www.centerforsocialmedia.org/). A qualitative approach tends to deal with the overall balance of all factors in a Fair Use evaluation more flexibly than an approach centered on the primacy of the fourth factor (market and value of work) and safe-harbor guidelines devised for the third (amount and substantiality of portion), which together tend to pre-condition judgment about a proposed Fair Use at hand.

USE SCENARIOS THAT ILLUSTRATE COPYRIGHT ISSUES

Applying copyright knowledge is necessary for determining how works might be used in specific DL situations. The following scenarios enable discussion of both Fair Use factors and the possible complications in arriving at decisions. The author has declined to make definitive *favors* or *disfavors* judgments in assessing each factor, sometimes because several variables that may apply can lead to differing conclusions. In any case, always remember that it requires an actual infringement challenge and judicial decision to decide the validity of any use built upon a Fair Use defense.

Case: Is the Play the Thing? And Do Students Need to Buy It?

SITUATION

An instructor teaches a theater course on "mastering dramatic construction" that is blended, combining online CMS components and activities with regular in-class meetings.

The course objectives are two:

1. A critical reading of six plays that will result in group discussion by all class members and then individual term papers by each student.

2. The reading of a final play with a different goal: the improvised construction of a new play by each of three groups of students. Each group
will assign each of its members a character from this play, that person's
obligation being to absorb the details of the character's life, imagine
the character in other circumstances, and contribute to group discussion and construction of a one-act play that uses the character. Each
group is then responsible for mounting a performance of their one-act
play before the rest of the class, whose members will critique it along
with the instructor, guided by what they have learned about dramatic
construction.

The instructor's course requirements include purchase (from the campus
bookstore) of the six plays studied in detail. (A print copy is also on library
reserves, but it won't be sufficient for 28 students in the time frame needed.)

But the instructor also wants the final play—which is a different choice
each time the course is given—to be used as source material for the group
exercise, and put into digital form for her students. By e-reserves service
policy, the library has to decline the request.

As a result the instructor approaches the CMS support office to help convert and mount the play on her course site. She argues that her students have
been asked to buy several play texts that they study directly and at length—
but doesn't think they should have to spend still more money on this particular one. It is central to one of the course's outcomes, she says, but the
play is a stepping stone for the work they have to do in the creative project
she's given each group.

Can the CMS support office justify honoring this request to duplicate the
entire play for her course?

Analysis: General Considerations

If all purchase, permission, or licensing alternatives are not feasible—aside from
the matter of whether they are required—then application of Fair Use would be
the main approach here. TEACH provisions alone, related to performance and
incidental reproduction for effecting that performance, are too limited for this
teaching situation. So appropriate support staff must scrutinize the four factors.

Fair Use Factor 1: Purpose and Character of Use

The purpose of using the work in question is educational—which is favored. Further, the character of its use is unusual and may be considered *transformational*. The
goal of the course here is not reading and study of the play for itself, but to treat it
as creative material for building student group exercises that demonstrate mastery
of dramatic construction. The collaborative construction of a new one-act play
out of preexisting characters in the copyrighted work does constitute a "derivative" work. In this, the situation is much like that of fan fiction created to spin further adventures of beloved fictional characters. But the special context of having

an educational purpose and environment strengthens claim for a transformative Fair Use under this factor.

Fair Use Factor 2: Nature of the Copyrighted Work

The work in question is highly creative and more highly protected by copyright, since it is a dramatic play. As suggested under our earlier discussion of Fair Use, though, we might also consider the original intention of the play's creation: this is different than the use to which it is going to be put in this course. Therefore a Fair Use evaluation on this factor may be mixed, not strongly favored or disfavored.

Fair Use Factor 3: Amount and Substantiality of the Portion Used

There is no question that use of the whole work makes a strong defense on other factors more necessary, even if it does not rule out a Fair Use overall. Reading of the entire play, by all of the students in their groups, is central to the teaching purpose: they need to have a complete sense of every character in order to create their own one-act plays successfully. So the amount being used under this factor is justifiable, when taken in context of the purpose of the use, under factor one.

Fair Use Factor 4: Effect of Use upon Potential Market for or Value of the Work

Here we deal with the final factor, which is commonly considered the most important—even though the meaning of *potential market* and *value* are not fixed in law for every situation.

First, assume that the play is in-print. These questions might then color our judgment of market impact and the work's value: How readily available is the work, and is it at reasonable cost in comparison with the other texts being studied and purchased by students? Is the work in-print as a first sale purchase copy, or only electronically via license instead, with some limitations that might compromise a Fair Use defense under copyright law? Regardless of the play's current in-print form, is the instructor in possession of an earlier lawful sale copy, which might serve to make a Fair Use?

These questions and their answers are context for a Fair Use decision, regardless of its outcome. The most crucial answers involve the forms in which the work is in-print, since there are two possibilities that could result:

1. The work is in-print as a purchasable non-digital text, with or without also being in digital form for purchase with license terms. In this situation, the text is either purchased by students in physical or digital form, or a Fair Use decision is made on the basis of the non-digital purchase version.
2. The work is only available in a licensed digital form, whether designed for teaching use and the educational market or only for individual purchasers of any kind (as in the iTunes or Amazon.com sales model). In this situation, Fair Use cannot be applied unless it uses a lawful copy of an earlier non-digital edition of the work (now out-of-print) as the basis. License terms for the digital version would make it unlikely that Fair Use evaluation could proceed based on such a copy.

How the instructor and her course use the work in the unauthorized electronic copy that would need to be created does impact the market for an in-print work. But this impact—if the use were to proceed—can be lessened by the following circumstances or conditions:

- The CMS targets a very specific audience and limits availability in a specific time period. If the instructor switches the exercise play every time she teaches the course, this also complies with a common (though not required) interpretation of a Fair Use as being of transitory or spontaneous in character rather than intended to continue indefinitely.[55]

- The play's electronic copy can also be protected from downloading and/or printing. This limits market impact by discouraging further unauthorized distribution beyond the class members.

- If the instructor has purchased a lawful copy of the work, the CMS service office, or the library in coordination, could archive it while the course is in process. Such a measure is not required in a defensible Fair Use but may strengthen that defense by establishing that the online version is substituting for a physical copy that is not otherwise in use simultaneously.

Together these added conditions document that a legitimate source of the work was used by the instructor and the services supporting her, and that efforts were taken to limit availability, distribution of copies, and market impact. If the work itself is also in-print under circumstances making it difficult to use in the way the instructor intends, that consideration also favors a Fair Use defense.

Concluding Analysis

The foregoing is an imaginative case where Fair Use might be justified. But the detailed and consistent application of policy, procedures, and technology to implement a defensible action is as important as having an imaginative and substantive rationale for defense. Every judgment and circumstance raised in the discussion could be involved both in policy and implementation for other teaching situations requiring less extreme defense and risk management of a possible infringement challenge.

It is also important to remember that not only established service policy and its application but also technology such as the CMS offer documentation of thinking and process that are valuable to a Fair Use defense. The instructor views the exercise play as having a process role that is neither primary course reading or supplementary reading—its use results in a transformational learning experience. The play itself may be chosen not for its high esthetic value but for an array of characters that can be used in dramatic construction by her student groups. These things may be regarded as subjective judgments, not objective facts (certainly, the playwright and publisher involved wouldn't agree with the instructor). But a clear purpose, careful thinking, and follow-through execution of the course itself—documented in teaching strategy and materials provided both within the CMS and the conduct of the live class—can buttress any Fair Use defense, as do service policy and its execution. Thus, the technology of distributed learning, which stretches conservative interpretations of copyright law, can sometimes help justify activities undertaken through its inherent capabilities to a greater degree than an instructor can in a physical classroom.

Case: Video Streaming without a License

SITUATION

A faculty member teaches a blended course for non-science majors on the history of science. It deals with the development of the scientific method and also the cultural environment in which it has occurred. The faculty member believes that engaging the students of his class—which consists of several sections, both online in the CMS and in multiple class meetings each week (F2F)—can be accomplished by asking them to consider the public role and reception of scientists and scientific practices over time in the modern world. A survey of cultural attitudes expressed in popular entertainment from the 1950s onward is part of his lesson plan. He'd like to use several period feature films as well as short documentaries in the online part of his course. Beginning with *Forbidden Planet* (1956), each film would be viewed by every student. He intends to have the initial discussion about the films F2F in the physical classroom. Later, group interactions online are planned in order to develop individual student insights. The library has most of the films he needs for the course; he owns a few commercial copies that he purchased for his own previous use in F2F teaching. One short industrial documentary is available from the Internet Archive and probably has no rights at issue anyway. With 63 students enrolled, it would be too time-consuming to conduct this aspect of the course via class screenings or through the library's physical reserves service: the multiple copies required for reserves viewing would be prohibitive to obtain, and perhaps even impossible for titles not currently in print. Online licensing may be available for some of the films; *Forbidden Planet* was produced by a major Hollywood studio and could be one of them. But a couple of films came from small independent companies that are now defunct; researching the transfer of rights for them could be labor-intensive and probably would still not yield a licensor, or so the instructor reasons. The research requirement for short documentaries might involve even more work and still fail to identify current rights owners. Can the library and the CMS support office justify helping the instructor conduct the course in this way—by preparing streaming versions of movies from videotape or DVD—without researching them for licenses or permission from copyright holders?

Analysis: General Considerations

As in the scenario of the complete play above, a narrow reading of TEACH would not suffice for meeting this instructor's science-and-sci-fi-movies-online teaching strategy, unless he could reconsider and adapt his teaching goal so that it requires only portions of the selected films. If the use of entire films in all cases is absolutely necessary, the lowest risk strategy would be to invest the professional research labor and the funds needed to vet them all and seek permissions or pay license fees. One or two of the instructor's obscure title choices might be in the public domain, or might be so difficult to trace for current owners that in effect they are orphan works (especially if already available on the public web). Still others may be readily licensed for DL-style course use (e.g., the Motion Picture Licensing Corporation and Swank Motion Pictures cover releases from many movie studios).[56]

The alternative to educational performance allowances is to apply the higher-risk strategy of a Fair Use evaluation, under the assumption that 110 does not limit it, or that it positively reinforces the educational purpose involved. In the remainder of this case analysis, we assume support services that are comfortable with applying Fair Use to assist the instructor.

Fair Use Factor 1: Purpose and Character of Use

We have a proposed use at the favored, non-profit educational end of the spectrum. But transformative use in the educational process is less obvious than in Scenario 1—and perhaps more challenging to establish here than with the play. Use of the play involved a specific collaborative class project that treated it as building material rather than a work of study in itself. Here, viewing the streaming films might result in less concrete learning activities—reflection and discussion in physical class and online in the CMS, and possibly in term papers completed. The outcomes are not as specific in detail this time. Still, if any educational processing of a work in these ways counts as transformative, then having this sort of evidence documented, preferably online but at least in F2F instruction, would be beneficial to a Fair Use defense.

Fair Use Factor 2: Nature of the Copyrighted Work

The documentary films are more favored for Fair Use treatment in their nature: more factual in content, and meant for an historical audience and interest.

All of the feature films are of a creative nature, and so are not strongly favored for Fair Use on this count. The feature films may vary, however, in their market availability for online use in an educational context. In the case of those films that are readily found as licensable, one can still consider: Is education a primary market for this content? Is its pricing comparable to other content designed for the educational market and also licensable? Answers that are negative or uncertain may tend to weaken an unfavorable judgment regarding the nature of the work.

Fair Use Factor 3: Amount and Substantiality of the Portion Used

There is no question that requiring students to view whole films compels a strong defense on other factors, especially a teaching purpose (under factor 1) that really does require students to watch the films in their entirety. If the instructor could really make do with clips from at least some of the movies instead, this compromise would strengthen a favorable judgment on this factor: portions selected for some films suggest that selectivity is also operating when other films require an entire viewing in a deliberate teaching strategy. However, if the complete use of each and every film is really important, and can be documented in the conduct of the course, then this fact should not result in an automatic no on this factor.

Fair Use Factor 4: Effect of Use upon Potential Market for or Value of the Work

First, assume that most of the films are either in print commercially, were at one time, or are otherwise available from presumably legitimate sources on the web (such as http://archive.org/ or even http://www.hulu.com/). To the extent that works are out-of-print or accessible on the web, it could be argued that their market and value are not heavily impacted by this proposed course use. Other films, in-print and perhaps also licensable for streaming, may indicate a more perennial popularity and market value. This market may still be primarily in physical copies, even where also distributed in a fee-per-access online environment. (See motion pictures vendor example, point 4 in the section "Complications to Infringement and Use: Licensing.")

So one might ask these questions: If an online market (on-demand service or license to serve content) might exist to support the teaching need, how developed is it? Does it cover the films needed? Is it timely and compatible with the CMS? Finally, does the market directed at educational use appear to be a major component of the general market for the films, and is pricing comparable to other educational materials designed for online courses? Answers to these questions may vary for each individual film. Note also that the final two-part question relates to the more probing consideration of factor one raised in the section "Fair Use (17 USC §107)—The Utility Doctrine for All" and also earlier in this scenario: the nature of each work can be viewed in terms of its original purpose and audience. In the end, evaluation of market here may fall anywhere in the range from favor to oppose Fair Use, applied to specific films or to the group as a whole, since all are involved in the overall teaching goal.

Concluding Analysis

This case is a provocative one in which the facts involving two of the criteria—use of the entire work and uncertain market conditions—oblige a strong defense on the first two factors in an overall evaluation. Their strength lies in the highly transformative as well as nonprofit educational use of the films in the course and the fact that even for the more creative (feature) films, this use may be viewed as distinct from the films' intended reception by audiences and their original market. Assuming that a decision favors Fair Use, for any or for all of the films, the defense can be enhanced by measures that the staff supporting the faculty member can take:

- Requests like this one could be subject to a formal review process for distinguishing integral class use in the CMS from trivial convenience or supplementary and voluntary viewing. In effect, the Fair Use evaluation process then benchmarks itself, whenever possible, to meeting the TEACH performance criteria of using material that is integral to the class and the teaching content—while remaining more flexible in other respects.

- Each film encoding for streaming would only entail a lawfully made commercial copy for its source. Web sources would be verified for probable authenticity, and merely linked (in the least *deep* way possible, if necessary). Any physical lawful copies of movies that are part of the media collection would not be circulated, except for media center viewing by users not in the general science course, but who still need access. Other lawful copies, such as the instructor's, could be archived by the library or other support office while used in the CMS. This measure helps strengthen a wise operating principle that streaming versions are substituting for purchased versions but do not expand their utility in two different media forms.

- Online viewings of each film could be tracked to verify its usage rate.

- In support of the use's transformative quality, encourage that the conduct and documentation of learning activity resulting from use of the films should occur online as much as possible.

- In anticipation of repeated use of the same film materials in future, for this course or any other, the library might set up procedures to explore licensing alternatives that accommodate the instruction need and fund them. This measure depends on the library or CMS support office's level of risk tolerance in repeated use of the same materials and how strongly they seem justified as transformative and fair. If copyright compliance policy and risk tolerance are more cautious, the institution might take alternative measures for repeated use: (1) adopt a licensing service for the same instructor, same course use in future; (2) attach a student course fee to support licensing, or require an individual video subscription service with streaming option (e.g., Netflix) where their catalogue matches course content; or (3) consider varying the video selections with each course repeat, when its subject content and teaching strategy can accommodate.

CONCLUSIONS: A SUMMARY ON STRATEGY

In supporting distributed learning with information resources, the user of copyrighted material—in the form of an instructor, library, instructional development or CMS office, and staff—has a small arsenal of options that can and must be applied creatively, carefully, and consistently. Meeting a wide range of teaching and learning styles across disciplines inevitably requires multiple approaches as well as qualifications.

Strategic Planning for Use of Resources in Distributed Learning

The following flow charts present a set of strategies that are helpful when considering use of copyrighted materials in DL. As such, they focus on independent judgment of fair use and performance rights in a controlled environment. These strategies do not address the long-established services of e-reserves and interlibrary loans, which are covered fully in chapter 6.

The context for the interpretation and use of these flow charts is as follows:

- Looking at copyright law in conjunction with the range of educational activities that serve DL, from traditional library services to online technologies for the virtual classroom, we can view the relative scope of potential action, as shown in Figure 1.

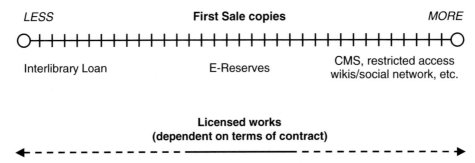

Figure 1: Relative Freedom of Unauthorized Use in DL

- The flow charts on the following pages show decision points in simplified form and without detailing complete criteria for qualifying activities that can be conducted by libraries and archives (§108), and under Fair Use (§107), the First Sale doctrine (§109a), and educational performance allowances (§110). Therefore, the user needs to address these decision points carefully, in the context of the copyright background information presented in this chapter and also in the context of the key works listed in the References. Other useful guidance in addressing these decision points can be found here:

  - The American Library Association Office for Information Technology Policy, *Section 108 Spinner* (http://librarycopyright.net/108spinner/), a handy interactive tool.
  - Columbia University Libraries/Information Services, Copyright Guidance Office (http://copyright.columbia.edu/copyright/), for checklists, forms and guidance on documenting activities related to libraries, archives, and Fair Use.
  - The most thorough set of detailed flow charts on evaluation and decision processes in library activities is in Peter B. Hirtle, Emily Hudson, and Andrew T. Kenyon, *Copyright and Cultural Institutions: Guidelines for Digitization for U.S. Libraries, Archives, and Museums* (http://ecommons. library.cornell.edu/handle/1813/14142).[57]
  - At several points, the strategy flow charts reference 17 USC §1201(a), which prohibits circumvention of access controls in works where these exist, with limited exemptions. The very latest classes of works announced for exemptions by the Librarian of Congress may permit circumvention of access controls on digital copies related to *some* uses in DL for the defined period during which the exemptions are in force.[58]

- Bear in mind that in for-profit DL services, decisions regarding use of copyrighted works are much more constrained than the uses addressed here.
- Documentation for each decision, action, and activity without permission is crucial, especially under Fair Use. The DL environment actually improves the docu-

mentation available, since class activities online are archived. If a transformative Fair Use is claimed for a work, the learning exchanges that accompany the use are important. That is, the number of displays or performances of a work by students may be logged, resulting discussion among students and faculty accumulated, as well as papers and other projects. (Should archived CMS activities be required as evidence in a Fair Use defense, though, participant identities might have to be omitted to meet privacy regulations.)

Summary Considerations in DL Support

1. Licensing is sometimes the most effective long-term solution.

Institutionally licensed resources, or permission services such as the Copyright Clearance Center's, may be the most cost-effective solution if/when their coverage is adequate and the institution's own copyright compliance policy and sense of risk management suggest it. Licensing terms maximize flexibility of educational use and the use may be repeated routinely over time. This option is the most risk-proof, but it demands adequate funding and advance planning on the part of faculty, librarians, and other professional staff. For example, if a course requires CMS use of a human resources video program on employee supervision whose licensing is expected to be expensive—and for which there is no adequate substitute programming—it may have to be budgeted for resource support, whether in the form of a course fee or library materials allocation. Future budget decisions can be shaped by recurrences of this need, addressing the unusual expenses involved in teaching certain courses; this is comparable to formalizing disparities in journal literature for various disciplines by differential funding allocations (e.g., more for the natural sciences than for the arts).

Licensing equivalents are pay-per-use subscription access, such as Films Media Group's Films on Demand (http://ffh.films.com/digitallanding.aspx), and clearance services for academic institutions such as plans provided by the Copyright Clearance Center (http://www.copyright.com).

2. U.S. copyright law in simplest application may not always be enough.

Every evaluation strategy in using a copyrighted work in a way that is not licensed or otherwise given permission must take into account miscellaneous factors beyond U.S. copyright law. Variations in international law, trademark rights, and rights of privacy or publicity may come into play in a given case.

3. Make copyright law provisions work in a complementary way wherever possible.

A positive evaluation of Fair Use can complement or extend the limitations on exclusive rights than benefit users in other parts of the copyright law—especially those under sections 108 (for qualifying libraries and archives) and 110 (for educational performances). Very often, almost no single provision of the law will

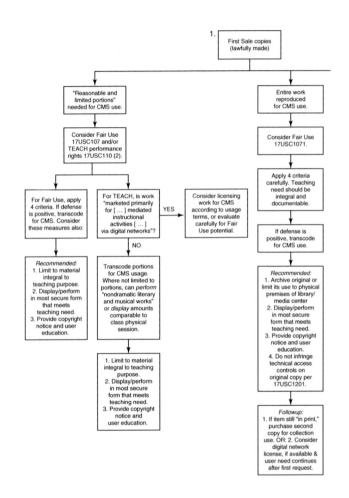

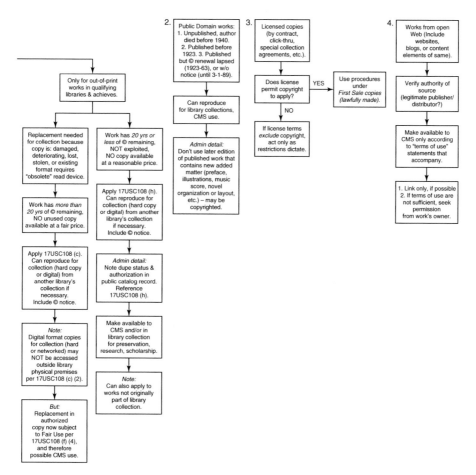

Flow Charts for Strategic Decision-Making Regarding the Use of Works

suffice to address a complicated need. One should be prepared to consider every relevant section that impacts the teaching need at hand.

4. Uses of works may tend to form predictable patterns—but decisions are seldom routine.

The application of copyright law to the use of works without permission, when not matched by a specific limitation (e.g., loan in copy authorized by the First Sale doctrine in section 109), often depends on Fair Use. It is important, however, to avoid easy, automated decisions that serve the institution's educational activities without due regard for the nature of the copyrighted material and of the instructional situation. Both faculty and service providers should also ask this question first: If I need to act without permission in using a work, what is the most direct and most limited solution that meets the educational need and prevents or discourages further unauthorized distribution to users and for purposes that are not intended by my action? An honest answer to this question should focus on true need, not merely desirable convenience for users. Since the services that support DL may have a vicarious or contributing infringement liability when decisions are too casual, the services should be an active collaborator with faculty in forming decisions.

5. A united front is always better: implement copyright decision making in a coordinated fashion.

A comprehensive and coherent policy related to copyright cannot be overestimated. Consider the range of activities involved, from the often established practices of copyright compliance for e-reserves and ILL services, to the instructional development and CMS support activities that meet more various needs within individually tailored course environments, and to self-service technologies provided to the end user, enabling their independent manipulation of works in any medium (from photocopiers to scanners and video production workstations). The more integrated the policy approach to meeting all of these services, the better. Very often, library professionals are in a leadership role here. It is easier to achieve integration when the offices involved—library, instructional development, and other CMS support units—are administratively related, but they often are not. Still, the investment of time and staff, and leadership, across administrative lines to cooperatively achieve integration pays off in multiple ways. A comprehensive strategy of copyright compliance results in easier decision making for knowledgeable staff responding to faculty and students, clearer education of service user expectations (reinforced across the offices), and an accumulation of documentable actions related to copyrighted works that form a consistent service history over time. In effect, a coherent and precise policy in action can demonstrate an approach to the law that is purposeful and responsible rather than arbitrary, variable, and contingent. The resulting policy-shaped service environment can strengthen any good-faith defense against a challenge of willful infringement (direct, vicarious, or contributory), should it occur. Therefore, coordination and integration of all copyright compliance policy administered by the services that support distributed learning should be a top priority.

Inevitably, library professionals have a key leadership role in understanding copyright and achieving a coordinated service policy in applying the law to benefit educational support activities online.

APPENDIX CASE: THE PUBLIC DOMAIN(?)
PHOTO—INSIDE THE CMS AND OUT

SITUATION

A faculty member teaches a DL course in women's studies in which each class, each semester, contributes to an ongoing project as part of their subject mastery. The project gathers and reviews resources on the history of women's rights and professional activities in each country of the western hemisphere. Resources for inclusion are those available via subscribed databases, in print, and openly accessible on the Internet. Each time she teaches this course, the students work collaboratively to research a particular country. They gather their findings within the CMS-related wiki (also restricted to class members), and develop the organization, features, and design of this expanding resource. The ultimate goal is to turn this serial project—created by four semesters of the course—into an open website sponsored by the university's women's studies institute. After that happens, future classes may contribute to expanding geographical coverage and maintaining the currency of contents.

The class now working on the project identifies a photograph of one of the most prominent American women journalists of the late 19th century. They feel her picture would be a perfect emblem of the project's intention, showing how far back in history women had valued and very public professional roles with influence. It is also a suitable entré to the website for American audiences, whom they expect will provide the greatest number of users when the resource becomes public.

But the instructor is uncertain about using the photograph without permission. It's true that it is no longer under copyright—being the work of a journalist photographer (freelance or staff) taken in 1895—but she also knows that the most widely known instance of this image comes from a major archive housing physical copies of many such historical photos. In the past 10 years this archive has licensed the right to distribute their inventory in digital form to a major software company. This particular photo is among those now licensed for various uses. Feeling compelled to check elsewhere for the photo—besides the low-resolution copies available from suspect sources on a few website blogs—she discovers it is also available in a photographic database that the library subscribes to. This could serve as a source for the photo that is higher in quality than the (unauthorized?) web reproductions and could allow the instructor to avoid the licensing service that might be expensive, especially when the project becomes an open website later on. At the same time, her students found the photo used in a published book biography of the journalist. The full plate reproduction includes a descriptive caption of the subject, and the citation: "Permission of the _____ Archive." This version can easily yield a scan of high quality that would meet any need in their project.

So . . . what should the instructor do? Inquire about the licensing costs, and decide later whether to seek funding that covers the course use and the eventual sponsored website use? Determine if the library database version of the photo can be used for the CMS wiki, and worry about the sponsored website later? Or just let her student's scan the journalist's photograph from the book biography, use it in both purposes, and assume that if they aren't justified by Fair Use then they certainly can claim public domain anyway?

ANALYSIS: GENERAL CONSIDERATIONS

This scenario offers two uses of the photo, and two potential applications of copyright law for each of them:

1. as part of a DL course in a CMS-related wiki project; and later
2. as part of an open educational website sponsored by the university but freely available to all search engines, web-crawlers, periodic "snapshot" storage by the Internet Archive.org or others and their users, public and private.

The initial question, however, involves the status of the photo itself and of the photo's source from which the project copy is to be made.

Discernable facts are:

- The photograph as a work is no longer covered by copyright, anywhere in the world. Its control by the archive that now licenses its digital distribution is based on physical possession. It is not presumed that the archive owns also an original negative or plate for the photo—just the most publicly known copy of it, from which other public reproductions have been authorized, such as the plate in the biography and perhaps even the image database that the library subscribes to. Are there other complications besides copyright law that might be involved here? A form of property law might apply to ownership of the source copy of the photo, which could conceivably condition the further reproductive uses that were authorized, such as the book biography and the digital versions licensed by the software vendor. This factor is not a strong likelihood, but could be researched by a legal professional. Use of the photo could also involve rights of privacy or publicity—but these are unlikely because the subject journalist is long deceased and no longer a celebrity.[59]

- The archival owner has contracted for digital distribution of its (presumably rare or unique?) collection of photos in the online environment, based on physical ownership of a copy of the photo. This copy may or may not be unique.

- The biographical book has reprinted the photo by permission of the archive. Publication occurred before the digital licensing service began years later. Nothing more is detailed about the terms of this permission in the book's credit information in the colophon.

- The copyright of the book, whether owned by the author or (more likely) assigned to the publisher, applies to the book's original contents as a whole, its arrangement and design. Discrete preexisting content elements such as this photo would not be covered by that copyright.

It is doubtful that copyright law applies in this scenario—directly to the photo itself or to any reproduction of it. Property law may conceivably apply. But such a claim on this basis, if asserted as the result of the use at hand, would probably treat it legally in a way comparable to copyright infringement.

Let us consider the scenario, then, as if copyright law did apply and TEACH or Fair Use could justify its use without license or permission.

Using the Photo within the CMS—Under TEACH

Within the course-related wiki, most of the major requirements of TEACH can be met.

- The CMS wiki provides directed access only to enrolled students (and it is assumed that the university has nonprofit status).
- The instructor initiated the request for the project's collaboration space in order to meet the instructional goals. The content is directly related to the instructional purpose of the course (assembly, construction, and design of an online subject resource by students who show their mastery of this cooperative activity related to the subject).
- The content is being made available for the entire length of the course, repeated for four semesters, which is suitable to the ongoing nature of this educational project.
- The features of the CMS wiki can be adjusted to prevent downloading and copying.
- Copyright education can be provided on appropriate use of project materials by the students. The amount of material displayed here (entire photo) is acceptable in comparison with display in a physical class.
- It is from a "lawfully made" copy in the book that published it.

Since we've accepted in theory the applicability of copyright law, we need to raise one concern, in two forms, that might work against TEACH: the licensed status of other versions of the photo (besides the book's). Would the digitally licensed version, authorized by the archive, represent the primary market for the photo now (assuming copyright were to apply)? Dealing with the answer could be avoided by using the library's image database version of the photo—but only if the terms of use for its subscription permit. In that case, TEACH might not have to be applied; the license may permit this use in the course wiki. The library alternative raises another complication down the line: If the photo is sourced from the database, it is probably usable under database terms only within a protected environment like the CMS or its restricted wiki. When the sponsored open website is launched, permission to use would be necessary, from either the database vendor or the software company that is authorized by the archive. Again, remember that we are treating the situation *as if* copyright law applies to the photo.

Using the Photo Under Fair Use—Both CMS and Open Website

Consider all four factors primarily in the context of open use on a public website, which is intended as the final destination of this course project. If unauthorized use in a CMS wiki is mostly defensible under TEACH requirements, it should be at least as defensible under Fair Use there. So the discussion below focuses on public website use.

Fair Use Factor 1: Purpose and Character of Use

Favored in this case, being nonprofit educational. The character of use is favored also as transformative, because it is meant to result in a new educational information resource that benefits scholars and other users among the public.

Fair Use Factor 2: Nature of the Copyrighted Work

The photo is documentary rather than artistic in nature. Its original intention was journalism in a long-past era. Use a century later, in an educational context, reinforces a favorable judgment for this factor.

Fair Use Factor 3: Amount and Substantiality of the Portion Used

Obviously the entire photograph must be used. Because it is necessary given the subject content of the work (a single portrait), this use of the whole work may receive lesser weight when balanced against favorable verdicts for the other factors—less weight than in the video streaming scenario, for instance.

Fair Use Factor 4: Effect of Use upon Potential Market for or and Value of the Work

Doubtless the original archive specimen of the photo is property that may be rare or unique in the world—thousands of such photos, after all, have built the archive's business—and from this fact derives its market value. The photo's use in a unique, public educational endeavor may not be in its favor—should a non-copyright property right come into play—because further capture and distribution of the photo by website visitors is probable. So care in presenting the photo in a way that discourages casual appropriation would help dilute any putative market impact that may be legally raised.

The following specific measures that limit impact, and strengthen a Fair Use defense generally are worth considering:

- Provide full credit information for the source of the photo, both for the archive, for the book publication from which the copy was derived, and even for the digital licensing source. If the library's image database license permits open educational website use, this should be credited, too, if the image is sourced from it. Too much information is never a drawback in this kind of use. Citing sources is both important for the scholarly record and can be useful to a viewer who wants to pursue licensed use.

- Apply technical measures to the photo image that discourage casual capture and reuse of it outside context of the sponsored website.

- Consider developing an explanation of the Fair Use justification for the website's non-original content, including this photo. Conditions of use for all of the website's original material should be spelled out, too. The strategy of educating site visitors is both useful guidance for ethical behavior, and a means of establishing a responsible, knowledgeable approach in creating and offering the resource. In short, it evidences "good faith" in any possible infringement action.

- Consider adopting a Creative Commons license for the entire website that helps legally protect against inappropriate reuse of both original and non-original elements. A suitable alternative might be the "Attribution—Noncommercial—No Derivative Works" license, found here: http://creativecommons.org/li censes/by-nc-nd/3.0/.

In conclusion, remember that this analysis and these measures assume that the photograph is subject to copyright or other property rights. But applying these measures regardless of the work's status is always advisable in an educational environment, especially a networked one. If protecting a work used without permission can still meet the teaching need effectively, this should be done as a matter of course.

REFERENCES

Key works are marked with an asterisk. Taken together, they provide a thorough view of U.S. copyright law provisions and of the existing scope of legal interpretation of this law. They also offer practical guidance in daily decision making. Use the latest edition of each work available.

* Armatas, Steven A. *Distance Learning and Copyright: A Guide to Legal Issues.* Chicago: American Bar Association, 2008.
* Bonner, Kimberly M. and Staff of the Center for Intellectual Property, ed. *The Center for Intellectual Property Handbook.* NY & London: Neal-Schuman Publishers, 2006.
Boyle, James. *The Public Domain: Enclosing the Commons of the Mind.* New Haven & London: Yale University Press, 2008.
Center for Social Media. *Best Practices in Fair Use for Online Video,* June 2008. http:// www.centerforsocialmedia.org/files/pdf/online_best_practices_in_fair_use.pdf.
* *Copyright Law of the United States and Related Laws Contained in Title 17 of the United States Code.* U.S. Copyright Office, October 2009. http://www.copyright.gov/ title17/.
* Crews, Kenneth D. *Copyright Law for Librarians and Educators: Creative Strategies and Practical Solutions,* 2nd ed. Chicago: American Library Association, 2006.
Dames, Matthew. "Intellectual Property: Library Schools and the Copyright Knowledge Gap." *Information Today,* 23, no. 2 (February 2006). http://www.infotoday.com/ it/feb06/dames.shtml.
Dean, Katie. "Cash Rescues Eyes on the Prize." *Wired,* August 30, 2009. http://www. wired.com/entertainment/music/news/2005/08/68664.
Fishman, Stephen. *The Copyright Handbook: How to Protect & Use Written Works,* 9th ed. Berkeley, CA: Nolo, 2006.
Gasaway, Laura N. "A Defense of the Public Domain: A Scholarly Essay." *AALL/LexisNexis Call for Papers,* 2009. http://works.bepress.com/aallcallforpapers/5.
Gasaway, Laura N. *When Works Pass into the Public Domain.* http://www.unc.edu/~unclng/ public-d.htm (last updated November 4, 2003).
Harper, Georgia K. *Copyright Crash Course.* University of Texas System. http://www.utsys tem.edu/ogc/intellectualproperty/cprtindx.htm#top.

* Hayes, David P. *Copyright Registration and Renewal Information Chart and Web Site,* 2009. http://chart.copyrightdata.com/sitemap.html.

Heims, M. & Beckles, T. *Will Fair Use Survive? Free Expression in the Age of Copyright Control. A Public Policy Report.* Brennan Center for Justice at NYU School of Law, December 2005. http://www.fepproject.org/policyreports/WillFairUseSurvive.pdf.

* Hirtle, Peter. B., Emily Hudson, and Andrew T. Kenyon. *Copyright and Cultural Institutions: Guidelines for Digitization for U.S. Libraries, Archives, and Museums.* Ithaca, NY: Cornell University Library, October 14, 2009. http://ecommons.library.cornell.edu/handle/1813/14142.

* Hoon, Peggy E. *The TEACH Act Toolkit.* North Carolina State University, 2008. http://www.provost.ncsu.edu/copyright/toolkit/.

"It's A Wonderful Life." *Wikipedia, the Free Encyclopedia.* http://en.wikipedia.org/wiki/It%27s_a_wonderful_life (accessed June 2009).

Kretschmer, Martin. "Artists' Earnings and Copyright: A Review of British and German Music Industry Data in the Context of Digital Technologies." *First Monday,* 10, no. 1 (January 3, 2005). http://firstmonday.org/htbin/cgiwrap/bin/ojs/index.php/fm/article/viewArticle/1200/1120.

McJohn, Stephen M. *Copyright: Examples & Explanations.* New York: Aspen Publishers, 2006.

Minow, Mary. "Library Digitization Projects and Copyright." *LLRX.com (Law Library Resource Xchange),* June 28, 2002. http://www.llrx.com/features/digitization.htm.

Netanel, Neil Weinstock. *Copyright's Paradox.* New York: Oxford University Press, 2008.

* Russell, Carrie, ed. *Complete Copyright: An Everyday Guide for Librarians.* Chicago: American Library Association, 2004.

* Stim, Richard. *Getting Permission: How to License and Clear Copyrighted Materials Online and Off,* 3rd ed. Berkeley, CA: Nolo, 2007.

U.S. Congress. House of Representatives. *Historical and Revision Notes, House Report No. 94–1476.* September 3, 1976. http://en.wikisource.org/wiki/Copyright_Law_Revision_(House_Report_No._94-1476).

* U.S. Copyright Office. *Circular 21: Reproduction of Copyrighted Works by Educators and Librarians,* November 2009 web revision. http://www.copyright.gov/circs/circ21.pdf.

U.S. Copyright Office. *Report on Copyright and Digital Distance Education,* May 1999. http://www.copyright.gov/reports/de_rprt.pdf.

U.S. Department of Health and Human Services. National Institutes of Health Public Access. *NIH Public Access Policy Details.* http://publicaccess.nih.gov/policy.htm.

NOTES

1. Matthew Dames, "Intellectual Property: Library Schools and the Copyright Knowledge Gap," *Information Today* 23, no. 2 (February 2006), http://www.infotoday.com/it/feb06/dames.shtml.

2. A recent application of this trend: "With the Blackboard Building Block, instructors and learners can select course texts, documents and other material from the Blackboard Learn™ platform and send to a Kindle device utilizing the Kindle Personal Document Service, enabling them to easily read and review a vast amount of information on campus, at home, at work or on the go." Blackboard Inc., "Blackboard Announces Support for E-Readers," (July 14, 2009), http://www.blackboard.com/Company/Media-Center/Press-Releases.aspx?releaseid=1307580&lang=en-us.

3. A unique exception to what is usually called the "idea/expression dichotomy" is the "merger doctrine"—which acknowledges that in special cases the expression of an idea can be unique and can take precedence over copyright protection. A mathematical formula, for example, would be an obvious example. See Lewis R. Clayton, "The Merger Doctrine,"

The National Law Journal (Monday, June 6, 2005), http://www.paulweiss.com/files/tbl_s29Publications/FileUpload5679/5645/MergerDoct.pdf.

4. However, note that databases can be copyrighted as "compilations" when they are comprised of "pre-existing materials or of data that are selected, coordinated, or arranged in such a way that the resulting work as a whole constitutes an original work of authorship" (17 USC §101).

5. David P. Hayes, *Copyright Registration and Renewal Information Chart and Web Site* (2009), http://chart.copyrightdata.com/, offers a table indicating the first eligibility of different forms of copyrightable works, under "Tree-View Chart on Copyright Law."

6. The U.S. had earlier become a signatory to the Universal Copyright Convention (adopted in Geneva in 1952), until modifications in U.S. copyright law made it compatible with the more dominant Berne Convention.

7. The full text and summary of Berne and other WIPO-administered treaties are available at the website of the World Intellectual Property Organization: http://www.wipo.int/treaties/en/.

8. Martin Kretschmer, "Artists' Earnings and Copyright: A Review of British and German music Industry Data in the Context of Digital Technologies," *First Monday* 10, no. 1 (January 3, 2005): introduction, para. 5, http://firstmonday.org/htbin/cgiwrap/bin/ojs/index.php/fm/article/viewArticle/1200/1120.

9. A chronological inventory of important copyright legislation and its relationship to technology is provided in Arlene Bielefield and Lawrence Cheeseman, "Technology and Copyright Legislation," in *Technology and Copyright Law: A Guidebook for the Library, Research, and Teaching Professions,* 2nd ed. (New York and London: Neal-Schuman Publishers, Inc., 2007), 19–44.

10. United States, Public Law 105-298: *Sonny Bono Copyright Term Extension Act* (1998), http://en.wikisource.org/wiki/Sonny_Bono_Copyright_Term_Extension_Act#Title_I.

11. United States, *Public Law 105-304: Digital Millennium Copyright Act* (1998), http://en.wikisource.org/wiki/Digital_Millennium_Copyright_Act.

12. The intricacies of the DMCA's anticircumvention provisions are covered in chapter 9 of Tomas A. Lipinski, *The Complete Copyright Liability Handbook for Librarians and Educators* (New York and London: Neal-Schuman Publishers, Inc., 2006), 265–99. It should be noted, however, that the latest round of anticircumvention exemptions, announced July 27, 2010, includes a very significant one for Fair Uses that are prevalent in higher education teaching: ". . . the incorporation of short portions of motion pictures [on DVDs] into new works for the purpose of criticism or comment . . ." For the full exemption text, see U.S. Copyright Office, *Rulemaking on Anticirumvention* (revised February 7, 2011) http://www.copyright.gov/1201/.

13. 17 USC §512, "Limitations on liability relating to materials online," explains the circumstances of protection and the need for a Designated Agent in order to be covered by them. The registration process for a Service Provider's agent is available at: http://www.copyright.gov/onlinesp/. "Service provider" is defined in 17 USC §512(k)(1).

14. Diderot and Condorcet quoted in John Ewing, "Copyright and Authors," *First Monday* 8, no. 10 (6 October 2003), http://firstmonday.org/htbin/cgiwrap/bin/ojs/index.php/fm/article/view/1081/1001. Source: Carla Hesse, *Publishing and Cultural Politics in Revolutionary Paris, 1789–1810* (Berkeley, CA: University of California Press, 1991), 101, 103.

15. A useful consideration of this issue in the fine arts is Dennis J. Gifford, "Innovation and Creativity in the Fine Arts: The Relevance and Irrelevance of Copyright," *Cardozo Arts & Entertainment* 18 (2000): 569–614.

16. Laura N. Gasaway, "A Defense of the Public Domain: A Scholarly Essay," UNC Legal Studies Research Paper No. 1495233 (2009), 3, http://ssrn.com/abstract=1495233.

17. Nimmer, quoted in Neil Weinstock Netanel, *Copyright's Paradox* (New York: Oxford University Press, 2008), 57.

18. For post-1977 works, an author and/or her family retain the statutory right to terminate copyright transfer after 35 years; for example, see Stephen Fishman, *The Copyright Handbook*, 9th ed. (Berkeley, CA: Nolo, 2006), 208.

19. A good resource for addressing relevant issues is *Scholarly Communication Toolkit*, (Association of College and Research Libraries, Scholarly Communication Committee, January 2009), http://www.acrl.ala.org/scholcomm/. For a professional faculty perspective, see: "Sample Intellectual Property Policy & Contract Language," (American Association of University Professors, n.d.), http://www.aaup.org/AAUP/issues/DE/sampleIP.htm.

20. See "NIH Public Access Policy Details," http://publicaccess.nih.gov/policy. htm. Legislative activity against the NIH-like policy mandate has been introduced since 2008, with its most recent iteration being *Fair Copyright in Research Works Act of 2009* (H.R. 801). Supporting the NIH approach, legislation promoting access to government-funded research results is currently found in *Federal Research Public Access Act of 2009* (H.R. 5037).

21. The interested reader can track pro-movement developments via Peter Suber, *The SPARC Open Access Newsletter*, http://www.earlham.edu/~peters/fos/, and *Open Access News: News from the Open Access Movement*, http://www.earlham.edu/~peters/fos/fos blog.html.

22. See the Shepard Fairey entry under sections 2.1, "The Hope Poster" and 3, "Legal issues with appropriation and fair use," *Wikipedia*, http://en.wikipedia.org/wiki/Shepard_ Fairey.

23. Kenneth D. Crews, *Copyright Law for Librarians and Educators*, 2nd ed. (Chicago: American Library Association, 2006), 103–05, provides a list of court decisions related to fair use and unpublished works.

24. Although this note anticipates upcoming discussion of the public domain in law, the website *Internet Sacred Text Archive* features an illuminating discussion of just how complicated rights can become in the international sphere. See owner J.B. Hare's "The Rider-Waite-Smith Tarot Card Copyright FAQ," http://www.sacred-texts.com/tarot/faq. htm, wherein he makes the case that these famous card images may be under copyright in the United Kingdom and the European Union but are not in the United States. He defends their use on his California-based website, but advises international visitors that doing more with the images than viewing them at his site may be contrary to their own countries' copyright laws.

25. For a more complete understanding of music and musical recording rights, see the Music Library Association's website (http://musiclibraryassoc.org/) and a concise legal exposition in Richard Stim, *Getting Permission: How to License and Clear Copyrighted Materials Online and Off*, 3rd ed. (Berkeley, CA: Nolo, 2007).

26. A concise detailed explanation of the film's history can be found in the "It's A Wonderful Life" *Wikipedia* entry under section 6, "Release: Ownership and Copyright Issues" (http://en.wikipedia.org/wiki/It%27s_a_Wonderful_Life). David P. Hayes, Copyright Registration and Renewal Information Chart and Website, (2009), http://chart.copyright data.com/sitemap.html, provides other examples of movies containing underlying copyrights under "Derivative Works," http://chart.copyrightdata.com/ch10.html.

27. Katie Dean, "Cash Rescues Eyes on the Prize," *Wired* (August 30, 2009), http:// www.wired.com/entertainment/music/news/2005/08/68664.

28. *Bridgeman Art Library, Ltd. v. Corel Corp.*, 36 F. Supp. 2d 191 (S.D.N.Y. 1999), para. 24, http://www.law.cornell.edu/copyright/cases/36_FSupp2d_191.htm.

29. For current status and background of this issue, see U.S. Copyright Office, *Orphan Works* (September 25, 2008), http://www.copyright.gov/orphan/.

30. Non-attribution of public domain materials was dealt with in *Dastar Corp. v. 20th Century Fox Film Corp.*, 123 S.Ct.2041 (2003); cited in Richard Stim, *Getting Permission: How to License and Clear Copyrighted Materials Online and Off*, 3rd ed., (Berkeley, CA: Nolo, 2007), 8/10.

31. An exploration of academic integrity in misusing source materials is Jon Weiner, *Historians in Trouble: Plagiarism, Fraud, and Politics in the Ivory Tower* (New York: New Press, 2005). Perhaps the book's most famous case involving contested misuse and fabrication from public domain records is that of Michael Bellesiles, *Arming America: The Origins of a National Gun Culture* (New York: Alfred A. Knopf, 2000).

32. Even websites offering public domain works may include copyrighted supplements that should be noted by the user. For example, from *Internet Sacred Text Archive,* http://www.sacred-texts.com/cnote.htm: "Some files are copyrighted because they are original material produced especially for sacred-texts. This includes index files, the sub-section graphics and any of the descriptive material. These files, graphics and text may not be reproduced in any form without the permission of the copyright holder, J. B. Hare. These files will have explicit copyright notices."

33. Classes of exemption granted, background, and current information on this subject can be found at U.S. Copyright Office, *Rulemaking on Anticirumvention* (revised February 7, 2011), http://www.copyright.gov/1201/.

34. For more tips appropriate to a specifc kind of copyright search, see Peter B. Hirtle, Emily Hudson, and Andrew T. Kenyon, *Copyright and Cultural Institutions: Guidelines for Digitization for U.S. Libraries, Archives, and Museums* (Ithaca, NY: Cornell University Library, October 14, 2009), chapter 8, 153–72, http://ecommons.library.cornell.edu/handle/1813/14142.

35. Examples from Laura N. Gasaway, "A Defense of the Public Domain: A Scholarly Essay" (*AALL/LexisNexis Call for Papers,* 2009), http://works.bepress.com/aallcallforpapers/5.

36. A lawsuit by three academic publishers against Georgia State University involving their use of e-reserves, course management system, and other distribution of copyrighted materials without permission, is the most prominent recent incidence of the "deep pockets" strategy. Among other sources, see "Georgia State University Sued Over E-Reserves," *Library Journal Academic Newswire* (April 15, 2008), http://www.libraryjournal.com/info/CA6552504.html.

37. *Encyclopaedia Britannica Educational Corp. v. Crooks,* 558 F. Supp. 1247 (1983).

38. Steven A. Armatas, *Distance Learning and Copyright: A Guide to Legal Issues* (Chicago: American Bar Association, 2008), 137. In regard to state sovereign immunity, a good application of this principle in an intellectual property case decision can be found in *College Savings Bank v. Florida Prepaid Postsecondary Education Expense Board,* 527 U.S. 666 (1999), http://caselaw.lp.findlaw.com/scripts/getcase.pl?court=us&vol=000&invol=98-149.

39. Recommendations for updating this section were released on March 31, 2008 in *The Section 108 Study Group Report,* http://www.section108.gov/docs/Sec108StudyGroupReport.pdf. The committee of copyright experts was convened as an independent group by the National Digital Information Infrastructure and Preservation program of the Library of Congress and by the U.S. Copyright Office.

40. The warning note for both the service location where the copy is made and for inclusion on the copy itself is specified in 37 C.F.R. §201.14:

Notice warning concerning copyright restrictions
The copyright law of the United States (Title 17, United States Code) governs the making of photocopies or other reproductions of copyrighted material.

Under certain conditions specified in the law, libraries and archives are authorized to furnish a photocopy or other reproduction. One of these specific conditions is that the photocopy or reproduction is not to be "used for any purpose other than private study, scholarship, or research." If a user makes a request for, or later uses, a photocopy or reproduction for purposes in excess of "fair use," that user may be liable for copyright infringement.

> This institution reserves the right to refuse to accept a copying order if, in its judgment, fulfillment of the order would involve violation of copyright law.

41. Neil Weinstock Netanel, *Copyright's Paradox* (New York: Oxford University Press, 2008) provides a full-length study of the interaction of copyright law and freedom of expression.

42. Two court decisions in recent decades have established that a commercial use of a copyrighted work without permission can still be a fair one. In *Campbell v. Acuff-Rose Music, Inc.*, 510 US 569 (1994), the use of the opening music and lyric from the song "Oh Pretty Woman" was considered to be parodic and sufficiently transformative to be defensible. In a lower court decision involving the plagiarism detection service Turnitin.com, a commercial Fair Use of entire student papers was judged sufficiently transformative; the U.S. Court of Appeals (4th Circuit) affirming decision on *A.V. v. iParadigms, LLC,* is available at http://pacer.ca4.uscourts.gov/opinion.pdf/081424.P.pdf. For other recent case examples that involve commercial uses, see Jonathan Band in the next Note.

43. In fact, at least one legal scholar has suggested an even more sweeping scope for transformative use, given recent case law: "If repurposing a work renders its use transformative, then arguably an educational use of a work created for a different market also is transformative." Jonathan Band, *Educational Fair Use Today* (Association of Research Libraries, December 2007), 13, http://www.arl.org/bm~doc/educationalfairusetoday.pdf.

44. See Robert Kasunic, "Is That All There Is? Reflections on the Nature of the Second Fair Use Factor," *Columbia Journal of Law & the Arts* 31, 529 (Summer 2008), http://www.kasunic.com/Articles/CJLA%20Kasunic%20Final%202008.pdf.

45. *Harper & Row v. Nation Enterprises*, 471 US 539 (1985), is often cited both for its relevance to the more limited scope allowed in unauthorized use of unpublished works and for its speaking to "substantiality of the portion" and the impact on the work's value and market. An excerpt from Gerald Ford's memoir, dealing with his pardon of Richard Nixon, was conveyed in galley to the *The Nation,* enabling it to scoop official article publication in *Time* magazine. Ford's memoir was scheduled for eventual book form also. The unauthorized excerpt of his pardon decision as president denied the author "first publication" (important to the legal decision, though not a defined right under copyright law), and also constituted the feature of his memoir most likely to be of interest to the public. Both the book's and the authorized *Time* article's value and market were negatively impacted by the scoop. On the other hand, parody is commonly understood (and successfully defended) as a privileged form of Fair Use—so long as the parody relates to the appropriated work itself, and the portion used is not a large part of it (as in *Campbell v. Acuff-Rose* in Note 29 above). The defensible parody should relate to the *content* of the work being parodied, not simply use its form or style.

46. See the case examples cited in Band, *Educational Fair Use Today.*

47. One legal scholar who has focused on the market factor closely is Mark A. Lemley, *Should a Licensing Market Require Licensing?* (Stanford Public Law Working Paper No. 917161, July 13, 2006), http://ssrn.com/abstract=917161.

48. Center for Social Media, *Code of Best Practices in Fair Use for Online Video* (June 2008), 11, http://www.centerforsocialmedia.org/files/pdf/online_best_practices_in_fair_use.pdf.

49. Consult Kenneth D. Crews, *Copyright Law for Librarians and Educators: Creative Strategies and Practical Solutions,* 2nd ed. (Chicago: American Library Association, 2006), Appendix B, 123–24. Also available as *Fair Use Checklist,* http://copyright.columbia.edu/fair-use-checklist.

50. For a history of the process, see U.S. Copyright Office, *Copyright and Digital Distance Education* (n.d.), http://www.copyright.gov/disted/.

51. Peggy E. Hoon, *The TEACH Toolkit* (North Carolina State University, n.d.), http://www.provost.ncsu.edu/copyright/toolkit/, offered a comprehensive resource on

the Act after its passage in 2002. The website now reflects the experience and perspective of academe in actually implementing TEACH provisions in online course practices. This author agrees that these practices most often rely on the Fair Use doctrine—but TEACH provisions, now reflected in section 110(2), are discussed in the text comparatively with Fair Use as a means to better understand both.

52. For a nuanced argument using this approach, see Library Copyright Association, *Issue Brief: Streaming of Films for Educational Purposes* (February 19, 2010), http://www.librarycopyrightalliance.org/bm~doc/ibstreamingfilms_021810.pdf. The scenario in the section "Case: Video Streaming without a License" draws on this approach in evaluating a Fair Use for a streaming video situation.

53. U.S. Copyright Office, *Report on Copyright and Digital Distance Education* (May 1999), viii, http://www.copyright.gov/reports/de_rprt.pdf.

54. Steven A. Armatas, *Distance Learning and Copyright: A Guide to Legal Issues* (Chicago: American Bar Association, 2008), 111–333.

55. *Spontaneity* is specified in the *Agreement on Guidelines for Classroom Copying in Not-For-Profit Educational Institutions with Respect to Books and Periodicals* (1976), published originally in H.R. 2223. These *Guidelines* are reprinted in U.S. Copyright Office, *Circular 21: Reproduction of Copyrighted Works by Educators and Librarians,* rev. November 2009, http://www.copyright.gov/circs/circ21.pdf, p. 6.

56. Licensing services for streaming movies to academic courses are available at the Motion Picture Licensing Corporation, http://www.mplc.org/, and Swank Motion Pictures, Inc., http://www.swank.com/.

57. Peter B. Hirtle, Emily Hudson, and Andrew T. Kenyon, *Copyright and Cultural Institutions: Guidelines for Digitization for U.S. Libraries, Archives, and Museums* (Ithaca, NY: Cornell University Library, October 14, 2009), http://ecommons.library.cornell.edu/handle/1813/14142, provides the most comprehensive and current guidance for applying copyright law when building digital collections. The collections themselves, once established, become available for distributed learning uses.

58. Rulemaking is authorized under 17 USC §1201(a)(1) every three years, and the current exemptions (published in the *Federal Register,* July 27, 2010) can be found at U.S. Copyright Office, *Rulemaking on Exemptions from Prohibition on Circumvention of Technological Measures that Control Access to Copyright Works,* http://www.copyright.gov/1201/.

59. For more information on the right of publicity and how it varies geographically in law, a good place to start is the website *Right of Publicity,* http://rightofpublicity.com/statutes.

6

ELECTRONIC RESERVES AND INFORMATION DELIVERY

John Schlipp

Jill Jones has been appointed as the new librarian responsible for copyright compliance and management of a mid-sized university academic library and its electronic reserves and interlibrary loan workflow. The library has established a budget for funding to support copyright fees for both library reserves and interlibrary loan. Jill has also been assigned to introduce a new library document delivery service for obtaining resources not available from her library's onsite or electronic collection. Her understanding of the Fair Use doctrine of the U.S. Copyright Act and the TEACH Act (both covered in chapter 5) are not the only areas related to intellectual property that she must know. Jill must also be familiar with other guidelines and policies that have been developed since the introduction of the U.S. Copyright Act of 1976. She will coach faculty, staff, and students on the ins and outs of Fair Use, the TEACH Act, the CONTU Rule of Five, and other related intellectual property topics. She will also publicize and promote her library's electronic reserves, interlibrary loan, document delivery, and other associated services essential for her university's expanding number of distance education students. Since the library is now paying for course reserve copyright fees, Jill is providing the instructors support, which may have been the responsibility of the instructors or of their departments before. As Jill's work responsibilities illustrate, she wears many hats and must juggle multiple roles tied together by her knowledge of and experience with intellectual property in an academic environment. She must have an understanding of digital classroom needs, and of the extent and limitations of delivering resources legally. This chapter is a basic introduction to what any librarian responsible for electronic reserves, interlibrary loan, document delivery, and associated areas needs to know in relation to intellectual property for distributed educational instruction to ensure that all are in compliance with the U.S. Copyright Act.

Distributed learning, as represented in information delivery services, relies on the support of electronic reserves, interlibrary loan, audio and visual media in course management systems, and copyright awareness. These information services are fundamental, as they are the ties to needed resources for distributed learners that are either licensed or not owned by a library. As we will discuss, understanding the following is vital for making certain that a library is copyright-compliant for distributed learning: the Fair Use doctrine, copyright guidelines such as the National Commission on New Technological Uses of Copyrighted Works (CONTU) Rule of Five, and database licensing agreements.

Copyright is confusing and challenging. Its complexity leads some libraries and educators to err on the side that everything is Fair Use. (See chapter 5 for a full description of Fair Use.) Conversely, others are so scrupulous as to fear copying or reproducing anything.[1] Establishing copyright awareness programs and policies help guide a library and instructors to avoid pitfalls. An example is the case of a Georgia State University copyright lawsuit (2008) brought by publishers claiming that the school distributed unauthorized works through its electronic course reserve systems.[2] Still, many notable experts on this subject, such as Laura Gasaway and Kenneth Crews, emphasize how librarians and educators must take control and exercise their Fair Use legal rights fully.[3] As librarians and educators, Crews affirms that we can only benefit from the legal exemptions (such as Fair Use) by understanding copyright. We must recognize options that the law allows and make decisions about copyright that best advance our educational purpose. If we do not manage copyright to our advantage, we could lose valuable opportunities for attaining our teaching and research goals.[4] Supreme Court Justice Sandra Day O'Connor perhaps expressed it best in reference to the Feist decision of 1991, stating that the primary purpose of copyright is to "build freely upon the ideas and information conveyed by a work . . . It is the means by which copyright advances the progress of science and art."[5]

ELECTRONIC RESERVES

Library course reserves provide a great service for instructors to offer outside readings to students that supplement their lessons. Since the introduction of electronic reserves (e-reserves), students now have 24/7 virtual access to reserve content. The Association of Research Libraries (ARL) describes e-reserves as a collection of digital course materials made available over one or more computer networks.[6] Library reserves may be available in either traditional (print) or electronic formats, but e-reserves have found greater favor among students of today's traditional classroom-based courses and are vital to the success of distributed learning students. It is fairly obvious that traditional reserves such as photocopied articles or entire books held at the students' host library would not be easily accessible to distributed students. With online technology, journal articles and many other library resources may be made available to all students remotely, with particular benefit to the distributed learning student. With the permission of the copyright holder, an entire book or an entire creative media resource such as music or film could be placed on e-reserve. However, such permission is not always so easy to obtain and can be costly. Without permission, the Fair Use doctrine only permits small portions and limited time use tied to classroom instruction.

Since distributed learning relies on e-reserves to support its courses, the open nature of the web potentially makes a school's reserves use presence more visible to the general public and commercial publishers. Despite few copyright-related lawsuits against educators, the open web activity should encourage educators to become better aware of copyright laws and Fair Use in order to avoid lawsuits and still provide resources tied to distributed learning.[7]

Library Copyright and Workflow Role

An important question about e-reserves now arises: Who should clear the copyright? In many cases copyright permission responsibility is shifting away from the teaching faculty to the library, which affords academic institutions a central location for management of both workflow and copyright compliance. Many schools use a special database or portion of an online course management system (CMS) to post their e-reserves. Libraries are well suited to handle copyright compliance and workflow because it generally fits into their existing role better than into that of the course instructors. Technology and copyright awareness are more aligned to what librarians do in their daily work routine.[8] Hence, librarians should act as copyright coaches for their customers, not as copyright police.[9]

To help manage the copyright compliance in the e-reserves workflow, library content e-reserves portals such as those found in a course management system (CMS) like Blackboard make it possible for the library to post copyright-compliant content into the online courses. An e-reserve folder may be placed in the Content Collection of any online course activated by the instructor for any active traditional or distance learning course.[10]

Copyright coaching provides an opportunity for the library to present copyright workshops and one-on-one copyright instruction in order to assist faculty with their instructional and research needs. Working together with instructors and their CMS also promotes a collaborative model of course development between the teaching faculty and the library. Together this coaching promotes greater integration of library resources and instruction in both distance education and traditional teaching. This collaboration demonstrates the "power of combining expertise, tools, and perspective to enhance teaching and learning."[11]

WHAT DO YOU THINK?

Who should deal with e-reserves and copyright? Who should clear copyright? The instructor or the host library? Who should pay for the copyright clearance? The instructor or the host library? What if the faculty decides to post their electronic reserves on their own course management system (CMS) and wants the library's help with copyright? Or should another party be responsible such as Information Technology, Legal Services, or another division of the school? What do you think?

Electronic Reserves Distance Learning Distinctions

Due to the physical difference between traditional and electronic reserves, copyright compliance and Fair Use analyses require extra precautions for online distributed learning. This is also critical due to most publishers' restrictive view of Fair

Use. Password restriction to a website or CMS access limited for those students enrolled in the course are the first step to lawsuit avoidance. Fair Use analysis and copyright permission record-keeping is next. Some e-reserves platforms such as Blackboard Library Content, DocuTek, and other similar systems provide copyright management tracking. If these are not available, then a library should maintain records in a paper file or through an electronic database to track use of a document. Finally, the library must obtain permission from the publisher or the author, when required, to document their copyright compliance.

As a rule, copyright fees are higher for the same resource utilized as an e-reserve compared to a traditional (paper) reserve. This is because the permission cost factor established by the copyright holder is usually based on the number of students enrolled in the class using the e-reserves, while the cost of a traditional reserve is based on how many physical copies (single or few) are held on reserve for students to share onsite at the library.

Workflow Database to Maintain Copyright Records

A number of libraries have developed their own databases that streamline the online faculty request process and improve the workflow of e-reserves and copyright compliance. This type of database could be built with three tables—reserve item, reserve instructor, and reserve copyright. Ideally, the database should be posted on the library's website. The database typically has two elements: 1) a customer view with an online instructor request form, and 2) a staff view, including document posting workflow and copyright compliance records. The staff view would have restricted access so that only library personnel may handle the workflow.

ROLE-PLAY A SITUATION

Your academic library has just introduced e-reserves with the school's implementation of a course management system (CMS) that permits posting documents on its student online course sites. This is a new service for faculty; they are accustomed only to traditional reserves where items are placed on reserve at the library circulation desk. You have posted an e-reserves policy on the library's website stating that all e-reserve requests must be submitted via an online order form. You request that faculty supply copies of any article or book chapter that is not held in the library's collection. Your policy states that the workflow to post the e-reserves on the course site may take up to one-week at the beginning of each semester. Professor Malo drops off handwritten request forms to the circulation desk for 30 articles, none of which are available among the library's journal collection. He asks you to post all of these articles for the next day. Come up with an outline of options on how to handle this situation and how you would present this to Professor Malo. Then find a friend or classmate to play the role of Professor Malo, while you present your response as the e-reserves librarian.

Fair Use or Permission to Use Works

Once the library receives the online faculty request, a Fair Use analysis or permission for copied works posted should be completed. Library copyright experts Kenneth Crews, Director of the Copyright Advisory Office at Columbia University Libraries, and Dwayne Buttler, professor and the first Evelyn J. Schneider Endowed Chair for Scholarly Communication at the University of Louisville libraries, have written a Checklist for Fair Use.[12] It has become the recognized standard for educators to use to determine if use of a document as a library reserve falls under the Fair Use umbrella. (See chapter 5 for a complete discussion of the four Fair Use factors.) The checklist uses the four Fair Use factors as established in the U.S. Copyright Act.[13]

Carrie Russell, Office for Information Technology Policy of the American Library Association, and author of *Complete Copyright: An Everyday Guide for Librarians,* suggests that understanding and utilizing Fair Use habitually may lessen potential liability in educators using copyrighted works. Kenneth Crews underscores, though, that educators should not become obsessed by exact numbers or percentages from some associations' published guidelines. Fair Use is not black and white. Lawmakers intentionally crafted Fair Use guidelines to be flexible for educators. Although recent technology has moved faster than the copyright laws, Fair Use guidelines generally apply for most educators' needs. Since the Fair Use doctrine is intentionally vague and lacking any specific mention of technology, it is technology-neutral. The interpretation of Fair Use may vary and is decided in courts of law. For example, some libraries only make use of Fair Use for articles posted as traditional or electronic reserves for the first semester utilized, while permission is acquired for use in subsequent semesters for the same document by the same instructor.[14] Fair Use does not stipulate this practice; this is a commonly accepted, conservative rule followed by most libraries based on the 1982 ALA *Model Policy* Section III-B, which is discussed later in this chapter. This question of use in a subsequent semester is interpreted in varying ways. Some librarians and instructors could believe that as a new class arrives for a semester, it constitutes a first time Fair Use for those class students. Each institution should determine its own policy based on its interpretation of the law and the technology available. However, be prepared to justify a more liberal interpretation of Fair Use for a copyright policy if necessary. Georgia Harper reinforces the one-semester idea in her view that the publishers "clearly believe that fair use has time limits."[15]

Fair Use conditions may differ depending on the types of customer use (e.g., library reserves, interlibrary loan, distributed learning course content posted by the instructor, or faculty and student research and writing). Also, the type of library determines different levels of Fair Use. There is a continuum between varying types of libraries and whether or not profit is concerned. The closer one's use of another's copyrighted works is related to a financial profit, the greater the risk of an infringement.[16] Academic, nonprofit libraries tend to have more liberal use of Fair Use for research and scholarship, while at the other end of the continuum, the specialty, for-profit libraries usually have very little Fair Use.[17] Yet more exemptions in favor of Fair Use may exist for specialty libraries than realized when individual cases are reviewed.

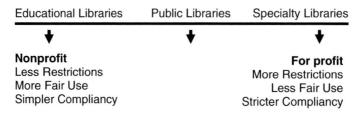

Fair Use Continuum by Library Type
Source: John Schlipp.

Durable, Persistent, Constant, Stable Links to Subscribed Databases

Many newspaper and journal articles utilized by faculty for their outside class readings may be available as full-text articles in a library's collection of databases. When a library has an agreement through its electronic database licensing contract, it could legally post URL links instead of actual e-reserves images of articles. Most databases provide persistent links to their URLs for uninterrupted posting of a document. There may be no need to ask for permission or to make an additional payment. Here is where database subscriptions have proved especially helpful for academic libraries. What's more, free and open web pages usually may be linked to an e-reserves site without any permission. A URL link is an address and considered a fact. Facts are not protected by copyright.[18] If a dispute ever occurs over linking, it should be addressed by getting permission and having the linked site sign and provide a written agreement.[19]

Educating faculty on how to post persistent URL links is another opportunity for librarians to collaborate with and coach instructors. The library could post a webpage with directions on how faculty should link the persistent URLs within their CMS. Some faculty may find their students prefer the outside readings posted within their CMS site rather than the library e-reserves location. This also provides the library an opportunity to assist with copyright permission for PDF documents posted that are not included in the library's databases.

What About the TEACH Act and Electronic Reserves?

The TEACH Act (covered in chapter 5) cannot be applied to e-reserves; Fair Use must be used instead of the TEACH Act. Since Fair Use is technology-neutral,[20] it may supplement the TEACH Act. If, however, the amount of the resource posted is a mediated instructional activity and comparable to what the instructor would use in face-to-face classroom instruction (i.e., its performance and display is analogous to the type that would take place in a live classroom setting),[21] then the TEACH Act guidelines could be applied for use within a password-protected CMS or e-reserves.[22] But the distributed instruction face-to-face equivalency aspect of posting documents under the TEACH Act should not substitute for coursepacks or supplementary readings for outside of the classroom instruction. If an instructor posted a current newspaper article or recent journal article excerpt to demonstrate a point of his distributed lesson, this might qualify as an electronic reserve. Caution should be exercised when utilizing this type of application as an e-reserve, as it is very narrowly allowed under the TEACH Act. Under current copyright laws, librarians and educators should utilize Fair Use or copyright permission for virtually all e-reserves.

OBTAINING PERMISSION TIPS AND CONDITIONS

Getting permission not only applies to e-reserves but also relates to interlibrary loan. When uncertain, ask for permission in writing. A permission request reference should include the resource title, author, page range, standard number (ISBN or ISSN), and date. It is a practical measure to insist for the permission reply to be in a permanent written format, including the name of the authorizing party. By no means rely on verbal, telephone, or cellular text messages. An email, telephone facsimile, or written letter with date and name of the permission-granting authorization should be saved in some type of copyright permission file.[23] To save time, the Copyright Clearance Center (CCC) is the first place to try to get permission. If a document used for library reserve is not registered with the CCC, contact the publisher or author directly. The U.S. Copyright Office offers a free online database at www.copyright.gov of copyright registrations (records since 1978) that may assist you in finding the author. Keyword searching for an author contact in a web search engine is another option. For e-reserves, it is practical to maintain a file or database that includes all related information for each document posted, such as source citation, instructor name and course, date posted, number of students, permission disposition, and cost.

According to the ALA, "Orphan Works" are those "whose copyright owners cannot be identified or found" after a realistic, good-faith search. If passed into law, the Orphan Works Act (OWA) may address the challenge faced by failing to find copyright owners. The still-pending act may provide some semblance of protection to libraries and researchers by limiting compensation to copyright owners who later materialize. The legislation, if passed, could even exempt libraries and nonprofit users "if they stopped using the item immediately." For updates on this matter, see the ALA "Issues and Advocacy" website, and keyword search "Orphan Works."[24]

In addition to not being able to find a copyright owner, other challenges may include no reply from the permission request, a cost-prohibitive copyright fee, or the copyright owner refusing permission. When this occurs, returning to a Fair Use analysis may guide you on what to do. Other options include replacing the work with an alternative work, using a smaller portion of the work, or conducting a risk-benefit analysis with legal counsel.[25] Most educators want to do the right thing. If copyright policies are posted and library awareness programs are presented, most educators will follow Fair Use guidelines or come to the library copyright specialist for help. The library can refer reluctant faculty to the copyright policies in the faculty handbook or on the library website.

WHAT WOULD YOU DO?

Professor Adkins comes to you and wants to post dozens of journal articles for outside class readings under the TEACH Act as e-reserves, when he should only make use of the TEACH Act for resources utilized as part of face-to-face equivalence instruction. Professor Miller's class textbook has not arrived at the bookstore in time for the first few weeks of class, and she needs to post a couple of chapters on her online course management system (CMS). You hear from another instructor that Professor Williams is posting journal articles and book chapters semester after semester on his online CMS without obtaining permission from any copyright holders. What can you do to support and assist teaching faculty to follow Fair Use guidelines (or the TEACH Act) for posting copyrighted works of others on a CMS? How do you coach faculty with advice without becoming known as the campus copyright patrol?

EDUCATOR GUIDELINES INTERPRETING FAIR USE

Over time, many special-interest library groups have developed related guiding principles interpreting Fair Use for librarians and educators to follow. Since Fair Use is technology-neutral, these guiding principles may support a conservative threshold to a Fair Use analysis for e-reserves when in doubt. Highlights of these include the following, which are covered in the next section of this chapter:

- 1976: *Agreement on Guidelines for Classroom Copying in Not-for-Profit Educational Institutions with Respect to Books and Periodicals*
- 1982: *Model Policy Concerning College and University Photocopying for Classroom, Research and Library Reserve Use*
- 2005: *Using Electronic Reserves: Guidelines and Best Practices for Copyright Compliance*, issued by the Copyright Clearance Center (CCC)

Classroom Copying Guidelines: Percentages of Use

Handouts of limited copyrighted works used in face-to-face nonprofit classroom settings are generally permitted if tied to the content of class instruction. An analysis of a Fair Use checklist such as the one prepared by Kenneth Crews and Dwayne Buttler is strongly recommended to verify that the limited use is indeed a Fair Use.

However, the question of percentage of copyrighted content use is not always clear according to the four Fair Use factors. The 1976 *Agreement on Guidelines for Classroom Copying in Not-for-Profit Educational Institutions with Respect to Books and Periodicals* (in this chapter, called *Classroom Guidelines*) covers the percentages of use published in House Report 94–1476.[26] The *Classroom Guidelines* were prepared by special-interest author and publisher groups as part of the committee reports presented to the congressionally enacted 1976 copyright revisions. The *Classroom Guidelines* were endorsed by the House Report as "a reasonable interpretation of the minimum standards of fair use" without being an official part of the fair use statute, Sec. 107. Two special interest groups (the American Association of University Professors and the Association of American Law Schools) declined to participate or endorse the *Classroom Guidelines* because they deemed them "too restrictive with respect to classroom situations at the university and graduate level."[27]

The section of the *Classroom Guidelines* on multiple copies for classroom use provides percentages of acceptable use and sets specific limits that are not quantified by the Fair Use guidelines. Remember that these guidelines were created for an analog environment decades before the digital world existed for education. Depending on your interpretation of the Fair Use doctrine, you may find these guidelines too restrictive for distributed education. Some scholars, such as Lindsey,[28] believe that this guideline is "the most conservative and least contentious ground of fair use." Laura Gasaway, another expert scholar on this topic, adds that although the *Classroom Guidelines* point towards "minimum" rules, many educational institutions apply the *Classroom Guidelines* as if they are "maximum rules."[29] These limits include brevity, spontaneity, and cumulative effect:

BREVITY

(i)   Poetry: (a) A complete poem if less than 250 words and if printed on not more than two pages or, (b) from a longer poem, an excerpt of not more than 250 words.

(ii) Prose: (a) Either a complete article, story or essay of less than 2,500 words, or (b) an excerpt from any prose work of not more than 1,000 words or 10 percent of the work, whichever is less, but in any event a minimum of 500 words.
(Each of the numerical limits stated in "i" and "ii" above may be expanded to permit the completion of an unfinished line of a poem or of an unfinished prose paragraph.)

(iii) Illustration: one chart, graph, diagram, drawing, cartoon or picture per book or per periodical issue.

(iv) "Special" works: certain words in poetry or in "poetic prose," which often combine language with illustrations and which are intended sometimes for children and at other times for a more general audience, that fall short of 2,500 words in their entirety. Paragraph "ii" above notwithstanding, such "special works" may not be reproduced in their entirety, but an excerpt comprising not more than two of the published pages of such a special work and containing not more than 10 percent of the words found in the text thereof may be reproduced.

SPONTANEITY

(i)   The copying is at the instance and inspiration of the individual teacher, and

(ii) The inspiration and decision to use the work and the moment of its use for maximum teaching effectiveness are so close in time that it would be unreasonable to expect a timely reply to a request for permission.

CUMULATIVE EFFECT

(i)   The copying of the material is for only one course in the school in which the copies are made.

(ii) Not more than one short poem, article, story, essay or two excerpts may be copied from the same author, nor more than three from the same collective work or periodical volume during one class term.

(iii) There shall not be more than nine instances of such multiple copying for one course during one class term.

Although the *Classroom Guidelines* have probably influenced more school library than academic library policies related to Fair Use, Kenneth Crews argues that these "guidelines are a constraint on the law's flexibility" and time-consuming to oversee. Fair Use factors are based on the law, while the *Classroom Guidelines* are not. The four Fair Use factors from the copyright law may provide greater security than guidelines such as these. Lindsey and Crews suggest that although these guidelines are a good starting point in a Fair Use analysis, there are no legal grounds for the guidelines to control Fair Use policy in higher education. Crews further claims that Fair Use is open to technology changes and educators' needs, while these guidelines may be too restrictive.[30] However, the *Classroom Guidelines* may be considered helpful, cautious measures to follow when a Fair Use analysis is uncertain (e.g., when two of the four Fair Use factors lean for and two lean against).

WHAT WOULD YOU DO?

A new media instructor wants to post an article from a highly creative film writing journal that features script excerpts of the Top Ten Films of the Year. It also reviews each film's background, such as cast, crew, photos, behind-the-scene trivia. The instructor wants to scan the article from a paper copy of the journal held in the library's collection. You help them to perform a Fair Use four-factor analysis. The analysis confirms that, due to the proprietary nature of the photos with multiple source credits and multiple scripts, only two of the four factors favor Fair Use. What would you do?

ALA Model Policy and the Kinko's Case

The *Model Policy Concerning College and University Photocopying for Classroom, Research and Library Reserve Use* was published by the American Library Association in 1982. The authors of this policy included ALA Legal Counsel Mary Hutchings of the law firm Sidley & Austin, with recommendation and support from the Copyright Subcommittee (ad hoc) of ALA's Legislation Committee, Association of College and Research Libraries (ACRL) Copyright Committee, Association of Research Libraries (ARL), other academic librarians, and attorneys. It was, "intended for the guidance and use of academic librarians, faculty, administrators, and legal counsel in response to implementation of the rights and responsibilities provisions of . . . the Copyright Law."[31] However, the ALA *Model Policy* was not approved by the U.S. Congress and did not represent any official meetings between librarians and publishers. The ALA *Model Policy* acquires much criticism for its statement in section III B—Permissible Photocopying of Copyrighted Works: Classroom Use, where "the distribution of the same photocopied material does not occur every semester."[32] For library reserves, some libraries found this too restrictive based on their Fair Use interpretation, while others have incorporated this into their library policy for workflow of handling reserves. This single-semester time limit factor has become the *de facto* policy for most libraries in the digital e-reserve setting, too. Yet the Fair Use doctrine in the copyright law includes nothing that supports a time limit in education for course reserves.

The first part of the ALA *Model Policy* reviews some of the requirements of the *Classroom Guidelines,* while the second part in section III C, "Permissible Photocopying of Copyrighted Works: Library Reserve Uses," states that at the request of faculty, a library may copy an entire article, book chapter, or poem for one copy placed on reserve. Section III C suggests the following regarding multiple copies in addition to the relevant sections of the Copyright Act:[33]

1. the amount of material should be reasonable in relation to the total amount of material assigned for one term of a course, taking into account the nature of the course, its subject matter, and level, *Copyright Act of 1976,* U.S. Code 17 (2005) §107 (1) and (3);
2. the number of copies should be reasonable in light of the number of students enrolled, the difficulty and timing of assignments, and the number of other courses that may assign the same material, *Copyright Act of 1976,* U.S. Code 17 (2005) §107 (1) and (3);
3. the material should contain a notice of copyright, see 17 U.S.C. §401;
4. the effect of photocopying the material should not be detrimental to the market for the work. (In general, the library should own at least one copy of the work.) *Copyright Act of 1976,* U.S. Code 17 (2005) §107 (4).

From what the ALA *Model Policy* implies, Gasaway believes that library reserves should not replace textbooks or legally acquired coursepacks; they are designed to supplement textbooks or coursepacks. Gasaway also states that the policy's second suggestion above regarding the number of reserve copies reproduced implies that "the library is better suited to make this decision than the faculty member."[34]

Comparison of Classroom Copying Guidelines and ALA Model Policy

The degree of user rights promoted under Fair Use is the major difference between the *Classroom Guidelines* (1976) and the ALA *Model Policy* (1982), according to Kenneth Crews. He observes four major dissimilarities:

1. Only the ALA *Model Policy* includes provisions for library reserves.
2. The *Classroom Guidelines* lists safe-harbor restrictions only, with no mention of any certain rights secured by the copyright law, while the ALA *Model*

Policy provides guidelines about unrestricted copying, permission requests, and legal liabilities and rights.

3. The *Classroom Guidelines* presents a statement of "minimum" standards adopted by higher education as a safe-harbor "maximum" limit of Fair Use to avoid lawsuits. This external pressure from publishers shapes a definition of Fair Use that may overwhelm educators' "internal obligations to best promote teaching and research." To support educational Fair Use, the ALA *Model Policy* opposes the "maximum" limits view by illustrating possible Fair Use scenarios outside the *Guidelines.*

4. The ALA affirms the quantitative standards in the *Classroom Guidelines,* except it highlights those as "the most conservative guidelines." As an alternative, the ALA guidelines state that complete articles may be copied, without counting words or authors.[35]

Kinko's Coursepack Case Affected Library Course Reserve Guidelines

The real Fair Use test that implicitly questioned the authority of the *Classroom Guidelines* (1976) and the ALA *Model Policy* (1982) was the 1991 decision in *Basic Books, Inc. v. Kinko's Graphics Corp.,* 758 F. Supp. 1522, 1526 (S.D.N.Y. 1991). Kinko's is a commercial photocopy retail chain.

A New York Federal District Court ruled that Kinko's Graphics Corporation infringed copyrights when it photocopied materials (including chapters of books and articles from periodicals) for sale to students as coursepacks for their university classes. The copyrighted works infringed included hardback and paperback editions of in-print and out-of-print trade and professional works, as well as textbooks. The 12 copied excerpts in the case ranged from 14 to 110 pages and from 5% to 24% of the works. In addition to ruling against further photocopying by Kinko's without permission of the copyright owners, the Court awarded the plaintiffs damages, court costs, and attorney's fees resulting in $2 million. The Court's decision in the case did not prohibit the reproduction and sale of anthologies, but rather the reproduction and sale of anthologies made without obtaining proper copyright permission or meeting the criteria of either the *Classroom Guidelines* or the statutory "fair use" provisions in Section 107 of the Copyright Act.[36]

The Federal Court reported Kinko's as the party who profited and was found liable for not obtaining permission to copy. The publishers were awarded over $500,000 in damages from Kinko's. Professors of three schools, New School for Social Research, New York University, and Columbia University asked Kinko's to make the copies for ranges of 3 to 132 students charging students $11 to $24 per coursepack.[37]

The Kinko's case not only affected the guidelines for coursepacks but added another layer of restricting guidelines to those already established by most colleges and universities for library reserves. It also serves as a warning for e-reserves. Crews observed that the court employed the statutory factors (Section 107. Limitations on Exclusive Rights: Fair Use) and easily found that three of the four factors, Purpose, Amount, and Market Effect, opposed Fair Use. The Purpose was considered commercial, since Kinko's was involved. In this case, the Amount copied (5% to 25%) was considered substantial and its Effect on the Market was seen as hindering the publisher's potential sale of books and photocopy permission royalties. Only the Nature factor favored Fair Use, since most of the copied materials were "factual works." The judge of this case refused to rule that all anthologies of photocopies, such as coursepacks, were unlawful. The decision was directed primarily against Kinko's for profit motive within the framework of Fair Use. The *Classroom Guidelines* that were utilized by the defendant were deemed as not appropriate for Kinko's use because they were created only for nonprofit educational use.[38]

Copyright Clearance Center Conservative View on Electronic Course Reserves

Another limiting document was published in 2005 by the Copyright Clearance Center (CCC) and it was entitled, *Using Electronic Reserves: Guidelines and Best Practices for Copyright Compliance.* Given the brokerage nature of the CCC as an intermediary between copyright holders and copyright users, it is not surprising that this document favors the publishers' perspective and should only be used as a conservative measure when establishing a library e-reserves policy. Congress established the need for and suggested the creation of the CCC as a national rights clearinghouse to assist educators in obtaining permissions during the introduction of the Copyright Act of 1976. CCC saves librarians and educators much time in obtaining permission for the use of copyrighted works. According to the U.S. Patent and Trademark Office, the CCC "is a voluntary, not-for-profit, industry-led licensing and infringement protection system for both electronic and paper-based works. CCC . . . completes approximately 2 million individual licensing transactions every year, collects over $100 million in royalties per year."[39] Although the CCC is a non-profit organization, it primarily represents publishers first as a liaison to libraries, since its copyright fees collected include a portion to cover the organization's administrative expenses.

It is common knowledge that publisher studies have recognized a decline of journal subscriptions for academic use.[40] One might question whether the 2008 lawsuit from publishers directed at Georgia State University was a result of such a decline. As the Yale University Library notes on its website, the CCC "investigates allegations of copyright infringement that involve works of its customers."[41]

Copyright compliance requirements for campus bookstores or photocopy centers making coursepacks vary greatly from library reserves. It is highly recommended to obtain permission and make copyright royalty payment when asked to do so, no matter the number of students or semesters a document is utilized. There are too many commercial aspects when a copy center is involved.

Audiovisual Fair Use Guidelines

Fair Use or the TEACH Act? That is the question. How might educators and librarians handle instructional audiovisual works such as films? Based on cautious guidelines such as those noted below, audiovisual resources posted may require either limited portion use or network streaming access of an entire work. Password-restricted access to the e-reserve site for students enrolled in the course may also sway Fair Use in your favor. Password restriction or network streaming demonstrate the Fair Use Purpose factor supporting the limited students of a specific class. The technology of streaming supports copyright protection as streamed resources are not saved to remote computers.[42]

The *Fair Use Guidelines for Educational Multimedia* offers conservative guidelines prepared by the Consortium of College & University Media Centers (CCUMC) for additional copyright compliancy in the classroom. As with the TEACH Act, the CCUMC guidelines are for face-to-face instructional equivalence online. These voluntary guidelines were the only part of the 1998 Conference on Fair Use (CONFU) report. Most of the major U.S. copyright owners participated in creation of the report and endorsed it.[43] According to Dr. Fritz Dolak at the University Copyright Center at Ball State University, there are four positive points for educational use of multimedia resources:

1. Some of the Copyright Law's Transmission Restrictions of the TEACH Act are minimized;
2. There is no need to seek permission to use the materials for two years (by then the project may be obsolete anyhow);
3. For those who like bright lines, the Multimedia Guidelines spell out in percentages and timed in minutes exact, limited types of copyrighted materials that can be used for a multimedia project; and,
4. Multimedia projects created under these CONFU Multimedia Guidelines can be used for remote, real-time instruction on a secure network.[44]

The *Guidelines* below offer examples of usable portion limitations of a single copyrighted work when presented in the classroom. As with the TEACH Act, these guidelines were not intended for e-reserves. Use of portions larger than the illustrations below may be permitted; educators should refer to the four factors of the Fair Use doctrine to determine if their desired use qualifies as Fair Use.

1. Motion media (e.g., film or video)—up to 10 percent or three minutes.
2. Text—up to 10 percent or 1,000 words.
3. Music/Lyrics/Music Video—up to 10 percent; 30 seconds maximum.
4. Photos/Illustrations—up to five from one artist.
5. Numerical Data Sets (e.g., databases)—up to 10 percent or 2,500 fields.[45]

WHAT WOULD YOU DO?

Professor Thomas wants to show a 20-minute clip to his online sociology class from *The Prestige*, a commercially released film of two rival stage magicians. The clip deals with human daredevil fascination of illusory magic as leisure entertainment in the late 19th and early 20th century, trade secrets, and deadly consequences. The total running time of the film is slightly over two hours. Although the story resembles many real-life examples of stolen tricks among stage magicians, it is a highly creative work. How might the instructor post this film on his course management system legally for an online class? What would you suggest to the instructor? Does this use fall under Fair Use, the TEACH Act, or require permission? What would you do?

The Music Library Association (MLA) has created the *Statement on the Digital Transmission of Electronic Reserves*. The MLA considers that the use of musical works for class reserves falls within the character of Fair Use. The MLA promotes digital audio clips of copyrighted recordings of musical works for outside class use in its *Statement*, under the following conditions:

- Access to such digital copies must be through library-controlled equipment and campus-restricted networks.

- Access to digital copies from outside of the campus should be limited to individuals who have been authenticated, namely, students enrolled either in a course or in formal independent study with an instructor in the institution.

- Digital copies should be made only of works that are being taught in the course or study.

- Digital copies may be made of whole movements or whole works.

- Either the institution or the course instructor should own the original that is used to make the digital file. The library should make a good faith effort to purchase a commercially available copy of anything that is provided by the instructor.

- The library should remove access to the files at the completion of the course.

- The library may store course files for future re-use. This includes the digital copy made from an instructor's original if the library has made a good-faith effort to purchase its own copy commercially.[46]

ELECTRONIC RESERVE LIBRARY POLICIES

Establishing an e-reserves policy is as essential for libraries as establishing a print reserves policy. Since there are no specific statutory exceptions that cover e-reserves, we must once again turn to Fair Use. Libraries and publishers have different ideas on what policies should be followed. An attempt to address the varying views was an objective of the Conference on Fair Use (CONFU) proceedings in 1996. With no common agreement at CONFU, guidelines for e-reserves were never produced. The lack of guidelines permits librarians to basically write their own policies and procedures.[47] One may easily browse the web to view various library e-reserves policies. Many library policies follow Fair Use influenced by the library reserves guidelines from the ALA *Model Policy*.[48]

TRY THIS!

Compare different e-reserves policies of two academic libraries posted on the web. You might compare your current academic library to another. Consider finding other libraries via a search engine or browsing other sites for which you are already familiar. Is the information provided in the policy detailed enough? Does the service look useful for distant users? Look at the details in the e-reserve policy, such as who is responsible for obtaining permission and who pays for the copyright. Is there a library copyright fee limit per document or per course? Does the library e-reserve policy state something about Fair Use and the TEACH Act? What type of technology is utilized to post the e-reserves online for student access? Does the library provide some type of training for instructors about copyright and Fair Use, such as an online tutorial or regularly scheduled workshops?

INTERLIBRARY LOAN/DOCUMENT DELIVERY—ONE STOP SHOPPING?

As the cost of journal subscriptions increase and most library collection budgets shrink or cannot keep up with inflation, it has become a challenge to collect every book or journal that we believe our users will need. Consequently, academic libraries rely on interlibrary loan and related delivery alternatives. According to the Interlibrary Loan Code for the United States, "Interlibrary loan is the process by which a library requests material from, or supplies material to, another library. The purpose of interlibrary loan as defined by this code is to obtain, upon request of a library user, material not available in the user's local library."[49]

Interlibrary loan activity helps libraries expand their *access* to resources unavailable to their local users beyond their locally *owned* holdings by borrowing from other libraries. ILL became a common practice in the mid-1950s when standardized ILL request forms were developed. During the 1960s, union catalogs and union lists of serial holdings emerged. Union catalogs listed holdings of a group of several libraries or collections. However, the delivery process of items lent was as not as quick as it is today. It could take over a month to obtain one book from a lending ILL source, as postal mail was the typical library request communication method. Journal article lending became more accessible as the cost and quality of photocopies improved in the 1970s. Once OCLC introduced its ILL subsystem in 1979, which used electronic requesting communication, the turnaround time improved for lending.[50] Consortia agreements were also introduced to enhance ILL services. Today, ILL electronic delivery of resources directly to patrons has transformed the role of libraries in delivering information to distance learners. Some ILL services also provide document delivery for when an item is not available via ILL, or due to copyright restrictions. The library may easily purchase a copyright compliant copy of an article from a publisher or document delivery website or acquire a book or media items from a bookseller within a few business days. We are no longer limited to what is available only in a lending library's collection.

First Sale Doctrine and Interlibrary Lending

If it weren't for the First Sale Doctrine (covered in chapter 5) from Section 109 of the Copyright Act, libraries would not even have the option to consider interlibrary lending. The First Sale Doctrine allows for a legally acquired copy of a copyrighted work to be sold, leased, lent, displayed, or disposed of without permission of the copyright owner. The doctrine does not cover copying or digitizing a work.

The First Sale Doctrine also supports libraries that want to sell used resources for fundraising, such as book sales. In theory, it permits a library to even lease parts of its collection to another library or museum if it so wished. However, when a library leases electronic resources (such as journal article databases) from a publisher, the contractual agreement may not permit lending to other libraries. Yet there is an exception in Section 109 of the Copyright Act for library lending of licensed works to other libraries, as discussed later in this chapter.

Journal Article Copies Obtained via Interlibrary Loan

Interlibrary loan could also include requesting copies of journal articles not owned by a library. However, as part of the workflow of ILL accepting article requests, the ILL support staff or librarian should verify that the journal is indeed not in their own collection. ILL customers could either overlook or not check the library catalog or journal holdings list before requesting an article. This is especially important with a library's electronic journal databases, since those could be easily retrieved by distributed learning student on their own. Sometimes a friendly reminder when the library's subscribed databases offer the request is a helpful library instruction measure that may serve the distance patron well in the future.

Since the commonplace use of photocopiers and the recent ease of electronic delivery, it has become exceptional for libraries to lend entire journal issues or bound volumes. Journal articles are now copied and delivered to a requesting library. As this method evolved, publishers expressed their concern for copyright infringement. Today, the Internet has made this process even more convenient and cost-effective, as we may easily scan journal articles and send via facsimile, Adobe® PDF files, or other electronic methods. However, the publishers' concerns over copyright infringement continue. So how do libraries copy and distribute journal articles legally? Section 108 of the U.S. Copyright Act[51] offers limitations on a copyright holder's exclusive rights, such as reproduction by libraries and archives. This allows libraries to make copies and to receive copies of articles, chapters, and other short works for purposes of private study and research. Fair Use does not play a major role within ILL as it comes from Section 107 of the Copyright Act.

Section 108(a) of the Copyright Act states that libraries may: "reproduce no more than one copy . . . of a work . . . or . . . distribute such copy," if the following conditions apply: (1) the copies are made without any commercial advantage; (2) the library's collections are open to the public or available to persons doing research in a specialized field other than those associated with the library; and (3) the copy or distribution of the work includes a copyright notice on the copy that this work may be protected by copyright.

Section 108(d) and (e) provide further limits:

- The copy becomes the property of the user;
- The library may copy no more than one article, one "other contribution" to a copyrighted collection, or a small part of any other copyrighted work (an exception may be allowed for when an entire work is extremely short, such as a pamphlet);

- The library or archive must prominently exhibit a warning of copyright where copy requests are placed (online or face-to-face order forms) in accordance with requirements issued by the Copyright Office:

Warning Concerning Copyright Restrictions

The copyright law of the United States (Title 17, United States Code) governs the making of photocopies or other reproductions of copyrighted material. Under certain conditions specified in the law, libraries and archives are authorized to furnish a photocopy or other reproduction. One of these specific conditions is that the photocopy or reproduction is not to be "used for any purpose other than private study, scholarship, or research." If a user makes a request for, or later uses, a photocopy or reproduction for purposes in excess of "fair use," that user may be liable for copyright infringement. This institution reserves the right to refuse to accept a copying order if, in its judgment, fulfillment of the order would involve violation of copyright law.[52]

Section 108(g) specifies that the allowances only apply to the "isolated and unrelated reproduction or distribution of a single copy . . . of the same material on separate occasions." The allowances do not pertain when the library, or its employees, is aware that copying is carried out for use of "related or concerted reproduction or distribution of multiple copies . . . of the same material," whether made on one occasion or over a period of time, and whether intended for aggregate use by one or more individuals. Nor does it apply where the library or its employees engage in the systematic reproduction or distribution of single or multiple copies of materials as a substitution for a subscription or purchase.

CONTU Rule of Five Guidelines

Based on the need to clarify Section 108(g) related to ILL, the CONTU (Commission on New Technological Uses of Copyrighted Works) Rule of Five guidelines[53] were developed by publishers, teachers, and librarians. If a library is indeed open to the public or others researching in a specialized field (outside its primary patron group),[54] the CONTU Rule of Five guidelines[55] supports a library's acquisition of limited photocopies or electronic copies of journal articles published within the last five years. Under Section 108(a)(2), for-profit academic institutions or profit-oriented company information centers could utilize the CONTU Rule of Five, but they would need to be open to the public or provide virtual access by offering document-finding services and ILL.[56]

The CONTU Rule of Five guidelines are such that for the current calendar year, borrowing libraries may not take delivery of more than five copies of articles from a single journal title published within the last five years. For example, the ILL staff receives a sixth article request for *Marmalade Magazine* during the current calendar year in October. The CONTU Rule of Five calendar does not start over until the first day of January each year. What are the options for ILL when the sixth ILL request for *Marmalade Magazine* arrives? Borrowing the journal from another library or canceling the request is the most prudent option but is not necessarily in the best interest of the ILL customer. As an alternative, the Copyright Clearance Center or commercial document delivery services are available when permission and royalties are necessary for the sixth copy. Purchasing pay-per-use, single-articles online from the publisher is another option. Document delivery service or publisher purchases usually cover the copyright royalties for individual customer use.

As noted above, the CONTU guidelines do not include those article requests over five years old at the date of request. Generally, it is considered that Section 107 of the Copyright Act related to Fair Use should cover those article requests that were published five years or later as the Effect on the Market is no longer significant. Exemption to follow the CONTU guidelines is permitted when the library owns a copy of the journal but it is not available due to being not yet received from the publisher, missing or stolen, or long overdue from borrowing patron. However, licensing contract agreements may supersede these exemptions for embargo periods of database journal issues.

The borrowing library must also specify whether its article request is copyright-compliant with the CONTU guidelines on the request form (paper or electronic). The borrowing library must clearly indicate on each request for photocopies whether it "Conforms to the CONTU Copyright Guidelines" (CCG) or "Conforms to the Copyright Act" (CCL). CCG is indicated when the borrowing library does not currently subscribe to a journal title, if it is of the first five copies from a journal title request for the current calendar year, and if the material requested was published within five years of the date of request. CCL is indicated on requested articles published five years before the date of the request or when the article copied is considered Fair Use under Section 107 of the Copyright Act. The borrowing library is responsible in maintaining the copyright compliance records. The lending library is not responsible for maintain copyright records.

WHAT WOULD YOU DO?

Sally is a distance education graduate student. She spends much time researching for her classes remotely from the library website. She has recently discovered that the interlibrary loan online request form is linked to the library's multiple journal databases that provide citation and abstract summaries of some articles not available in full-text from the library. She is able to click one-button to request these articles. For a new issue of a journal for which the library does not subscribe, she requests six articles via interlibrary loan. Shortly after she submits her requests, she gets an email message from the interlibrary loan service that due to copyright restrictions the library is unable to get the sixth article. She comes to you and states that she really needs this article to complete her research paper. As the head of the interlibrary loan service, what would you do?

Lending Resources to Distance Learners

Some libraries send books, media, and other physical resources to their distance learners. Once again, the First Sale Doctrine as presented in Section 109 of the Copyright Act[57] permits lending of books. Remember, it states that once you buy a copyrighted work, you have the right to redistribute the single copy as you see fit without permission of the copyright holder. Other resources delivered to distance learners include physical resources obtained through ILL from lending libraries, article copies from journals supplied by the library or lending libraries, and access to the library's electronic resources, such as journal databases and eBooks.

The manner in which libraries distribute books and physical non-print media to their distance learners varies. Zheng Ye Yang's 2006 article from the *Journal of Academic Librarianship* reports a survey of 62 libraries by their various information delivery types and levels for their own libraries' holdings:

1. The majority (79.0%) of the libraries (49 out of 62) offer free document delivery services of their library-owned journal articles to their distance users. Forty-five (72.6%) of the 62 libraries also send their library-owned books to the distance users' homes, even if the users live overseas. Of those 45 libraries that send their own books to the distance users, eight (17.8%) subsidize the entire shipping cost for the users; five (11.1%) charge users for the shipping cost; and 32 (71.1%) require users to be responsible for the return shipping cost.
2. When it comes to interlibrary loan, fifty-three (85.5%) of the 62 libraries offer free ILL service to the distance users, however, 32.1% (17 out of 53) do not send ILL books to their distance users—they only send articles.[58]

Some libraries in this survey reported not delivering physical items such as books and media materials acquired through the ILL process due to lending time-limitations and the borrowing library's responsibility to lending libraries. Another concern may involve the ILL Code of Responsibility by the borrower for lost or damaged items in transit. Distance students may also rely on the public library close to their home or workplace for some materials not available through ILL.

ILL Codes, Consortia Networks, and Reciprocal Agreements

There are codified polices that assist the interlibrary loan daily workflow. The primary code that virtually all ILL departments follow is known as the *National Interlibrary Loan Code*,[59] also available as the *Interlibrary Code for the United States*[60] with supplementary guidelines to clarify the original *National Code* document. The *Code* promotes open-minded ILL policies for state, regional, and local applications. These groups often create their own code based on the *National Code*. State and regional policies are usually tied to consortia, network, or reciprocal agreements that assist with tight budgets. These groups may work together to garner sharper pricing or licensing terms of resources such as databases. Networks may be created at the local level to provide express courier services and reciprocal agreements. *A Model Interlibrary Loan Code for Regional, State, Local or Other Special Groups of Libraries* was made available by the American Library Association in 1984. It was "intended to provide guidelines for any group of libraries interested in developing an interlibrary loan code to meet special needs."[61]

ILL codes are also helpful for clarifying who is responsible for what (e.g., borrowing libraries are responsible for any damaged or lost items borrowed). Many libraries post the *National ILL Code* for their customers to view on their websites.

There are supportive ways for libraries to ensure some free ILL transactions. A consortium of libraries may offer its members priority access to interlibrary loan. Those libraries in the consortium may direct ILL requests to each other first and receive the item at no charge. Separate from consortia agreements, libraries may establish ILL reciprocal agreements where they provide one another materials via ILL at no charge. When a library sets up its ILL workflow, it could select from libraries that lend at no charge as part of its consortium membership or from reciprocal free lenders. Otherwise, lending libraries may charge for their ILL services. The *National Code* is helpful when consortia create and implement their own codes for lending and borrowing agreements.

ILL/Document Delivery Cost-Recovery and Fees

Some nonprofit lending libraries may charge a fee for ILL book loans or copied articles. When this occurs it is usually qualified as a cost-recovery. Although this is more common with for-profit and specialty libraries, or document delivery services, there are a few public libraries and academic libraries that may charge small fees to offset their supplies and labor for their ILL workflow. Consortium and reciprocal agreements mentioned above may reduce or eliminate the fees.

Cost-recovery is defined differently by different information delivery services. In most instances, the fees are associated with value-added services. Understanding actual costs usually involves cost-accounting methodology that classifies the cost as either direct or indirect. Direct costs are more obvious and include staff salaries, photocopy expenses, ILL technology expenses, database fees, capital equipment, telecommunications, mail, and postage. Indirect costs are not as noticeable and include building use, equipment use, maintenance, general library operations, and administrative support.[62]

ILL Non-Print Audiovisual Format Resources

In 2006, an ACRL (Association of College & Research Libraries) Media Resources in Academic Libraries Review Task Force affirmed that academic libraries may collect non-print media resources that are as "vital and diverse" as any print collection in an academic library.[63] As use of media resources increases, so does the number of non-print ILL requests to support distance learners. One need only look at the online explosion of audio and visual materials provided on blogs, social networking, and amateur film sites. Some libraries do not lend any non-print media materials, while others may lend to their consortium or only to those libraries that lend media. Some electronic resources such as computer software may contain licensing restrictions for one user at a time, which is not conducive to interlibrary lending. Making copies of audiovisual resources is not considered an ILL function, unless the copying is considered to be a Fair Use. Generally, non-print audiovisual resources are lent to traditional and distributed learner ILL customers.

The ALA provides guidelines for Interlibrary Loan of Audiovisual Formats (1998).[64] The ALA comprehensive format guidelines:

> are intended for use by libraries and other agencies that provide loans of audiovisual material in all formats to fill study, research and information needs. Audiovisual materials include, but are not limited to videotapes, videodiscs, multimedia CD ROMs, audiotapes, compact discs, records, 16 mm films, 35 mm slides, realia [real life objects which complement instruction or class activity] and photographs.

Although the *National Interlibrary Loan Code for the United States* (1993) may apply to this format, the ALA audiovisual guidelines offer specific principles for audiovisual materials. The basic principles of the policy promote lending audiovisual materials to other libraries as freely as possible in a way that supports loss and damage.

A recent concern for librarians in lending media resources deals with licensing. See more on licensing below in the "Licensing Implications" section. Similar to computer software, some audio and visual resources are no longer sold, but are instead licensed, to libraries. Licensing potentially allows the copyright holder to take away some statutory rights including the First Sale Doctrine of the U.S. Copyright Act. In this scenario, the library is restricted in ILL lending, and it may prohibit lending to its own customers. Some video producers of instructional films on DVD from media services generally associated with educational classroom use have been involved in legal action against educators. When purchasing audiovisual resources, watch for any licensing restrictions associated with the materials. Some signs to look for include shrink-wrapped packaging with a fine-print license, a "splash page" in addition to the customary FBI copyright notice, or other special sales terms posted in the publisher catalog or on the website.[65]

However, David Ensign proposes that there may be exceptions to lending licensed works in Section 109(b)(1)(A) of the Copyright Act. "Under some circumstances, individuals and institutions may not be permitted to lend or lease computer programs or sound recordings, but specific provisions included in the Copyright Act permit nonprofit libraries and educational institutions to lend these items to one another."[66]

Copyright and Fair Use knowledge are vital to working within the law for interlibrary loan. Gretchen McCord Hoffmann states that we should know the rules and when they apply and follow them. She also emphasizes knowing your institution's policy about copyright and ILL. When in doubt, always consult your institution's legal counsel for any questions. And most importantly, maintain documentation related to the workflow of all ILL and library reserve activity.[67]

DOCUMENT DELIVERY—PURCHASE ON DEMAND

Commercial document delivery services are available for both nonprofit and for-profit libraries. Usually these services will ensure that their delivery of documents are copyright compliant for a specific library's needs.[68]

Document delivery means different things to library customers. To some, the document-on-demand commercial service provides them with hard-to-locate documents and ensures copyright compliancy. To distance learners, the library's scanning service offers copies of in-house journals.

Ronald Dekker and Leo Waaijers define document delivery as bridging the gap between where the customer is and where the document is. Dekker and Waaijers expand the explanation from two perspectives, the user and the library. A user sees a document delivery service as a transparent and reliable way of obtaining a document, while a library sees document delivery as a known quality service and efficient process that fills the gap between the customer and the requested document. User-friendly, seamless access (as much digital delivery as possible) to hybrid collections of both paper and electronic resources is also fundamental in meeting the needs of the document delivery customer.[69]

From the point of view of library customers, ILL and document delivery are the same thing. They see only a method of borrowing books and other media or obtaining copies of articles not available from their library at the time of their request. Document delivery is vital for distance learners because it may be the only access they have to needed resources for distributed learning research. Hence, document delivery services may continue to move toward purchasing and acquiring books, non-print media, and journal articles in lieu of interlibrary loan borrowing. This is a growing popular trend and an effective collection development method, especially where research patrons need a specific resource. Also known as "purchase instead of borrow" or "just-in-time," this collection development method has been researched and reported in library literature often.[70]

Distance learning and traditional ILL patron requests may positively influence collection development policies. For ILL requests, in some cases it is more cost effective to buy an item than to borrow it. In addition, libraries can use ILL statistics to supplement their acquisition choices. The titles purchased from ILL requests tend to circulate more frequently than those selected by traditional collection development methods. Of course, it should always be remembered that collection development literature supports the principle of pay-per-use ILL or document delivery request (access) over traditional collection development acquisition (ownership).[71]

Some libraries have integrated a purchase-on-demand document delivery service of outside sources into an automated interlibrary loan workflow (see "Pay-Per-Use Document Delivery" sidebar). Contemporary library literature affirm this effective acquisition practice, where intangible resources such as full-text journal articles are available via "pay-per-view" and are purchased by a library and given to its customer to keep and never added to the library's permanent holdings.[72]

PAY-PER-USE DOCUMENT DELIVERY

See http://nku.illiad.oclc.org/illiad/FAQ.html#a1 for details on how the W. Frank Steely Library of Northern Kentucky University integrated ILL and an outside source document delivery service. Guidelines were required to coordinate a purchase-on-demand for when an ILL request is too new to borrow via ILL, when there is no potential free lender, or when an item or article is not available after attempting requests from first potential five lenders. Most funding for this service was made possible by cancellation of high-cost/low-use journal subscriptions. (Journal use statistics were maintained and viewed over a period of time.) The Library now follows a just-in-time model, rather than just-in-case, for resources that the Library does not hold. It locates and purchases journal articles as needed from publishers or document delivery services rather than subscribing to high-cost/low-use journals. Once the article is purchased, it is delivered electronically to the customer.

The Library has added new journal databases to meet the needs of customers as well. Since both document delivery purchases and library databases provide added electronic versions of articles, this is also conducive to the needs of distance learners. For books and non-print media resources, the Library attempts to purchase from an online bookseller such as amazon.com first in order to expedite the delivery for the customer. Otherwise, the library uses established vendor sources such as Baker & Taylor. When the book or media resource arrives, it is rush-catalogued and then the customer is contacted via email to pick up the item at the library. For distance learners, the item is sent directly to the patron. The average turnaround time for books and non-print media is usually two weeks from the initial ILL request.

Source: Lois Schultz, *Soaring High Two Years Past the Crossroads,* PowerPoint presentation about pay-per-use document delivery in an academic library ILL department at Ohio Valley Group of Technical Services Librarians 2008 Annual Conference, "Technical Services Taking Flight: Soaring to New Heights of Innovation," Dayton, Ohio, May 16, 2008

TRY THIS!

Interview a librarian who specializes in library course reserves or an information delivery service. Either interview the person at their workplace or consider taking them out for coffee. Ask them if they would mind answering questions about their duties and responsibilities, including how they obtain permission for using or obtaining copyright-cleared copies of works posted as e-reserves and/or copyright-restricted interlibrary loan requests. See if they might provide examples of: (1) How they obtain permission (e.g., Copyright Clearance Center vs. author or publisher requests); and (2) If they obtain copyright-cleared copies of works from a commercial service, what is their procedure?

ILL/DOCUMENT DELIVERY CUSTOMER POLICIES

A borrowing policy for a library's ILL customers that provides details on the service should be readily accessible for review. Interlibrary loan model policies among libraries depend on Section 108 of the Copyright Act and the CONTU Guidelines.[73] Many interlibrary patron borrowing policies are posted on library websites that serve as model policies for comparison. In many cases a separate policy regarding ILL and document delivery for distance learners may be posted in a special section for distance learning students. Library association and consortium journals, newsletters, and conferences are another area where libraries may learn how to develop their policies for ILL and document delivery services. Some libraries provide a highlight policy page that links to a detailed Frequently Asked Questions format to present policy information, such as http://library.nku.edu/about_the_library/policies/sourcefinder_policy.php.

TRY THIS!

Compare different distance education user ILL/information delivery policies of two academic libraries posted on the web. You might compare your current academic library to another. Consider finding other libraries via a search engine or browsing another site for which you are already familiar. Does the ILL/information delivery service look useful for distant users? Looking at the details, for example, does the library provide delivery of books and media, and if so, does it pay for shipping expenses both ways via postal mail to the distance user? Does the library provide document delivery of articles that were not located via ILL or that were copyright-restricted? Does the library provide easy access for questions or feedback from distance users?

LICENSING IMPLICATIONS TRUMP FAIR USE

For electronic journal databases to be utilized for e-reserves, your library acquisitions should negotiate for the permission to use the electronic journal content for reserves and possibly ILL lending. Licensing almost always overrules Fair Use, since a legal contract is involved. If Fair Use is not mentioned, it could still apply at a more restricted degree. The publisher may stipulate any requirements. Libraries should carefully examine any contractual details to be aware of what is defined for ILL, e-reserves, authorized users, and any other research use of the licensed content. It's best to get licensing agreements in print. One should never rely on any verbal agreements.[74]

Most licensing agreements permit only distribution of database articles to that library's intended audience (e.g., academic library's school faculty, staff, and students; public library's patrons; corporate library's company employees). For academic libraries, the authorized users should be defined as broadly as possible to include distance learners.[75] Distribution outside of the intended audience is usually prohibited, unless the library negotiates use for ILL lending. It cannot be emphasized enough how important contract negotiations are for libraries related to "right to use" conditions for ILL lending. A library has the right to ask for reasonable revisions in a contract that helps its customers.

For libraries dealing with database acquisitions, there are three basic licensing agreement categories:

1. Statutory or Compulsory License—Third parties such as libraries legally make use of copyrighted works without the copyright owner's authorization as long as the use complies with legal requirements and royalties are paid when applicable. This is more the exception than the rule. The Digital Performance Rights in Sound Recordings is one of six compulsory licenses accepted by U.S. copyright law. It likely would not apply to licensing of databases for library acquisition.

2. Shrink-Wrap License—Also known as Click-On, are licensing agreements that are non-negotiable. Everyone is familiar with this type of licensing, which is associated with computer software and some online resources. A

buyer or user of the resource agrees to the terms by virtue of opening the package or clicking on an "I Accept" agreement. It is usually associated with a single user of the resource, and it is not intended to be reviewed for negotiation. However, as a conservative measure, libraries should review those agreements that are unclear with their legal counsel to avoid any legal risks for the library and its parent institution.

3. Negotiable License—Mainly associated with library acquisition of leased databases. Since most library databases are intended for use by a larger-scale community than most Shrink-Wrap single users, negotiation is important to define terms and conditions for their specific users and obtain a competitive price.[76]

LIBRARY LICENSING 101

The introduction of the DMCA (see chapter 5) and growing use of licensing agreements have diminished applications where the First Sale Doctrine may apply in a digital setting such as electronic delivery to distance learners. Since licensing agreement contracts may be overloaded with many legal terms and unclear conditions for librarians, it is helpful to have your institution's legal counsel review the fine print in the negotiation process. To help learn the jargon of and how to negotiate licensing agreements, here are examples of supportive books written from the perspective of librarians on this subject:

1. Lesley Ellen Harris, *Licensing Digital Content: A Practical Guide for Librarians,* (2009), American Library Association;
2. Becky Albitz, *Licensing and Managing Electronic Resources,* (2008), Chandos Publishing;
3. Fiona Durrant, *Negotiating Licenses for Digital Resources,* (2006), Facet Publishing;
4. Stephen Bosch, et al., *Guide to Licensing and Acquiring Electronic Information,* (2005), Scarecrow Press.

eBooks and related reader products had originally created much controversy when online bookseller Amazon prohibited lending its popular Kindle electronic device. Libraries have utilized Kindle and eBook titles with great success. However, Amazon's initial Terms of Use prohibited such shared use. Finally, Amazon granted Kindle users the right to borrow and read eBooks from public libraries in 2011.[77] With the growing popularity of Smart Phones such as Apple's iPhone, how soon will it be before libraries are able to negotiate to provide more full-text eBook titles directly to patron Smart Phones from a library's website? Blackboard CMS offers an application for utilizing online courses from an iPhone. Could this develop into a new area to support distributed education textbooks in the future?

WHAT WOULD YOU DO?

A music composition software program is not available via ILL. So your library decides to purchase the software. The acquisition librarian has confirmed that your library's patron-use computers will operate the software. However, the software website displays a licensing notice that states the software may be used by only one user at a time. Since the licensing agreement makes this one-user at a time condition, as the ILL manager what would you do?

DIGITAL RIGHTS MANAGMENT (DRM)

The ALA defines Digital Right Management (DRM) technology as a way "to control access to, track and limit uses of digital works."[78] DRM consists of practices such as encryption, watermarks, and password restriction incorporated into the technology that delivers information. Some digital media content publishers maintain that DRM technologies are essential to prevent revenue loss due to unauthorized copying of their copyrighted works. Conversely, others argue that conveying control of the use of media from consumers to the media will lead to loss of existing Fair Use rights and suppress innovation in the flow of information and ideas.

At first glance, DRM may not appear to affect distributed learning to a large extent. However, librarians and educators should be aware that it exists. The ALA Office for Information Technology has issued *Digital Rights Management: A Guide for Librarians, version 1,* prepared by Michael Godwin in 2006. In it, Godwin remarks on the limits of DRM related to exemptions to copyright ownership such as Fair Use and how "librarians, and citizens at large, should care about DRM because they have much at stake both in the balances built into our copyright law, and in the technologies, such as personal computers and the Internet, that might be restricted or controlled in order to protect copyright interests. The choices our society makes now about how we may use copyrighted works and about the technological protections for such works will affect us for a long time to come. This is why, as we work through our understanding of DRM, we need to make sure we understand the traditions and principles of copyright as well . . . Although there is a tendency on the part of some people to equate copyright interests with other kinds of ownership and property interests, under our legal system copyright is actually significantly different."[79]

DRM could negate Fair Use, especially for interlibrary loan or document delivery. As with licensed databases, there may be agreements associated with single purchased digital copies of articles or database digital copies permitted for ILL lending. Since this technology, as it relates to copyright law and licensing agreements, is developing, librarians and educators should keep an eye on the latest DRM developments and DRM's impact on ILL and document delivery customers. One such development is middleware software that has been developed to authenticate and authorize individuals through an online negotiator process that works on behalf of DRM vendors and DRM users. Hypothetically, an educator using DRM content might request to make Fair Use copies of document through middleware online prompts without requesting permission directly from a copyright holder.[80]

ROLE-PLAY A SITUATION

Your academic library is considering document delivery for distance users, including both the library's onsite sources and items purchased directly from publishers or commercial document delivery services. A budget has been planned to support this program. As the librarian manager of this new service, your current ILL support staff will coordinate the workflow. Your library director has asked you to prepare a proposal that presents how you will initiate and operate such a service. Come up with an outline for what you would propose. Then find a friend or classmate to role-play the director while you present your proposal as the ILL librarian.

CONCLUSION AND FUTURE TRENDS

What does the setting for e-reserves and information delivery look like for the future of distributed education? Will e-reserves and other information delivery services such as ILL and document delivery continue to develop as distributed education and traditional course use of electronic resources increase? As libraries continue to evaluate their collection use and cancel low-use and high-cost journal subscriptions, will an *access versus ownership* philosophy further support e-reserves and other information delivery services? How will mash-ups (e.g., video remixing) and transformative expression of creativity and thought affect the Fair Use of related resources via electronic mailing lists, electronic texting, social networking, mobile smart phone learning, and so on? As the Digital Library Federation reports, new technologies are "transforming ILL, blurring the lines between ILL and document delivery services, and shifting costs" while improving information delivery service quality for our customers.[81] As this chapter has illustrated, distributed learning librarians and educators must not only be "technology literate" but "information literate" with regard to both social and ethical legal responsibilities related to intellectual property and CMS.

ACKNOWLEDGMENT

The author thanks Dwayne Buttler, J.D., professor and the first Evelyn J. Schneider Endowed Chair for Scholarly Communication at the University of Louisville's University Libraries, for his related Fair Use and TEACH Act expertise.

NOTES

1. David M. Marcovitz, "Copyright, Technology, and Your Rights," in *Advances in Educational Administration: Vol. 8. Technology and Education: Issues in Administration,*

Policy, and Applications in K12 Schools, ed. Sharon Y. Tettegah and Dr. Richard C. Hunter [Advances in Education Series Volume 8] (London: Elsevier, 2006), 73–84.

2. Andrea L. Foster, "In Lawsuit, University Asserts That Downloading Copyrighted Texts Is Fair Use," *Chronicle of Higher Education,* (June 27, 2008), http://chronicle.com/article/In-Lawsuit-University-Asse/942/.

3. Laura Gasaway, *Growing Pains: Adapting Copyright for Libraries, Education, and Society* (Littleton, CO: Rothman & Co., 1997), xii.

4. Kenneth D. Crews, *Copyright Law for Librarians and Educators: Creative Strategies and Practical Solutions* (Chicago: American Library Association, 2006), viii.

5. *Feist Publications, Inc. v. Rural Telephone Service Co.,* 499 U.S. 340,349 (1991).

6. Cindy Kristof, *Electronic Reserves Operations in ARL Libraries: A SPECK Kit* [Series] Flyer 245 (Chicago: Association of Research Libraries, May 1999).

7. William W. Fisher and William McGeveran, *Digital Learning Challenge: Obstacles to Educational Uses of Copyrighted Material in the Digital Age: A Foundational White Paper* (Cambridge, MA: Berkman Center for Internet & Society at Harvard Law School, August 2006), http://cyber.law.harvard.edu/media/files/copyrightandeducation.html.

8. Rachel Bridgewater, "Shifting Responsibility for Electronic Reserves Copyright Permissions from the Academic Departments to the Library: From Confusion to Cooperation," *Journal of Interlibrary Loan, Document Delivery & Electronic Reserve* 18, no. 2 (2008): 141–52; David McCaslin, "Processing Electronic Reserves in a Large Academic Library System," *Journal of Interlibrary Loan, Document Delivery & Electronic Reserve* 18, no. 3 (2008): 335–46; Tomas A. Lipinski, *Copyright Law and the Distance Education Classroom* (Lanham, MD: Scarecrow Press, 2005), xi.

9. John Schlipp, "Coaching Teaching Faculty: Copyright Awareness Programs in Academic Libraries," *Kentucky Libraries* 72, no. 3 (2008): 18–22.

10. Blackboard Inc. "Creating Course Content—Leveraging Existing Content," *Bb Quick Start Guides* (Washington, DC, 2008 promotional brochure).

11. Kim Duckett and Dede Nelson, "Evolution of a Librarian: Instructional Designer Partnership in Higher Education," in *Academic Librarianship by Design,* ed. Steven J. Bell and John D. Shank (Chicago: American Library Association, 2007), 74–77.

12. Crews, *Copyright Law for Librarians and Educators,* 124.

13. Kenneth Crews and Dwayne Buttler, "Fair Use Checklist," Columbia University Libraries, Information Services, Copyright Advisory Office, http://copyright.columbia.edu/fair-use-checklist.

14. Carrie Russell, *Complete Copyright: An Everyday Guide for Librarians,* (Chicago: American Library Association, 2004), 25–28; Kenneth Crews, *Copyright, Fair Use, and the Challenge for Universities,* (Chicago: University of Chicago Press, 1993) 22–25; Crews, *Copyright Law for Librarians and Educators,* 60–62; Andrew Richard Albanese, "Down with E-Reserves: Confusing, Contentious, and Vital, E-Reserves Fuel Higher Education—And an Ongoing Copyright Battle," *Library Journal* 132, no. 16 (2007): 36–38; and Janet Brennan Croft, "Electronic Reserves," *Journal of Interlibrary Loan, Document Delivery & Information Supply* 14, no. 3 (2004), 21–35.

15. Georgia Harper, in "Using the Four Factor Fair Use Test: A Note About Time Limits" on the University of Texas webpage, http://copyright.lib.utexas.edu/copypol2.html. "Fair Use of Copyrighted Materials," affirms that publishers believe there is a time limit to Fair Use, http://www.utsystem.edu/OGC/intellectualProperty/copypol2.htm#note; Georgia Harper, on the webpage "Fair Use Guidelines for Electronic Reserve Systems," provides guidelines for library reserves based upon the Conference on Fair Use (CONFU) in 1997. Section D entitled, "Storage and Reuse," states that permission from the copyright holder is required if the resource is reposted for the same class at a future date, http://copyright.lib.utexas.edu/rsrvguid.html.

16. Schlipp, "Coaching Teaching Faculty: Copyright Awareness Programs in Academic Libraries," 18–22.

17. Dave Zielinski, "Organizing Your Message: Copyright and Fair Use," *AllBusiness — Presentations,* http://www.allbusiness.com/services/business-services-advertising/424 5041-1.html.

18. *Feist* (1991) supports that facts themselves (such as a URL hyperlink) are not copyrightable. For more, see Matt Jackson's (April 1997) related article, "Comment: Linking Copyright to Homepages," *Federal Communications Law Journal,* 49 Fed. Com. L.J. 731.

19. Stanford University Libraries, *Stanford Copyright & Fair Use: C. Connecting to Other Websites,* http://fairuse.stanford.edu/Copyright_and_Fair_Use_Overview/chapter6/ 6-c.html.

20. Purdue University, *University Copyright Office: Fair use analysis,* http://www.lib. purdue.edu/uco/CopyrightBasics/fair_use.html.

21. *Technology, Education and Copyright Harmonization Act,* Public Law 107–273, *U.S. Statutes at Large* 116 (2002): 1910, codified at 17 U.S.C. §110(2), 112(f) (2005).

22. Crews, *Copyright Law for Librarians and Educators,* 62.

23. Richard Stim, *Getting Permission: How to License & Clear Copyrighted Materials On-line & Off,* (Berkeley, CA: Nolo, 2004). Stim's book also provides ideas on how to write letters to contact the author/publisher.

24. Originally named the Orphan Works Act of 2006, it has subsequently been re-named the Orphan Works Act of 2008, where it passed in the Senate but was stalled in the House. There are plans to reintroduce it in 2011. There are numerous references on the web as ORPHAN WORKS ACT (OWA) with no year since it has been reintroduced. Keep abreast of this act at the ALA website: http://www.ala.org/ala/issuesadvocacy/copy right/orphan/index.cfm. See also Peter B. Hirtle et al., *Copyright and Cultural Institutions: Guidelines for Digitization for U.S. Libraries, Archives, and Museums* (Ithaca, NY: Cornell University Library, 2009), 171–72.

25. Crews, *Copyright Law for Librarians and Educators,* 111–12.

26. *Copyright Law Revision,* U.S. Congress. 94th Cong., 2d Sess. (1976). H. Doc. 1476: 68–70. "Agreement on Guidelines for Classroom Copying in Not-for-profit Educational Institutions with Respect to Books and Periodicals, March 1976."

27. Marc Lindsey, *Copyright Law on Campus,* (Pullman, WA: Washington State University Press, 2003), 27.

28. Ibid.

29. Laura Gasaway, "Copyright Considerations for Electronic Reserves," in *Managing Electronic Reserves,* ed. Jeff Rosedale (Chicago: American Library Association, 2002), 116–18.

30. Crews, *Copyright Law for Librarians and Educators,* 60–64; Lindsey, *Copyright Law on Campus,* 27.

31. American Library Association, *Model Policy Concerning College and University Photo-copying for Classroom, Research and Library Reserve Use, March 1982,* http://www.cni.org/ docs/infopols/ALA.html.

32. Gasaway, "Copyright Considerations for Electronic Reserves," 118–21.

33. *Copyright Act of 1976,* USC 17 §107 (2005).

34. Gasaway, "Copyright Considerations for Electronic Reserves," 118–21.

35. Crews, *Copyright, Fair Use, and the Challenge for Universities,* 51–52.

36. Association of American Publishers, *Questions & Answers on Copyright for the Campus Community* (New York: Association of American Publishers, 2006), 25.

37. *Basic Books, Inc. v. Kinko's Graphics Corp.,* 758 F. Supp. 1522, 1526 (S.D.N.Y. 1991).

38. Crews, *Copyright, Fair Use, and the Challenge for Universities,* 53–55.

39. United States Patent and Trademark Office, *Technological Protection Systems for Digitized Copyrighted Works, Written Comments of Copyright Clearance Center, Inc.,* January 14, 2003, http://www.uspto.gov/web/offices/dcom/olia/teachcomments/copyrightcc.pdf, Docket No. 2003-C-006.

40. Crews, *Copyright, Fair Use, and the Challenge for Universities,* 97.

41. Yale University Library, *Liblicense: Licensing Digital Information—Licensing Resources,* http://www.library.yale.edu/~llicense/liclinks.shtml.

42. Sidney Eng and Flor A. Hernandez, "Managing Streaming Video: A New Role for Technical Services," *Library Collections, Acquisitions, & Technical Services* 30, no. 3–4 (2006): 214–23.

43. Consortium of College & University Media Centers, *How the Fair Use Guidelines for Educational Multimedia Help Educators,* http://ccumc.org/node/209.

44. Fritz Dolak, Ball State University, Copyright & Intellectual Property Office, "Overview of the Fair Use Guidelines for Educational Multimedia," http://cms.bsu.edu/Academics/Libraries/CollectionsAndDept/Copyright/FairUseTEACH/ComplyingWith-TEACH/CONFUGuidelines.aspx.

45. Consortium of College & University Media Centers, *Fair Use Guidelines for Educational Multimedia,* http://www.ccumc.org/copyright-matters/fair-use-guideline.

46. Music Library Association. Statement on the Digital Transmission of Audio Reserves. *Digital Reserves—Copyright Guide for Music Librarians,* http://www.musiclibrary assoc.org/copyright/Resources/DigitalReserves.

47. Crews, *Copyright Law for Librarians and Educators,* 62–63.

48. Gasaway, "Copyright Considerations for Electronic Reserves," 121.

49. American Library Association, Interlibrary Loan Committee, *National Interlibrary Loan Code for the United States, 1993,* RQ, 33, no. 4 (Summer 1994): 477–79.

50. Kate Nevins, "An Ongoing Revolution: Resource Sharing and OCLC," *Journal of Library Administration* 25, no. 2–3 (1998): 65–71 and co-published simultaneously in *OCLC, 1967–1997: Thirty Years of Furthering Access to the World's Information,* ed. K. Wayne Smith (New York: Hayworth Press, 1998), 65–71.

51. *Copyright Act of 1976,* USC 17 §108 (2005).

52. *Code of Federal Regulations,* title 37, vol. 1, sec. 201.14 (2008), pages 485–86.

53. For more on the CONTU Rule of Five see http://www.copyright.gov/circs/circ21.pdf.

54. *Copyright Act of 1976,* USC 17 §108(a)(2) (2005).

55. *1975 Senate Report on the New Copyright Law,* Senate Judiciary Committee, 94th Cong., 1st sess., (1975): S. Rep. No. 94–473, 70–71.

56. Hirtle, *Copyright and Cultural Institutions,* 109–11.

57. *Copyright Act of 1976,* USC 17 §109 (2005).

58. Zheng Ye Yang, "Improving Turnaround Time for Document Delivery of Materials Owned But Not on the Shelf: A Case Study from an Academic Library," *Journal of Academic Librarianship* 32, no. 2 (2006): 200–204.

59. American Library Association, Interlibrary Loan Committee, *National Interlibrary Loan Code.*

60. American Library Association, RUSA Reference Guidelines, *Interlibrary Loan Code for the United States, 2001,* http://www.ala.org/ala/mgrps/divs/rusa/resources/guide lines/interlibrary.cfm.

61. American Library Association, Coalition for Networked Information, Information Policies, *Model Interlibrary Loan Code for Regional, State, Local, or Other Special Groups of Libraries, 1984,* http://www.cni.org/docs/infopols/ALA.html.

62. Yem S. Fong, "Pricing and Costing in Fee-Based Information Services," *Journal of Interlibrary Loan, Document Delivery & Information Supply* 10, no. 1 (1999): 63–73.

63. Guidelines for Media Resources in Academic Libraries Review Task Force, Association of College & Research Libraries, *Guidelines for Media Resources in Academic Libraries, 2006,* http://www.ala.org/ala/mgrps/divs/acrl/standards/mediaresources.cfm.

64. Video Round Table, American Library Association, *Guidelines for the Interlibrary Loan of Audio Visual Formats, 1998,* http://www.ala.org/ala/mgrps/rts/vrt/profession alresources/vrtresources/interlibraryloan.cfm.

65. Carol Simpson, "Interlibrary Loan of Audiovisuals May Bring a Lawsuit," *Library Media Connection* 25, no. 5 (February 2008): 26–28.

66. David Ensign, "Resource Sharing and Copyright among Library Consortia Members," in *Growing Pains: Adapting Copyright for Libraries, Education, and Society*, ed. Laura Gasaway (Littleton, CO: Rothman & Co., 1997), 151–71.

67. Gretchen McCord Hoffmann, *Copyright in Cyberspace 2: Questions and Answers for Librarians* (New York: Neal-Schuman Publishers, Inc., 2005): 42.

68. James S. Heller, "Impact of Recent Litigation on Interlibrary Loan and Document Delivery," *Law Library Journal* 88, no. 2 (1996): 158–77, for libraries wishing to implement their own document delivery.

69. Ronald Dekker and Leo Waaijers, "Beyond the Photocopy Machine: Document Delivery in a Hybrid Library Environment," *Interlending & Document Supply* 29, no. 2 (2001), 69–75.

70. Access (just-in-time) vs. ownership (just-in-case) collection development research affirms more effective fulfillment results for researcher document or book requests. This collection method may require shifting funds from the traditional ownership (just-in-case) acquisition for journal subscriptions and books to accessing (just-in-time) to fill requested journal articles and books on demand. See the following articles for more: Kristine J. Anderson, et al., "Buy, Don't Borrow: Bibliographers' Analysis of Academic Library Collection Development through Interlibrary Loan Requests," *Collection Management* 27, no. 3–4 (2002): 1–11; Sharon A. Campbell, "To Buy or to Borrow, That is the Question," *Journal of Interlibrary Loan, Document Delivery & Electronic Reserves* 16, no. 3 (2006): 35–39; Gayle Rosemary Y.C. Chan, "Purchase Instead of Borrow: An International Perspective," *Journal of Interlibrary Loan, Document Delivery & Electronic Reserves* 14, no. 4 (2005): 23–34; Suzanne Ward, "Books on Demand: Just-in-Time Acquisitions," *The Acquisitions Librarian* 14, no. 27 (2002): 95–107; Suzanne Ward, Tanner Wray, and Karl E. Debus-López, "Collection Development Based on Patron Requests: Collaboration between Interlibrary Loan and Acquisitions, "*Library Collections, Acquisitions, and Technical Services* 27, no. 2 (2003): 203–13.

71. Bruce R. Kingma, *Economics of Access Versus Ownership: The Costs and Benefits of Access to Scholarly Articles via Interlibrary Loan and Journal Subscriptions* (New York: Haworth Press, 1996): 1–79. Co-published simultaneously in the *Journal of Interlibrary Loan, Document Delivery & Information Supply* 6, no. 3 (1996): 1–76.

72. Audrey Fenner, "Introduction: Managing Digital Resources," *Managing Digital Resources in Libraries* (New York: Haworth Press, 2005): 1–2. Co-published simultaneously in *The Acquisitions Librarians*, no. 33–34, 1–2.

73. Crews, *Copyright, Fair Use, and the Challenge for Universities*, 99–101.

74. Leslie Ellen Harris, *Licensing Digital Content: A Practical Guide for Librarians*, (Chicago: American Library Association, 2009), 112; Stephen Bosch, et al., *Guide to Licensing and Acquiring Electronic Information* (Lanham, MD: Scarecrow Press, 2005): 53.

75. Harris, *Licensing Digital Content*, 72–73.

76. Fenner, *Managing Digital Resources in Libraries*, 11–12; Bosch, *Guide to Licensing and Acquiring Electronic Information*, 53–57.

77. Cris Ferguson, "Technology Left Behind—Throwing Kindling on the eBooks Fire," *Against the Grain*, April 2008: 84; Julie Bosman, "Kindle Users to Be Able to Borrow Library E-Books," *New York Times*, April 20, 2011, http://www.nytimes.com/2011/04/21/technology/21amazon.html.

78. American Library Association, *Digital Rights Management (DRM) and Libraries*, 2007, http://www.ala.org/ala/issuesadvocacy/copyright/digitalrights/index.cfm.

79. ALA Office for Information Technology, OITP Technology Policy Brief, "Digital Rights Management: A Guide for Librarians version 1," 2006, prepared by Michael Godwin, http://www.ala.org/ala/issuesadvocacy/copyright/digitalrights/DRMfinal.pdf.

80. Russell, *Complete Copyright*, 104; Pramod Jamkhedkar, et al., "Middleware Services for DRM," Communication Systems Software and Middleware, COMSWARE 2007, 2nd International Conference on, (January 7–12, 2007), 1–8. http://www.ece.unm.edu/~drake/products/COMSWARE_07.pdf.

81. Denise A. Troll, "How and Why are Libraries Changing?" *Digital Library Federation*. Draft, January 9, 2001, http://www.diglib.org/use/whitepaper.htm.

7

PUBLIC, STATE, AND
SCHOOL LIBRARIES

Ruthie Maslin

Public libraries complement formal education by providing a resource base and platform for people of all ages to participate in lifelong learning.[1]

[T]he public librarian in the United States has long held a strong sense of his mission to serve the unserved . . . from the founding of A.L.A. in 1876 to the enactment of the Library Services Act in 1956, the principal goal of public librarians was to make their institutions available to every citizen.[2]

Libraries have long had a strong commitment to distributed learning, and it has been an integral part of their mission as we can see from the following mission statements:

- **Seattle Public Library:** "We strive to inform, enrich and empower every person in our community by creating and promoting easy access to a vast array of ideas and information, and by supporting an informed citizenry, lifelong learning and love of reading."[3]
- **El Paso Public Library:** "The El Paso Public Library serves our diverse community through information access, cultural enrichment and lifelong learning."[4]
- **New York Public Library:** "The mission of The New York Public Library is to inspire lifelong learning, advance knowledge, and strengthen our communities . . . We inspire lifelong learning by creating more able learners and researchers. We:
  - Teach learning and information-navigation skills
  - Provide tools, resources, and great places to work
  - Engage in great exploratory conversations
  - Ask and answer questions that encourage patrons to challenge their assumptions

- Support creativity, research, and problem-solving
- Bring people together to spark creative synergies and learn from each other."[5]

Every library and every librarian, regardless of type or location of the library, participates in distributed learning in some way on a regular basis. Whether it is answering a chat reference question or helping a customer navigate database articles, setting up a remote classroom session or making full-text books and articles available on the library's website, the future of 21st century libraries is tied to the future of distributed learning.

The foundation was laid in the 19th and 20th centuries and ranged from the Pack Horse Librarians of the 1930s in Appalachia to the rise of bookmobiles nationwide in the 1950s and 1960s. Books by mail, deposit station collections, and prison libraries formed a strong base. This continually growing structure has been and will be continually reconfigured by technology. While public libraries briefly shifted mid-20th century to more of a leisure function in the community, the rise of rapidly changing technology in the late 1990s and continuing into the 21st century has shifted libraries back toward an information-providing model. Public libraries' commitment to helping their customers and communities bridge the digital divide has driven that culture of learning and access. Libraries today are charged not only with providing people *access* to information through technology but also with teaching them how to use technology to access that information. They are both purveyors of distributed learning and facilitators of it.

Additionally, libraries pursue a somewhat unique mission in that they serve their customers from birth to death. As a result, *lifelong learning* has quickly risen as a key element in library mission and service statements, especially with public

Pack Horse Librarians on horses ready to begin their rounds outside of the Pack Horse Library in Hindman, KY. (Photographer, George Goodman, 1876–1961) Reproduced with permission from the University of Kentucky Archives: KUKAV-64M1–2885.

In Kentucky, Lexington Public Library bookmobile service affected distributed learning through much of the 20th century. (Photo courtesy of the Lexington Public Library)

libraries. Lifelong learning means libraries do more than provide equity of access to information. It means libraries actively engage customers in learning activities throughout their lifetimes.

The International Federation of Library Associations and Institutions (IFLA) has defined lifelong learning on an international scale:

> Lifelong learning can be defined as all purposeful learning activity undertaken on an ongoing basis with the aim of improving knowledge, skills and competence. It contains various forms of education and training, formal, non-formal and informal, e.g. the traditional school system from primary to tertiary level, free adult education, informal search and training, individually, in a group setting or within the framework of social movements.
>
> All these forms of education and training rely on working methods developing the individual's ability to search for information and develop knowledge actively and independently. Libraries have the potential to make a difference between a traditional system of formal education and a broader system of learning. Libraries are socially inclusive places, offering a broad choice of different media and professional guidance in information search. In my view, they must therefore supplement the classroom and the traditional textbook.[6]

This chapter will examine some of the current trends in distributed learning in public, state, and school libraries. While the specifics of what is taking place may change as rapidly as the technology updates, the potential of distributed learning in libraries is limitless—the whole universe of knowledge and learning lies open and accessible to you and your customers.

PUBLIC LIBRARIES

Public libraries have long served as information connectors, joining customers with information they need and want. Traditionally, that connection has happened on-site. Library buildings contained both information and information professionals, and so people came to libraries for information. In the 20th century, however, technology began its rapid shaping of our concept of information, both *what* and *where* it is. Suddenly, information wasn't just in the library—it was somewhere out there in cyberspace. Public libraries responded to technological changes, keeping true to their mission of connecting people with information. Bridging the first wave of the digital divide meant providing customers with access to personal computers and then to the Internet and World Wide Web. The second wave brought a new challenge: bridging the digital divide now meant providing customers with something even more abstract than an entré to cyberspace—it was access to bandwidth and the speed and power to navigate cyberspace.

Educating the Electorate

Anyone who has been around public libraries long enough or taken just about any beginning library science course knows that the argument for the very existence of public libraries is predicated on the need for an educated electorate to sustain our democratic process. In the mid to late 19th century, this train of thought led in part to the establishment of the identity of the public library as a true and broad-based educational resource. "Mann, Bernard, and their followers held that an intelligent and educated electorate is essential to a democracy, and in the great system of public education which they foresaw the public library was to be a true 'people's university'."[7]

This notion of the "people's university" is perhaps the clearest iteration of the role of public libraries in educating the electorate and its most current incarnation—distributed learning. Cleveland Public Library's vision statement says it well:

> "The People's University" is to be the learning place for a diverse community, inspiring people of all ages with the love of books and reading, advancing the pursuit of knowledge, and enhancing the quality of life for all who use the Library.[8]

Numerous other public libraries have also assumed the "people's university" moniker and have embraced to varying degrees all that entails, from proctoring exams and providing off-campus classroom space to facilitating online learning and teleconferencing classes.

This notion of the library as university is echoed in one of the most memorable statements of Daniel J. Boorstin, who served as Librarian of Congress from 1975 to 1987:

Libraries remain the meccas of self-help. They remain as they have always been, the most open of open universities—institutions of the highest learning, where there are no entrance examinations, no registration fees, no examinations, and no diplomas, and where one can enter at any age. There we make available the great teachers of all ages and all nations.[9]

That statement was part of "The Indivisible Community," a speech he made at the 1976 annual conference of the American Library Association in Chicago. During his tenure, Boorstin continually emphasized this educational imperative for libraries throughout the United States, our "Republic of Letters."

A "Learning Culture"

Public libraries as both seats and conduits of learning are not uniquely an American notion. The desire for an educated populace is one of the most basic of modern civilization, and public libraries around the world have embraced distributed learning. A 2003 British strategy document produced by the Department for Culture, Media and Sports identified several critical roles public libraries play in supporting learning at all levels. The *Framework for the Future: Libraries, Learning and Information in the Next Decade* advised that "libraries should provide the foundations for a learning culture." Libraries, the report noted, are uniquely positioned to foster learning as exploration and self-development in an environment that draws together learners of all ages, offering informal group and individual learning opportunities.[10]

"Learning" is slowly replacing "education" in such policy statements, recognizing both the formal and informal elements of learning *and* learning as a lifelong process. Gradually the focus is shifting from teacher-centered learning to student-centered learning.[11] This is the niche public libraries are able to fill so well, since emphasis on individual information seekers' needs goes to the heart of the library mission.

On the Road

We return to the case of Cleveland Public Library. Throughout its 141-year history, CPL has worked to stay current with the needs of the consumer, each one a potential "student" of the people's university. But as we have seen in so many cases, technology and its rapid changes drive currency in today's public libraries. CPL's late 20th century directors embraced technological advances—under Andrew A. Venable Jr.'s leadership, CPL became the first U.S. public library to offer eBooks for customer checkout.[12] CPL's 21st century history reflects that as well. On November 26, 2001, CPL rolled out its new mobile library, dubbed "The People's University on Wheels." Part of Cleveland Public Library's Branches and Outreach Services, the 32-foot mobile library provides all the services a customer could access at any other library location, including books for all ages, magazines, videos, compact discs, books-on-tape, and DVDs. The unit contains computers with software and Internet access, and a wheelchair lift and adaptive technology are provided for special-needs patrons.

While bookmobiles continue in many areas to expand customers' ability to access library materials, today's public library outreach work is increasingly focused on expanding customers' ability to access learning. In 2010, the Lexington Public Library in Kentucky expanded its outreach services to include mobile computer and job skills training. Funded by an $82,000 grant from the John S. and James L. Knight Foundation, the mobile computer initiative provided for the hiring of a full-time teacher/coordinator and the purchase of two complete and self-sufficient mobile labs. The labs contain laptops for 10 students and one instructor, a wireless printer, a generator, and a mobile hotspot box. With the mobile lab program, teaching can occur anywhere the lab can go. Customers can access library resources through the library's website where they are, even if they don't have their own computer.

Through outreach efforts like this, public libraries have been able to distribute learning quite literally throughout the communities they serve. As librarian Charles Lyons notes,

> An opportunity is emerging for libraries to build on the community focus they have always embraced and become more involved with the flow of local information—both as producers and coordinators of local data. Local search engines, government entities, local media (newspapers, television, radio), and the locals themselves (the residents of the community) are just a few of the sources that contribute to the wide range of information swirling throughout a community. By leveraging new technologies and reinvigorating their efforts on storing, organizing and creating information about their communities, libraries can build on their status as valuable and trusted local community assets and become, if not the princip[al] soloist, a distinct voice among a whole chorus of local information providers.[13]

Using new technologies in innovative ways is at the heart of today's distributed learning in public libraries, as it has been in the past. Library websites offer 24-hour access to much of the same information customers can get in the library. State and regional online library networks make it possible for even the smallest libraries to connect their customers to databases and other proprietary online sources.

Shortening the Distance

If "necessity is the mother of invention," then budget reduction is the mother of innovation. Public libraries have traditionally seen use increase in tough financial times. Even as economic shifts may force libraries themselves to slash budgets, lay off staff, and cut hours, the demand for library services typically grows during these times as customers turn to libraries to fill their most basic needs for connection, entertainment, information, and learning. Distributed learning originating from other sources helps libraries fill the gaps. Libraries have always found ways to provide information in tight times, often looking increasingly to free sources of information and expanding their purchasing power with fee-based services through consortium development. The technology infrastructure is already in place—most libraries have teleconferencing and high-speed data connections at the ready—all that is lacking is the instruction. These sites are easy to navigate and offer a wide range of educational opportunities for both public and staff:

- Online Programming for All Libraries (OPAL) is an international collaboration to provide web-based training. Libraries and other non-profit organizations pay an annual membership based on the number of "seats" in their online learning rooms, with the cost ranging from $100 to $1,000. OPAL uses Talking Communities web conferencing software that allows "voice-over-IP online conversations, text chatting, co-browsing, document sharing, and more. Live online events can be recorded, archived, and podcast with ease." OPAL programs include book discussion programs, writing workshops, staff training, and virtual tours.[14]

- WebJunction is an online learning community whose services are targeted to libraries and library staff. Self-paced online courses are offered free or at low cost. The learning community model also provides a variety of options for more informal and peer-based learning to flourish.[15]

Libraries are also developing and managing their own online classes. Library staff often teach these classes, adding the "people's professor" hat to the already-full list of duties for public librarians. A variety of open source software is available to make these endeavors inexpensive and easy to manage. Some of the most popular include the following:

- Dokeos—Offers both standard course management tools and Flash-based videoconferencing to facilitate live trainings remotely. It is available in Dutch, English, French, and Spanish.[16]

- Sakai—A Java-based Collaboration and Learning Environment (CLE) product that is used in hundreds of universities, schools, and organizations around the world.[17]

- eFront, claroline—Available in 35 languages, ILIAS Learning Management—available in 23 languages, and OLAT.[18]

By making learning opportunities available online through their websites, public libraries around the world are shortening the distance customers must travel to access learning opportunities. These services are also available to users in the library. In this case, the notions of distance and distributed learning merge—resources are made available to a wide variety of users in diverse locations. For example, San Bernardino Public Library in California (www.sbpl.org) recently began a trial program offering free language learning, including ESL, to customers through its website. The language training is through Mango Languages, a company that focuses on the language learning needs of libraries. In 2010, Warren County Public Library in Kentucky began offering language classes through its website using Cengage Learning's Powerspeak (www.bgpl.org). Reference and Technical Services Manager Holly Hedden says the library started the online language classes in response to high customer usage of traditional print and audio language learning materials and customer requests for computerized language learning. "I hope it will be a good resource for travelers who need to familiarize themselves with other languages and also as a supplement for students who are studying languages," Hedden said. The program is too new to have a statistical track record, but staff have high hopes for the program.[19] This is how innovation begins—a need arises, and libraries look for solutions, often embarking on untested waters.

As part of their mission to support lifelong learning, public libraries have not left the younger customers behind when it comes to distributed learning. Many public libraries now offer extended-hour remote learning opportunities to younger users. Elementary through high school students can access teachers and tutors through live online homework help programs such as Tutor.com. Libraries subscribe to the services and make them available to cardholders through their library websites.

STATE LIBRARIES

State libraries have an interesting charge: they may provide information services to state employees and often to state legislators, they offer support and services for libraries throughout the state as well as the employees of those libraries, and they serve the information needs of the public, particularly with regard to archives, records, and other special collections. This broad-based mission makes them an ideal environment for the development of interesting and cutting-edge distributed learning activities.

Training for Library Staff

Providing continuing education opportunities for library staff throughout the state can be a daunting challenge, especially when a state library is serving a very large geographic area. It is perhaps this challenge that has pushed state libraries to the forefront of distributed learning. Limited funds, a broad range of educational and training needs, and large distances to travel make distributed learning an ideal solution in many cases. In a clear example of public libraries' commitment to equity of access for all users, the Utah State Library's Distance Education site articulates the scope of this challenge—"to provide equal access to information and library resources to all Utah residents by providing . . . training and services for our customers—in their communities where they work and live—in the effective performance of their public responsibilities, and in the use of rich and diverse information technologies and resources."[20] The site makes use of Moodle, an Open Source Course Management System (CMS) that is used by educators around the world to create online dynamic web sites for their students.[21] Course offerings range from Library Trustee Enrichment to Grant Writing for Libraries.

The Texas State Library & Archives Commission offers a rich compendium of distance learning resources for library customers and library staff. The website also explains in depth how various iterations of remote learning work, explores best practices from around the country, and discusses both satellite teleconferencing and videoconferencing as distributed learning options.[22]

Leveraging Resources

Because of their size and broad service missions, state libraries are able to make resources available to libraries that otherwise would not be able to afford them. Access to databases for customers and staff ranks high on this list of resources. Maine's Virtual Library sports a colorful interface and catchy name—MARVEL!— attracting users of all ages to access databases and other learning support resources online. The State Library of Kansas has a downloadable media section on its website where library cardholders across the state can virtually check out and re-serve books 24 hours a day. Available formats include Mp3 and iPod compatible audiobooks, video, music, and more.[23] The Kentucky Virtual Library—KYVL—offers a mix of free learning support resources and ones available either to library card holders from the state or onsite in member libraries.[24] One popular KYVL resource is the Kentuckiana Digital Library, whose mission speaks to the heart of distributed learning:

> The Kentuckiana Digital Library is built to enhance scholarship, research and lifelong learning through the establishment of access to shared digital archi-val collections in the state of Kentucky. It also provides guidance and instruc-tion for Kentucky libraries, archives, historical societies and museums on applying appropriate technologies used in the production of digital library resources.[25]

SCHOOL LIBRARIES

College students around the world are earning degrees online. They access their college or university's library virtually, and they have nearly the same access to materials as their on-site counterparts. But where do elementary and secondary schools fall into the mix with regard to distributed learning? After all, students *go to* school—school doesn't go to them. Or does it? In fact, this is where some of the most cutting-edge ideas are coming from with regard to distributed learning.

The Branson School Online in Colorado, started in 2001, is an excellent case in point. "Branson School Online is an accredited, diploma-granting, K-12 pub-lic school," their website states. "We operate within a school district in the State of Colorado, just like the school district you happen to live in. We are a local governmental agency governed by a locally elected Board of Education, which is empowered by Colorado Revised Statutes."[26] This is not an adjunct learning interface—it is a full-time public school with a regular student body, accredited teachers, graduations, and honor rolls. The only difference is that students attend school in their own homes. Just like any other public school, there is no tuition cost. In its commitment to bridge the digital divide separating "haves" and "have nots" with regard to technology and connectivity, the school district loans laptops to students for the entire school year and reimburses their families $20 per month to help cover the cost of Internet service.

What is perhaps even more interesting is that this is not an isolated case. There are hundreds of Internet-based public schools across the country. Some offer online courses that supplement face-to-face classroom sessions, and some offer a complete online curriculum.

"We're attracting a lot of 21st century students who are excited about learn-ing in their own element, and on their own schedules, instead of being in a traditional setting, where they get a predetermined 50 minutes of instruc-tion," said DeLaina Tonks, director, Open High School of Utah.[27]

Libraries Without Books?

In 2009, the prestigious Cushing Academy located just west of Boston did the unthinkable. School administrators decided to clear the library's 20,000 books from the shelves. They reconfigured the library as a learning center, filled with technology to connect students with, well, books. They were just books in a different format. EBooks and online books, digital resources, and state-of-the-art connectivity comprise the new library's holdings. Electronic readers filled with digital materials replaced dusty volumes of encyclopedias. "Instead of a traditional library with 20,000 books, we're building a virtual library where students will have access to millions of books," said Cushing Headmaster James Tracy. "We see this as a model for the 21st-century school."[28]

Not all school libraries are ready to take that plunge, but there can be a happy medium. A Dutch team of educators and innovators have developed a unique library product that integrates a physical school library with a virtual one. The twist is that the virtual library is not merely a list of links and databases; it builds on the participatory nature of Web 2.0 to construct a "virtual school library where pupils can study [and] work but also play, discover, experience and create."[29]

> We are aware children, youngsters, learn everywhere, in their multiple styles, through unexpected sources and strategies, and so on. We have to incorporate the new digital tools and resources in our "school librarians' toolkit:" the digital school library services are a way of actively engaging our children in their learning process, making them acquire reflective skills of posing and solving an information-seeking problem. As I could see, a learner or a group of learners are guided by the school librarian and the teacher in this new environment. Children can learn autonomously and, at the same time, they are not alone: their learning process is facilitated and fostered by their school librarian and teacher, using both traditional and new tools and resources, through "Fac-Totem 2.0."[30]

These types of hybrid libraries and distance learning interfaces are indicative of the move by educators around the world to meet "digital native" students where they best interact and learn—in a multi-platform, multi-format, highly interactive environment. A good example of this is the Hawaii eBook Library, which provides access to 500,000 eBooks and 23,000 Mp3 audio books. The eBook Library is committed to "Making Reading Fun for the Students of Hawaii." While there is a charge for membership, it is minimal—$8.95 annually for individuals to join. If schools or institutions want to purchase memberships for students, the price drops to $2 per student.[31] By making resources like these available easily and at low cost, kids *are* reading. To borrow from Dr. Seuss, a book's a book, no matter how it looks. Supporting reading by providing books in the formats kids and teens want is becoming an increasingly important consideration for both school and public libraries.

Barry Joseph is the Online Leadership Director for Global Kids, Inc., an independent non-profit organization in New York with a mission to "educate and inspire urban youth to become successful students, global citizens and community leaders by engaging them in academically rigorous, socially dynamic, content-rich learning experiences." He describes these hybrid learning environments as "distributed learning networks," the most important places in kids' lives where learning occurs. He described one student's distributed learning network as consisting of

> Not just at home, school and church but also . . . digital media, like MP3s, SMS and social networks, and at youth-serving institutions . . . Some are places that require her presence, like school, while others are opt-in, like MySpace. But the learning she gathers across the nodes in her network are preparing her to succeed in the classrooms, workplaces, and civic arenas of the 21st Century.[32]

The challenge, Joseph suggests, is to ask ourselves, "What do youth need to understand and strategically navigate their distributed learning networks? And how can youth-serving institutions support youth to document the associated learning that address 21st century skills that so often go unrecorded?"[33] One approach to empowering young people to take charge of their learning and make more sense of their distributed learning networks is "to focus on youth's existing assets through both digital tools and offline activities to help them see the contours of their networks, understand their role as they traverse their learning nodes, and enhance their abilities to make connections amongst them."[34]

CONCLUSIONS

The concept of distributed learning enfolds a bit of irony: its subset of distance learning involves learners, educators, and often resources separated from each other physically, yet its most powerful applications continually create and recreate connections among learners, educators, and resources, bringing them together in increasingly meaningful ways. A 21st century view of distributed learning necessitates a reorienting of one's notion of distance and connectedness. In the same way, libraries today are continually reorienting their concept of connecting information seekers with information. Very basic questions emerge: *Where* is the library? *Where* are the books? *Where* are the customers? The paradigm doesn't just shift, it constantly morphs. They are *here* and *there*. While early efforts still brought materials, people, and teachers together, technology has created many new facets of the issue.

Bowman notes, "[Distributed learning] . . . allows teachers, students, and content to be located in different noncentralized locations so that instruction and learning occur independent of time and space."[35] Libraries that embrace distributed learning find their impact on and connection to the community expands. Budget woes may force branch hours to be cut, but cyberspace never shuts its doors. Libraries can have 24-hour access to their customers, and customers have 24-hour access to library resources and services. Further, the library service model shifts even further toward more individualized customer-centrism. Today's library customer has access to an exponentially expanding array of information resources, and librarians often serve more as guides through the information—in many cases, libraries provide not only access, they also provide the road map. As Bates notes, "Distributed learning has further been defined as a student centered approach, which uses the possibilities of new technology to offer opportunities for active learning and communication. This gives the teachers [and librarians] possibilities to adapt the learning environment to the user (student) to be able to meet the needs of different groups and has the potential to offer both high-quality and cost-effective education."[36]

NOTES

1. Robert Newton, Audrey Sutton, and Mike McConnell, "Information Skills for Open Learning: A Public Library Initiative," *Library Review* 47, no. 2 (1998): 125–34.

2. John Colson, "The United States: An Historical Critique," *Library Services to the Disadvantaged*, ed. William Hartin (Hamden, CT: Linnet Books, 1975), quoted in John W. Fritch, "Electronic Outreach in America: From Telegraph to Television," Libraries to the People: Histories of Outreach, ed. Robert S. Freeman and David M. Hovde (Jefferson, NC: McFarland, 2003), 66.

3. Seattle Public Library, *Mission Statement*, http://www.spl.org/default.asp?pageID=about_mission.

4. El Paso Public Library, *Mission Statement*, http://www.elpasotexas.gov/library/ourlibraries/strategicplans/mission.asp.

5. New York Public Library, *Mission Statement*, http://www.nypl.org/help/about-nypl/mission.

6. Britt Marie Häggström, "The Role of Libraries in Lifelong Learning Final Report of the IFLA Project under the Section for Public Libraries," *IFLA* (March 2004): 2, http://archive.ifla.org/VII/s8/proj/Lifelong-LearningReport.pdf.

7. Jesse Hauk Shera, *Foundations of the Public Library: The Origins of the Public Library Movement in New England 1629–1855* (Chicago: University of Chicago Press, 1949): 247.

8. Cleveland Public Library website, http://www.cpl.org/index.php?q=node/24.

9. John Y. Cole, ed., *The Republic of Letters: Librarian of Congress Daniel J. Boorstin on Books, Reading, and Libraries, 1975–1987* (Washington, DC: Library of Congress, 1989): 29.

10. Sarah McNicol and Pete Dalton, "Broadening the Perspectives on the Learning Process in Public Libraries," *The New Review of Libraries and Lifelong Learning* 4, no. 1 (2003): 28.

11. Ibid., 27.

12. David D. VanTassel and John J. Grabowski, "Cleveland Public Library," *The Encyclopedia of Cleveland History*, http://ech.case.edu/ech-cgi/article.pl?id=CPL.

13. Charles Lyons, "The Library: A Distinct Local Voice?," *First Monday* 12, no. 3 (2007), http://firstmonday.org/htbin/cgiwrap/bin/ojs/index.php/fm/article/view/1629/1544.

14. "Online Programming for All Libraries (OPAL) website," http://www.opal-online.org/factsheet.htm.

15. "Webjunction" website, http://www.webjunction.org/.

16. "Dokeos" website, http://www.dokeos.com/.

17. "Sakai" website, http://sakaiproject.org/.

18. "eFront," http://www.efrontlearning.net/; "Claroline.Net," http://www.claroline.net/; "ILIAS Learning Management," http://www.ilias.de/docu/goto_docu_root_1.html; "OLAT: Your Open Source LMS," http://www.olat.org/website/en/html/index.html.

19. Holly Hedden, personal interview with author, March 2010.

20. "Utah State Library Distance Education Site," http://library.utah.gov/moodle/.

21. "Moodle" website, http://moodle.org/about/.

22. Texas State Library and Archives Commission, Resources for Librarians, http://www.tsl.state.tx.us/ld/pubs/dl/.

23. "State Library of Kansas website," http://kansas.lib.overdrive.com/C5C010B6–9F85–4662-B2C1-D8F3D67270A8/10/378/en/default.htm.

24. "Kentucky Virtual Library" website, http://www.kyvl.org/.

25. "Kentuckiana Digital Library" website, http://kdl.kyvl.org/.

26. "Branson School Online" website, http://www.bransonschoolonline.com/index.cfm?pID=2308.

27. Bridget McCrea, "Open Content in Practice: A Virtual High School in Utah Shuns Textbooks and Relies on Open Content for 100 Percent of its Coursework," *THE Journal*, http://thejournal.com/Articles/2011/03/02/Open-Content-in-Practice.aspx?Page=2.

28. David Abel, "Welcome to the Library. Say Goodbye to the Books. Cushing Academy Embraces a Digital Future," *The Boston Globe*, September 4, 2009.

29. Lesley Farmer, "Lourense Das's Innovation Awarded," *Newsletter for IFLA Section No. 11 School Libraries and Resource Centers*, 2009, 48, http://www.ifla.org/files/school-libraries-resource-centers/newsletters/june-2009.pdf.

30. Luisa Marquardt, "Lourense Das awarded for 'Fac-Totem 2.0!,'" *IASL Meeting Place Blog*, February 5, 2009, http://iaslonline.ning.com/profiles/blogs/lourense-das-awarded-for.

31. "Hawaii eBook Library website," http://www.hawaiilibrary.com/.

32. Barry Joseph, "Using Alternative Assessment Models to Empower Youth-Directed Learning," *Breakthrough Learning in a Digital Age Blog*, October 23, 2009, http://breakthroughlearning.blogspot.com/.

33. Ibid.

34. Ibid.

35. Maureen Bowman, "What Is Distributed Learning?," *Tech Sheet* 2, no. 1 (1999), http://techcollab.csumb.edu/techsheet2.1/distributed.html.

36. Anthony Bates, "Technology for Distance Education: A Ten-Year Perspective," in *Distance Education: New Perspectives*, ed. Keith Harry, Magnus John, and Desmond Keegan (London: Routledge, 1993).

8

ACADEMIC LIBRARIES, MARKETING, ACCREDITATION, AND SUPPORT

Arne J. Almquist

As we saw in the chapter one time line, academic libraries have long worked to effectively support their students and faculty, regardless of physical location. In the pre-digital age, libraries endeavored to provide remote users with as many traditional resources and services as were practical. The rise of digital technologies and the expansion of electronic collections and information have not only made that task easier but also caused a shift in the issues of virtual and real library support as well. In fact, many services, once considered unique to distant customers, are now mainstream—provided, expected, and used by all. This chapter presents an overview of the development of academic library distributed and virtual support efforts, briefly discusses accreditation, examines aspects of marketing of virtual library services, and suggests a new focus for future library virtual support projects in the establishing of a distributed learning support center in the library itself.

THE DEVELOPMENT OF ACADEMIC LIBRARY SUPPORT SERVICES FOR DISTRIBUTED LEARNING

Regardless of the type of extra campus instruction, whether delivered as a correspondence course, interactive video, or online, the challenge for academic libraries and librarians has revolved around equity of access between distant and on-campus users as outlined in the Association of College and Research Libraries' *Standards for Distance Learning Library Services* (see chapter 2 for a in-depth discussion of the *Standards*). Before the development of robust technologies and extensive digital collections, providing that equity of access was difficult, mainly due to the limitations of physical materials, distribution venues, and services. Distant users were plainly at a disadvantage to on-campus users, with, at best, access to a fraction of the materials and services available to those on campus.

Indeed, the development of advanced information technologies leveled the playing field and revolutionized the academic library's ability to serve its customers.

Today, distributed users have access to collections at a level virtually identical to that available to on-campus users as librarians effectively negotiate licensing for registered off-campus users, institute fast document delivery tools, and use a variety of communication channels. For example, in 2010 at the W. Frank Steely Library, Northern Kentucky University (NKU), 92 percent of journal collections, most of the standard reference sources, a growing collection of electronic books, and databases of audio and video recordings are at the fingertips of all users, available 24 hours per day, seven days per week, regardless of the user's physical location. Government documents are readily available via the Internet and users can freely access millions of electronic books from online libraries, such as those provided through Google Books Projects, Project Gutenberg, and many others. The library's online catalog linked into its website allows quick access and a portal to information.

While the effort to provide online services has lagged behind the development of online collections, great progress has been made in that area as well. Electronic reserves are now the rule rather than the exception, with libraries addressing copyright issues in an effort to provide the best service for the most people. Interlibrary loan and document delivery services are freely available to students and faculty via online interfaces. (John Schlipp discusses copyright in regard to document delivery and e-reserves in chapter 6.) For example, Steely Library's unique SourceFinder service combines interlibrary loan, document delivery, and a user-driven acquisition service into a single, easy-to-use interface, allowing all users to obtain materials not currently held in the library's collections.[1] An increasing proportion of reference assistance is being provided through electronic means. Online tutorials, subject guides, and librarians embedded in classes are all helping to provide access to services unaffected by time or location.

Students and faculty are demonstrating their preference for the convenience of online access through their patterns of usage. According to the 2009 LibQual+ user survey, administered at NKU's Steely Library, of the 81.95 percent of respondents who indicated that they used library or other information sources on a daily basis, 66.67 percent stated that they referred to an online search engine, such as Google or Yahoo, while 15.28 percent accessed the library through its online interface. Only 20.37 percent of daily users stated that they travelled physically to the library to use information resources.[2]

Ten to fifteen years ago, citation databases made up the majority of online library resources—full-text resources were rare. Those instructors wishing to assign a fully online reading list were limited to a very small subset of available sources. Today, distributed users, virtual librarians, and professors have the entire spectrum of information resources at their fingertips, including text (books and journal articles), and audio and video recordings. Mobile computing, most notably the use of iPhones, iPads, and eBook readers like the Kindle, further extend the range of electronic resources.

DIPLOMA MILLS AND ACADEMIC ACCREDITATION

No discussion of distributed learning and academic libraries would be complete without mention of diploma/degree mills and accreditation in the virtual world.

Diploma and Degree Mills

Diploma mills have been a bane of academic existence since the beginning of the higher education experience and are not unique to online learning. In 1883, the *Pacific Medical and Surgical Journal and Western Lancet* exposed the "Bellevue Medical College of Massachusetts" as a bogus diploma mill. After receiving a suspect diploma, the Illinois State Board of Health's secretary set a trap by having a man "connected with the press" apply to the college for a diploma. In the application letter, the applicant used poor spelling and grammar, but was readily accepted nonetheless. The president of the bogus school was once a physician who had been expelled from the profession. After this exposure, both the phony president and dean were arrested and held on criminal charges.[3]

What are diploma or degree mills? Simply put, such counterfeit operations offer a diploma in exchange for money. Some charge exorbitant fees and award credit for what is frequently termed "life experiences."[4] Diploma mills issue a fake degree from a real college. Degree mills hoodwink students by awarding what appears to be a genuine degree from a fake college. Throw into this mix unaccredited institutions of various quality and you have a potential minefield awaiting the virtual student.

"Diploma mills and degree mills both sell academically meaningless degrees that are purchased by dishonorable customers with the intent of defrauding prospective clients and employers."[5]

According to an informal survey he performed in 2007, Alan Contreras estimated that 20 percent "of legally operating U.S. degree-granting institutions are unaccredited" and "about two-thirds of these are religious colleges, but almost 300 are secular and offer courses in traditional fields such as business, psychology, law, and so on."[6]

In addition to universities and colleges, private unaccredited correspondence schools operated for many years offering useful and legitimate courses. In 1958, two articles in *Popular Mechanics Monthly* discussed those that catered to men (predominately) interested in increasing their vocational knowledge in order to change jobs or increase their pay. Experts in their fields, these teachers made "a real effort to keep students interested, peppering them with brochures, newsletters, pep talks, as well as long personal letters and handwritten comments on exams."[7] Offering courses teaching advanced skills such as engineering, accounting, drafting, television repair, and the like, these correspondence courses reached many people not able to attend a formal institution. Hardly diploma or degree mills, these unaccredited schools served, and continue to serve, a very real need, as do the for-profit institutions as epitomized by the University of Phoenix, an online accredited for-profit university.

Already in 1958, "the number of students has doubled in the past decade, and will almost certainly double again in the next."[8] This is mirrored in statistics that are more current. According to the findings published in *Class Differences: Online Education in the United States, 2010,* more than 5.6 million students were taking at least one online course during the fall 2009 term, which was an increase of nearly one million students over the number reported the previous year (4.6 million). The growth rate for online enrollments exceeded that for the overall higher education student population with online growing at 21 percent and growth overall less than 2 percent. The study found that almost 30 percent of higher education students take at least one course online.[9] The 2010 study further highlighted some patterns that could well determine academic library support efforts. The number of chief academic officers who declared that online learning was "critical" to their institution's long-term strategy rose to 63 percent from 59 percent in 2009. For-profit institutions showed the largest increase from 51 percent in 2009 to 61 percent in 2010. As more institutions add online learning to their strategic plans, the need for library support for online students remains a key concern for librarians.[10]

Perceptions of Distributed Learning

Some in higher education have held the opinion that distributed learning (DL) was inferior to a face-to-face learning experience in a classroom. Rather than seeing DL as simply a different method of dissemination, they considered it an inferior substitute, or worse, and somehow not as rigorous as its face-to-face counterpart. Conversely, learners wondered if they would receive the same quality of education online as in a classroom and whether online work would be considered positively by employers. Potential employers questioned the quality of online work and closely examined the credentials of schools.

These concerns have diminished as the use of the Internet as an educational and social communications medium has become more widely accepted. According to a 2008 Excelsior College/Zogby International online survey of business executives nationwide, 83 percent of those surveyed strongly believed that online degrees were as credible as those earned in a face-to-face program. This majority judged the online degree by considering the institution's accreditation, the quality of its graduates, and its name. A small number, 5 percent, said they would judge the degree based on whether or not the institution was fully online or part of a brick-and-mortar campus.[11]

As acceptance has increased, so have the number of online courses and fully online degree programs. In 2011, eLearners.com listed over 250 accredited online colleges, online universities, and online schools in the United States, offering online Bachelor's, Master's and Doctoral degrees in numerous fields.[12]

Ideally, the main consideration was and should be an understanding of what constitutes effective teaching and learning regardless of distribution method. Olcott addressed this in 2005 when he wrote:

> Face-to-face and distance learning are mutually reinforcing learning interventions. When misinformed politicians, resistant faculty, and institutional administrators who have not had a creative leadership idea of late approach distance learning, they simply fall back on the adage that distance learning is inferior teaching and learning compared to teaching and learning traditional, face-to-face instruction. Did they ever think that the quality and pedagogical effectiveness of what goes on in traditional classrooms might be pretty poor examples/models for aspiring teachers and trainers?[13]

"Distance education is defined, for the purposes of accreditation review, as a formal educational process in which the majority of the instruction occurs when student and instructor are not in the same place. Instruction may be synchronous or asynchronous. Distance Education may employ correspondence study, audio, video, or computer technologies."[14]

In reports sponsored by the Alfred P. Sloan Foundation (such as *Class Differences: Online Education in the United States, 2010,* quoted here and above) the investigators measured the attitudes of academic leaders toward online education. In the first report from 2003, they found that 57 percent of academic leaders "rated the learning outcomes in online education as the same or superior to those in face-to-face."[15] Seven years later, in 2010, that level had increased to 66 percent. They also measured the differences between public and private nonprofit institutions and for-profits finding that "over three-quarters of academic leaders at public institutions report that online is as good as or better than face-to-face instruction (compared to only 55.4% of private nonprofits and 67.0% of for-profits)."[16]

Of course, if transcripts do not carry a note showing whether the student completed the class face-to-face or online, how would an employer know how it was delivered? Generally, transcripts show online and face-to-face classes equally without any distinction or identifier.[17] While standards vary by institution, those for online instruction can be far more demanding than those for face-to-face classes, which may not be as closely supervised. As noted above, there are legitimate non-accredited institutions, but most colleges and universities strive for accreditation. Accreditation is one way to identify legitimate online courses.

Accreditation

Accreditation standards take into account web-based, blended, and face-to-face courses. Unlike other countries, where accreditation is controlled by the government, it is voluntary in the United States. Accreditation is a self-regulatory mechanism based on meticulous review and evaluation following a wide-ranging set of standards. Institutional accreditation keeps an institution viable and forces it to periodically examine its effectiveness. Along with an assessment of operations and policies for DL and face-to-face courses, academic library services are also evaluated as a key factor in effective support of academic programs.

Bonnie Gratch-Lindauer, in her article comparing regional accreditation standards (2002), specifically addressed the issue of distributed learning support services:

Every commission [accreditation agency] has either a separate policy and/or statements embedded within the standards relating to distance learning and electronically delivered offerings. They all have separate procedures in place to review degree programs that are offered in whole or part at a distance. Found in all the regional higher education commissions' standards is the requirement that institutions provide evidence of how students and faculty will access information resources and services and how library and information services will be evaluated in an electronic teaching and learning environment. Some of the commissions require additional evidence, such as how students will learn to use online resources effectively and how these resources are incorporated into the course.[18]

Six major regional associations are authorized to accredit public and private schools, colleges, and universities in the United States, including distance education programs offered at those institutions. Each regional association operates only within its designated area; each accredits the entire school, not individual programs. All are recognized by the U.S. Department of Education (USDE) and the Council for Higher Education Accreditation (CHEA). The CHEA is the regulating body that watches over accreditation agencies and guards against non-authorized accreditation mills. The regional agencies listed below are the primary higher education accreditation agencies in the United States:[19]

1. Middle States Commission on Higher Education—Delaware, the District of Columbia, Maryland, New Jersey, New York, Pennsylvania, Puerto Rico, and the U.S. Virgin Islands.
2. Commission on Institutions of Higher Education, New England Association of Schools and Colleges—Connecticut, Maine, Massachusetts, New Hampshire, Rhode Island, and Vermont.
3. North Central Association of Colleges and Schools, The Higher Learning Commission—Arizona, Arkansas, Colorado, Illinois, Indiana, Iowa, Kansas, Michigan, Minnesota, Missouri, Nebraska, New Mexico, North Dakota, Ohio, Oklahoma, South Dakota, West Virginia, Wisconsin, and Wyoming.
4. Northwest Commission on Colleges and Universities—Alaska, Idaho, Montana, Nevada, Oregon, Utah, and Washington State.
5. Southern Association of Colleges and Schools Commission on Colleges—Alabama, Florida, Georgia, Kentucky, Louisiana, Mississippi, North Carolina, South Carolina, Tennessee, Texas, Virginia and Latin America.
6. Western Association of Schools and Colleges, Accrediting Commission for Community and Junior Colleges and the Western Association of Schools and Colleges, Accrediting Commission for Senior Colleges and Universities—California, Hawaii, the United States territories of Guam and American Samoa, the Republic of Palau, the Federated States of Micronesia, the Commonwealth of the Northern Mariana Islands, and the Republic of the Marshall Islands.

To illustrate the requirements for distributed learning, let's examine several of the Southern Association of Colleges and Schools Commission on Colleges (SACSCOC) Comprehensive Standards. Standard 3.4 covers all educational programs including on- and off-campus, blended, and distance learning programs and courses regardless of distribution method. All of an accredited institution's programs must adhere to standards, putting distributed learning and face-to-face instruction on the same level.

Standards 3.4.4 and 3.4.7 in the *Principles of Accreditation* refer to the quality of an institution's courses and programs. Standard 3.4.4 deals with the accredited institution's acceptance of transfer credits and other learning experiences external to the receiving institution and fixes responsibility for academic quality on the institution upon whose transcript coursework or credit is recorded—the host institution. 3.4.7 stipulates that the accredited institution ensures the quality and compliance of those courses and programs "offered through consortial relationships or contractual agreements."[20]

Standard 3.4.11 requires that accredited institutions assign "academically qualified" individuals to coordinate each major of a program. 3.4.12 discusses the institution's use of technology and the availability of technology training to students. This, of course, is critical to the success of an online instructional program. Students must be at least functionally proficient in the use of basic computer applications, such as the course management system.

Standard 3.8 is more germane to the subject of this chapter, as it deals with library resources in support of academic programs. 3.8.1 refers to the adequacy of library facilities and information resources, 3.8.2 requires that users have access to library instruction, and 3.8.3 describes the requirement that sufficient qualified library staff be employed "to accomplish the mission of the institution."[21]

Sufficient library resources are critical to the success of any academic program, definitely including those that are online. As described earlier in this chapter, the rapid development of online and networked technologies has revolutionized the provision of library services to both on-campus and DL students. As a result, the greater issue in regard to support of distributed learning students is most likely provision of a satisfactory program of library instruction.

Luckily, again technology has come to our rescue. The same course management systems used to provide credit-bearing courses and programs can be very effectively used to provide instruction in the use of library resources and services. The library website itself can be used to provide access to valuable user assistance. For example, the NKU Steely Library website includes long lists of custom tutorials and research guides.[22]

Embedded librarian programs further support the SACSCOC standards. Where instructors are willing and there are enough librarians available, librarians can be added as members of online courses, providing students with unprecedented access to an individual librarian. Students often build a better working relationship with the librarian in the non-threatening and more personal environment of the online course system.

Questions for you to consider about the SACSCOC standards:

- What if the lending practices of the home institution restricts checkout of certain materials or formats (e.g., DVDs) to library-use only?
- How do these restrictions mesh with the requirement to make items available to off-campus students on an *equivalent* basis? (Remember also the *ACRL Guidelines* we examined in chapter 2.)
- Should off-campus students be allowed to view the item at home while on-campus students may not? This is especially a concern for non-print media, such as microforms, 16 mm film, slides, and other physical media not available digitally.

What about organizations that specifically offer accreditation of distance/online learning programs? There are national and international accreditation agencies, many of which are approved, like the regional agencies listed above, by the USDE or the CHEA or both. One such is the Distance Education and Training Council (DETC). CHEA lists the DETC's scope of accreditation as "higher learning institutions in the United States and international locations that offer programs of study that are delivered primarily by distance (51 percent or more) and award credentials at the associate, baccalaureate, master's, first professional and professional doctoral degree level."[23] Established in 1926 as the National Home Study Council, the DETC is a nonprofit (501 c6) educational association based in Washington, DC, and operates as "a voluntary, non-governmental, educational organization that operates a nationally recognized accrediting association, the DETC Accrediting Commission."[24]

The International Accreditation Organization (IAO) operates worldwide to accredit higher education and vocational institutions providing education for working adults offered through any method of distributed learning or face-to-face.[25] It, like many others, is not accredited by either the CHEA or the USDE.[26]

MARKETING: A CRITICAL BUT OFTEN NEGLECTED COMPONENT

The appropriate marketing of distributed and virtual library services is integral to their success. A good start is to identify and address challenges that the library's users encounter as well as to brand or label library services so that they are easily identified as offerings of the library. However, to be most effective, libraries need to move beyond the simplistic, traditional understanding of marketing as advertising and develop a marketing orientation throughout the organization. An organization operating under this model seeks to offer services that serve actual and perceived needs rather than simply pushing services offered by the library. In addition, libraries supporting virtual users must make a significant effort to make full use of the tools that the new technologies have made available, such as using metatags to achieve high rankings in search engines to social media marketing using Facebook, Twitter, LinkedIn, and the like. Customizing the virtual library based on users' individual needs and bringing information to people when and where they need it are other key components.

Indeed, given the competition online, libraries must look at how other libraries, companies, and nonprofits market their services, how and why they are or are not successful, and what parts can be used effectively within a budget. Innovation is key, and many online applications are free to use. Consider word-of-mouth marketing using Twitter, for example. Dell Outlet (computers) earned $1 million in sales within six months when customers came to their site from Twitter.[27]

By definition, marketing is concerned with building effective two-way communications channels to more efficiently link producers with consumers—in this case, linking librarians and library staff with faculty, students, the community, and other learners, who may be worldwide. A properly implemented marketing program provides enhanced tools to develop strategies that improve awareness among users while also providing an important feedback channel to determine the actual and perceived needs of users. If we do not take perceived and actual user needs into account, our customers' points of view, when creating services and adequately build awareness of our offerings, we will waste precious resources on collections and services that will be underutilized. We will continue with the increasingly obsolete collection-centric model and miss the opportunities provided by the service-centric, or facilitating, model that promises to better serve our 21st century clientele. As Alison Circle in her article about marketing trends succinctly noted: "When we focus on our collections, electronic databases, or—heaven forbid—library FAQs, without first establishing an emotional connection, I worry about the future relevance of our great institutions."[28]

Effective marketing of library and information services is a vital segment in every type of library and information services organization today. Customer-centered marketing is at the core of successful service, and understanding the marketing mix and creating value is vital.[29]

Marketing and Libraries

Marketing has been a hot topic among librarians over the past 30 years, and marketing techniques, such as promotion and advertising, have been used in American libraries since the late 19th century. Numerous articles and books support many different aspects of library marketing.[30] Acknowledging the importance of marketing, the American Library Association (ALA) and the Association of College and Research Libraries (ACRL) offer marketing information as part of "@ your library®, the Campaign for America's Libraries." The marketing toolkit includes people profiles, case studies (including those promoting virtual services), and statistics as well as customizable, downloadable publicity materials such as logos and slogans.[31]

Most librarians who are firmly ensconced in the virtual realm realize the importance of marketing because they see the trends and the tools potential customers use daily. Unfortunately, there are still those who have not moved beyond a basic understanding of marketing to that deeper understanding referred to as a marketing orientation. In fact, the equation "marketing = advertising" is still prevalent among many librarians who do not have the time, training, or support to fully implement a marketing plan.

This narrow definition of the term has the twin effects of limiting the potential benefits of marketing and of leaving some librarians with negative perceptions of the concept. When seen as simple promotion and advertising, marketing can be perceived as an activity that is beneath the dignity of the academic library. This lack of respect for marketing concepts can also lead to an ad hoc approach to awareness-building rather than a systematic approach based on targeted markets, strategic imperatives, and user needs.

Similarly, we tend to define our markets very narrowly. When we approach the issue of marketing solely from an advertising/promotion perspective, we see our users as the sole target group. We ignore other important constituencies, such as donors, upper administrators, and political leaders. We also do not tend to segment the user population into target markets. The overall result is a scattergun approach rather than one that is systematic and strategic.

What does this have to do with distributed and virtual learning? While academic libraries in the traditional face-to-face setting can definitely benefit from a more systematic application of marketing principles, the traditional face-to-face educational environment provides channels for communication that are weakened or do not exist in the case of a distributed clientele (of course, the online environment brings with it communications channels that are unavailable in the face-to-face environment). Low user awareness means that library resources go unused, resources are not projected in ways that most effectively and efficiently meet user needs, and users are frustrated and dissatisfied. The potentially powerful communication channel of direct contact between librarian and user, facilitated by technology, is not established, leading to a continuing cycle of low awareness and low usage. An effective marketing effort, making full use of the new channels offered through online access to offset the loss of traditional face-to-face channels, offers libraries the ability to build strong levels of communication with their users, in the long run, perhaps surpassing those in the traditional educational environment.

Are Librarians Accepting of Marketing?

A number of studies have focused on the perceptions toward, and acceptance of, marketing by librarians. A 2001 survey of New Jersey public librarians sought to identify attitudes toward marketing and the relationships of those attitudes to various personal characteristics. These characteristics included the librarian's age, number of years of experience, level of education, coursework or classes in marketing, and experience with marketing efforts.[32]

While most respondents indicated a positive view toward marketing, reactions varied based on personal demographics. Administrators, those with longer professional experience, and those who had had training and experience with marketing techniques reacted most positively. A follow-up study found a similar level of acceptance, but it suggested that much of the apparent acceptance could be related to the fact that a pro-marketing position had become socially acceptable.[33]

In both studies, negative responses correlated with fewer years of professional experience, lack of experience with marketing efforts, and lack of training in marketing techniques. Negative attitudes on the part of librarians were positively correlated with the statement, "Marketing is not a high priority in my library." This suggests the importance of the work environment—in particular, the organization's goals, mission, and vision statements—and the support of leadership in building employee acceptance of the marketing concept.[34]

The results of the studies suggest that while the environment may be conducive to the growth of marketing efforts, additional work needs to be done to build librarians' understanding and acceptance of marketing principles. Possible solutions include introductory marketing survey classes in graduate library degree programs and ongoing training sessions for librarians and staff. Strong commitment on the part of library administrators is also important if employees are to fully buy into the marketing concept.

Building a Working Definition of Marketing

To build a broader perspective toward the marketing concept, it may be helpful to consider the American Marketing Association (AMA) definition of marketing:

> Marketing is the activity, set of institutions, and processes for creating, communicating, delivering, and exchanging offerings that have value for customers, clients, partners, and society at large.[35]

An important tenet of this recent definition is that marketing does play a role within society at large and that marketing can accomplish good things rather than be a tool solely for financial benefit. This is certainly a value that should resonate with the profession of librarianship, which is geared toward helping others to achieve.

Marketing is an organizational function, arguably as important to the library as cataloging and reference. And yet it is also a cross-functional process, requiring participation by staff and administrators at all levels of the library. Implemented properly, it is a process that provides a two-way communications flow between organization and user. This allows the organization to identify the needs of a group, create or tailor products and services to meet those needs, and build awareness of solutions among members of the group.

Marketing is about the exchange of value. As Stephen Abram noted: "Whether we like it or not, people pay, whether there's a monetary transaction or not. They pay for their library visit with time, taxes, prestige, and their own success. . . . We fail to merchandise our offerings in a way that is engaging and culturally relevant."[36] A lack of merchandising affects *user perceptions,* which in turn determine the value of the library's services or products. A database may cost the library $35,000 per year. You may pay staff $80,000 to $100,000 per year to provide interlibrary loan and document delivery services. You may pay $200,000 per year in wages and salaries to provide extensive online instructional and reference services. If the database is not used, users are not going to local libraries to try to find materials and use interlibrary loan services, and no one takes advantage of educational and reference opportunities, the perceived value to the patron is nil. If users do not perceive value because services and products are not being used, then the deliverables are lacking, the services or resources are not relevant to the users' real or perceived needs, or, more likely, the library's message is not being effectively communicated.

Obviously, the value placed into exchange by the academic library is the utility of its services and information resources. Academic libraries, and libraries in general, are commonly not revenue-producing units. Since third parties (the parent institution) rather than the actual user provides financial support or payment for services rendered, what is the value exchanged in "payment" between the user and the library? The answer is the usage or demand that users have for the library's resources and services. This usage does have a value to the library, most notably by justifying continued or expanded funding.

Defining Multiple Markets

Other constituencies also provide value or support to the library and must be treated as markets within a strategic marketing implementation. These include donors, administrators of the parent organization, and government officials. While these are important to all types of libraries and provide value to the library through philanthropic support, increased administrative and financial support, or political support for the library, they are often more critical to the academic library in the age of distributed learning.

Distributed and virtual learning efforts may be viewed as outreach activities, providing the university with a powerful tool for projecting resources in the solution of societal problems. It is an extension service that can increase the geographic reach of the institution, opening new markets and expanding enrollment. It can increase enrollment without growing the requisite support infrastructure (parking, health center, etc.). The increasing importance of distributed and virtual learning to the central mission of the university brings opportunities for marketing to new constituencies, all of whom can have a profound effect on the overall efforts, health, and growth of the library.

For example, upper administration, seeing the potential of increased revenues and larger markets through distance learning, will often be sensitive to the need for support to DL students. The library can benefit by building awareness and support among users that could lead to additional resources for the purchase of online resources, benefiting both distant and on-campus users. Donors and government officials can provide the library with stronger support if library services are perceived as being critical to the success of particular distributed learning projects that may address social problems or particular constituencies.

Clearly, then, it is important to define multiple constituencies or markets in order to better tailor our message, build awareness among the various groups, and meet the various needs of the library. Marketing, after all, requires markets, that is, a group of people with similar needs who are willing to exchange something of value with an entity that offers products or services to satisfy those needs.[37] It is important to cast a wide net when thinking about markets. While we generally focus on our users, we should realize that markets exist within all stakeholder groups, including our users, employees, present and potential donors, funding authorities, legislators, taxpayers—in short, anyone who has a stake in the successful operation of the library.

We determine our markets by segmenting a population. Segmentation is based on the premise that people in a given group will behave similarly when deciding whether or not to use our services.[38] This can be done by breaking the population into groups based on demographics (faculty, graduate students, upper/lower division undergraduate students), by discipline (architecture, art, biology, genealogy, etc.), by stakeholder type (user, donor, political leader) or into any logical grouping that brings together people of common interests or needs. Users of distributed and virtual services, whether they are real distance students/faculty or they are traditional on-campus clientele, could be treated as a distinct market segment.

Marketing is about meeting needs. Too often, we promote or advertise services that we are most comfortable with and have been providing since the dawn of time, or services that are easiest for us to produce. We tend to promote products and services that we develop or select internally to meet needs that we ourselves perceive. This is known in the marketing field as a production orientation.[39]

One function of marketing is to focus on determining needs through market research, and then to design and provide services that will meet those real and perceived needs. If we are successful in this effort to determine needs and then to develop services to meet those needs, promotion and advertising can be done to develop awareness rather than to sell the services. If services and collections meet real or perceived needs, they will sell themselves once users are aware.

Defining Markets in the Online World

Another valuable plot of virtual real estate is in your school's course management system. Packaging library information alongside course assignments and the syllabus will definitely get your material notices. Additionally, gaining the endorsement of a professor increases credibility and improves the odds that students will actually pay attention to your content. In this manner, the library becomes part of the classroom instead of a supplemental service.[40]

Cultural shifts and changing paradigms affect marketing and no more so than in libraries. Competition from online services is everywhere. When people can't figure out the library databases, or find them too hard to find or use, they turn to readily available and easy-to-use search engines. As Stephen Abram warned: "Know your customers better than Google—or you'll lose."[41] Why do people go to Google? It's fast. It's easy. It's free. Can the library make the same claim?

How are customers defined or categorized in the virtual world? Market research is the key. Consider which communications media most appeal to your audience— there may be more than one or two. Social media, print-based brochures, radio, television, Internet, mobile devices, word of mouth, and proximity, use whatever is necessary for communication. Be where your customers are. Be in their face if necessary—link from course home pages, embed in assignments, appear on the front page in search engine results, link from other websites. Take a prominent part in the learning experience. Don't let people satisfice with simple search engine results—use different search engines to illustrate concepts. Connect with users on a personal level. Use a "Meet the Librarian" corner, including a photograph and contact information, or include a personalized welcome email, audio, or video message, and link to social media pages.

The list is virtually endless.

On the other hand, don't forget feedback. Feedback is an extremely important component of this effort. Focus groups (preferably facilitated by people from OUTSIDE of the library), LibQual+, surveys, and so on, are all needed to provide feedback.

Even if you are working mainly in the virtual world, you need to be visible in the physical world. You still need to show that you are a part of the educational structure of the university and that there is still a need to connect with faculty and administrators in the physical campus environment. Establish a University Library Advisory Committee and select representatives of the colleges, Faculty Senate, and Student Government Association to serve as a communications channel. Visit informally with teaching faculty and attend their departmental meetings. Go to graduation ceremonies and student association meetings. Check out online pages and social media sites to see how the library is being perceived. Make use of your physical as well as virtual space. Many libraries feature coffee bars and computer labs bringing students into the library who may never have come before and aggressively connecting the physical with the virtual. Today's face-to-face student is often also a potential virtual student.

If academic libraries are to survive as vital resources in a very competitive environment, they must actively work to get information about their services and resources out to users—all users, those on-campus, off-campus, and anywhere in the world.

> With convergence (i.e., the ongoing movement of virtually all information, text, audio, video) to the digital bit stream, the need for librarians to understand technology—and to embrace it rather than to fight to retain the status-quo—will be critical if we are to remain relevant into the future.— Arne Almquist.

A One-Stop Virtual Learning Support Center in the Academic Library—Revisioning the Academic Library

Academic libraries sit uniquely positioned at a crossroads in the learning process, where they have the opportunity to integrate information content, technology, and information literacy skills and to serve a role that is both high-tech and high touch. Librarians are well suited to provide a highly valuable and effective role as the neutral brokers of skills, support, and services.

A library-coordinated and administered center for virtual teaching and learning support would benefit from the distinctive position of the academic library within the college or university as well as from the wide range of librarian perspectives. After all, school libraries have been the media center hub of their schools for a long time and have served in the role of instructional support. This is because librarians excel at making pertinent, unbiased, and authoritative information accessible. They are adept in finding, selecting, acquiring, synthesizing, and organizing information. The center of learning is the library.

A one-stop center housed and administered by an academic library provides faculty with the varied support services necessary to help them make the transition from traditional face-to-face instruction to the online environment. It would also support them once they are firmly installed in the online environment. Pulling together talent from various disciplines, the library center is the place to help faculty to create effective courses, stimulate quality and provide quality benchmarks, incorporate pertinent information from authoritative online resources (including library resources as well as information available freely on the web), and provide critical networking and mentoring support.

Many such centers exist, but most are external to the library. The University of Central Florida's Center for Distributed Learning offers a three-tier faculty support program that addresses the pedagogical, logistical, and technological issues necessary for successful online course development and delivery.[42] The Center for Learning Enhancement, Assessment, and Redesign (CLEAR) at the University of North Texas assists "faculty in the creation, design, implementation, and assessment of distributed learning courses" while serving "as the liaison for various administrative and technical support functions, thereby saving faculty's time, talent, and creative energies for their students."[43] The State University of West Georgia Distance & Distributed Education Center "facilitates collaboration among university colleges and departments to deliver quality distance instruction, faculty and student services, and initiatives." The Center offers workshops, lecture taping, and course development.[44]

At an earlier stage in the development of distributed learning, many academic libraries supported development in terms of production services (video, audio, print) and media collection and distribution (16 mm film libraries, followed by video, DVD, and other media formats and distribution methods.) In the 1970s, community college learning resource centers, sponsored by the National Science Foundation, provided computer-assisted instruction under the title: Time-Shared Computer-Controlled Information Television (TICCIT).[45] The Technology-Assisted Curriculum Center (TACC), operated by the J. W. Marriott Library at the University of Utah, "supports faculty, instructors and students with technology-enabled course design, development, and delivery services. We collaboratively connect people and instructional technologies for effective, efficient education."[46]

> David Lipsky, head of Cornell University's Distance Learning Office, stated that "There are arguably other models, but I'd rather have the librarians than the technologists take the lead in virtual education. The librarians know the content, and it should be the content that dictates the technology, not the other way around."[47]

Combining technology with the best practices of pedagogy, an academic library is uniquely positioned to effectively support faculty training in the virtual world: training in course management systems, instructional design, production, and research. A one-stop center would induce and inspire interaction and collaboration between all players in the virtual realm: faculty, students, librarians, staff, and administrators. Barry Willis pointed out, when virtual learning was still in its infancy, that "for many years, and with few exceptions, technical managers have played a more dominant role than educators in distance planning and implementation."[48]

The center's organization includes the following areas:

1. Instructional Design/Pedagogical Technique

   - Consultation
   - Training—both hands-on and online
   - Evaluation, best practices
   - Quality Matters or other rubric

2. Instructional Technology

   - Training—Hands-on, group, one-on-one, online opportunities
   - Consultation/ongoing support
   - Learning Resources Repository

3. Information Literacy

- Consultation
- Information literacy course modules

4. Production Services

- Consultation
- Organization and planning
- Production (creation of graphics, audio and video clips, programming)

5. Networking and Mentoring

- Facilitation of discussions
- Facilitation of peer mentoring
- Facilitation of collaborative partnerships between all constituencies—including students

6. Events

Production Services

Instruction and skill-building aside, the emphasis of the One-Stop Center is focused on stimulating course and program production while improving the quality of instruction—not on turning out faculty who are fully trained in every minute aspect of the tools of instructional technology. The object is not to turn out as many finished and accomplished technologists as possible. The center needs instead the unique pedagogical skills, subject knowledge, and dedication of skilled, experienced faculty. The example of "teaching one to fish so that he may feed himself" aside, in many cases, it will be much more efficient to perform services for faculty than to teach them how to perform complex technology tasks themselves. While it is true that teaching one to fish can help a person to feed him/herself, in the modern world, we obtain our fish from professional fishermen through an efficient distribution system. We need to employ each person's skills in the most efficient and effective way possible. In many cases, this means pairing teaching and subject skills from one person with hands-on production skills from another.

The amount of work provided by the One-Stop Center in support of the creation of an online or blended course could be weighed when determining a faculty member's ownership of a course. The percentage of ownership could be adjusted downward based on the amount of assistance received from center staff. Creative work provided by center members would be considered work for hire.

Students

The other often-missing dimension is the online student. Online students need support, particularly at an early point in their careers as online learners. In the online environment, students should take a more active role in their own learning, becoming part of an active learning community. To do this, students must be acclimated to the environment and must have good command of the operation of the course management system's student interface. A truly comprehensive support center would provide training for students to make them skilled users of the course management system and competent users of technologies used to create and post electronic assignments. With their deep interaction with students, librarians would work hand in glove with other specialists to provide these skills.

CONCLUSION

A One-Stop Center administered by an academic library provides the opportunity for effective support for all players in distributed learning. It streamlines the process of online development and makes it convenient for users to get help where and when they need it. Librarians have long accepted and used technology to its fullest potential. Operating equally well in a virtual or physical environment, librarians, virtual librarians, cybrarians, by whatever name they are known, have their fingers on the pulse of campus services.

NOTES

1. Northern Kentucky University, W. Frank Steely Library, "SourceFinder," http://nku.illiad.oclc.org/illiad/logon.html.

2. Northern Kentucky University, W. Frank Steely Library, LibQual+ Results, 2009.

3. "Bogus Diploma Mill in Massachusetts," *Pacific Medical and Surgical Journal and Western Lancet* 25, no. 8 (January 1883): 357–61. The journal reported that the original letter to the university read: "Mr. Rufus King Noyes Esq Boston Mass-Dear Sir Will you pleas Inform me what are the Requirements and feas for Graduation at Your College alos how long your corse of lectures is Yours Truly VB Kelly p S I have bin redin medesin about a year."

4. The Higher Education Opportunity Act, signed into law in 2008 by President George W. Bush, defines a diploma mill as an entity that may offer "for a fee, degrees, diplomas, or certificates, that may be used to represent to the general public that the individual possessing such a degree, diploma, or certificate has completed a program of postsecondary education or training; and (ii) requires such individual to complete little or no education or coursework to obtain such degree, diploma, or certificate; and (B) lacks accreditation by an accrediting agency or association that is recognized as an accrediting agency or association of institutions of higher education (as such term is defined in section 102) by—(i) the Secretary pursuant to subpart 2 of part H of title IV; or (ii) a Federal agency, State government, or other organization or association that recognizes accrediting agencies or associations." U.S. Department of Education (DOE), "Diploma Mills," http://www2.ed.gov/students/prep/college/diplomamills/diploma-mills.html.

John and Mariah Bear, authors of *Bears' Guide to Earning Degrees by Distance Learning,* exposed diploma mills in the correspondence era and continue to expose them. See Quackwatch, "Diploma Mills," http://www.quackwatch.com/04ConsumerEducation/dm0.html.

5. Alan Contreras and George Gollin, "The Real and the Fake Degree and Diploma Mills," *Change: The Magazine of Higher Learning* (March 1, 2009): 40.

6. Ibid., 38.

7. Martin Mann, "Plain Facts About Correspondence Schools, Part 1: What are they Like?" *Popular Science Monthly* 172, no. 2 (February 1958): 278.

8. Martin Mann, "Plain Facts About Correspondence Schools, Part 2: What can they do for You?" *Popular Science Monthly* 172, no. 3 (March 1958): 234. It is interesting that part of this article included a survey detailing what employers thought about correspondence graduates. They discovered four different attitudes: 1. any education is good; 2. each case needs to be addressed according to the individual; 3. correspondence study is acceptable,

but face-to-face training is to be preferred; 4. correspondence study is inferior and unacceptable.

9. I. Elaine Allen and Jeff Seaman, *Class Differences: Online Education in the United States, 2010* (Babson Survey Research Group, 2010), 2, http://sloanconsortium.org/publications/survey/pdf/class_differences.pdf.

10. Ibid., 2–7.

11. Zogby International, *Poll: Online Degrees Earn Wider Acceptance in the Business World* (April 17, 2008), http://www.zogby.com/templates/printnews.cfm?id=1482.

12. eLearners.com, *Online colleges, universities and schools*, http://www.elearners.com/colleges/index.asp. eLearners includes those online colleges, universities, and schools that choose to list their online degree programs, certificates, diplomas, programs, and online courses with eLearners.com.

13. Don Olcott, Jr., "A Funny Thing Happened on the way to the Distance Learning Research Forum," *Distance Learning* 2, no. 4 (2005): 42–43.

14. Bonnie Gratch-Lindauer, "Comparing the Regional Accreditation Standards: Outcomes Assessment and Other Trends," *The Journal of Academic Librarianship* 28, no. 1 (2002): 18.

15. Allen and Seaman, *Class Differences*, 3.

16. Ibid.

17. The lack of distinction between online and face-to-face courses on transcripts is common. Oregon State University Extended Campus's website prominently noted that "[o]ur accredited online degrees and programs appear the same on your OSU transcript as do on-campus degrees and programs at Oregon State University." Oregon State University, *Online & Distance Degrees,* http://ecampus.oregonstate.edu/online-degrees/. This is also the case at Indiana Wesleyan University, which notified potential online students through its website, stating: "Course objectives, major learning activities and assignments, and assessment criteria are essentially the same for online and onsite courses; no distinction is reflected on your transcript. *You will earn the same degree online as you would in a classroom.* The only difference is where you hold your class discussions and where you submit your assignments." Indiana Wesleyan University, IWU Online Degree Programs, http://www.indwes.edu/Admissions/Online/Online-Delivery/.

18. Bonnie Gratch-Lindauer, "Comparing the Regional Accreditation Standards: Outcomes Assessment and Other Trends." *Journal of Academic Librarianship* 28, no. 1/2 (2002): 14.

19. United States Department of Education, *Regional and National Institutional Accrediting Agencies,* http://www2.ed.gov/admins/finaid/accred/accreditation_pg6.html.

20. Southern Association of Colleges and Schools Commission on Colleges, *The Principles of Accreditation: Foundations for Quality Enhancement* (2010 ed.) (Decatur, GA: SACSCOC, 2009), http://www.sacscoc.org/pdf/2010principlesofacreditation.pdf, 26.

21. Ibid.

22. See http://www.nku.edu/research_help/.

23. Council for Higher Education Accreditation, *2010–2011 Directory of CHEA-Recognized Organizations* (Washington, D.C.: CHEA, 2011), 7, http://www.chea.org/pdf/2010_2011_Directory_of_CHEA_Recognized_Organizations.pdf.

24. Distance Education and Training Council, *About Us,* http://detc.org/about.html.

25. International Accreditation Organization, *About IAO,* http://iao.org/iao/about.asp.

26. Jennifer Williamson, *Online College Accreditation 101,* Distance Education.org, http://www.distance-education.org/Articles/Online-College-Accreditation-101-12.html. Williamson provides lists of quite a few accrediting agencies and their approval status.

27. Claire Cain Miller, "Dell Says It Has Earned $3 Million From Twitter," *New York Times,* June 12, 2009, http://bits.blogs.nytimes.com/2009/06/12/dell-has-earned-3-million-from-twitter/.

28. Alison Circle, "Marketing Trends to Watch," *Library Journal* (2009): 29.

29. Robert D. Stuart and Barbara B. Moran, *Library and Information Center Management*, 7th ed. (Westport, CT: Libraries Unlimited, 2007), 119.

30. Specific information on library marketing may be found in several sources and a number of books. Matuozzi summarizes five articles dealing with branding and marketing in libraries. (Robert N. Matuozzi, "Library Public Relations: Recent Articles on Marketing and Branding in University Libraries," *Public Services Quarterly* 5, no. 2 (2009): 135–138.) Nancy Dowd, Mary Evangeliste, and Jonathan Silberman offer some relief to the overtaxed librarian in *Bite-sized Marketing:Realistic Solutions for the Overworked Librarian* (Chicago: American Library Association, 2010). Peggy Barber and Linda Wallace examine WOMM (word of mouth marketing) in *Building a Buzz: Libraries & Word-of-Mouth Marketing* (Chicago: American Library Association, 2010). Susan Webreck Alman offers *Crash Course in Marketing for Libraries* (Westport, CT: Libraries Unlimited, 2007). Suzanne Walters has given librarians a marketing text just for them in *Library Marketing That Works!* (New York: Neal-Schuman Publishers, 2004). *Marketing Concepts for Libraries and Information Services* by Eileen Elliott de Sáez (London: Facet Pub., 2002) and *Marketing/Planning Library and Information Services* by Darlene E. Weingand (Englewood, CO: Libraries Unlimited, 1999) also offer good advice.

31. Association of College and Research Libraries, *Marketing @ Your Library*, http://www.ala.org/ala/mgrps/divs/acrl/issues/marketing/index.cfm. See also the "Toolkit for Academic and Research Libraries," 2007, http://www.ala.org/ala/issuesadvocacy/advocacy/publicawareness/campaign%40yourlibrary/prtools/toolkitfinaltext2.pdf. The authors articulate the need for marketing based on a changing student population that includes "distance education students, international students, adult learners and others involved in new teaching and learning methods." They further bemoan declining literacy rates and a lack of ethics leading to an acceptance of plagiarism and copyright violation. They call for academic librarians to take the lead "in teaching students both 21st century research skills and the respect for scholarship and research that undergird free access to information" (11).

32. Marilyn L. Shontz, Jon Parker, and Richard Parker "What Do Librarians Think About Marketing? A Survey of Public Librarians' Attitudes toward the Marketing of Library Services," *Library Quarterly* 74, no. 1 (2004): 67.

33. Richard Parker, Carol Kaufman-Scarborough, and Jon C. Parker, "Libraries in Transition to a Marketing Orientation: Are Librarians' Attitudes a Barrier?" *International Journal of Nonprofit and Voluntary Sector Marketing* 12, no. 4: 324.

34. Shontz, Parker, and Parker, 71, 73.

35. American Marketing Association, *Definition of Marketing*, http://www.marketingpower.com/AboutAMA/Pages/DefinitionofMarketing.aspx.

36. Stephen Abram, *Out Front with Stephen Abram: A Guide for Information Leaders*, compiled by Judith A. Siess and Jonathan Lorig (Chicago: American Library Association, 2007), 96.

37. William D. Perreault, Joseph P. Cannon, and E. Jerome McCarthy, *Basic Marketing: A Marketing Strategy Planning Approach* (Boston: McGraw-Hill/Irwin, 2008), 61.

38. Patricia H. Fisher and Marseille M. Pride, *Blueprint for your Library Marketing Plan: A Guide to Help You Survive and Thrive* (Chicago: American Library Association, 2006), 44.

39. Perreault, Cannon, and McCarthy, *Basic Marketing*, 16.

40. Brian Mathews, *Marketing Today's Academic Library: A Bold New Approach to Communicating with Students* (Chicago: American Library Association, 2009), 122.

41. Abram, *Out Front*, 31.

42. Sally A. McCarthy and Robert J. Samors, *Online Learning as a Strategic Asset, Vol. 1: A Resource for Campus Leaders* (Washington DC: Association of Public and Land-Grant Universities, 2009), 29, http://www.aplu.org/NetCommunity/Document.Doc?id=1877. The report mentioned library support in Appendix F, "Benchmarking Study: Campus Questionnaire." In this area, the survey sought to discover best practices that could be shared

with others in online learning. It is under the heading "Student Life Cycle Issues" that libraries are listed along with other services: "provision of student services such as registration, advising, financial aid, and library resources to online students; adjustments to service delivery toward students who are more likely to study part-time and therefore take a longer time to complete academic programs; practices regarding student retention and success in the online environment; and verification of student identity and the administration of proctored examinations and other issues specific to technology-mediated education" (p. 66).

43. University of North Texas, *Center for Learning Enhancement, Assessment, and Redesign,* http://clear.unt.edu/. CLEAR is under the Vice Provost for Learning Enhancement and is managed by a Director and Assistant Director.

44. State University of West Georgia, Distance & Distributed Education Center, http://www.westga.edu/~distance/aboutus.html.

45. Gloria Terwilliger, "Forecasting the Future of Community College Learning Resources Centers," *Library Trends* 33, no. 4 (1985): 523–538.

46. The University of Utah, Technology Assisted Curriculum Center, *TACC Mission,* http://www.tacc.utah.edu/about/tacc_mission.html.

47. Ron Chepesiuk, "Internet College: The Virtual Classroom Challenge," *American Libraries* 29, no. 3 (1998): 52–55.

48. Barry Willis, "Enhancing Faculty Effectiveness in Distance Education," in *Distance Education: Strategies and Tools* (Englewood Cliffs, NJ: Educational Technology, 1994), 279.

INDEX

ABOUT THE EDITORS
AND CONTRIBUTORS

ARNE J. ALMQUIST, Associate Provost for Library Services, Steely Library, Northern Kentucky University (NKU). Arne's interest in distributed learning can be traced back to his work as head of the LAN (local area network) Management department at the University of North Texas (UNT) Libraries, where he developed the initial microcomputer network and locally held networked library resource systems. As Assistant Dean of Libraries at UNT, he sat on the TexShare Advisory Board for several years and taught Library Management in a hybrid face-to-face/ interactive video/online environment at the School of Library and Information Sciences at UNT. Arne served on the UNT Center for Distributed Learning Steering Committee. As Associate Provost for Library Services at NKU, he was one of the key people who created the Bachelor of Library Informatics program, taught by Steely Library faculty (available online), and in the creation of "Bridging the Gap: Supplying the Next Generation of Librarians to Underserved Counties of Rural Kentucky," a project of NKU, the Kentucky Department of Libraries and Archives, and Bluegrass Community and Technical College, funded through a nearly $1 million Institute of Museum and Library Services (IMLS) grant. A second IMLS grant awarded in 2011 expands the project into West Virginia. Arne holds a PhD in Information Science from UNT and served as president of the Cincinnati Rotary Club (2010–2011).

SHARON G. ALMQUIST, adjunct instructor, library and information sciences, University of North Texas (UNT), began her career as a music cataloger and reference librarian in the music library at the University of Buffalo, where she graduated with an M.L.S. in Library Science and an M.A. in Music History. She moved to Texas and cataloged music and media at UNT. Leaving cataloging, she became head of the Media Library and Multimedia Development Lab at UNT where she achieved the highest rank as a librarian, Librarian IV. Leaving UNT when her husband (Arne) accepted the position of associate provost for library services at Northern Kentucky University, she concentrated on teaching both face-to-face and virtually. As a virtual instructor, she has taught at various institutions in addition to UNT, such as the University of Kentucky, Northern Kentucky University, and Bluegrass Community and Technical College. She designed the "Distributed Learning Librarianship" course, SLIS 5369, at UNT, which she has taught in the spring semesters since 2003.

CARLA CANTAGALLO, Distance Learning Librarian, W.T. Young Library, University of Kentucky (Lexington). Carla holds a M.S. in Library Science from the University of Kentucky and a B.A. in English from Regis College. She has served twice as the Distance Learning Librarian at the University of Kentucky. Carla has held her current position since 2005 and was the "Extension Librarian" at U.K. from 1989 to 1990, when she moved to the Reference Department. She has also served as Adjunct Faculty for the School of Library and Information Science (Master Degree Program), at the University of Kentucky. As an adjunct professor, she taught the required course LIS 601 "Information Seeking, Retrieval and Services." During her first semester in Library School, Carla was a distance learner herself.

JEFF CLARK, former Assistant Dean, Media Resources, James Madison University, Harrisonburg, VA. Jeff currently holds the title of Faculty Emeritus at James Madison University (JMU). He received a Master's in Library and Information Science from the University of California, Los Angeles, in 1978 and began his professional experience specializing in academic reference services. Since 1982 most of his work has centered on academic media librarianship. In this role at JMU he developed and sustained a specific interest in copyright and intellectual property and supported the media center and other library related services in that area. For over 20 years he worked with teaching and library faculty, as well as campus legal counsel, to address copyright law policy and application, both in the physical and online campus environments, including streaming video licensing and fair use practices. Since 2000, Jeff has made copyright-related presentations at CCUMC (Consortium of College and University Media Centers) annual conferences, served as one of CCUMC's key representatives in U.S. Copyright Office hearings, and since 2003 has served as a copyright guest consultant for Sharon Almquist's online course "Distributed Learning Librarianship" at UNT. He continues to consult and present on copyright issues as they apply in the academic environment.

MELISSA DENNIS, Outreach & Instruction Librarian and Assistant Professor at the University of Mississippi. Melissa received her MLIS from the University of Southern Mississippi in 2006, and her BA in English from the University of Mississippi in 2002. After six years of working in Mississippi academic libraries, Melissa's job now focuses on teaching and researching instruction technologies, distance learning and outreach within academic libraries.

LEORA M. KEMP, Founding (and former) Virtual Librarian, Department Head, University of North Texas at Dallas Library. Says Leora, "I have a distinct memory of my mother saying to me, while I was still in high school, that she knew I would never go to college. Maybe that was the motivation I needed to set high goals and keep going until they were accomplished. After high school, I got my undergraduate degree in English, and then a master's in religious education. Although I did some teaching and some social work, I continued working in libraries, which I had started doing in high school at the age of 14. After several years and several jobs (mostly in libraries), I went back to school to obtain my master's in library science (MLS) while working full time in the university library. It was not long after this that computers entered our lives in more and more ways. While I've never 'been in love with them' (as I was once accused), I've always been intrigued with what they can do. Had the Internet and online library science classes been available earlier, I would have had that MLS much sooner. Before my current position as 'virtual librarian' at the University of North Texas at Dallas (UNTD), I had worked in all kinds of libraries—school, special, public, and academic. Being given the opportunity to help create the library at UNTD (a branch located 50 miles away from the main campus), shortly after it opened in 2000, I quickly became an advocate for distance education and how libraries can support it. Over the past 11 years, I have learned a lot about different ways to deliver library services and that libraries are no longer 'museums for books.' I also saw many, many changes in libraries and librarians since I entered this profession at age 14. I constantly have to tell people that we (at UNTD) may have a small room, but we have a HUGE library. (Someday there will be a separate library building.) Students and faculty alike are amazed when they find out what they can get from their library, whether or not they are in the building. The job as virtual librarian at UNT Dallas was the most fun job I ever had. Few people get an opportunity to help build a university from the ground up and, with it, a real library of the 21st century. I retired from UNTD on March 31, 2011, but I look forward to continuing my relationship with the UNT Dallas library—in a volunteer capacity—for many years to come."

BRAD MARCUM, Distance and Online Education Program Officer at Eastern Kentucky University Libraries (EKU) in Richmond, Kentucky. Brad has worked in libraries since 1998. Brad splits his time between working with EKU's regional campuses and online students and faculty and is an active conference presenter and author on distance librarianship issues. He received his MLS from the University of Kentucky in 2003 and has worked with distance education since that time.

RUTHIE MASLIN, Director, Madison County Public Library, Kentucky. Ruthie formerly was manager of Outreach Services for the Lexington Public Library, Lexington, Kentucky (LPL). She came into the field of librarianship as a second career after beginning as a part-time Librarian Assistant with LPL in 2001. The more she worked in Outreach Services, the more she felt drawn to that type of community work, so she began pursuit of an MLS in 2006 and received her degree the next year. Prior to entry in the library world, Ruthie worked in the non-profit sector in literary arts and adult literacy organizations. Her undergraduate degree is in journalism, and she worked in TV and print journalism as well as in public relations for a number of years. She has continued a sideline of freelance writing and editing throughout her career, and she has published several books, including most recently, *Library Contests: A How-to-Do-It Manual*, co-written with Kathleen Imhoff and published by Neal-Schuman in 2007. Ruthie has also been an adjunct faculty member at Bluegrass Community and Technical College since 2001, teaching developmental reading and writing as well as study skills.

TRENIA NAPIER, Coordinator, Research, Noel Studio for Academic Creativity, Eastern Kentucky University. Trenia has worked in libraries since 2003. The Noel Studio is a collaborative venture between EKU Libraries, EKU's Department of English & Theatre, and EKU's Department of Communications. Trenia received her MLS from the University of Kentucky in 2008.

JANA REEG-STEIDINGER, Reference/Distance Learning Librarian at the University of Wisconsin-Stout located in Menomonie, WI. She is presently Distance Learning Librarian as well as Reference Work Group Leader at the University of Wisconsin-Stout. She received an MLS degree from the University of Minnesota and an Education Specialist degree in Library Research from UW-Madison. Jana has been at UW-Stout since 1982 and delights in the advances in library technology and distance learning she has witnessed.

JOHN SCHLIPP, Assistant Professor of Library Services and Extended Collection Services Librarian, Northern Kentucky University, Highland Heights, KY. John is responsible for copyright compliance of interlibrary loan, document delivery, electronic reserves, distance learning, and faculty inquiries. He has been active in intellectual property, as the Patent & Trademark Librarian at the Public Library of Cincinnati & Hamilton County (OH) and before that as manager of the document delivery department of the Procter & Gamble Research Library in Mason, OH. Prior to receiving his MSLS from the University of Kentucky in 2000, he worked in the communications industry for 15 years. John's published works include articles and book reviews on communications and intellectual property and an educational intellectual property awareness program for teens and young adults entitled *Creative Thinking* (http://CreativeThinking.nku.edu). He served as an associate editor of the *Encyclopedia of Northern Kentucky* (University Press of Kentucky, 2009).

CINDI TRAINOR, Coordinator for Library Technology & Data Services at Eastern Kentucky University in Richmond, Kentucky. Cindi has worked in libraries since 1990 and Cindi received her MLS at the University of Kentucky in 1994, and has professional experience at The Claremont Colleges, the University of Kentucky, and Rend Lake College.